AMERICAN BASSES

AN ILLUSTRATED HISTORY & PLAYER'S GUIDE

BY JIM ROBERTS

D1567531

Backbeat Books

Published by Backbeat Books
600 Harrison Street
San Francisco, CA 94107
www.backbeatbooks.com
Email: books@musicplayer.com

An imprint of the Music Player Network, publishers of *Bass Player*, *Guitar Player*, *Keyboard*, and other magazines.
United Entertainment Media, Inc.
A CMP Information company

CMP
United Business Media

© 2003 by Jim Roberts. All rights reserved. No part of this book covered by copyrights hereon may be reproduced or copied in any manner whatsoever without written permission, except in the case of brief quotations embodied in articles and reviews. For information contact the publishers.

Distributed to the book trade in the US and Canada by
Publishers Group West, 1700 Fourth Street, Berkeley, CA 94710

Distributed to the music trade in the US and Canada by
Hal Leonard Publishing, P.O. Box 13819, Milwaukee, WI 53213

Cover design and photo by Paul Haggard
Flag Bass designed by Gary Weidner for Lakland Musical Instruments
Text design by Michael Cutter
Composition by Michael Baughan

Library of Congress Cataloging-in-Publication Data

Roberts, Jim (James H.)
American basses : an illustrated history & player's guide / by Jim Roberts.
p. cm.
Includes bibliographical references (p.) and index.
ISBN 0-87930-721-8 (alk. paper)
1. Guitar makers—United States. 2. Bass guitar—Maintenance and repair. 3. Bass guitar—History. I. Title.

ML1015.B35R628 2003

2003040439

Printed in the United States of America
03 04 05 06 07 5 4 3 2 1

Dedication

To Lloyd Loar,
who had the right idea,
and Leo Fender,
who made it work.

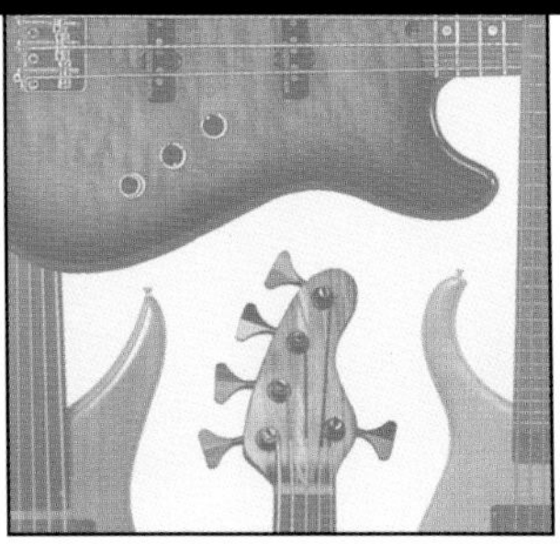

Table of Contents

I love basses. I love everything about them—the way they look, the way they feel, and especially the way they sound. I own nearly 40 bass guitars, and I play each of them at different times for different reasons. Every one has its own unique voice, and they each help me to expand my stylistic and sonic range by bringing out different aspects of my musical personality. Together, they're proof that we're living in a Golden Age of bass guitar building—as the instruments and stories in this book eloquently attest.

Leo Fender's invention of the Precision Bass in 1951 was the "big bang" of the modern electric bass guitar, and the reverberations of his creation are still resonating throughout the musical universe. The bass began the 20th century as a barely audible support instrument relegated to the back of the bandstand, but the introduction of the electric bass did much more than just make the bass louder and more portable, as Leo had intended. During the 1960s and '70s it liberated the role of the bass player in popular music, and by century's end bassists could be seen and heard performing solo and stretching out in front of the band, as well as maintaining and expanding the bass's traditional function—and anywhere and everywhere in between. (This phenomenon is well documented in Jim's previous book, *How the Fender Bass Changed the World*, which I highly recommend to any music fan with an interest in the history of instruments.)

The evolution of bass guitar building over the past 50 years has paralleled the progressively more prominent role of the bass in all types of music. Rock, jazz, funk, reggae, hip-hop, R&B, and even country music have become more bass-friendly as musical styles cross-pollinate and developments in recording technology expand the sonic territory available to the bass. Builders have responded to the needs of those players who are pushing the limits of their instruments, and this interaction leads luthiers, musicians, and the music itself in new directions.

This book also tells a story of American individuality, ingenuity, and innovation, and the classic conflict of art versus commerce. There are as many approaches and styles of bass building as there are luthiers. Many builders have taken the basic ingredients as a starting point and put their own spin on the tradition. Some have started with a clean slate and focused on design aesthetics with as few preconceptions as possible, while others have concentrated on refining the sonic and technical aspects of existing designs. Each bass is unique—a product not only of its maker's vision but also its owner's personality, stamped upon the instrument through years of use (and sometimes abuse).

Basses can be works of art, but they are also supremely functional tools for making music. The defining musical characteristic of the bass guitar is flexibility. The same instrument can be played in many different ways—fingerstyle, slapping, tapping, thumping, flatpicking—and its sound can be radically altered through such techniques as muting as well as technical considerations such as setup and string type. This versatility gives the bass a remarkable range of sounds, allowing it to function in a wide array of musical situations and push the music in new directions. Add to that the myriad variations in playability, appearance, and tone available in today's instruments, and the musical possibilities are—in the words of Alembic's Ron Wickersham—"almost infinite."

When fate creates the right match of player and instrument, the result is memorable music. From Motown lynchpin James Jamerson's legendary P-Bass and Jack Bruce's Gibson EB-3 to Jaco's fretless Jazz Bass and Stanley Clarke's Alembic, the list goes on and on. And while many great bassists are associated with a particular model, there are others, such as John Entwistle and Tony Levin, who have played a variety of instruments over the years as their music changed and they searched for the perfect combination of sound, playability, and appearance.

There are a number of parallels between builders and players. Many luthiers started out as musicians, and some continue to play as well as build. Among bass makers you can find conservative traditionalists and radical innovators, commercial success stories and those unconcerned with making money—just as you can among players. Creative self-expression is the primary motivation for many of these builders, just as it is for the musicians who play their creations.

This book offers a much-needed appreciation and insight into the hard work and artistic vision of those who make the instruments that inspire bassists to create the music we love. On behalf of all bass players, past, present, and future, I would like to say thanks to all of the luthiers who have changed our world and made it a better place.

Dave Pomeroy

Nashville session bassist, producer, and solo artist Dave Pomeroy has recorded with Chet Atkins, Emmylou Harris, Elton John, Alison Krauss, the Chieftains, Trisha Yearwood, and many other artists. All of the sounds (except for Dave's voice) on his 2002 solo album, Tomorrow Never Knows, *were created with basses—33 of them. He is also the leader of the instrumental group Tone Patrol and of the All-Bass Orchestra, both of which record for his label, Earwave Records (www.davepomeroy.com). Pomeroy was a* Bass Player *columnist from 1997 to 2001, and leading bass builders have frequently consulted him about instrument design, construction, and sound.*

ACKNOWLEDGMENTS

I'm greatly indebted to all the individuals who took the time to be interviewed and/or to collect and send materials and photos—large boxes filled with them, in some cases. Many luthiers wrote detailed accounts of their building careers and company histories especially for this book, and I greatly appreciate their efforts. Special thanks go to the builders who wrote the "Inside Info" sidebars, which provide valuable glimpses into the life, work, and knowledge of the skillful and accomplished people who build bass guitars.

None of this would have happened without the fine folks at Backbeat Books, of course. First on my thank-you list is Richard Johnston—friend, colleague, co-conspirator, and editor nonpareil. I'm also indebted to publisher Matt Kelsey, whose support encouraged me to get this project going and whose suggestion for "some how-to material" inspired the "Inside Info" sidebars. Thanks also to production editor *extraordinaire* Amy Miller, designer Michael Cutter, layout-and-scan man Michael Baughan, proofreader Greg Isola, and the sales-and-marketing dynamic duo of Kevin Becketti and Nina Lesowitz.

As I was completing the manuscript, I was saddened to learn of the early and untimely death of Backbeat sales manager Jay Kahn. I'd gotten to know Jay when we collaborated on the promotion of *How the Fender Bass Changed the World*, and I was greatly looking forward to brainstorming with him again. He was smart, capable, hard-working, funny, and—above all—a good guy. As the song says, only the good die young.

Dave Pomeroy, who wrote the excellent Foreword, has been a good friend since 1994, when he came to me with the idea of an all-bass concert, hosted by *Bass Player*, at the Summer NAMM show in Nashville. The show was a rousing success and became an annual event. (The 1996 edition was captured on a video appropriately titled *The Day the Bass Players Took Over the World*.) Dave is an incredibly enthusiastic guy, always bubbling with ideas, and it was great fun to collaborate with him again. He's also a superb bass player whose work has graced dozens of recordings. Thanks, Dave!

There are many direct quotes in the book. Most of these came from my own interviews or from written material provided to me especially for this book. In places where I have used a quote originally given to someone else, I have identified that person and/or named the publication in which it appeared. Whenever possible, I worked from primary sources—my own interviews or material supplied directly to me by the builder or company—when writing the company profiles. I supplemented this with information from the publications listed in Sources. I used the Internet extensively, but I was wary of information from websites other than official company sites. The Web is a vast source of information, much of it wrong. Whenever there was a conflict between sources regarding dates, specifications, or other factual matters, I tried to go straight to the builder for clarification. When that wasn't possible, I used my judgment. Despite my efforts to check facts, it's inevitable that errors have crept into the book. I'll do my best to correct them in future printings. In some places I have interjected my thoughts and opinions about the importance (or lack thereof) of certain people, places, events, and instruments. Take these with a grain of salt.

My deepest thanks and love are reserved for my wife, Susan, and our children, Miles and Nadia, who remained calm even after I answered their question "Oh no, you're not writing another book, are you?" with a "Yes."

INTRODUCTION

On my first day as editor of *Bass Player*, I went to Tom Wheeler's office for a meeting. Tom, the longtime editor of *Guitar Player*, was serving as BP's editorial director, a job that required him to teach me how to put together a magazine. After we had reviewed the line-up for *BP*'s Spring 1990 premiere issue, Tom reached into a box, pulled out a book, and handed it to me. "Here," he said, "you can use this to start your reference shelf." It was a hardcover copy of the first edition of *American Guitars*, Tom's classic history of the U.S. guitar industry.

After returning to my office, I opened *American Guitars* and began to read. Tom's profiles of the builders, peppered with quotes and colorful reminiscences, were informative and fun to read. He had a gift for describing instruments in memorable ways. ("Novices sometimes confuse reverse and nonreverse Firebirds," he wrote, "which to a collector is like confusing Errol Flynn and Elmer Fudd.") The company histories told you who, what, where, when, and why; the product listings were detailed and exhaustive; the photos showed you people and places and cool-looking instruments—lots of them.

I had been writing about music and musicians for more than 20 years, but this side of the music industry was new to me. At that time, I had never been to NAMM, the musical-instrument trade show, or visited a shop where basses were made. I didn't know much about lutherie or how a builder's choice of materials and construction techniques made his instruments look and sound distinctive. But I wanted to learn. And as I soaked up the information in Tom's book, a thought formed: someday, I'd like to write a book like this about bass guitars.

That thought stayed with me during my seven years as *Bass Player*'s editor. Before *BP*, the bass guitar had always taken a backseat to the guitar in music magazines and books. Our premiere issue, the one Tom and I were talking about on the day he gave me a copy of *American Guitars*, included an article about early P-Basses written by the noted Fender historian Richard R. Smith. Many *BP* issues after that had accounts of developments in the history of the bass guitar, some of them incorporated in product reviews, others in feature articles and columns such as John J. Slog's "The Great Basses." As editor, I felt it was important to chronicle the history of this still-new instrument, one that had been—and remains—profoundly important as a creative force.

After I stepped down as *BP*'s editor, I wrote a column that ran on the magazine's back page for four years. One series of columns, called "How the Fender Bass Changed the World," examined the musical and cultural impact of the electric bass guitar following the 1951 introduction of the Fender Precision. I later expanded those columns into a book of the same name, published by Backbeat Books in 2001. My next series was about bass builders. For each column, I interviewed a well-known builder, asking questions about how he got started as a luthier and what his philosophy was as a designer and builder of basses. While doing this, I realized I was collecting valuable material for the book on bass builders that I'd been thinking about for more than a decade.

I began to formulate a plan for the book and quickly discovered that the interviews I'd done for my column barely scratched the surface. There were many more builders to consider—more than 100, ranging from one-man shops to large corporations. After getting the green light from Backbeat to write the book, I decided that the ideal title was *American Basses*. Although I wanted to do some things differently from what Tom Wheeler had done, *American Guitars* was clearly my inspiration. So I called Tom and asked for permission to use the name. That might not have been necessary, legally, but I couldn't imagine doing it without Tom's blessing—which he gave. By choosing that title, I've also acknowledged that I hope my book will approach the level of excellence that Tom achieved (and that his 1992 update enhanced). I also hope it will be almost as much fun to read.

Why just *American* basses? The reasons are both philosophical and practical. The bass guitar was invented in the United States, and most of the milestones in its development have happened here. (A more accurate title would be *North American Basses*, as I've included makers from Canada and acknowledged Fender's Mexican operation.) That's not to imply, however, that only American basses are worthwhile. Today, many fine bass guitars are made abroad, and I've provided a brief overview of the international scene in the piece entitled "Across the Pond(s)." This is far from comprehensive, and there's plenty of room for another book called, perhaps, *World Basses*. On the practical side, it would have been impossible to squeeze even a few international builders into this book and do them justice. There simply wasn't room.

Why just bass *guitars*? Again, there was a practical consideration. I thought about including makers of electric upright basses, but soon discovered there are as many of these as there are makers of bass guitars. I've included some builders who make both electric uprights and bass guitars, but my accounts focus on the latter. I've also included information about what I call "hybrid" basses: instruments that are bass guitars in most aspects of their design and construction, but are played in an upright position. When considering these, I used thc "36" Rule": if the scale length was 36" or less, the instrument was fair game; if the scale length was greater than 36", I excluded it. Arbitrary, to be sure, but I had to draw the line somewhere. There is, once again, room for another book, one that focuses on the world of electric uprights. (Perhaps it will be written by my friend and colleague Mikael Jansson, who has accumulated a wealth of information about these instruments.) As for acoustic uprights, that's a vast and highly specialized area that involves centuries of instrument making. It's also largely a European saga.

One of the challenges of accurately documenting the many bass models some builders offer is what I call "The Curse of NAMM." For more than a century, the mid-winter NAMM* trade show has been the major merchandizing event in the American music industry. In a cavernous convention hall—in Anaheim or downtown Los Angeles in recent years—manufacturers display their wares to store owners, who place orders for the upcoming year. Journalists and other hangers-on cruise the aisles, finding out what's new. (There's a second, smaller show in the summer, although fewer orders are placed there. It's been held in Nashville since the mid 1990s.)

Because so much business is done at NAMM, manufacturers are under pressure to display "new and improved" products every year. Sometimes the changes are minimal, like a new pickup or finish color; sometimes entire product lines are replaced or revamped. With the changes often come new names (and higher prices). Every company wants to give the impression that its line is better every year, so merchants will be enticed to place larger orders.

It's not good business to say, "Well, we've got the same old stuff," when your competitors are blaring the news about their hot new gear. This means basses rarely remain the same for long. What could be essentially the same instrument will get a facelift, or be repackaged as a signature model, or get a trendy new name. Because of the ongoing advances in electronics and hardware technology, many bass guitars are outfitted with new pickups, preamps, bridges, tuning machines, and other components almost every year. In this book, I've tried to note the truly important changes without getting bogged down in superficial details. That means, inevitably, that some changes have been glossed over in my accounts. If you want to know more about how a bass or series has changed over the years, I encourage you to dig into the company's catalogs,

* The acronym means "National Association of Music Merchants," although the organization that presents the trade show is now officially called the International Music Products Association.

product literature, and website (see Addresses), and to look for books that focus on a particular company's history (see Sources). Because the bass guitar is such a new instrument, the information that's available is spotty—but there's sure to be more every year.

As you look through this book, you may think of a builder whose instruments you know and discover he hasn't been included. I can think of a few myself. While I did try to err on the side of completeness, I had to consider my goal of writing a history and not just assembling a catalog of builders. If a luthier or company was making basses at the time of writing (2001–02), I did my utmost to make sure they were included. In a few cases, repeated requests for information were ignored—but most of those builders are here anyway, because I had sufficient material from secondary sources, such as brochures, websites, buyer's guides, magazines, and books. A few of them aren't, because I just didn't have enough material to work with. (Sorry, guys, but I tried.)

For builders no longer in business, I applied a "historical significance" standard. Thus, defunct companies such as Harmony and Mosrite are profiled while some others are not. They were included because, in my opinion, they played a notable role in the story of the bass guitar. I may have omitted some builders who should have been included and included some who could have been left out—the decision making that's part of the history-writing process is always subjective. (Feel free to express your thoughts about where I goofed by writing to me c/o Backbeat Books.)

This is a book about musical instruments and the people who make them. Bass players have a secondary role here, although many are mentioned because of their influence on bass design and production. If you want to know more about the musical significance of the bass guitar, I humbly suggest that you read my book *How the Fender Bass Changed the World*, and also investigate *Bass Heroes*, *The Bass Player Book*, and *Playing from the Heart* (all from Backbeat), as well as such fine studies of important players as Dr. Licks's *Standing in the Shadows of Motown: The Life and Times of Legendary Bassist James Jamerson* (Hal Leonard) and Bill Milkowski's *Jaco: The Extraordinary and Tragic Life of Jaco Pastorius* (Backbeat).

In the end, *American Basses* is a love story. I've been infatuated with the sound of the bass guitar since I was a teenager, and my affection was deepened by learning to play bass, working as a professional bassist, interviewing and writing about bass players, evaluating instruments as a product reviewer, and getting to know the people who build basses for a living. For most of them, it's a matter of the heart, too. They could probably make more money in some other line of work, but they love the artistry of designing a bass, the feel of the wood in their hands, the thrill of hearing that first note come from a new instrument. I've tried to capture some of that emotion in my accounts of their lives and their basses, so you can feel it, too.

Jim Roberts

A NOTE ABOUT TERMINOLOGY

I've tried to use standard musical-instrument terminology throughout, but some of it is jargon that may not be familiar to all readers. I assume, for instance, that you know what a humbucking pickup is or how a semi-hollow bass differs from a solidbody bass. If you don't, there are a number of gear glossaries available, including one in *The Bass Player Book*. To save space in the text, I've employed these acronyms and initials:

ABG: acoustic bass guitar. I use this term for any hollowbody bass that resembles a traditional acoustic guitar, even if it's acoustic/electric (equipped with a pickup).

CNC: computer-numeric controlled. This is usually found in the expression "CNC machine," a computer-controlled power tool used by instrument makers to precisely cut, shape, and rout bodies, necks, and other parts.

EUB: electric upright bass. A standup instrument that emulates the function of an acoustic upright bass but is equipped with one or more pickups. Some EUBs have bodies; others are "stick" basses that are little more than extended necks with pickups attached.

OEM: original equipment manufacturer. Some builders assemble instruments using components made by subcontractors. Such components are called "OEM parts" because their manufacturer was not the builder who produced the final instrument.

P and J: common pickup designs. The letters are derived from the classic Fender basses. A P-style pickup is a split-coil model similar to those found on Precision Basses after 1956. A J-style pickup is a narrow, bar-shaped model similar to those found on Jazz Basses; a bass with two of these pickups is said to have a JJ configuration. Combining a P-style pickup (neck position) with a J-style pickup (bridge position) produces a PJ configuration. These initials are often used just to describe the shape of the pickup; the coil configuration and construction may be very different from the original Fender models. They are sometimes applied to other components as well: a bass with a P-style body has a body similar to that of a Precision Bass; a bass with a J-style neck has a slim, narrow neck like a Jazz Bass, etc.

DESIGNING A BASS: THREE VIEWS

Starting from Scratch

By Ned Steinberger

What is a bass guitar? Four, five, six, or even seven low-pitched strings, stretched over a fingerboard, with a nut, bridge, tuning hardware, and pickup, and a structure capable of holding it all together. Most bass guitars on the market today are still pretty close to Leo Fender's original statement of 1951. This confirms both the genius of Leo Fender (as if there were any doubt) and the conservative approach of most musicians. Can you imagine going into your local Chevy dealer and purchasing a model that was designed more than 50 years ago? Some of us are bound to wonder about new instruments that reflect developments in music and technology we experienced in the latter half of the 20th century. What more can a bass guitar be?

■ Ned Steinberger, 2003.

I try to distill an instrument to its basic elements, scope out the essential task each performs, and then clear my mind of preconceived notions of how these tasks should be accomplished. My goal is to evolve the structure of the instrument to enhance its function and aesthetic. Others may have a specific sound or visual statement in mind when designing a new instrument. The trick is not to become attached to any idea early in the process. The most fun—and the most difficult—part of designing an instrument involves a process of trial, error, and discovery. The first headless bass I made was a complete disaster, leading (after the initial despair) to a realignment of my thinking about structure and sound that has become the cornerstone of my work. It can take a daunting effort to get from point A to point B—only to find that C has suddenly become obvious, and it's time to start over!

It's exhilarating to blast off into infinite space, leaving the firm earth of established design parameters behind, but it's easy to get lost. The only method of navigation I know requires the ability to develop a viable concept and the determination to pursue it relentlessly. Every decision involves compromises among competing factors, such as weight, balance, tone, and aesthetic considerations, but the process needs to be driven by uncompromising loyalty to the underlying concept. When every element, from the overall configuration to each detail of the hardware, combines to support a whole that is greater than the sum of its parts—that's when it gets interesting.

Reconciling functional and aesthetic considerations is always a big challenge. Sound may be the bottom line, but the way an instrument feels and speaks to a player visually is a crucial part of the relationship. I concentrate on finding the shape that best expresses the logic of the design, to help a player understand and feel comfortable with the instrument. Hardware, graphics, and surface treatment should be used to enhance a shape that's pleasing on its own, rather than attempting to distract the eye from a shape that's not. I almost never get it right the first time, which is why I have learned to make softwood models for trying out my aesthetic ideas. Making a new, complete instrument directly from the drawing board can be time consuming, costly, and too slow for a fluid development process. Insights and changes inevitably follow from seeing and holding the three-dimensional form. If I don't like the shape of the horn, I just cut it off and glue on a new one. Tuners, hardware, strings (under low tension), and weight can be added to the model to clarify balance and playability issues.

There should be some ideal or dream to propel a design forward. The key for me is to stay focused on the dream, so each step is directed toward a common goal. Starting from scratch can make for a daunting journey, but when it all comes together it can be extremely rewarding.

Ned Steinberger and NS Design are profiled on page 136; his work on the original Steinberger headless bass is detailed on page 170.

■ Rich Lasner with a Modulus Quantum 5.

Making a Concept Come to Life
By Rich Lasner

My ground rule No. 1 for beginning a bass design: the new model should address content, cost, design, or performance issues in a way that surpasses what preceded it. The concept can range from a bass with quality and features that a year ago would have cost $200 more to an entirely new instrument based on ideas never before tried.

When I begin the process, there are a number of issues I consider right up front. My guiding philosophy is to listen to as much new bass music as possible and imagine what roadblocks the instrument presents to the player. This exercise creates a rough idea of the direction I'll head in. Second, I think about the image of the company I'm designing the bass for. Regardless of whether a company is large or small, it has a "design DNA"—identifiable form/function/concept factors that define the brand. In an automobile, these kinds of factors make a Ferrari recognizable as a Ferrari, rather than as a Honda. Basses are no different. I spend time analyzing the overall form to assess what will make this new bass a clear part of the lineage, whether you can see the headstock logo or not. For instance, I'm not likely to begin work on a multi-laminated neck-through exotic-wood bass with a tilt-back headstock and state-of-the-art onboard electronics when the company's image is based on bolt-on, maple-neck, alder-body basses with flat headstocks and minimal electronics.

Once I have a feel for the cues that make the instrument project its connection to the line, I can approach the new design from several different directions. One common route is to evolve an existing instrument, either in response to the market—players requesting a new function, or adding a feature needed to stay competitive—or to make a clear improvement, the need for which has made itself obvious over time (such as individually adjustable bridge saddles for better intonation). Another consideration that generates new design concepts is reaching beyond what a company already offers to enter a new market. The growing popularity of 5-string basses spurred the development of many new features. Since most companies entering the 5-string arena hadn't built a 5-string before, a wealth of new ideas hit the scene: longer scale lengths, wider necks, improved hardware, better electronics, and advanced neck-reinforcement techniques. In a case like this, a clean sheet of paper may be the best route to innovation.

If the design is an evolution of an existing bass, we'll put together a test mule made from a current model. Cosmetic perfection is not an issue—I'm going for form and function at this point. Modifications to body or neck shape can be performed quickly to check out the results. The same holds true for hardware and electronic improvements. New parts are simply installed and tested. It usually takes numerous attempts to get the revised shape right and find the control and pickup placement that works. While the mule is being tested, drawings of the evolving shape take form.

As recently as ten years ago, a new bass design started with a full-size pencil drawing. Making corrections to the drawing was as simple as erasing what you didn't like. But there are two major drawbacks to using a hand drawing: first, the design is in two dimensions, so you don't really know what the finished instrument will look like until you build one; and second, you'll later need another set of technical drawings to make templates (if the bass will be made by hand) or to drive a computer-driven router program (if the instrument will be made on CNC machinery).

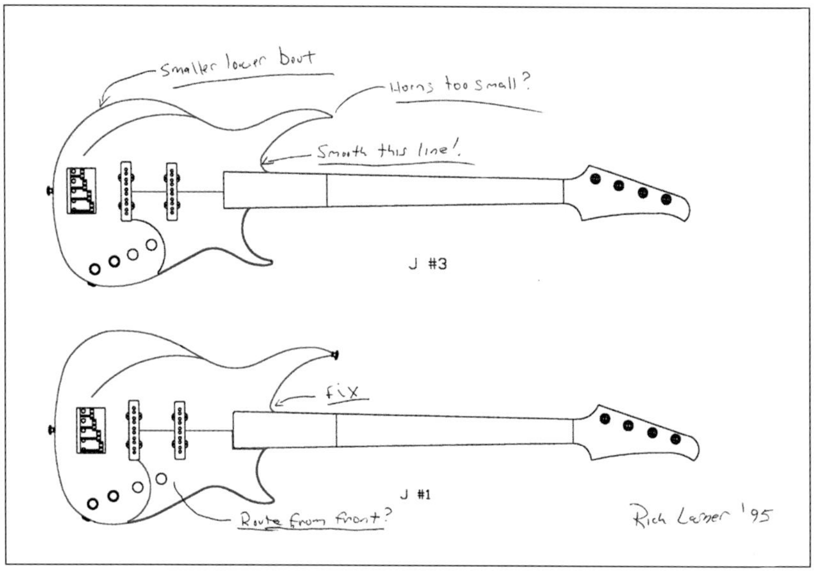

■ Work-in-progress: a new J-style bass design takes shape.

The advent of CAD (computer-aided design) programs and related CAM (computer-assisted manufacturing) programs both simplified and complicated the design task. Drawing in the computer is more complex than drawing by hand, in most cases. You need to learn not only how to work the computer, but also how to use the CAD program. There are many parameters to deal with if you will be sending the drawing to a CAM system, which will control the CNC machine and run the program that makes the instrument. In hand-drawing, the flow of the pencil line is guided by your drawing ability. Erasing tiny parts of a line and redrawing them has no effect, except to change the shape of the line. Computer drawings of complex shapes include hundreds or thousands of tiny line segments. These segments must flow smoothly into each other, or the computer-controlled router will either stop at the end of each segment or create sharp angles where one line ends and the next begins. (I learned this the hard way.) For me, the greatest advantage of using CAD to realize a bass design is the ability to positively check the fit and dimensions of such crucial areas as the neck pocket, pickup routs, and scale length. Computer drawings also allow you to store repeated parts like bridges, pickups, and tuners so there's no need to draw these items over and over.

Once you've decided on the final form and the content of the new bass, prototypes are made. The protos will be used either as a standard to check production models against, or, in the case of companies that contract production out to other factories, to gauge how closely the instruments they receive are adhering to the original design specs and details. This may seem like overkill in this age of precision automated manufacturing, but I once had the experience of rejecting several hundred instruments from an outside factory because they were so far off from the original shape they wouldn't fit in the cases made to hold them!

Once a bass is in production, the design process for that instrument is done. You then move on to the refining phase. If a bass sells well and stays in production for several years, I like to revisit the design and initiate changes that will make it better. Seeing a design you've worked on out in the world is like watching your kids grow up.

Rich Lasner has designed and built basses and guitars since 1974, working for Yamaha, Ibanez, Peavey, and Modulus Guitars. In 2003 he took a position with Line 6 as Director of Instrument Product Lines.

■ Bill Conklin, 2003.

Breaking the Rules

By Bill Conklin

If you're a budding luthier who wants to get into bass design and construction, or maybe a player who wants to design a custom instrument, my first and foremost words of advice are: Remember there are no rules, and there is no wrong or right. There are certain physical limitations you must consider, such as the scale length, which determines nut, bridge, and fret placement and allows the instrument to be built so it plays in tune all the way up the neck. But beyond the basic physics, the door is wide open for virtually every facet of the bass guitar—born of your imagination, mixed with the builder's creativity, without boundaries.

I look at bass design quite differently now than I did when I started. Back then it was all about flash and fashion. Wild and crazy shapes were paramount in my decisions, followed by unusual finishes and maybe even some outlandish inlays. Today's Conklin line exhibits a more refined approach. I now have a simple way of evaluating a potential design: If the body style is classy enough for me to envision a legendary blues or jazz player using it 15 or 20 years from now, then I'm happy with it. If it seems too goofy to stand the test of time, then I shy away from it.

A good design should have traditionally inspired lines yet still incorporate some innovative detailing. Beyond that, key design factors include perfect balance and playability, easy access to all frets and controls, and a special emphasis on making the instrument lightweight and comfortable. So when you begin to create your own designs, don't just take an old P-Bass and trace it. Use your imagination and come up with something tastefully original—move the chains, raise the bar, set new standards. It doesn't have to be earthshaking, but push yourself a bit to come up with a new way of doing something. The same principles hold true for construction details, finishes, inlays, and electronics.

While we've pulled off some electronics wizardry over the years, I would encourage young designers to think about the application of the instrument. Always try to get the most versatility out of the fewest controls. If the bass is going to be used mainly in live situations, keep it fairly simple and easy to use, with only the bare essentials. A studio musician may want a few more bells and whistles, but try not to make it too confusing or overloaded to the point that there are problems with power consumption or noise. Everyone seems to like having some sort of onboard EQ, and I've become fond of parametric systems. I also like what piezo pickups can do for a bass, and lately MIDI seems to be more and more prevalent. Trying to decide which options are best can be tough, but in the long run I think having only what you will really need and use makes the instrument most effective.

Bill Conklin of Conklin Guitars is profiled on page 41.

BUILDING A BASS: THE QUEST FOR TONE

By Michael Tobias

■ Michael Tobias, 2003.

Among the many goals we luthiers must keep in mind as we design and build instruments—including comfort, playability, and flexibility—none is more important than tone. There are many paths that lead to tone, and for each of us the path is different.

Even though two bassists are using similar equipment, one player's sound will possess subtleties and nuances that are different (or absent) in the tone of the other. Like snowflakes, no two of us are alike—we don't have the same ears, the same fingers, the same muscles in our hands and arms. And we may not share the same idea of what constitutes good tone.

The path I have chosen as a luthier is based on my early interest in acoustic instruments. When I started building guitars, I was struck by the tone qualities of different woods. One way luthiers check for this is with "tap tones," which we use to judge the resonant qualities of different pieces of wood.

1. The quest for tone begins with the right wood. My wood supply includes ash, alder, poplar, several types of maple, wenge, walnut, zebrawood, redwood, buckeye burl, and several species of rosewood and ebony. When gluing a body, we combine woods to create an instrument with the right sound for the customer.

2. The tops and accent veneers are glued and clamped. They will stay clamped overnight.

3. The body halves are carefully joined to show off the bookmatched tops. After gluing, the body blanks are milled to thickness.

4. The bodies are bandsawn to 1/8" from their true perimeters to minimize tear-out and chipping when they're pin-routed.

5. Body shapes are routed by attaching a template to the blank and running the shape along a guide pin while the router cuts the blank to shape.

6. The interior pockets—pickup routs, neck pocket, and control cavities—are also cut on the pin router.

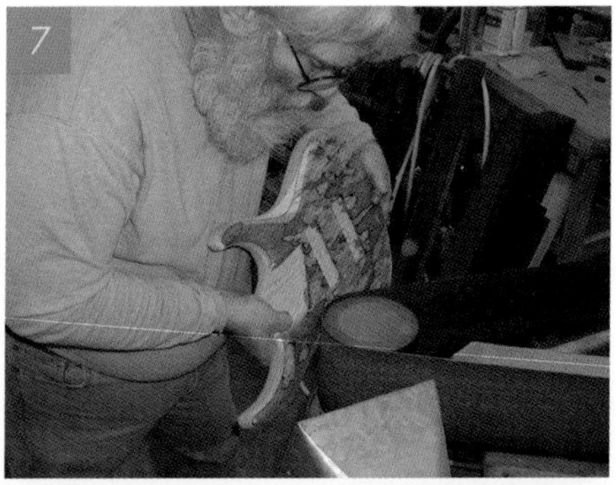

(For an accurate comparison, it's best to use samples that are the same size.) Tap tones are generated by holding a piece of wood firmly, but with as little contact as possible, and then striking the wood sharply. You can use a fingertip, knuckle, or something else; the most neutral tapper is a piano hammer—the doubled felt does not add any coloration, allowing you to hear a more natural sound.

I used to buy acoustic-guitar backs, tops, and sides that were rough-milled to approximately the same size. While tapping the pieces, I noticed there were differences from piece to piece within the same species. Pieces that were cut from the same log or flitch (a longitudinal section of a tree trunk) had similar, but not identical, characteristics.

I found that stiffer woods yielded brighter-sounding guitars. Instruments with thick tops and heavy braces were darker and less resonant. Mahogany and maple backs and sides yielded guitars that were brighter and sometimes sweeter-sounding than ones with rosewood, walnut, or koa—they did not, however, have the warm, rich bass response of the darker woods. To investigate further, at one point I built a batch of guitars that were essentially the same except for one component, so I could observe the difference each modification made.

If this doesn't seem to relate to electric basses, consider that the electric bass is first and foremost an *acoustic* instrument. If you amplify a 2x4, it will sound like an amplified 2x4. That in itself may not be bad, but it may not be what you need to get the

7, 8, 9. I use the drive pulley on my edge sander to shape the arm and belly cuts to make the basses more comfortable in playing position.

job done. You need an instrument that sounds good acoustically; if a bass sounds good without amplification, then it usually sounds good with amplification. (Sometimes not, since many other factors are involved, including the strings, the pickup, the electronics, the rig, the venue, and the player.)

The Elements

The tone of wood is the result of many components, and you can analyze and describe it in a variety of ways. I'll try to do it here in non-scientific terms that will be meaningful to players.

One way to explain the different tone qualities of different types of wood is to rate them in terms of hardness. Simply put, hard woods have a sound that is brighter, clearer, more articulate, and more conducive to a sharp attack than soft woods. If a bass is made entirely of hard woods, what you hear predominately is the attack and the fundamental. Soft woods are more sensitive, allowing you to hear the swelling of overtones as a note sustains. By combining hard and soft woods, a builder can take advantage of both qualities—if the recipe is right.

A second, even more simplistic way to rank woods is by color: light woods are generally brighter than dark woods. Sound silly? Think about it—light-colored woods such as maple, alder, ash, and poplar are all brighter sounding than dark woods such as walnut, koa, zebrawood, and rosewood.

A third factor in tone is weight/density. Lightweight wood is brighter than heavy wood. The perfect example is swamp ash (also called light ash or southern ash). Lighter pieces of swamp ash have sweet treble response and punchy midrange—but if the wood is too light, the bass response is weak. Heavier pieces lack the sweetness in the treble and that nice midrange, but they have a fuller, rounder low end.

The tone of a piece of wood is a combination of these elements. For instance: Bubinga is an extremely hard wood, even harder than eastern rock maple. It does not have a brighter sound than maple, though, because it is much heavier. Bubinga and such other hardwoods as rosewood and gonçalo alves contain large amounts of oil, wax, or resin; this tends to darken their tone, even though they are hard.

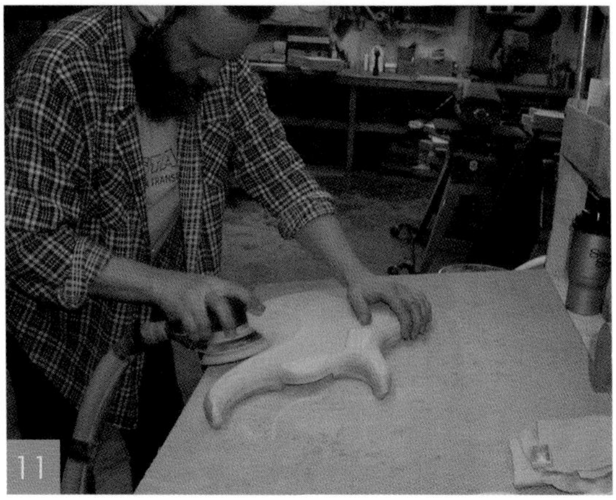

10, 11. After the rough shaping is completed, the bodies and necks are step-sanded through four different sandpaper grits.

12. Color is applied, if called for. This part is like fingerpainting—blending the colors to get the desired effect really makes the grain stand out. After sealing, the bodies and necks are topcoated with a catalyzed acrylic urethane.

photo essay continues

13. We use a table saw to cut the desired angle on the neck blank for the peghead. The pieces are glued up to make a neck blank.

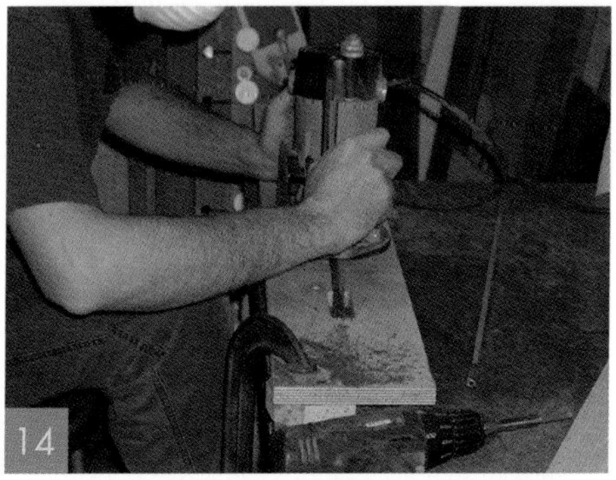

14. A drop-on template is used to rout a channel for the trussrod.

15. After the trussrod is fitted, the fingerboard is glued on. The neck is trimmed and the initial round-over is done on the pin router.

Lamination

Should we make "hippie sandwich" basses out of exotic plywood? If so, what is the purpose, other than aesthetics? Laminating different woods certainly can make instruments more beautiful, but it's possible to overdo it. Too many pieces means too many glue joints—and glue does not have desirable resonant characteristics!

Nonetheless, by carefully combining woods you can focus on particular tone qualities. Different configurations yield different results: a maple neck with a maple fingerboard is generally brighter than a maple neck with a rosewood fingerboard. When making a body, putting a hard top on a soft back can make the low end clearer and more articulate but still retain the desired qualities of the softer wood for the high end and midrange.

A laminated neck has more structural stability if it's properly made—that is, by correctly matching the grain and the moisture content and correctly clamping it in assembly. Lamination also affects the neck's "Q" (quality factor). Here's what that means: Each piece of wood has a resonant peak. When you laminate several pieces, you create a system with multiple resonant peaks at different frequencies. The laminated piece should have the average of these resonances as its peak, and (in theory, anyway) this average Q should make the neck less prone to accentuate one peak, and thus respond more evenly.

Laminating creates an interaction between the pieces, and it generally makes the neck stiffer. Greater stiffness raises the resonant frequency—to a point, one hopes, where the peaks do not match the notes on the neck, thus diminishing dead spots.

16, 17. The fingerboard is rough-radiused and the back of the neck is carved to shape on this belt sander. Abrasive sculpting!

Neck Attachment

Neck-through-body basses respond differently than bolt-ons. Neck-throughs have more sustain and a higher fundamental content in their notes, especially in the low end. This can be adjusted by using different body woods—lighter woods, for instance, reduce low-end accentuation. Bolt-ons seem to lack this fundamental response in the low end, especially with the low *B* on a 5-string. (I believe the mechanical neck joint contributes to this.) This characteristic of bolt-ons is often perceived as a "tighter" sound, thanks to a trick of the human ear.

The ear (or, more precisely, the brain) has the ability to "fill in" the missing components of the sound spectrum. Without the actual fundamental in place to muddy the sound, the ear is able to "extrapolate" the fundamental from the upper partials. The telephone is an example of this principle in action. When you talk on the phone, the mechanism (which is really a miniature bass-reflex cabinet) is not capable of transmitting the fundamental, especially if you're a man with a fairly deep voice. Yet the person on the other end hears it just fine.

Composites

High-quality, properly seasoned wood is becoming increasingly scarce. Some sources have disappeared altogether, and the rape of the rainforests has raised not only prices but also the consciousness of many people around the world. Consequently, many builders are buying wood from suppliers who harvest from sustained-yield forests or who sell recycled wood.

Other builders have taken a high-tech approach. Graphite and composite materials have made a great contribution to the music industry in recent years. Whether used for light, super-stiff reinforcements, for parts, or for complete instruments, these materials are making quite an impact. They offer increased sustain (thanks to greater rigidity) and more stability (because they're less susceptible to atmospheric conditions).

If those materials are so superior, you ask, why doesn't everyone use them? (I'm sure the people who sell fiber and resin would like to know, too!) Well, you know what they say about opinions being like belly buttons: everyone has one, and they're all different. Not everybody wants to use the same materials, and luthiers' different choices lead to many different tones for players. Diversity is good, no?

18, 19. The shaped neck is mounted on an adjustable deck that supports its entire length during final radius and leveling before frets are installed.

20. Frets are pressed on with an arbor press, using a torque wrench to make sure they're set consistently.

photo essay continues

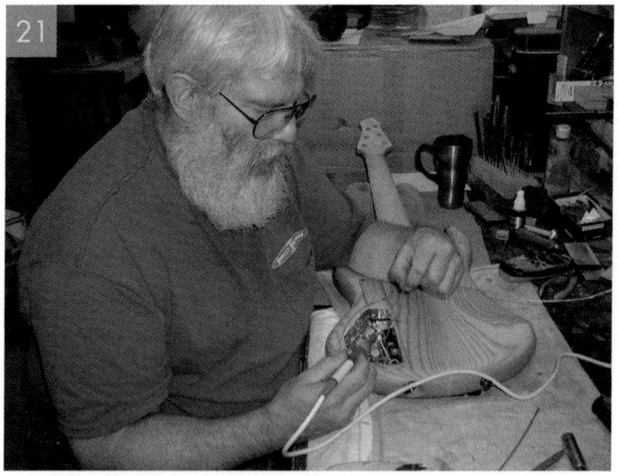

21. After fitting the neck and setting the bridge, the electronics are installed in the control cavity, which is shielded with copper foil.

22. The string height is set and measured at the last fret, the neck is adjusted, and the pickup height is set according to the string height.

23. After stretching the strings and checking the string height and neck adjustment one more time, the intonation is set using a strobe tuner. Once everything is correct to my satisfaction, the instrument is ready for delivery.

Other Factors

Aside from wood and its composite cousins, there are many other factors that influence an instrument's tone, including the hardware and the finish. Pickups and electronics are also important, but I will leave that subject to others.

There are many approaches to building hardware for a bass, and many different materials are used. The bridge might be made of brass, aluminum, or steel—or a combination—and each of these metals has a different effect on the tone. The mass of the bridge also affects sustain and attack. In general, brass is considered to be favorable to sustain while steel and aluminum are brighter sounding. The most important aspects of bridge construction are: (1) good contact between the parts, (2) a well-defined "witness point" for the string, and (3) sufficient saddle movement to allow for proper intonation.

Finish—the bane of the bassmaker's existence—also plays an important part in determining the tone of an instrument. I believe there must be a compromise when choosing a finish: you have to balance the need for protecting the instrument with the finish's sound-dampening effect. A finish that's too thick kills an instrument's resonance; one that's too thin does not offer enough protection.

Modern materials technology now offers finishes that provide good protection from rock & roll sweat, even when the finish is applied in thin coats. As long as the buildup is not too thick, the resulting tone can be outstanding. There are also blends of tung oil and urethane that can offer the traditional look and feel of a hand-rubbed finish with much greater resistance to moisture and skin oils. They don't, however, offer much protection from scratching and denting. These oil finishes require greater care than lacquer or urethane sprays—but I'm really fond of the way they sound.

There are cases when a piece of wood sounds significantly better with a certain type of finish. I once built a bass with a body made of very light swamp ash that received an oil finish. The instrument's tone was okay but a bit mushy and lacking in crispness. For some reason, we had to refinish it; the oil was cleaned off, and the bass was shot with polyester. When we plugged it in, lo and behold—it had gained brightness and clarity.

Adapted from an article in Bass Player, *May/June 1994. Used by permission. Michael Tobias and MTD are profiled on page 130; his work on the original Tobias basses is detailed on page 179.*

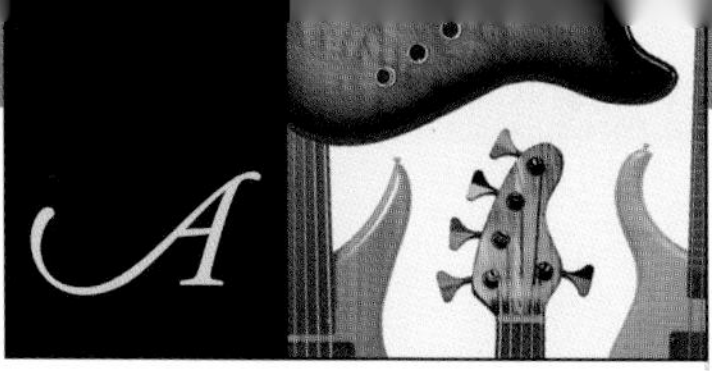

A BASSES

Albey Balgochian is a bass player who builds basses. Or maybe he's a bass builder who plays bass. Either way, it means that Balgochian brings a player's sensibility to every instrument he handcrafts in his Waltham, Massachusetts, shop.

Albey has been a professional bassist since 1966. In the early '70s, when he stopped touring to help raise his son, he took a job in the shop of Peter Kyvelos, restoring and repairing uprights. In 1976 Balgochian built his first electric bass, combining what he'd learned from Kyvelos with affection for his vintage Fender hybrid ('64 P-Bass body/'62 J-Bass neck) to create his own 4-string. "With each bass I made, I fine-tuned my design," he says. "When I finished #9, my Fender was given a well-deserved rest." (Albey liked #9 so much it became his main instrument for more than 15 years.)

At first Balgochian built all his basses to order, working on them whenever he had time off between gigs. In 1996 he standardized some of his ideas in the Jade Bass, a J-style 4-string with an alder or swamp ash body, maple or rosewood fingerboard, passive pickups, and an optional preamp. Even when new, the slim "handworked" neck of a Jade Bass feels like one from a well-worn vintage Jazz Bass. Unlike a Fender, though, it sports 21 frets. (As a player, Balgochian was bugged that Fender basses came up one note short of three octaves.) He also teamed with Darryl Jones to create a signature model, based on the Jade but tailored to Jones's preferences. Like the '66 Jazz Bass that Darryl used on tour with the Rolling Stones, it has an alder body and rosewood fingerboard.

■ A Basses Jade Bass Classic 4.

Balgochian's other standard model is the World Bass, which he calls "the ultimate fretless." It has an extra-long ebony fingerboard and an alder body with an oil-finished figured-maple top. A hand-carved flame-maple top is optional. The 2002 version features Lane Poor pickups and a Basslines 3-band EQ; it can be ordered with a piezo-equipped wooden bridge. Albey also builds electric upright basses, each of which is specially designed. His EUB creations include the Picasso Bass made for Darryl Jones, with a *D* extension on the *E* string, and a fretted upright built for Reggie Scanlon.

Balgochian believes that his steady work as a player—in recent years, he has led his own Band of Peace while playing in several other ensembles—gives him an edge over other bass builders. "The player in me strives to physically reproduce the sound that I hear in my head," he says, "and the builder in me has designed a bass that produces a strong, clear bass tone that is present in every musical situation."

ACACIA

After he founded Acacia in 1987, Matt Friedman built every bass himself. "The main focus of Acacia," he said, "has always been the beauty and diversity of the woods used"—and he offered a tremendous range of choices, from the familiar maple and swamp ash to such rarities as pink ivorywood and snakewood.

■ Acacia Custom Series 5-string.

Acacia basses fall into three main styles: Custom Series, Emotion Series, and Grüv Bass (originally called GLB, for Great Little Bass). As the name implies, Custom Series neck-through basses could be tailored to just about anything a customer wanted, and Friedman said he built everything from a 3-string tuned *BEA* to a "14-string guitar/bass/banjo/harp … thing." String spacing, scale length, fingerboard radius, neck feel, and the choice of pickups, electronics, and hardware could all be specified. And the wood, of course. His Emotion Series basses were 35"-scale neck-through fretless instruments equipped with a single magnetic pickup and a hand-carved ebony piezo bridge. The Grüv Bass, described as an

■ Alembic Distillate.

"exotic jazzy bolt-on," combined modern technology with a vintage-inspired look. Features included a swamp ash body, 35" scale length, 24-fret five-piece laminated neck, J-style or soapbar passive pickups, and an extra-strong five-bolt neck attachment. It was available as a 4- or 5-string, fretted or fretless. Late in 2002 Friedman announced he was closing up his shop and would no longer be taking orders for new basses, though he would continue to honor warranties.

ALEMBIC

If Leo Fender's invention of the Precision Bass was the first historic landmark in the development of the electric bass guitar, then the formation of Alembic was the second. By uniting sophisticated electronics with strikingly original woodworking, Alembic elevated bass building to an art form, opening the door for dozens of talented luthiers to express themselves in the creation of beautiful, great-sounding, premium-priced instruments.

Alembic began as more of a concept than a company. Credit for formulating the concept goes to San Francisco's Owsley Stanley, also known as "The Bear," mentor and supporter of the Grateful Dead. Owsley had the idea of assembling a "dream team" of technical experts to improve the Dead's sound both in live performance and on recordings. His first recruit was Ron Wickersham. "In 1969 I was working at Pacific Recording, where I had built the first multi-track console with a separate mixdown section," says Wickersham. "The equipment attracted all the famous San Francisco bands, and in the process of recording them we would find limitations in their gear. If the musician was willing, I would improve the signal circuits in the instruments and amplifiers. One of the bands we worked with was the Grateful Dead, who were recording *Aoxomoxoa* at the time. One of their associates, The Bear, persuaded my wife, Susan, and me to move to a pink warehouse in Novato … [and] that's really where Alembic got started."

■ Alembic Spoiler 5-string.

Sonic Alchemy

The word "alembic" is an ancient alchemy term that means a vessel where something is refined or purified, and the sheds behind the warehouse where the Dead rehearsed soon became the center for Alembic's sonic-purification research. The original focus was on making better live recordings, to help the band critique its work, and on upgrading the sound system. "We also worked on the instruments," says Wickersham. "It was there that the first active electronics were placed in an instrument—Phil Lesh's Guild [Starfire] bass, which had Hagstrom pickups made in Sweden. The pickups had winding inductance of several Henries, so the high frequencies were getting lost in the cord to the amp. We found that isolating the cord's capacitance would bring out the highs while preserving the tone in the lows. And we found that even a 6" cable from the pickup to the electronics moved the self-resonance down about an octave, so the preamp was built right on the terminals of the pickup." (Although Wickersham is correct in asserting Alembic's leadership in developing truly effective instrument-mounted electronics, the idea had been tried earlier: in 1962 the Burns Company of London mounted battery-powered preamps with bass and treble boost in its TR2 basses.)

Recording engineer Bob Matthews came to the warehouse to work with the Wickershams, and then Rick Turner joined the team. Turner had gigged as a folk and rock guitarist on the East Coast, and he learned guitar repair and lutherie while working at various music stores, including Dan Armstrong's shop in New York City. "When I got out to the West Coast in 1968, one of the things I decided to do was to become an *electric* luthier," says Turner. One of his first projects was a bass guitar that he built in 1969 for Jesse Colin Young, the leader of the Youngbloods. "The Youngbloods' secretary was Phil Lesh's girlfriend, and after she saw the bass I'd made for Jesse, she introduced me to Phil," says Turner. "He invited me out to the pink warehouse in Novato, where I met everyone and we got along famously."

Turner showed Wickersham some of the things he'd been working on, including the sliding pickups he'd built for Young's bass. "Ron had started measuring pickup frequency response, and mine were way beyond anything he had previously measured, although the output was low," says Turner. "He had already started designing low-noise preamps that he was building into the Guild Starfire pickups and getting great results with that, so pickup output was simply not an issue: you need output, you create it." Turner had previously experimented with installing guitar effects directly into instruments, so Wickersham's approach made perfect sense to him. They were off and running.

■ The Alembic logo, on the cover of a mid '80s catalog.

Alembic's early instrument projects included the installation of low-impedance pickups and active electronics in Guild Starfire basses used by both Lesh and the Jefferson Airplane's Jack Casady. Their work expanded rapidly, and when the space in Novato became too cramped Wickersham and Matthews moved Alembic to 320 Judah Street in San Francisco. Turner moved in, and in the summer of 1970 Alembic became a formal business, with Wickersham, Matthews, and Turner as shareholders. Another "Alembicized" Guild Starfire, with quadraphonic electronics, was created for Lesh. When this bass was plugged into the Dead's Alembic-created "Wall of Sound" PA system, it produced a sound Turner describes as "like a really big and really great pipe organ."

Alembic #1

In 1971 Turner built the bass known as Alembic #1 for Casady. Originally conceived simply as a test bed for various experiments, this neck-through-body, 32"-scale 4-string became the first high-end electric bass. ("It wasn't supposed to be a work of art," says Turner, "but I got carried away.") Carved from zebrawood, purpleheart, and maple, it had an ebony fingerboard inlaid with abalone and silver designs, and the position markers were tiny red LEDs along the side of the neck. For maximum sonic flexibility, there were interchangeable sliding pickups riding on brass rails and modular onboard electronics. "The electronics were supposed to be like the modules in a recording console," says Turner. "There would be a master output module and an input module for each pickup, with the idea that we could switch to different kinds of EQ, no EQ, and so on. As Ron designed different types of filtration, the bass could be fitted with them and we could try them out." There had never been anything like it—or its $4,000 price tag, as *Guitar Player* noted in a feature article that extolled the instrument's innovative design and construction.

Alembic continued to expand, taking over Pacific High Recording Studio in San Francisco in 1972 and moving instrument production to a Cotati farm that Turner had rented. "It was an old chicken ranch," he says. "We had the production facility in the barn, and the spray booth was in one of the chicken shacks. There were woodburning stoves to

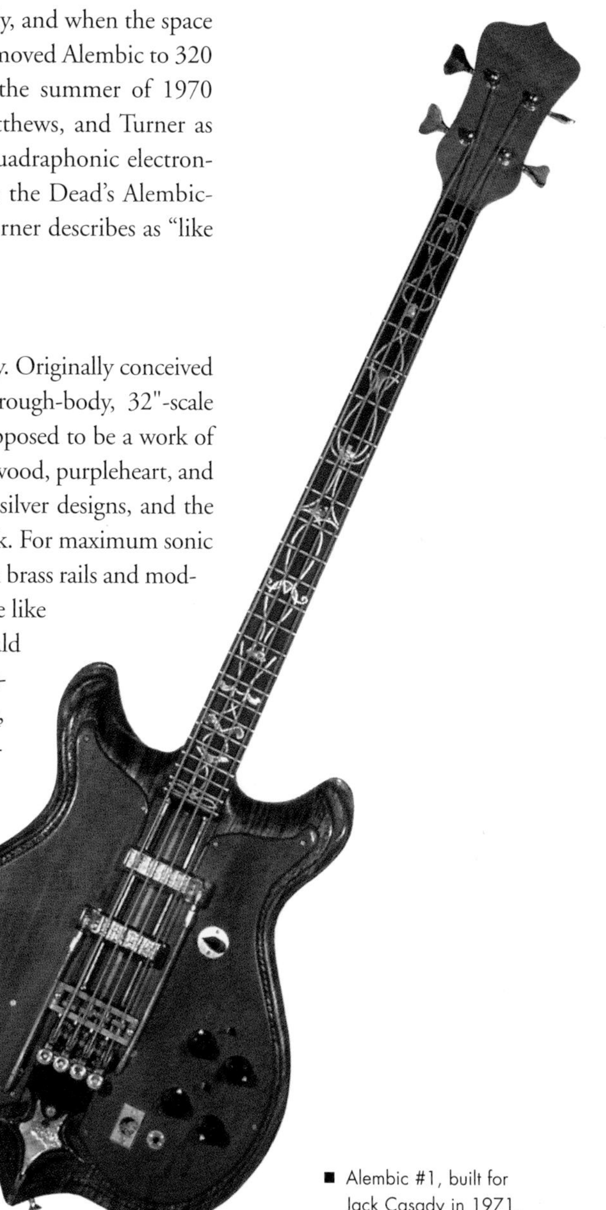

■ Alembic #1, built for Jack Casady in 1971.

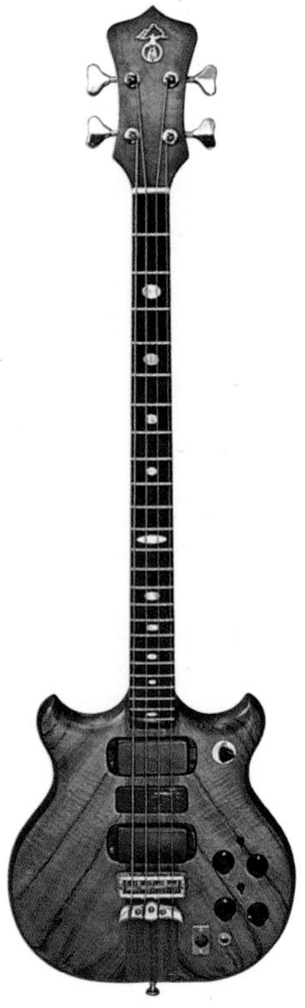

■ This 1976 Alembic short-scale 4-string was the first bass guitar with a graphite neck.

■ Alembic bass with Modulus Graphite neck, circa 1977.

keep us warm in the winter—and we had lots of wood." The local fire marshal was horrified, but he didn't shut them down because there were plenty of doors to escape through if the whole thing went up. The Wickershams set up their electronics operation in another barn in Sebastopol, and within months the most sophisticated electric basses ever conceived, to that point, were being built in two barns in rural Northern California.

Alembic's first business breakthrough came after the publication of a 1973 article in *Rolling Stone*. "They had a special 'pro audio' section that included Alembic," says Ron Wickersham, "and it caught the attention of the president of L.D. Heater, a musical-instrument distributor in Beaverton, Oregon. He called to see if we'd be interested in making production instruments. Susan negotiated a deal, and that was the beginning of Alembic's transition to becoming a full-scale manufacturer." L.D. Heater was a subsidiary of Norlin, a conglomerate that also owned Gibson and several other musical-instrument companies at the time. Norlin's management had instructed Heater to find "cutting-edge products" to sell, so they placed an initial order for 50 Alembic instruments—an astounding number for a tiny outfit used to building them one at a time.

Turner readily admits that he was baffled by the mechanics of instrument production at first. He began to see the light after visiting a toilet-seat factory in nearby Sonoma. "I went there, stared at their production line, and figured out how it worked," he says. "I got to see how jigs and fixtures worked with conventional woodworking equipment like shapers and routers. After that, I figured out how to tool up to make the instruments faster."

As Turner was gearing up the chicken-ranch factory, Bob Matthews left the company. At the time, Alembic was also operating a retail store in San Francisco, selling their own instruments and electronics as well as other high-end audio gear. But by 1974 they had sold both the recording studio and the store, which became Stars Guitars. "By '75 instrument production was really becoming the main thing," says Turner. "We were building instruments for the Dead, the Airplane, Santana, Crosby, Stills & Nash—the list went on and on."

Stanley Steps In

Alembic's success in the instrument market got a huge boost in 1973 after Turner went to see Stanley Clarke, who was using a Gibson EB-2 at the time. "We were playing at a club in San Francisco," Clarke recalled in a *Bass Player* interview, "and this guy came up to me and said my playing was great but my sound was atrocious. It was Rick Turner, who was with Alembic. He had a bass with him, so I tried it out. It was like a new bass player was born that night—suddenly, I could play anything I heard in my head." Clarke immediately switched to Alembic basses, and the success of his 1974 solo album, *Stanley Clarke*—with its cover shot of Stanley playing an Alembic—was a breakthrough both for virtuoso electric bass playing and for Alembic. "That really put us on the map," says Turner.

"The success of the sound brought other musicians to seek improvements," notes Wickersham, who attributes the power of Alembic's bass tone to the combination of a through-body neck with a sustain block and brass hardware. "We postulated that the strings should be isolated from the instrument's body—we could enhance sustain by reflecting energy back into the string rather than losing it to the body. So we placed a mass block under the bridge, which provided the desired effect. We also realized a traditional bone or plastic nut was different from the metal of the frets, so we used a brass nut."

Turner says that collaborating with great musicians was one of the most satisfying aspects of this period in Alembic's history. "I believed we were equal partners," he says, "and I really wasn't interested in working with musicians who didn't accept that." Rick likes to tell the story of John Paul Jones's visit to the Cotati factory, at the height of Led Zeppelin's popularity. "I took him to lunch at this hot dog place where he had to bus his own table—and he *thanked* me for it. He said that he couldn't go out in London or New York without being mobbed, so this was great for him."

In 1976 Alembic's deal with L.D. Heater ended, and they signed on with Rothchild Musical Instruments, a distributor that specialized in elite musical products. It was run by Paul Rothchild, whose claim to fame was producing the Doors. In that year they also met Geoff Gould, a bass-playing aerospace engineer who came to Alembic with the idea of building basses with graphite necks. Turner worked with Gould to create a bass with a short-scale graphite neck, which they displayed at the January 1977 NAMM show. John McVie of Fleetwood Mac bought the bass, and Turner received a patent on the concept. Several more Alembic basses with graphite necks were produced before the patent was assigned to Gould's new company, Modulus Graphite [see Modulus].

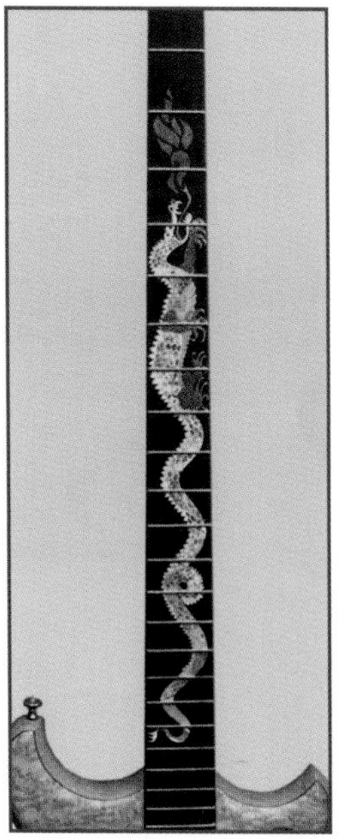

■ Many Alembic basses have elaborate decorative elements, such as this dragon inlay.

Alembic unified its operations in 1977, moving into a facility on Industrial Drive in Cotati. Production was up to about 25 instruments a month, the vast majority being electric basses. (Alembic has always made guitars, too, but basses are their claim to fame.) In 1978 disagreements within the management group reached the flash point, and Turner left the company. The deal with Rothchild also ended, and Alembic took over its own distribution.

To Santa Rosa

Since then Alembic has been operated by founders Ron and Susan Wickersham, assisted by a close-knit group of family members and associates. In 1979 the company moved to Foley Street in Santa Rosa and introduced a new bass, the Distillate, which featured traditional Alembic concepts in a lower-priced instrument than the original Series I and Series II models. The product line has continued to expand, with new models being added almost every year.

Alembic relocated once again, in 1991, to its current location on Wiljan Court in Santa Rosa. All of the current basses feature neck-through-body construction except for the set-neck Epic. The other models are distinguished primarily by their different body shapes, most of them designed by Susan Wickersham. All pickups and electronics are made in-house. A wide variety of woods, inlays, and electronics options are available, making each Alembic virtually a custom bass. In 2002 list prices for a dozen different models ranged from $2,250 for the Epic to more than $10,000 for a Series II 6-string. From time to time, Alembic creates special "landmark" instruments, such as the limited-edition 25th Anniversary Bass, offered in 1994, which sold for a cool $25,000.

"Music starts as an original thought, heard inside your head before you even touch the string," says Ron Wickersham. "The instruments we build succeed by not interfering with the release of that thought, preserving faithfully the subtle differences in expression and letting the sound flow unmolested to the audience."

■ Alembic Series I (left) with Standard Point body shape and Series II with Standard Omega body shape.

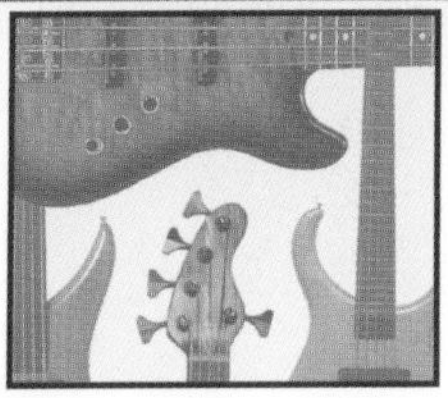

A FIELD GUIDE TO ALEMBIC BASSES

By Susan and Mica Wickersham

In 1969 Ron Wickersham began development of what would become Alembic's Series I/Series II pickups and active electronics. Our PF Series was unlike anything ever seen before in musical instruments: low-impedance pickups with preamps. By 1972 our repair shop had expanded, and instrument production began. First there was the Standard Point body shape, made originally for Jack Casady. It was designed so that you had to place it on a stand. (One of the most common repairs we performed before we started making instruments was fixing pegheads that broke because the instrument had fallen over after someone leaned it against an amp or a wall.) That was also the year Stanley Clarke got his first Alembic, a short-scale bass with features that would come to be known as Series I—although at the time we didn't use model names.

By 1973 Ron's PF electronics had evolved to Version 6. Most of the instruments we were making used the PF-6 electronics, although Alembic has always been a custom shop, so variations found their way into many one-off jobs. Some basses even had Superfilters onboard—talk about a forest of knobs!

It wasn't until 1975 that the Series I and Series II model names were introduced, at the suggestion of our distributor. By then the Standard Omega shape and the Small Standard shape for short-scale basses were common. All Series I and Series II basses have both top and back laminates (though not always matching on early examples) and two outputs: ¼" and 5-pin. Four-string basses were usually fitted with five-piece through-body necks in various combinations of maple, purpleheart, walnut, cherry, and birch. By 1979 we had made the maple and purpleheart combination our standard.

In 1976 we made a short-scale, graphite-neck bass for John McVie—it was the first graphite-neck bass, with a neck supplied by Modulus Graphite founder Geoff Gould. From 1976 to 1985, many Series I and II basses and a few Distillates and Spoilers were made with graphite necks.

The Distillate was introduced in 1981. It blends the Standard Point and the Small Standard body shapes, with a flat bottom. Distillates were our first standard-issue mono-only basses. The first Distillates were made exclusively for Japan. These special basses had only one pickup, a brass front-mounted electronics plate, and an LED indicator. By 1982 we were making two-pickup Distillates for the U.S. and other export markets, most in medium scale (32") with five-piece maple and purpleheart through-body necks. Typically, Distillates had a mahogany body with an exotic top laminate. We dropped the Distillate from our catalog in 1990, but they are still available by special order.

John Entwistle wanted the Exploiter body. He bought 15 Series II basses with this shape in a variety of woods, most with his signature note-name inlays on the fingerboard and sterling-silver spider webs on the body. We made lots of Spoilers and Distillates in the 1980s with this body shape. Contrary to how it might appear, this is one of the best-balancing body shapes.

The first Spoilers arrived in 1982; they were solid koa with three-piece maple through-body necks and 32" scale lengths. A decal of the Alembic logo was used on the first 50 or so, and we learned quickly that the cast-bronze logo was a must for all Alembics. By 1983 we were making them with multi-laminate bodies like the Distillates. Spoilers were dropped in 2000, but like the Distillate they are available by special order—it's not like we threw the templates out!

The Scorpion shape was really many different shapes, but all versions had "pistol grip" horns and a Heart Omega bottom. The most popular one was a version we made for Germany, about three-quarter scale of a Standard Point blended with the Spoiler. Scorpion was never a dedicated model but an optional body shape for all models.

In 1983 we started promoting our Activator line of pickups and electronics by installing these systems in Spoiler basses—and the Persuaders were born. Because of the similarity between the models (differing only in electronics and pickups), Persuaders were dropped in 1990 in favor of the Essence bass.

The Signature Series began in 1985. These were designed to give the overall look and feel of our top-of-the-line Series I and II basses, but at about half the price. We achieved this by making a simplified electronics package and using a standard wood combination that we could make in groups, rather than one at a time. The Stanley Clarke came first, and by the end of 1985 the Mark King model was introduced. In 1992 these became the Signature Deluxe models when the

Signature Standards came out. The Standards were $1,000 less than the Deluxes and varied only in the wood configurations.

The first Elan was made in 1988 for a customer in Japan who wanted an Alembic version of the Fender Jazz Bass (the "H" in the Elan serial number stands for "Hojin"). Elans were the only Alembics whose standard body wood was maple. Long-scale three-piece maple through-body necks were standard issue for Elan basses.

The year 1989 marked our 20th anniversary—so we celebrated with a new model, aptly named "20th Anniversary." It was a limited edition of 200 pieces with stylized three-quarter Omega bodies and five-piece maple and purpleheart through-body necks. Bodies were either maple with a quilted-maple top and back or walnut with a figured-walnut top and back. For electronics, we used a control layout like a Series I, with a standard mono/stereo switch, but 20th Anniversary models do not have the 5-pin jack.

Elans were a bit large for some customers, so in 1990 we introduced the Europa. It's an inch narrower than an Elan, with more tapered horns. The Europa took the mantle from the Distillate and used a similar circuit, replacing the pickup-selector switch with a pan pot. Our familiar five-piece maple and purpleheart through-body neck is found on Europas.

In 1990 we introduced the Essence bass. It draws its lower body half from the Small Standard with the upper horn extended so it will balance in a long-scale bass. The Essence is our smallest body—narrower than most guitars. Originally supplied with a flame-maple top and maple body, Essences now have a standard mahogany body and a choice of tops.

Nineteen ninety-three was an "epic" year—the first time we made a set-neck model. The key feature was having the inner surface of the horns part of the same curve. The body borrows its bottom curve from the Elan, but a little more rounded. Epics have a thin polyurethane finish that closely resembles oil, so you can still feel the texture of the wood.

To mark our 25th anniversary we released a limited edition of 25 Sterlings. These basses are richly inlaid on

the fingerboard with nearly 400 separate pieces of sterling silver, wood, copper, mother of pearl, and abalone, all done by hand. Sterlings are also the only models that come standard with an ebony and maple neck and burl-rosewood top and back.

To make the Rogue, we merged an Essence into the Europa and then stretched the horn to match the length of the Series II 6-string custom in the 1990 brochure. Everyone loved that shape, but it was really quite enormous. The Rogue captures the feeling of that bass, but in a much more manageable size. Rogues first hit the scene in 1995.

With the Epic's success, we decided to introduce another set-neck bass in order to have more choices in this style of construction. As the set-neck version of the Europa, the Orion differs only along the inner surface of the horns. Epics and Orions have mahogany bodies and maple necks. Later versions include small walnut pinstripes in the neck laminates.

In 1999 we brought out the Excel, our latest set-neck bass. It's really curvy like a Spoiler, but even more circular. This body has the most extreme inner-horn curve. The Excel is also the only bass we offer standard with an ash body.

A Word About Wood

We dry all our wood to the same moisture content (7 percent), taking into account that in the gluing process moisture will be added. Body and neck woods are gathered together before gluing to "equalize" the moisture, in the tradition of fine piano building.

We use a variety of woods in various combinations depending on the model we're constructing. We use maple as the primary wood for both its beauty and stiffness. We use ebony laminates when fundamental sustain is wanted or required. It's an expensive option, so it's not standard on any model.

Originally we used walnut for neck laminates, in various combinations with other woods. We stopped using walnut in favor of purpleheart, which is stiffer and more stable thanks to its very straight grain. Ebony laminates emphasize the sustain of a note's fundamental, while all other woods focus the energy in the second harmonic (which is true of all stringed instruments). In combination with certain body woods, like those in the rosewood family, the resulting sound is phenomenal.

In the beginning, we did a lot of experimenting with wood and electronics looking for ideal combinations to achieve certain tonal results. In the early days we used myrtle, birch, mahogany, maple, and walnut as core woods. We finally decided on mahogany as the standard body-core wood. Its neutral color and tone are the foundation we build upon. Mahogany also looks nice with any top and/or back wood. By adding laminates of select tonewoods, we influence the instrument's overall sound and also practice respectful conservation of these valuable materials. Maple is used in the core when an exceptionally bright tone is wanted—a maple top, core, and neck would make a *very* bright-sounding bass.

Flame koa contributes to a warm sound, and vermilion is our favorite on fretless basses. An ebony fingerboard on a fretless produces a melodic "pretty" sound, while pau ferro makes the tone more growly. Our favorite combination of woods for overall bass performance in any musical situation is a cocobolo top and back and through-neck construction with ebony laminates. The sound is very strong and clear, with big bass response, piano-like highs, and amazing fundamental sustain.

We chose neck-through construction so the strings would terminate on both ends of the neck's main beam structure. This minimizes the effect of the body wood, since the main beam structure reflects the energy back into the string. We want the vibration of the string, and thus the output of the instrument, to be as uncolored as possible, to reproduce all the spectral content without favoring one frequency more than another. With a bolt-on joint there's also a loss of energy at some frequencies when compared to the response of a full-length beam structure.

When making a laminated neck, we carefully select the wood to have opposing grain structures. This greatly increases neck stability over long periods of time, compared to a neck made of a single piece of wood. On some models we use purpleheart laminates, which are stiffer than maple. By utilizing laminates of different stiffnesses in the same structure, we see fewer effects of beam resonance, and therefore have more even response—one of our primary goals.

The body is laminated because we want to be able to provide a beautiful wood on the surface. Due to the way we make our basses, the choice of top-laminate wood affects the sound less than it might with another type of bass.

When a musician has specific requirements, we work closely with that person to build the right tool to create his or her music—there's an almost infinite number of wood, shape, hardware, and electronics combinations.

WHY ACTIVE?

By Ron Wickersham

Our primary goal at Alembic in the late '60s was to create better recordings of the live-performance musical experience of the San Francisco bands. The work on bass electronics came from that. The musicians were pushing the limits of sound systems, which at that time were based on systems from the motion-picture exhibition market and did not extend to the acoustic levels desired (especially at frequencies lower than 120Hz), or were derived from high-end hi-fi gear. As we made progress in this area, a few musicians became interested in what could be done for their instruments.

Phil Lesh and Jack Casady were using Guild Starfire basses that had been modified by Owsley Stanley with switchable capacitors to give them a broader tone range, and made quieter by shielded cabling inside—but Phil and Jack could hear more top end acoustically than came through the speakers. The problem was that the pickups were loaded down considerably by the guitar cord's capacitance. For studio recording we made very short cables of low-capacitance co-ax (not the rubber-insulated, high-impedance microphone cables that were the standard issue). My background in broadcasting and hi-fi electronics—magnetic phono cartridges and tape heads—led me to realize that putting the first amplifier close to the pickup would improve this further.

We first examined Guild pickups, which had pole-pieces that could be adjusted in height to control each string's output. These were typical of pickups at the higher end of the impedance range found in commercial basses of that time. In prototyping a matching amplifier, I was surprised to find that even a 4"-long shielded wire lopped off an entire octave of high-end response. To get the best response, it was necessary to reduce the lead length to zero, so the electronics were built onto the terminals of the pickup. The circuit chosen was a Darlington-connected monolithic circuit, the CA3018, manufactured by RCA. It was connected as an emitter-follower since no gain was required because the signal level was adequate. And it's the most simple circuit, requiring only one resistor and one capacitor in addition to the device. (The Alembic Blaster preamp is an upgrade of this circuit with a modern JFET device.)

■ Ron Wickersham lab-tests an Alembic.

The results were amazing. The pickups' response went up more than three octaves, and the clarity this brought to the fingering skills of the musicians revealed the true character of the music. One of Jack Casady's instruments included an inductor as well as a selection of eight capacitors, and the under-damped two-pole low-pass filter response was introduced. On Phil Lesh's instruments, the passive low-pass filter was upgraded to a state-variable filter. (This filter design eventually became the Alembic Superfilter SF-2.)

We took what we learned on these early experimental instruments to the design of our own electronics. We scaled back the impedance of our pickups by using fewer wire turns and a unity-permeability core structure, so the preamps could use up to a 12" connecting cable without loss of high frequencies. The work with filters led us to select an active low-pass filter for our standard tone control, which also had the benefit of closely resembling the behavior of naturally resonating acoustic instruments.

■ Ampeg AUB-1, introduced in 1966.

AMPEG

Everett Hull began his company with the idea of making the bass louder. His first innovation was a microphone inserted into the body of an upright bass through the endpin (or peg) hole: an "amplified peg," thus the name Ampeg. Early ads for the product touted it as "The Answer to the Bass Man's Prayer." It was sold with the 18-watt 1x12 Bassamp, and Hull focused most of his subsequent efforts on improving the amplifier part of the equation. By the late 1960s, Ampeg was renowned for such groundbreaking (and wall-shaking) innovations as the B-15N "flip-top" amp and the mighty SVT, with its 300-watt tube power amp and two 8x10 cabinets.

Ampeg has also offered bass instruments from time to time, including the fiberglass-bodied Baby Bass electric upright (still a favorite of Latin players) and an array of bass guitars, some of them interesting if not especially influential. The prime example would be the Horizontal Bass of 1966. In the early 1960s Ampeg had been importing bass guitars made by Burns of London, but the company's management decided it was time to take a more aggressive market position. Dennis Kager, an employee who had been doing setup work on the Burns instruments, was asked to design a new bass guitar to be built in Ampeg's New Jersey factory. He came up with something truly original: a strangely shaped solidbody bass with *f*-holes that went completely through the body. Kager wanted the bass to have a 4-in-line headstock shaped like an "A," but the scroll headstock of the Baby Bass was used instead—and to this day these Ampegs are usually referred to as "scroll basses."

Even more important than the weird body or the scroll headstock was the decision to offer the Horizontal Bass in both fretted and fretless models. The AUB-1 (the designation meant "Ampeg unfretted bass") was the first production fretless. It didn't make much of a ripple at the time, but it was an important milestone in bass guitar design: the instrument that Leo Fender had created as an antidote to the "imprecise" upright had come full circle. Both the AUB-1 and its fretted partner, the AEB-1, featured a scale length of 34¼" (more or less; the engineering wasn't very precise) and a bridge-mounted diaphragm pickup called the "Mystery Pickup," presumably because it was out of sight. The tailpiece was positioned all the way at the end of the body, so total string length was 47".

Ampeg's product line had always been strongly influenced by the needs of acoustic bassists—Everett Hull was often pictured with his upright in company photos—and the fretless fingerboard, scroll headstock, and diaphragm pickup all reflected this. In the case of the latter, it was chosen to allow the use of gut strings, which wouldn't work with a conventional magnetic pickup. This would appeal to acoustic bassists, it was hoped, although very few Ampeg basses were actually equipped this way. And the "Mystery Pickup" lacked the punch of a magnetic, which is why some of the scroll basses that are still around have been modified with a magnetic pickup.

A former coffin maker named Mike Roman designed another version of the scroll bass, the ASB-1. Commonly called the "Devil Bass," it had an even more bizarre body, with long, pointed horns and triangular body cutouts. A fretless version, the AUSB-1, was also offered, although very few of these odd basses were made,

■ Ampeg AEB-1 (left), ASB-1 (center), AMB-1 (right), and SSB (front) basses.

with or without frets. They were just *too* strange, even for the '60s. The short-scale (30½") SSB and SSUB basses completed the line; these had conventional solid bodies, magnetic pickups, and 4-in-line headstocks that looked like Kager's original concept for the Horizontal Bass.

Ampeg was acquired by Unimusic in 1967, another example of the conglomerate onslaught that overwhelmed the music industry after CBS purchased Fender in 1965. In 1968 the scroll basses were updated with magnetic pickups and renamed the AMB-1 and the AMUB-1. Too little, too late—by the end of 1969, production ceased. Ampeg licensed the production of Japanese-made scroll bass knockoffs in the late 1980s, but the instruments were available only in Japan.

In 1971 Ampeg was acquired by Magnavox and made part of the Selmer division, known for its band instruments. The Ampeg-brand basses offered by this version of the company came from overseas: Japanese-made Stud basses and several Hagstrom bass models, built in Sweden. None of these were memorable, although the Big Stud and Little Stud 4-strings probably deserve to be in some sort of marketing hall of fame, just for their names.

Ampeg was sold again, to Music Technology Inc., in 1980, and one more time, in 1985, to current owner St. Louis Music. (The movement of the Ampeg brand across the music industry is like the tale of a journeyman ballplayer being traded from team to team.) St. Louis Music has done much to restore Ampeg's position as a first-line amp manufacturer, but its efforts in the instrument business have mostly been as an importer of Japanese and Korean instruments, except for the "Ampeg Classic Bass" reissues of the late 1990s.

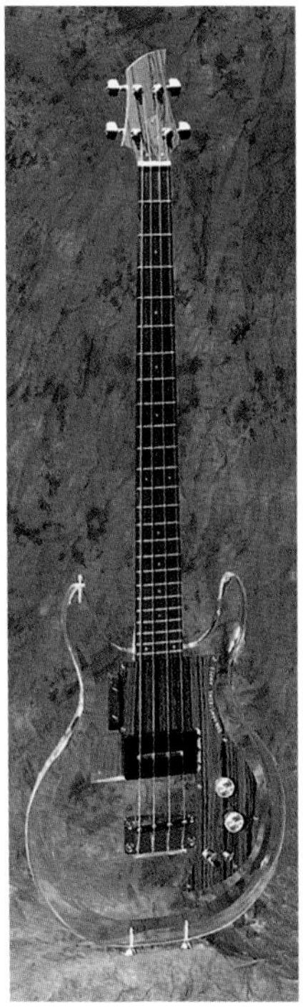

■ Ampeg "See Through" bass, designed by Dan Armstrong.

In 1997 Ampeg offered new versions of the scroll basses built by Bruce Johnson of Johnson's Extremely Strange Musical Instrument Company in Burbank, California. Johnson made a number of improvements while keeping the look of the original instruments; the new scroll basses, logically enough, were designated AEB-2 and AUB-2. Production difficulties eventually doomed this promising reintroduction, although Johnson continued to build the instruments on a limited basis. At the same time, Ampeg also introduced an improved reissue of the Baby Bass, built by Steve Azola.

The other famous Ampeg electric bass is the Plexiglas-bodied instrument designed by Dan Armstrong, which was introduced in 1969. Armstrong, who was widely admired for his skillful modification and repair work, chose the plastic material because it could be worked like wood, offered superior sustain, and presented a striking new look. His short-scale (30½") "See Through" bass had a 24-fret bolt-on neck, one stacked-coil humbucking pickup co-designed by Armstrong and Bill Lawrence, and a wood-grain Formica pickguard. A few of these basses were made with black-plastic bodies, and about 150 fretless models were built just before production ended in 1971. One of them ended up in the hands of Jack Bruce, who played it on a mid-'70s tour.

Like the scroll basses, the Dan Armstrong bass returned as an Ampeg reissue in the late 1990s. The new basses were built in Japan and had a number of refinements, including a better bridge and interchangeable "Deep Bass" and "Bright Bass" pickups made by Kent Armstrong (Dan's son). They were offered in both clear and smoked Plexiglas; a budget model, with a basswood body and Basslines pickup, came on the market in 2000.

SEE ALSO: AZOLA, JOHNSON'S EXTREMELY STRANGE MUSICAL INSTRUMENT COMPANY

■ Axtra LMF 5-String.

AXTRA

Founded by Bill Michaelis in 1985, Axtra Guitars of Kenosha, Wisconsin, is a "custom specialty" shop that builds instruments to order. Designs range from traditional J-style basses to more radical concepts like the LMF, a Steinberger-ish headless model with a five-piece rosewood and maple neck. Both bolt-on and set-neck basses are available, in 4-, 5-, and 6-string configurations that emphasize playability and good value.

AZOLA

If you've attended a Concours d'Elegance—a classic car show where only the finest vehicles are displayed—you know the exacting attention to detail that distinguishes the prize-winning entries. In the world of automotive restoration, these shows are the Olympics; the craftsmen who work on Concours cars are as far beyond local body-shop workers as world-class athletes are from guys playing softball in the park.

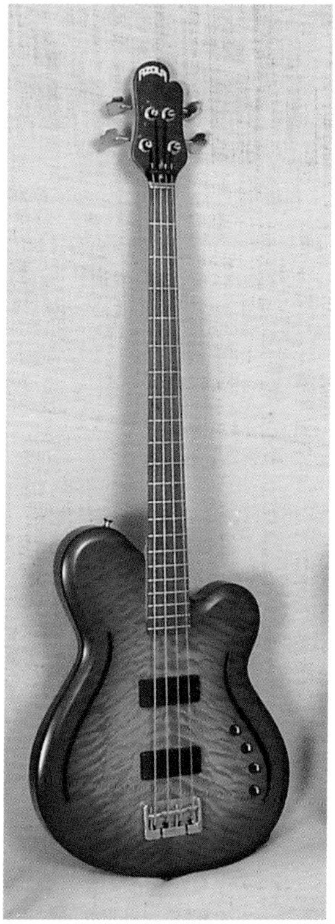

■ Azola Nouveau Bass.

Restoring old cars might seem like odd training for a luthier—but for Steve Azola, it was the perfect preparation. "I learned about materials and fabrication, fine paint work, and making things straight," he explains. "I was working mostly with metal, of course, but when I did get into instruments, I had the eye already."

Azola grew up outside of Baltimore and displayed an early affinity for the low end. "I guess I was just drawn to the bass. I played tuba in the school band, starting in fourth grade, which led me to listen to the bass end of things. I began playing bass guitar in 1968, when I was 13. I had a Univox violin-body bass, like everybody else." Steve took lessons and progressed rapidly. By age 15 he was playing in bands with older kids and earning enough money to buy better gear. "That was the early '70s, so I started doing what everybody else did—messing with my instruments. I took a beautiful '64 Jazz Bass, carved a big groove in the body, and put on a humbucking pickup. I did that kind of stuff to several basses."

In 1973 Azola graduated from high school and began working in a body shop. He was still gigging a lot, and he built his first semi-original instrument in 1974, grafting the through-body neck of a semi-hollow Rickenbacker 4005 onto a '62 Jazz Bass body and installing DiMarzio PJ pickups. ("It has come to be known as the 'Fenderbacker,' and I still have—it's sitting in my dining room.") Steve continued to tinker with his basses and do occasional modifications for friends, but he wasn't thinking about building instruments as a career.

■ Azola Deco Bass.

In 1978 Azola moved to California, a car-crazy state where his bodywork skills were greatly appreciated. "A friend got me a job in a shop that did nothing but Corvettes, and later on I worked in shops with old-time guys from England, where I learned how to do really detailed work." As his skills improved, Steve got better and better jobs, working on both cars and motorcycles. Then, in the early '90s, he got into playing music again. "I was playing blues, so I got a Fender bass and an SWR amp. Then I got into 5-strings, and I realized I wanted to make one of my own. I liked the old Fender Telecaster Basses, so I built a 5-string that was like a Telecaster Bass with a Music Man pickup."

Steve married his wife, Jill, in 1990. Shortly after the wedding, he made an offhand comment to her about how he liked the look of the old Ampeg Baby Bass electric uprights. "Soon after that, one became available—a 5-string. The owner was a motorcycle guy, so I traded him some paint work for the bass. Once I had it, I saw how they were being used in Latin music, and I saw ads for replacement parts. I started thinking, There's got to be a reason parts are available—a lot of guys must be using these. I got the idea that the world needed a new, modernized Baby Bass, maybe made with different materials." Azola called Ampeg to see if they objected to him building an updated version of the bass, which hadn't been in production since 1972. Ampeg didn't, and Azola Music Products was off and running.

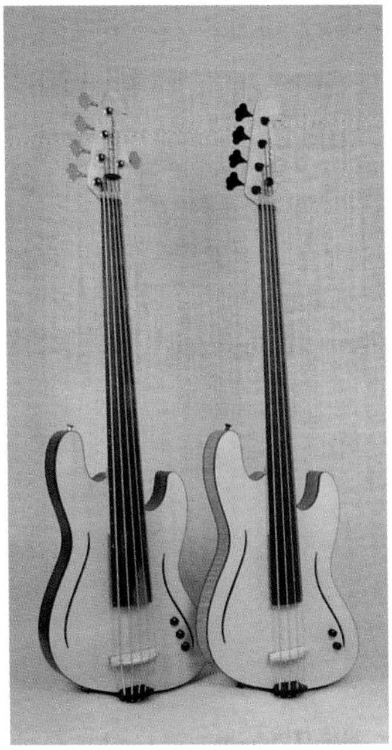

■ Azola Jazzman fretless 5- and 4-strings.

The Azola Baby Bass got a warm reception at the January 1994 NAMM show, and Steve returned home with a fistful of orders. Within months, he was building basses full time. He went on to develop several versions of the Baby Bass, from the vintage-style 4-string with fiberglass body to a fully carved acoustic version. In 1996 Azola introduced the Bug Bass, a moderately priced "stick" bass that's the mainstay of the line; it's available in several different models. Steve has also collaborated with fellow luthier Martin Clevinger on the Stradibass and Virtuoso EUBs.

Since 1998 Steve Azola has also built bass guitars. His vintage-style Jazzman was originally offered in solidbody and semi-hollow models, but Steve abandoned those in favor of a hollowbody version. Available fretted or fretless, as a 4- or 5-string, it has a spruce top with distinctive *f*-holes and a piezo pickup system with active EQ. The Deco Bass is Steve's tribute to the great archtop-guitar builders like John D'Angelico, expressed as a bass. It can be ordered with either a laminated or carved body, and there are "limitless" options, including 5- and 6-string versions. Azola's most recent bass guitar is the aptly named Nouveau, a futuristic double-cutaway instrument he describes as "really versatile in its sound and uses."

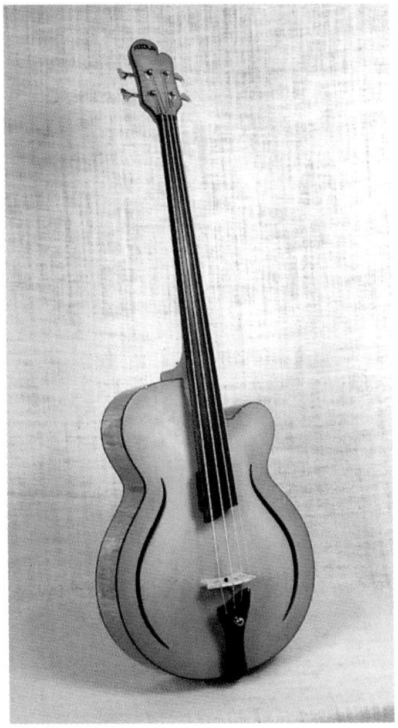

■ Azola Deco Bass fretless.

In 1999 Steve and Jill Azola moved to "Rancho Bajo" in Ramona, California, near San Diego, where they run the business themselves. "We don't rely on anyone else to do work for us," says Jill. "We have complete control over when and how the work gets done. Maintaining quality standards is essential to our reputation, and you lose that when you relinquish control by having things done by subcontractors."

Comparing bass building to his days in the car business, Steve says, "I went a lot of places and won a lot of awards—but in the end, it was the car's owner who got the prize. It's personally rewarding now to build something and stick my name on it."

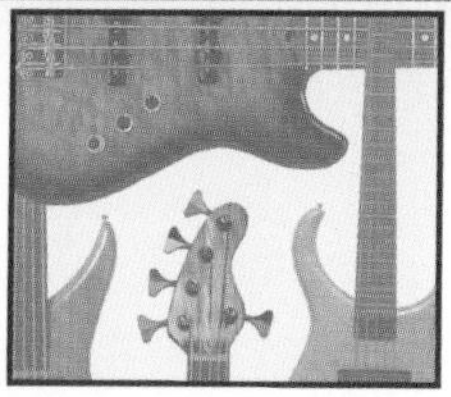

THE LUTHIER'S WORKSHOP: TOOLS AND SAFETY

By Steve Azola

Have you ever thought about working on, or even building, your own instruments? The ability to turn an idea into something tangible, playable, and useful in the real world is the culmination of many lessons learned. But consider how quickly your life can change if you're injured while woodworking. The impact could be dramatic: as a bassist, you might lose your ability to express yourself, and your capabilities as a woodworker could also be impaired. It's not a pretty picture—and it hurts.

One morning I was trying a new construction method to improve the strength and integrity of one of my bass designs. It was a simple idea, involving a straightforward procedure on the table saw. But in a blink this task turned into one of those life-changing moments because something slipped. The injury could have been much worse—the dado blade chewed about ¼" off a couple fingertips on my left hand—and I consider myself lucky. But after that experience, I've started hearing the voice of the New Yankee Workshop's Norm Abrams in my head: "Let's take a minute to talk about shop safety."

■ Steve Azola with the "Fenderbacker" he made from parts in 1974.

Here are some of my thoughts about woodworking shop organization and safety. I certainly don't know everything, just what works for me. The creative process is pretty complicated, and there are times when you simply cannot make any mistakes. Armed with inspiration and the right tools, see what you can do—and be careful.

■ A clean, well-organized work space is essential for shop safety.

Self-Preparation

The most important factor in the bass-building process, and the most critical tool, is yourself. Your attitude, mental preparation, and focus are the keys to safe and fruitful work. Don't overestimate your strengths and abilities, and be sure to recognize your potential vulnerabilities. Set your mind to the tasks at hand, and tune in to all of the aspects of the job ahead. Don't try to work when you're preoccupied or worn out from a gig the night before. Educate yourself thoroughly, ahead of time, with all available printed and Internet resources. Use common sense in preparing yourself physically for what you need to do—don't wear loose clothing or let long hair dangle. Try to limit distractions in the shop. Music choices should provide an inspirational backdrop for your work and should not intrude on your concentration. Don't be afraid of your tools and machinery, but give them the healthy respect they deserve.

Shop Setup and Maintenance

Create an environment conducive to focus and productivity. With enough planning and forethought, your shop will be a place that draws you in and keeps you there willingly. It should be clean, properly ventilated, and well-lit. Make it as pleasant as possible for what you want to accomplish. Allow adequate space for woodworking, assembly, and storage. Lay out your tools efficiently, with economical use of the available area, but with enough room to move around the machines. Most equipment should be hooked to a dust collection system; this keeps chips away from the cutters, which prevents clogging and lets them perform effectively.

Climate Control and Wood Storage

Most experts recommend that shop humidity levels be kept at about 40–45 percent, with a consistently moderate temperature, for proper wood storage. Install an accurate thermometer and humidity gauge (hygrometer). In most areas, humidity falls in the winter and rises in the summer. Air conditioning can lower humidity levels as well as air temperature. Heaters dry the air as they warm it, so you may need to use a humidifier to maintain optimum levels during cold weather. Let newly acquired wood stabilize for at least a few weeks before working it. Unfinished wood needs to be kept in a fairly stable climate-controlled environment to avoid warpage and splitting.

■ Many jobs are done with hand tools and hand-held power tools.

Common Shop Tools and Safety Tips

Most of my lutherie skills are self-taught, so I've developed distinct opinions about useful tools and the safest ways to employ them. While many of my contemporaries use big industrial-strength machines, I prefer smaller, less intimidating equipment. Although some say the bigger machines are safer, and I know they do their jobs well, my experience makes me comfortable with more manageable tools.

Here are the basic tools I use for instrument making, along with some tips for using them:

Hand tools and hand-held power tools

Along with hand files, scrapers, and sanding blocks, hand-held power tools such as drills, jigsaws, and sanders are probably the first items you'll need to acquire for your bass-building endeavors. They're small versions of the more serious machinery used in big woodworking shops. I've found that effective hand-tool use begins with securing the wood carefully, and then applying the tool to the work piece.

Though you could use small tools for most aspects of a bass-building project, you'll sacrifice precision and efficiency. In my opinion, you're best served investing some time, effort, and capital in basic shop machinery and setup.

Table saw

The table saw is typically the most-used tool in traditional woodworking shops, generally for dimensioning lumber and making straight-line cuts. But I find I don't use it much for most instrument-making tasks. When I do, it's usually with the dado blade installed for radiusing fingerboards. It's an intimidating machine that demands the utmost respect. The best and safest way to approach a table saw is to use push sticks and fixtures to hold your wood, so your hands are completely clear of the blade.

Bandsaw

I use a bandsaw for rough-shaping almost everything. It's relatively safe and not too overwhelming to master. Best utilized for cutting shapes and working with thick pieces of wood, it leaves a fairly rough-cut edge—sanders address that later. If you're working with an oddly shaped piece, make a fixture to send it safely through the saw.

Sanders (belt, drum, disc)

Many different types of sanders have found their way into my shop to handle final shaping. They do most of the work after I make basic cuts with the saws. They're relatively safe machines, with the exception of the large edge sanders, which tend to grab a workpiece if you offer it up to the belt at the wrong angle. I find it's best to keep the belt, discs, and drums fresh (sharp or new), as the expense for new abrasives is less costly than the time wasted using dull ones. Watch your fingertips, or you can give yourself a pretty aggressive manicure.

Routers (table, pin, hand)

Routers are used for neck profiling and radiusing, cavity cutting, and body radiusing. Overhead pin routers are among the most dangerous tools in a shop, which is probably why I don't even have one. Though the pin router is a highly productive machine, the potential danger outweighs the possibility of faster work. Imagine a

■ Steve hand-cutting a nut slot on an upright neck.

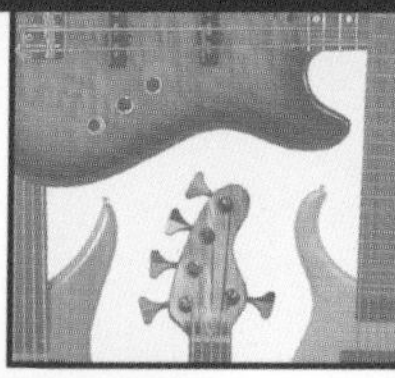

■ Steve clamps the kerfing on a bass body.

5-horsepower motor spinning a blade at 20,000 RPM, with nothing between it and your hands but a chunk of wood. One wrong move and your hand gets sucked into it. I do have a couple of inverted pin routers, which put the motor under the table with the cutter poking up through a hole. The cutting is done down at table level, and your hands are above everything, in relative safety. These can still be dangerous, so—as with most other tools—build a fixture to hold your wood and keep your hands out of harm's way. Be sure to feed the wood into the cutter in the proper direction. Make cuts in several passes rather than a single deep one.

Shaper

A shaper is a larger, more heavy-duty version of a table router, and it can be even more dangerous. For my instrument building, I find I don't need one.

Drill presses

Because my metal hardware is cast in aluminum, drill presses are invaluable for machining it. A mill drill is especially accurate for machine-drilling precision holes in any material. A drill press is relatively harmless, but for most operations it's important to securely clamp the workpiece to the table. Always use sharp bits and proper drilling speeds for specific materials. Don't try to drill all the way through in one stroke. Use repetitive strokes in incremental depths until you achieve the desired depth.

Jointer

A jointer is used primarily to flatten and true boards for precision glue joints. It can be extremely dangerous because the blade is rotating in plain view as you feed in the wood. Use push tools to propel the wood through, keeping your hands away from the blades.

Planer

A planer accurately mills wood to the desired thickness, turning rough lumber into usable material. Most of the cutting mechanism is inside the machine—so the real safety issue is to avoid being pulled in. As your high-school shop teacher told you: don't wear loose clothing, keep your tie tucked in, and put your long hair in a ponytail.

Remember that these are just tips—detailed safety instructions for all this equipment could fill volumes. It's critical to understand the proper operation and maintenance of every machine and tool you use. Read the manuals thoroughly so you know how each tool works and what it will do. Machines should be properly set up and aligned. Keep all metal tables cleaned and derusted. Apply a surfacing spray, which allows wood to glide smoothly through cutting tools. Keep all cutters, bits, blades, and abrasives sharp for maximum efficiency and best results. Use push sticks to move boards through saws, and use push pads to propel boards through jointers. Acquire plenty of clamps, in a variety of sizes, for gluing and to use with drill presses and hand tools.

Fixtures and Jigs

Take the time to make fixtures and jigs to support and guide your workpieces. They'll make your life much easier and safer, and will likely prove to be some of the most important tools you use. In the long run, you'll benefit from the improved efficiency and consistency they provide. Many large companies have full-time employees devoted to pattern-making. Take full advantage of all available resources offering diagrams and ideas for fixtures and jigs that can be adapted to meet your specific needs. Templates and patterns, which start life as paper drawings, can be transferred to wood, plastic, or metal for repeated use. Most routing operations will require some form of jig, fixture, or pattern.

Inspiration and Creation

Instruments are the tools used in the creative process of music making, performing beautifully in the right hands. Expressing yourself with woodworking tools as a luthier can be equally rewarding. There is no "how to" manual for building the instrument that exists in your imagination. So you will no doubt spend countless hours working out design details and feasible construction methods, which is how I spend a lot of my time. Breathing life into my basses brings me great fulfillment. I wish you the same sense of satisfaction in your own endeavors.

■ The Azola assembly room, with soldering bench.

B.C. RICH

In its heyday B.C. Rich was the Alembic of heavy metal, building elaborate, expensive, neck-through-body instruments with complicated active electronics controlled by rows of knobs and switches. The more outrageous, the better, and the razor-sharp horns and swooping curves of such B.C. Rich models as the Bich, Warlock, Eagle, and Mockingbird were unmistakable. These were basses created for pounding out bone-crunching riffs in giant arenas, preferably while leaping around amidst clouds of smoke.

Oddly enough, the company was founded by a luthier who learned his craft building classical and flamenco guitars. Bernardo Chavez Rico didn't get interested in electric instruments until the early 1970s, when he made a few custom guitars modeled on Fender and Gibson models. He quickly warmed to the task, and by the end of the decade Bernie Rico was firmly established as a wild and crazy guy, both in his personal life (he loved hot cars and flashy clothes) and his instrument designs.

In 1976 Rico drew the Mockingbird body shape, the story goes, on a cocktail napkin; the first Mockingbird he built was a short-scale bass. More futuristic and flamboyant designs followed, some of them co-designed with Neil Moser. Many were quite similar on a functional level; it was the *look* of an instrument that appealed to Rico, and the more eye-catching he could make it, the more he liked it. ("If you're going to do something," he once said, "do it with flair.") According to Michael Wright, Rico proclaimed the Wave—introduced in 1983—as his finest bass design.

■ B.C. Rich Bich 8-string.

Rico's loyal customers included Gene Simmons of Kiss—whose first Punisher bass was built by B.C. Rich in the early '90s—and dozens of metalheads. He also sold instruments to session greats like Bernard Edwards and Nathan Watts, who didn't care about stage presence but were attracted by the tonal flexibility of Rico's creations.

At first all B.C. Rich instruments were built in Los Angeles, but production of lower-priced models eventually moved offshore to Japan and Korea. In 1990 Rico sold his design licenses to a company called Class Axe, and he was not involved with the company again until 1994, when he opened a new factory in Hesperia, California, with sons Joey and Bernie Jr. New B.C. Rich bass models like the Bernardo and Exclusive were introduced, and a custom shop operation was set up. Bernie Rico died in 1999, but production of U.S.-made and imported B.C. Rich basses continues under the ownership of corporate conglomerate HHI.

BENAVENTE

In 1995, faced with the need for a student project in his CAD/CAM course, Chris Benavente decided to build a guitar. "It took about six months for me to complete it, but to my amazement it actually worked," he says. "Our local luthier told me that I had a knack for this sort of thing and should pursue it—and Benavente Guitars was born." Benavente's first bass design was the 219 Series, which he still produces. It's a neck-through with a double-cutaway body featuring an extended upper horn for better balance. EMG electronics are standard, and it can be built from a wide variety of woods as a 4-, 5-, or 6-string. Other Benavente models include the J150, a neck-through J-style bass, the 219-B, and the Singlecut.

■ Benavente Singlecut 5-string.

BOLIN

SEE NS DESIGN

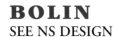

■ Born To Rock F4b.

BORN TO ROCK

Looking for the perfect bass for a submarine voyage or an extended stay in the tropics? The Born To Rock F4b, designed by Robert Kunstadt of New York City, might be just the thing. Made of hand-welded and polished aluminum tubing, the patented F4b is strong and stable, yet incredibly light. The neck/pickup/bridge unit is attached with pivot joints, so the strings themselves hold it in place, eliminating the tension problems that cause wooden necks to warp. And there aren't many headless basses that have *full-size* tuning machines attached to the body.

BREEDLOVE

The Breedlove Guitar Company, founded in 1990, is a small production shop in central Oregon that builds 80 to 100 acoustic instruments a month. In 1993 they created ten prototype SWB acoustic bass guitars, one of which was displayed at the NAMM show. These 32½"-scale 4-strings had distinctive single-cutaway walnut bodies topped with red cedar or Sitka spruce, mahogany necks, and an ebony pinless bridge. They were never put into production, but in 2002 a company spokesman indicated that Breedlove was considering a new series of acoustic bass guitars.

■ Breedlove SWB acoustic bass guitar.

BRIAN MOORE

Perhaps because of its founders' connection to Steinberger Sound, Brian Moore Guitars is a company known for instruments that are just a bit *different.* A designer by trade, Brian Moore was working for Ned Steinberger when he met Patrick Cummings in 1991. At the time, Cummings was a Gibson executive overseeing Steinberger (which Gibson had acquired in 1986) and several other divisions. With financial backing from Kevin Kalagher, who had done printing work for Steinberger, Moore and Cummings launched Brian Moore Guitars in 1992.

The company's first offering was the MC/1, a high-tech guitar that combined a neck-through composite structure with a curved wooden body similar to that of the Spector NS. In 1997 Cummings collaborated with Michael Tobias to create the TC/4 and TC/5 basses. They had swamp ash bodies with optional figured-wood tops, 21-fret bolt-on maple necks, active or passive Basslines pickups, and the same "comfort contoured" body shape as the

■ Brian Moore TC/5 (left) and TC/4.

MC/1. The tuning keys on the sculptured headstock were in a unique 1+3 configuration on the 4-string and 2+3 on the 5. Another out-of-the-ordinary feature was the placement of the output jack in a recess on the back of the body ("keeps output cable hidden away and snug behind your guitar strap," said the literature). Scale length on both models was 34". RMC piezos were optional, with a MIDI-ready upgrade available.

Brian Moore's "Why not?" philosophy is also evident in the Korean-made iGuitars, equipped with RMC 13-pin MIDI connectors. Conventional models, without the connectors, are dubbed the i2000 series. This line includes the i4 and i5 basses, neck-through instruments with figured-maple tops, 24-fret necks, and the same unusual headstock design; a MIDI-ready version, for use with the Roland V-Bass system, was being tested in 2002. The company also announced plans for new U.S.-made basses to replace the discontinued TC series.

BRUBAKER

Baltimore-area luthier Kevin Brubaker has been building basses since 1993, turning out a small number of custom-made instruments each month. The bodies of his instruments are carved to produce what he calls "center mass construction," with the outer edges thinner than the middle. All Brubaker basses have bolt-on necks with a deep inset that reaches about halfway into the body. Kevin uses a 34⅝" scale length on all of his basses, finding this "in-between" length a good compromise for both manufacturing and playability reasons.

Brubaker, a working bassist himself, offers three models—NBS, Protégé, and Lexa—all available as 4-, 5-, or 6-strings. The main difference between them is body shape. The NBS can be ordered with either a 22- or 24-fret neck. It has an ash body, maple neck, and Bartolini pickups; a large number of options and upgrades are available. The 22-fret Protégé is available with either a single Bartolini humbucker or a pair of Bartolini J-style pickups. The Lexa is a 24-fret model with similar options as the NBS models.

■ Brubaker 5-string with "center mass construction."

BUNKER

If innovation were the only requirement for recognition in the musical-instrument industry, then Dave Bunker of Puyallup, Washington, might be as esteemed a figure as Leo Fender. In 1955, when the solidbody electric guitar and bass were still in their infancy, Bunker conceived a doubleneck instrument called the Duo-Lectar, which combined guitar and bass necks played by tapping the strings. With assistance from his father, Joseph (a violinmaker), Bunker built one. The first version had 6-string necks for both guitar and bass, but Bunker later changed the bass neck to the more familiar *EADG* configuration.

The Duo-Lectar never caught on—probably because it required a radically different playing technique—but Bunker himself showcased its sound in a well-received Las Vegas lounge act. In the 1960s, Leo Fender reportedly tried to buy the rights to the instrument (Bunker wasn't interested), but the guitar-and-bass, two-hand tapping concept was later revisited in such instruments as Emmett Chapman's Stick [see Stick].

■ Bunker Galaxy BTX500 5-string.

Bunker never gave up on his original idea, which he continued to perfect through several generations of instruments and several companies. In the late 1980s, he helped to establish PBC Guitars of Coopersburg, Pennsylvania. PBC produced several instruments using Bunker's touch technology, including the 355H Electro-Mute bass. Scott Malandrone, reviewing it in *Bass Player*, was impressed with its solid construction and good sound; he noted that the bass's Electro Mute system, which electronically mutes strings not being played, provides cleaner sound for any player and also makes it possible for disabled musicians to play the instrument with one hand.

While at PBC, Bunker did subcontracting work for the large Japanese company Hoshino, producing such instruments as the Ibanez ATK bass, which featured Bunker's Tension Free Neck. Another novel design concept, it has a separate headstock attached to the body with a steel bar, thus eliminating string-tension stress on the nut-to-body length of the neck. (Bunker came up with the idea in the 1950s while discussing conventional neck design with engineers at Boeing, where he was working at the time.) As interesting and well-made as the PBC instruments were, they didn't yield commercial success for Bunker. When the company went bust in 1996, he moved back to his native Pacific Northwest and started again with Bunker Guitar Technology.

The contemporary Bunker Touch Guitar is a vastly refined version of the Duo-Lectar. The key to its sound is a unique electronics configuration. "The strings are all electronically separated from each other," explains Bunker. "They have a very small DC voltage fed to them, and the frets are a common ground—the same as your jack output. When you touch the string to the fret, that string turns on its own pickup. You get only the pure sound of the string vibration without any of the unwanted scraping, sliding, hum, hiss, thumping, or ambient sounds normally associated with electric guitars and basses. As soon as you remove your finger, the string is off and no manual muting is required. You can move any place you wish as fast as you want and will get no unwanted string noise."

The 32"-scale bass has a Tension Free Neck and another innovative Bunker-designed feature: the Through Body Bridge. Each string is attached to its own individual bridge unit, a precision component milled from bell brass. It has a fine-tuning knob and two steel mounting posts that go through the body and are attached to a "reflection plate" on the back of the instrument. (A somewhat different version of the through-body bridge concept was developed by the now-defunct 2TEK Company of Kent, Washington, in the late 1990s.)

Bunker also builds standard bass guitars that feature the Tension Free Neck and Through Body Bridge. His Sunstar model is a solidbody instrument available as a 34"-scale 4-, 5-, or 6-string, headed or headless, with EMG or Bill Lawrence pickups. The Galaxy solidbody and Astral hollowbody basses are available as 4- or 5-strings. In 2001 Bunker's Touch Guitar was honored by inclusion in an exhibit called "Objects for Use: Handmade by Design" at the American Craft Museum in New York City.

Dave Bunker's son, David L. Bunker, also builds instruments with a specialized "Floating Neck" design. Sold under the Treker name, his Utah-made Pro-Star basses come in 4-, 5-, and 6-string configurations. He also offers custom instruments with a wide variety of construction and electronics options. For more information, go to www.trekerguitars.com.

CA GUITARS

They say it doesn't take a rocket scientist to build a bass—but sometimes it does. Composite Acoustics (CA) was launched in 1997, when Ellis Seal left his job as an aerospace engineer at Lockheed Martin and began to prototype all-composite acoustic instruments. Using innovative fabrication techniques and his patented "Acoustic Tailoring" bracing system, Seal created a carbon-fiber dreadnought that compared favorably to high-quality wooden guitars. In 2001 CA expanded its Lafayette, Louisiana, facilities, and a year later it began to produce Vortex acoustic bass guitars, 34"-scale 4-strings available fretted (F4) or fretless (FL4). Equipped with Fishman electronics, these jumbo-size instruments have a "soundport" on the upper bout.

■ CA Guitars Vortex F4.

CARL THOMPSON

"I just got mad one day and made a bass," says Carl Thompson. The object of his anger was a borrowed Fender 4-string, which he found neck-heavy and awkward to play. "Playing is hard enough without struggling to hold up the neck. I wanted to fix that."

Thompson grew up in the western Pennsylvania town of Pitcairn, where he learned guitar from his father. He also helped out in his dad's workshop, where the projects included a crude electric bass guitar they put together in 1942. After reinforcing the body of a Kay archtop guitar with a center block, the Thompsons attached a homemade neck and mounted a dual-coil pickup. They then took a set of gut bass strings and modified the sections that passed over the pickup with a coating of conductive paint and some hand-wound steel wire. Young Carl played this electric bass himself on some of the family's home recordings.

Thompson moved to New York City in the late 1960s at the urging of a friend, bassist Russell George. He hoped to make his mark as a jazz guitarist, but he soon discovered that the city was loaded with talented players. Using the skills he'd learned at home, Thompson went to work in Dan Armstrong's shop on 48th Street, doing repairs and modifications. He still gigged at night, sometimes doubling on electric bass, and that's when he got irked wrestling with a Fender.

Before he began to build, Thompson went to the library and took out a book on the great violinmaker Antonio Stradivari. Carl absorbed the information about working with wood and creating an instrument to fit the player's hands and body. That was useful—even inspirational—but he lacked the practical experience to achieve the results he wanted. "I didn't have woodworking chops of any kind," he told Tom Mulhern in *Guitar Player*. "I never really studied it. It just came to me. It think it's a desire: if you put your head into it and you have any kind of talent for it, you'll be able to do it." Thompson also gives credit to Mrs. Keck, his fifth-grade teacher, who instilled in him the basic principles of mathematics. Too many builders, he says, fail to understand the math of music, leading to faulty bridge placement and other design flaws that diminish the tone of their instruments.

■ Carl Thompson left-handed 4-string, 1978.

Armed with both knowledge and desire, Thompson forged ahead, building instruments by hand and sometimes using his mistakes to creative advantage. The characteristic Carl Thompson heel block, for example, came about because of a problem with the neck mortise on his first bass. "I figured I could add a piece of maple to the neck and start over with a fresh hole," he told Mulhern, "but I thought it might look like I was trying to cover up something. So I tried a piece of ebony and put it on like a heel block, and carved it so the neck flowed right into the body. It serves two purposes: first, it enhances the beauty of the instrument;

■ Carl Thompson 4-string #5-17-2000.

■ Carl Thompson fretless 4-string #7-31-02.

second, we can easily change the angle of the neck to the body by increasing or decreasing the taper of the block."

By 1974 Thompson had gained a foothold as a builder, producing custom instruments at a time when there were few basses available, other than Alembics, that were not mass-produced by large companies. His career got a boost after one of his repair customers, Stanley Clarke, made an unusual request: could Carl build him a 4-string tuned an octave *higher* than a bass? Although Thompson had made only a handful of instruments, he was more than willing to tackle something different—so he created the first piccolo bass: a 34"-scale fretless equipped with a special set of D'Addario strings. Clarke soon found that the instrument lacked clarity without frets, so Thompson installed them. And when Stan the Man played this piccolo bass on the *School Days* album and gave credit to its builder in the liner notes, Carl Thompson suddenly became a new star in the bass-building universe. A few years later, when Clarke's piccolo bass was damaged, Thompson built him a new one, this time using a 32" scale for brighter tone.

Not long after he built the first piccolo bass, Thompson got another unusual order. Session bassist Anthony Jackson came to him with an idea for a "contrabass guitar" with six strings tuned *BEADGC*. "My first reaction," Carl told Mike DuClos in *Bass Player*, "was, 'Crazy guy! Six strings, low *B*—what are you talkin' about?' Anthony said he wanted to extend his range, but I told him the first thing we'd have to do is lengthen the scale—34" just wouldn't be enough. To get that *B* to sound right, we'd have to stretch it; it's simple physics. He agreed, but he was so used to playing his Fender he wasn't sure if he could deal with the longer scale—so we ended up making it 34". It was a difficult but worthwhile experience." (Thompson's initial assessment would prove to be correct, and most contemporary 6-strings have a 35" or 36" scale length.)

In 1975 Thompson delivered the first true 6-string bass, with a low *B*, to Jackson, who used it on tour with Roberta Flack and in the studio with saxophonist Carlos Garnett on the album *Let This Melody Ring On*. Jackson was unhappy with the instrument's tight string spacing, though, so he returned to Thompson's shop. Carl tried out some other ideas—including one test bass with a 44" scale—before Jackson moved on to Ken Smith to build his next contrabass. (Smith had been one of Thompson's earliest instrument customers, and Thompson assisted Smith's 1976 entry into the business by assembling the body blank, based on Ken's drawing, for the first Ken Smith bass.)

Thompson enjoyed steady business during the late '70s and early '80s, building one-of-a-kind basses for a procession of top players who made the pilgrimage to his Brooklyn shop. By 1990 things had slowed down, and he was contemplating retirement—and then Primus mastermind Les Claypool ordered a fretless 6-string, setting off another publicity boom. "Les has been great," Thompson told DuClos. "He found one of my basses in a shop, loved it, and sought me out. . . . He's made it possible for me to reach more people."

The Les Claypool Bass comes as close to being a standard model as anything Thompson has made, although all of his instruments are individual creations. Even so, most of them are instantly recognizable thanks to their distinctive scroll-shaped horns. Thompson carves the bodies from a wide range of woods, often combining such unusual choices as zebrawood, padauk, bubinga,

■ Carl Thompson Les Claypoo
fretless 6-string.

bocote, and birch with the more familiar maple and mahogany. Scale length can be 32", 34", 36", or 38". Thompson favors oil finishes for their natural feel and ease of maintenance. He likes to build his own bridges from a single piece of ebony in order to maximize string contact, but he recognizes that many players like to change string gauges, so his basses can be ordered with adjustable metal bridges. Pickups and electronics are chosen from various sources to meet the needs and playing style of each customer. Carl Thompson basses are often much lighter than they look (some weigh as little as six pounds), and they all have impeccable balance—of course.

While Thompson is grateful for the recognition he has received, he's quick to share the praise. When interviewed, he invariably mentions the players who have given him good ideas, and he thanks such associates as Joel Frutkin, Ronnie Blake, Mike Parisi, and "a girl named Serena" for their contributions to the design and construction of his basses. He also points out that he still practices more than two hours every day, which keeps him focused on what's important: "For me, it's just the music."

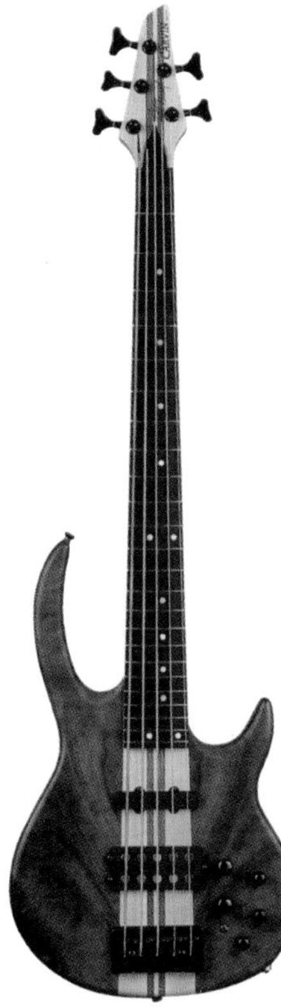

■ Carvin BB75 Bunny Brunel 5-string.

CARVIN

In the 1940s, shortly after Leo Fender and Doc Kauffman set up shop as K&F Manufacturing, a Hawaiian-style guitarist named Lowell Kiesel started his own California-based music-products business, the L.C. Kiesel Company. Working out of his Los Angeles home, he made and sold guitar pickups, soon adding lap steels and amplifiers to the line.

In late 1949 or early 1950, Kiesel changed the name of his company to Carvin, in honor of his sons Carson and Gavin. The family moved to Covina, California, and by the mid '50s their product line expanded to include solidbody electric guitars. Then as now, most Carvin products were sold directly to customers via a mail-order catalog, rather than through a dealer network. In 1959 Carvin introduced its first basses, modeled after the company's SGB guitar, a single-cutaway model that looked like a deformed Les Paul guitar. Carvin also offered a double-neck model with 4-string bass and 6-string guitar necks. Throughout the 1960s and '70s, Carvin updated its two or three bass models in lockstep with its guitar line, rolling out redesigned bodies and electronics that mirrored changes in the guitars. Some imported basses were also sold under the Carvin name.

In 1968 Carvin relocated to Escondido, California. The company's bass and guitar models became more sophisticated during the late 1970s and '80s, with the introduction of exotic woods like koa, active electronics, upgraded hardware, and distinctive sharp-horned bodies designed by Mark Kiesel. Carvin offered neck-through-body construction in 1988, and the LB neck-through basses emerged as one of Carvin's most popular lines. The series includes the LB20 (passive) and LB70 (active) 4-strings, the LB75 5-string, and the LB76 6-string, as well as the BB75 Bunny Brunel signature 5-string.

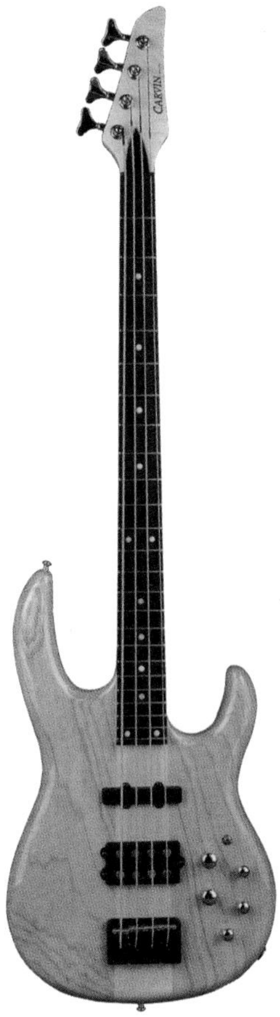

■ Carvin LB70.

In 1995 Carvin moved again, to an 80,000-square-foot factory in San Diego. During the '90s the company enhanced its LB series with more premium-wood choices (such as figured claro walnut), graphite-reinforced necks, and continuing improvements to the pickups and electronics, including an optional piezo-bridge system. In 1996 the semi-hollow AC basses were introduced, available fretted or fretless, 4- or 5-string. The bargain-priced B4 and B5 bolt-on basses were added in 1998. In the '90s Carvin opened retail showrooms in California and Europe, but the bulk of the company's business is still by mail order, and still at low direct-sale prices. In 2002 it was possible to order a U.S.-made neck-through-body LB76P 6-string with 18-volt active/passive electronics including the piezo-bridge system—for less than $1,000.

■ Chandler Royale 12-string.

CHANDLER

Paul and Adrian Chandler of Chico, California, started out in the guitar-parts business and have been making instruments since 1991, most of them retro-style electric guitars, slide guitars, and lap steels. They've offered a few basses over the years, including the Continuum (a J-style fretless in kit form) and the Hi-Fidelity Bass (available with a choice of wide/large, wide/slim, or narrow/slim neck profile). In the bass world, though, Chandler is probably best known as a builder of 12-strings. (In its usual configuration, a 12-string has four bass strings tuned *EADG* with two octave strings alongside each—although other tunings are possible.) In 1996 the Chandlers built a Flying V–style 12-string, festooned with a Miller Genuine Draft logo, for Allen Woody of the Allman Brothers Band. A little later, working with Tom Petersson of Cheap Trick, they created the Royale 12-string. It has a full 34" scale length, unlike the 30" or 32" on many other 12s. The laminated-maple neck is reinforced with a graphite slab to withstand the considerable string tension. Three pickups are nestled in the single-cutaway body: a P-style in the neck position and two humbuckers. A variety of flashy finishes is available, including "SuperSparkle" metallic paint.

CHARVEL

SEE JACKSON

CITRON

For Harvey Citron, building basses is a natural extension of interests nurtured during his late-'60s days as an architecture student at City College of New York. "I started out as a musician," he explains. "I had a Martin guitar and played in bands when I was 11 and 12 years old. Early on, I played with [drummer] Carmine Appice, who lived on my block in Brooklyn. I stopped playing for a while, and then I started again when I was in college, which is where I met Joe Veillette."

Veillette was an aspiring guitarist who was curious about instrument construction—largely because his guitar kept breaking. "Joe decided it would be a good idea to learn how to make guitars so he could fix his neck," says Citron. "And then a friend told him about a class being taught by [well-known luthier] Michael Gurian. Joe took the class, and he got so enthralled with making guitars he decided to start doing it himself."

■ Citron CB5.

Citron, who was working as an architect and playing in bands at night, would drop by to watch his friend's progress. Veillette was focusing on acoustic guitars, but he had also started a solidbody electric that languished unfinished in the corner. "Every time I'd go over there," recalls Harvey, "I'd say, 'Joe, when are you going to finish that electric?' One day he just handed it to me and said, 'You finish it.'"

The idea intrigued Citron. With the help of Bob Castaldo, an assistant in Dan Armstrong's shop, and Sal Palazolla, who worked with pickup maker Bill Lawrence, he figured out how to install the electronics. "The woodworking still wasn't done," Harvey says, "so I went to Joe's shop, and we stayed up for two nights finishing that guitar. Witnessing this thing come to life was an incredible turn-on."

Invigorated by their success, Citron and Veillette began to build prototypes for their original solidbody bass and guitar designs. At the time, Harvey was also testing guitar strings for the Vinci company. Tom Vinci took an interest in the Veillette-Citron instruments, and he invited the novice luthiers to share his booth at the June 1976 NAMM show in Chicago. "We were amazed at the reaction to the prototypes," recalls Harvey. "Some friends of ours who were also working with Tom Vinci were there, and when they saw the reaction they said, 'Wow, this is great. How 'bout if we sell your instruments?' They decided they were going to buy everything we made, and suddenly we were in business."

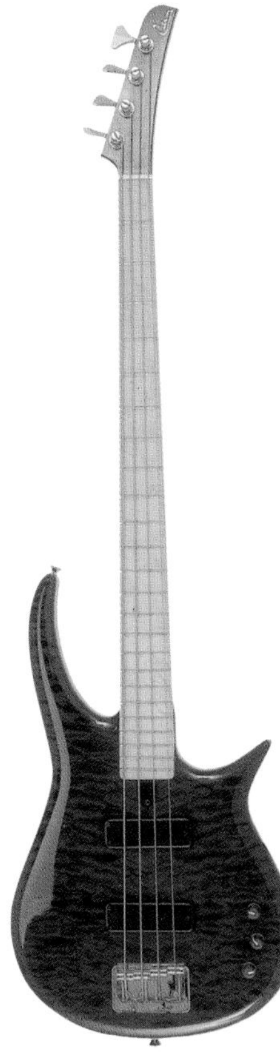
■ Citron BO4.

Citron says the V-C bass prototype was an Alembic-inspired neck-through-body instrument made of laminated maple with black dyed-wood strips between the laminations. The 32"-scale 4-string had an ebony fingerboard and "probably" 24 frets. They handcrafted the brass hardware in their shop. Harvey wound the pickups himself, mounting them in black-Plexiglas boxes and casting them in polyester resin. He has always been fascinated by the art of creating pickups. "Right from the start, I was asking: What happens if you use a heavier or lighter gauge of wire? What if you use less wire? What happens if the coils aren't even?" says Citron, who has wound his own pickups throughout his building career.

The quick acceptance of the V-C designs led to a partnership that lasted for eight years. The company produced both basses and guitars, but was more successful selling bass instruments. The line included neck-through-body double-cutaway 4-string and 8-string basses in both single- and dual-pickup configurations at three price levels: Standard, Classic, and Limited Edition. The top-of-the-line Limited Edition basses featured 3⁄16" tops made of selected ebony, rosewood, koa, or walnut. The Series S basses, shown in the company's final brochure, had an unusual body shape reminiscent of the Guild Jet-Star Bass. Made of solid maple with a curly maple top, they were available with one or two V-C single-coil pickups.

Since Veillette-Citron dissolved in 1983, Harvey has worked as an independent designer and luthier. The Citron line includes solidbody 4-, 5-, and 6-string basses in neck-through (NT) and bolt-on (BO) versions as well as the piezo-equipped acoustic/electric (AE) models, which Harvey has built in both conventional and headless 4- and 5-string configurations. The 4-string models have a 34" scale length; 5- and 6-string basses add another inch. All Citron basses have laminated quartersawn necks for maximum stability and stiffness; they are made of three

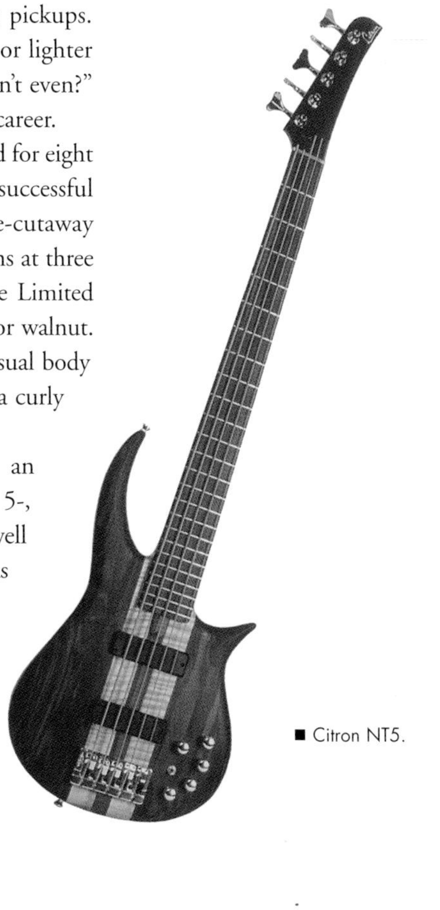
■ Citron NT5.

pieces of hard-rock maple on all models except the AEs, on which two pieces of mahogany and one piece of maple are used.

In 2001 Harvey Citron added the CB basses to his line. These instruments have 2"-thick chambered bodies made of swamp ash or mahogany, and they fall, sonically, between his solidbody models and the hollowbody AEs. Standard electronics include an Aguilar 18-volt preamp and a pair of Citron humbucking pickups that are wound with two different gauges of wire to produce a distinctive throaty tone.

Jazz bassist Steve Swallow worked with Citron to develop a personalized version of the AE5, tuned *EADGC*, that has a 36" scale length, one magnetic pickup, and a wooden piezo bridge with adjustable saddles. To get the string balance Swallow wanted, Citron re-engineered the bridge to include six piezos (two for the *E* string, two for the *A* to *G* strings, and two for the *C* string) connected to three discrete buffer circuits. Their collaboration continued on another custom instrument, equipped with piezos only.

Citron points out that living and working in the close-knit musical community of Woodstock, New York, makes it easy for him to share ideas with Swallow and other top players. Their input, he says, has been instrumental in helping him to create new bass designs. "I love working out problems," he says. "That's why I do this."

■ Citron AE4 (left) and AE5.

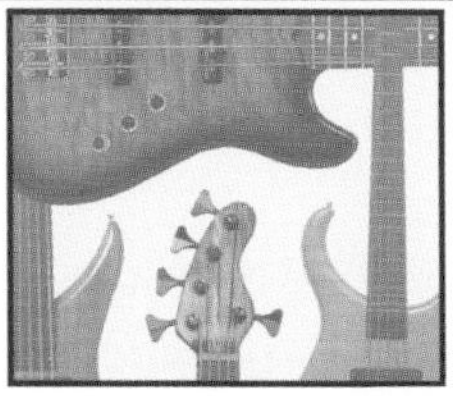

DEMYSTIFYING BASS SETUP

By Harvey Citron

A lot of players think when they find a bass that feels great to them there's some kind of magic associated with it. While there may be something mysterious at work in the tone—no two pieces of wood sound exactly alike—setup can be measured and understood. If you can measure a setup you like, you can duplicate it on another bass. Or if you want to change it, you'll know precisely what to change.

There is no setup that works for everyone. I've read articles that state a bass neck should always be dead straight, or it should have precisely this much or that much bow. That's ridiculous. When I set up basses for Doug Wimbish, he insists on very low action and a straight neck. He says, "I don't care if it buzzes." His playing style allows him to play with that setup and make magic. Tony Levin has a more normal setup with a little bit of bow: the lowest string (*E* or *B*) about 1/8" off the fingerboard at the last fret, and the *G* string about 3/32" or less at the last fret. This works for him. Steve Swallow plays with action that is over 1/4" off the last fret on the *E* string, and some bow. This works well for him. Don't be afraid to use what works for you.

The factors that affect the way a neck feels are shape, scale length, fingerboard radius, neck width at the nut, neck width at the last fret, string spacing at the bridge, string spacing at the nut (which, along with the string spacing at the bridge, will dictate the clearance to the edge of the fingerboard), how the fret ends are dressed, neck bow, individual string height, and how low the nut is cut. Some of these (like scale length) are aspects of the instrument's construction and are hard (or impossible) to change. Others can be adjusted during setup. Let's go through it step by step.

The first thing I do is tune the bass to pitch and adjust the trussrod, if needed, to the correct amount of bow for the player. I hold down the low string (*E* or *B*) at the first and last frets, and view the amount of space under the string in the middle of its length. You can measure that with a set of feeler gauges. If I think the trussrod needs adjustment, I'll loosen the strings and turn the trussrod nut. Turning the nut clockwise (tightening) will straighten the neck if it's bowed; turning it counterclockwise (loosening) will produce more bow if the neck is too straight. When I'm satisfied with the trussrod adjustment, I tune the bass and make sure that I still like what I have. If not, I'll adjust the trussrod again.

■ Harvey Citron, 2003.

Next I adjust the heights of the individual strings at the bridge. For this I use a machinist's 6" steel ruler, measuring with the side that's marked in 32nds of an inch. Here are the steps: Put the bass in playing position and check the string height by placing the ruler at the last fret and looking under the string. Adjust each string to a height that works for you, but remember that the string heights should follow the fingerboard's curvature. That kind of adjustment makes the strings feel comfortable, and it can be done correctly only by measuring carefully. If you start with 3/32" at the last fret on the *G* string and want to end up with 1/8" at the last fret for the *E* or *B* string, you'll need to make each string slightly higher than the preceding one. If you look closely, you can see that distinction. After you've adjusted string height, tune the instrument and check for buzzes. If there is a buzz, the action might be too low for your playing style. Buzzes can also be caused by a high fret.

Check the nut height. The lower the strings are, the better the intonation will be—but if the nut is cut too low, the strings will buzz if you play hard. The strings should also follow the fingerboard curvature at the nut. This can be precisely checked with feeler gauges, but I do it partly by feel.

Last, check and set the intonation: Tune up and play the harmonic at the 12th fret. Then play the fretted note at the 12th fret. If the fretted note is sharp, make the string's vibrating length longer by moving its bridge saddle back; if the fretted note is flat, make the string's vibrating length shorter by moving its bridge saddle forward. Do this in small increments so you don't go past the correct pitch.

Don't be afraid to experiment—and have fun!

■ Clevinger Jr. basses, 1987.

■ Clevinger Piezo Archtop.

CLEVINGER

Since Martin Clevinger is best known for the electric uprights he's been designing and building for the past 20 years, you might guess he started as an acoustic bassist who was looking for a louder, more portable instrument that retained the sound and feel of his beloved bass fiddle. Well, guess again.

"In 1966, when I was 14, I got a Kay electric guitar for Christmas," recalls Clevinger. "Other friends got guitars, and we formed a band. Three guitars didn't make it, so somebody had to take the fall—I think we drew straws—and I became the bass player. I tried to do it by playing single notes on a guitar tuned as low as I could make it go, but it became apparent that to compete with other bands we'd have to buy a real bass."

That "real bass" turned out to be a Zim Gar 4-string purchased at Phil Tofoya's guitar shop, a few blocks from Jimi Hendrix's house in South Seattle. "It had a full [34"] scale and a big, baseball-bat neck with a flat fingerboard and tiny banjo frets. We had no idea how to tune it; I think we took the *E* string down to *C*. The action was so high, it was playable only when it was tuned down anyway." Armed with his Zim Gar—and a fake ID—Clevinger began to work in clubs around Seattle, laying down the groove for rock and soul bands. By 1968 he'd earned enough to buy a better axe. "I couldn't afford a P-Bass, so I got a Fender Mustang for $189. It played like a dream, and from then on I was hooked on Fenders." Martin later acquired several early Fenders, including a '51 Precision.

In 1969 Clevinger rented a Czech-made upright and began to study with Ron Simon of the Seattle Symphony. "I don't know how to explain why I did that, except that a lot of the music I was listening to at the time—the mid to late '60s—still had upright. The Supremes' 'Love Is Here and Now You're Gone' had two bass fiddles playing in unison, a magnificent sound. I wanted to make those deeper sounds." And thus the two sonic strands that eventually intertwined in the Clevinger Bass—vintage-Fender punch and the upright's deep fundamentals—began to come together.

Martin moved to the San Francisco Bay Area in 1975, where he immersed himself in jazz. "I was playing straight-up bebop with Vince Wallace and other local players from 1978 to '81, but I had not lost touch with the bass guitar. It didn't make sense to me that the double bass had not evolved into an electric form—at least not one that I could find on the market." Clevinger was unaware of the early "bedpost basses" such companies as Rickenbacker and Regal offered in the 1930s; he later discovered them when he began to do patent searches. "But I had seen the Ampeg Baby Bass, and George Benson came to town with Wayne Dockery playing a Framus electric upright back in 1969, when I was still in Seattle. Ultimately, I got both a Zorko and a Framus Triumph. After suffering with these late-'50s instruments for two years, I decided it was up to me to build an acceptable electric upright."

Although he had taken wood and metal shop in school, Clevinger had no training as a builder. Undaunted, he drew up plans for what he thought would be a workable instrument, bought a slab of maple, and went to work. "I used a Dremel tool until it burned out," he laughs. "I thought, Well, I don't think I'm going to be able to do this with my own tools. So I went looking for job shops to prototype the parts." He assembled the first Clevinger Bass prototype in 1981, and it worked well enough to be played on gigs. "I kept it for a long time and used the hell out of it," says Martin.

Clevinger immediately began to tinker with his design, trying different configurations, woods, neck shapes, hardware, and (especially) pickup designs. "I've always believed this is an electric double bass of the bowed-string family, so I wasn't satisfied with any pickup system that didn't respond to the nuances of bowing. My early

IN SEARCH OF THE PERFECT PICKUP

By Martin Clevinger

In 1973 the first of what would become an endless series of pickup experiments involved the rewiring of my Fender Mustang Bass, which received an experimental quadraphonic array. This separated the strings, allowing individual EQ of each. Two Fender Rhodes pickups per string produced an array of eight pickups wired in series, with separate outputs for each string, just enough to get an output level—and it was hum canceling!

In search of different sound qualities, I began more experiments using an old Kent hollowbody bass guitar as my "bread board." (It was a rather distorted approximation of a Beatle bass with a 30" scale.) This was to be my guinea pig in a quest for tone beyond the bland zone. I also spent hundreds of hours studying old patents at the patent clearinghouse in Sunnyvale, California. Coil-less designs—ones in which the strings themselves were part of the coil scheme—appeared to be one possible way to escape the sonic signature of standard magnetic pickups.

The first operable prototype was a new system of my own design fitted to the Kent bass. The sound was surprisingly different: all of the harmonics along the entire length of the string appeared to be more present and of equal loudness. The magnets could be hidden in various places, as there was no bobbin or visible coil. (The appearance of a bass guitar with no visible pickup was quite shocking in 1976.) To get enough output, I used a step-up transformer electrically connected to the string balls.

The first prototype was promising, so I built a second. This time I used a P-Bass copy equipped with a newly designed hum-canceling step-up transformer. A sectioned brass bridge, for insulated electrical string connection, was constructed; this provided for series or parallel connection of each string. The results were spectacular with regard to the evenness of all harmonics and a more acoustic-like tone and dynamic response. There was little choking of high frequencies, and none of the peaky resonances common with pickups of that day.

While improving this beta prototype, I realized that a great deal of magnetomotive force was necessary to induce sufficient signal for a reasonable output level. At that time, large ceramics were the strongest magnets available. (The incredibly strong and focused rare-earth magnets common today were not yet available.) Undue magnetic pull over large areas of the strings is undesirable, as it interferes with vibration, decreasing sustain. I later realized that magnets and their coercive forces were the enemy of good string vibration.

■ Martin Clevinger, 2003.

My old roommate and longtime friend Dr. Steve Jacques (an electrical engineering grad from Berkeley who attended MIT, received a Ph.D. in biophysics, and taught at Harvard) was of great assistance in my quest. Together, we had built a headphone practice amp for guitar and bass—this was about 15 years before the Rockman. Steve dubbed this little amp the "Dynamic Environment" because the magnetic pickups on our guitars would acquire stray noise from power lines and appliances as we walked about, playing our instruments while wearing white lab coats, pocket protectors, and geeky '60s headphones.

Hoping that the size and strength of the magnets could be minimized, I reasoned there might be a more efficient way to boost the weak string signal. It would be best to dispense with the passive step-up transformer, I decided, and instead use an active transistor amplifier to increase gain. In one day, with help from Dr. Jacques, I built a very-low-impedance amp using a grounded-base transistor circuit. *Voila!* We were able to reduce the magnets' coercive force as well as their size, while at the same time eliminating the costly transformers. We were going to set the world on fire with this new bass guitar with the voodoo tone and no visible pickups!

Where is it now? Well . . . part of the quest for acoustic bass tone and response was achieved quickly by removing the frets from the prototypes. The fretted experiments that followed are now relegated to the dusty shelves, awaiting revival by some ambitious innovator who must face the challenges of implementing the proper high-resistance alloy required for the frets. It's necessary to treat the frets with acid or gun bluing and then put hard lacquer over that. We tried some epoxies, as well as hard-plastic frets of the Micarta/melamine family, but all of these have a shorter lifespan than standard nickel-silver frets—which can't be used because they short out the system, causing clicks and pops.

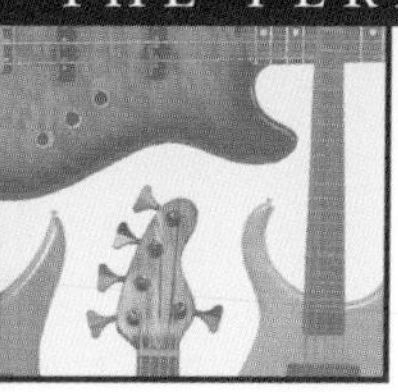

I consulted with the engineer who had invented magnesium-oxide plating (MGO), which is on every electric-stove burner ever made. It was his opinion that the frets might be treated with MGO, but the market size for this product was then (and remains) below the necessary size for this type of production. On top of that, I knew that frets needed milling maintenance, so plating was not really an option. In spite of this insurmountable obstacle, this technology was promising enough that I received two U.S. patents. But I knew I had to find a more practical scheme to achieve the same sonic benefits.

Through intuition and additional patent searches of many pickup schemata—including esoteric Hall-effect systems, optical-type pickups, capacitive or plate-condenser pickups, various dynamic diaphragm arrangements, and too many other Rube Goldberg systems to recall—I began work in earnest on an elegant way to efficiently link strings to piezoelectric materials. This was truly an uphill battle, as the piezo materials presented a whole new set of problems. (It was fairly simple to make a bad-sounding piezo pickup, but getting acceptable tone was something else.) I eventually achieved a marketable and manufacturable configuration that was used in the Clevinger Jr. bass guitars.

I met Richard McClish in 1988, and we discussed pickups with polyphony: one pickup for each string. I went forward with a combined system of discrete piezo saddles designed by Richard (RMC pickups), Bartolini magnetic pickups, and my acoustically resonant compliant piezo bridge/pickup as an underpinning for the RMC pickups. Richard and I still collaborate on electronics, and he has been essential in the development of our MIDI systems. I have continued to develop fully passive bass guitars, although the knowledge gained in my years of pickup experiments has yet to be fully expressed in the instruments still on the drawing board.

■ Clevinger UltraLight, 1979.

designs had magnetic pickups, which don't work very well for bowing, and more than 250 different bridge/pickup designs have been sold in our production models since 1983."

In addition to a wide variety of EUBs, Clevinger has also built several different bass guitars. The Clevinger Jr., available in fretless 4-, 5-, and 6-string models, was introduced in 1986; it had a poplar body, bolt-on maple neck, and 35" or 36" scale length. In 1988 it was upgraded with new electronics that included a Bartolini magnetic pickup and piezos that Clevinger co-developed with Richard McClish of RMC. This model was in production for three years.

While focusing primarily on EUBs in the 1990s, Clevinger prototyped several bass guitars, including an archtop fretless. He eventually introduced the MJ Wide Five, which offers sophisticated electronics in a traditional configuration. The name is derived from its string spacing: a full ¾" between strings at the bridge, the same as a Fender P-Bass—but with five strings. It has a 35" scale length, a bolt-on 24-fret neck (neck-through is available), and a hybrid pickup system with two magnetics and bridge-mounted RMC piezos that can be connected to an optional MIDI preamp.

The original Clevinger designs have evolved into a large and ever-changing product line that includes both EUBs and bass guitars. "We have over 30 standardized models in production—from classic reissues to cutting-edge MIDI systems," says Martin. "Trying to keep up has kept us working around the clock, but behind it all is just the idea of making better basses."

CONKLIN

How did a guy who wanted to play guitar like Ace Frehley end up building 7-string basses? For Bill Conklin, the turning point was high school wood shop. "I had been playing in garage bands since I was 14," he explains, "and I liked to make drawings of guitars—mainly what I'd call 'fashion' guitars, things like star-shapes and V's. So in my senior year I decided I'd try to build a guitar in wood shop. I made one that was shaped like an M-16 [rifle] and got a really good grade on it. When I played that guitar in a band, people asked, 'Where'd you get that?' And when I told them I'd made it, they would say things like, 'Man, you ought to do that for a living.' Well, that really got in my blood."

The idea of building guitars stayed in Conklin's head during his days as a student at the University of Missouri at Rolla, where he studied geological engineering. "Throughout that time, I kept dreaming and drawing. I came home after my third year with the design for a thing I called the Quick Co-Necked Doubleneck. It was a modular doubleneck guitar system; you could put together a 6-string/12-string guitar or a fretted/fretless bass—whatever. I thought I was going to set the world on fire with this thing."

■ Conklin Sidewinder basses, including the 15th Anniversary 7-string (right).

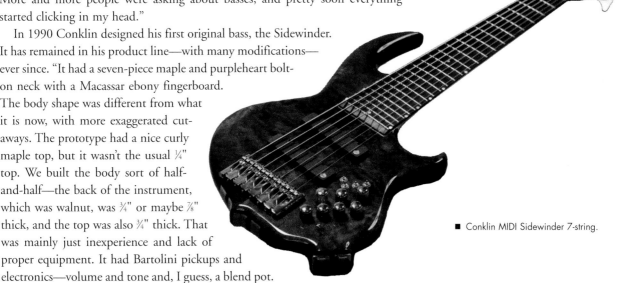

No blazes broke out. After several attempts to find a manufacturer who would license his doubleneck system, Bill decided to start his own company. In late 1983 he began acquiring tools and contacting guitar-parts suppliers. Forgoing his last year of college, he turned his parents' two-car garage into a shop and launched Conklin Guitars.

Conklin notes that although he had actually started out playing bass (briefly), his initial building focus was solely on guitars. "At that time, basses were sort of a mystery to me. I'd look at the ones made by Alembic and Ken Smith and drool over them, but something about the bass seemed out of reach." That attitude began to shift in 1987, when he got a custom order to build a "hot-rodded" Rickenbacker 4001 copy. It was the first bass Conklin Guitars produced. "Then in 1989 and '90, for some reason we started getting a lot of requests for basses. More and more people were asking about basses, and pretty soon everything started clicking in my head."

In 1990 Conklin designed his first original bass, the Sidewinder. It has remained in his product line—with many modifications—ever since. "It had a seven-piece maple and purpleheart bolt-on neck with a Macassar ebony fingerboard. The body shape was different from what it is now, with more exaggerated cutaways. The prototype had a nice curly maple top, but it wasn't the usual ¼" top. We built the body sort of half-and-half—the back of the instrument, which was walnut, was ¾" or maybe ⅞" thick, and the top was also ¾" thick. That was mainly just inexperience and lack of proper equipment. It had Bartolini pickups and electronics—volume and tone and, I guess, a blend pot.

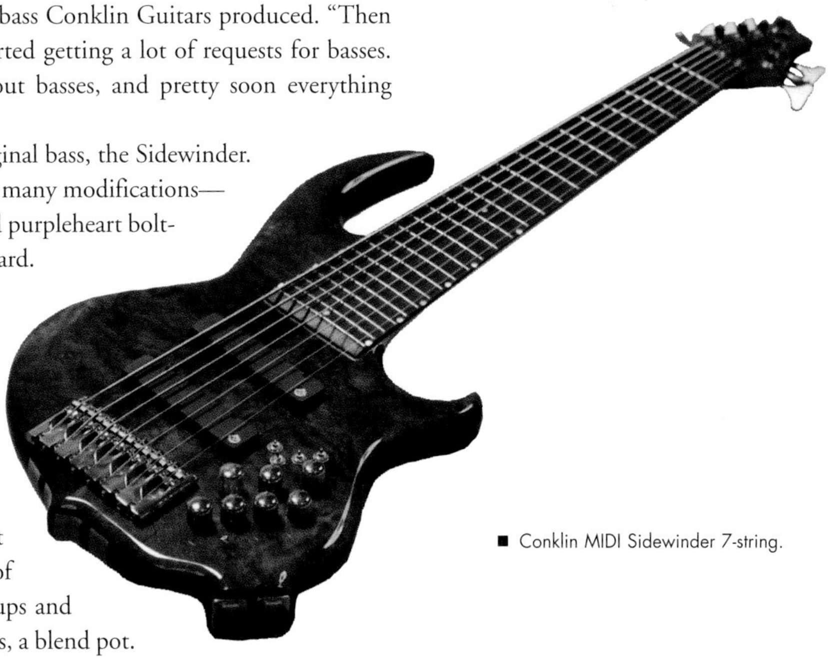

■ Conklin MIDI Sidewinder 7-string.

■ Conklin New Century Series Club 5-string.

And because I was a total greenhorn to the bass world, we built it like a guitar. The back pickup was close to the bridge, like a humbucking guitar pickup, and the neck pickup was right at the end of the fingerboard. And did I mention that it was a 6-string? I wanted to do something different, right from the start."

Conklin took that Sidewinder 6 to his first NAMM show, in January 1991, and got a positive response from both players and dealers. Bass orders started to roll in, and Bill began to refine the look and sound (not to mention the pickup placement) of his instruments. "The real kicker came in 1992, when we got an order for a 7-string bass tuned from low *E* to high *B♭*. While we were working on it, everyone who came by the shop flipped, so we built two in our new Sidewinder body style and took them to the next NAMM show." The 7-string, usually tuned *F#BEADGC* or *BEADGCF*, soon became Conklin's trademark bass.

Bill has also built 8-strings—not the usual 4-string bass with octave pairs but instruments with eight bass strings tuned *F#BEADGCF* or *BEADGCFB♭*—as well as a 9-string leviathan, created for Bill Dickens, that stretches from low *F#* to high *B♭*. Conklin created a special hollowbody 7-string to celebrate the company's 15th anniversary in 1999, and a hollowbody option has remained in the catalog since then. Customers can also order doublenecks in just about any combination, fretted or fretless. The electronics of these basses can be as radical as the string configurations, with stereo wiring, bridge-mounted piezos, a MIDI interface, and the LightWave optical pickup available. There are some subtle touches, too, including a locking output jack, "off-sides" position markers (inlaid in the top edge of the neck), and the smoothly contoured "neck-through-body-feel" heel on the bolt-on models.

Conklin neck-through basses are built to order in the company's Springfield, Missouri, shop; a wide range of styles, woods, and options are available, including scale lengths of 34" or 35" or a "multi-scale" (fanned-fret) fingerboard. Many Conklin instruments feature three-dimensional carving and "melted" tops created by joining exotic woods in unusual dripping or flowing designs. The ultimate Conklin custom creation—although it's hard to choose one—might be a melted-top doubleneck that pairs a 28-fret 7-string neck with a 7-string fretless.

In 1996 Conklin standardized some of the most popular Sidewinder configurations as the New Century series. These 4-, 5-, 6-, and 7-string basses were originally made with cherry bodies, although Conklin later switched to swamp ash; other woods are available. They all have a 34" scale length, Bartolini soapbar pickups, and bolt-on laminated necks incorporating purpleheart for stiffness and strength. Three price levels are offered: Club, Tour (with a figured-maple top), and Session (with a two- to five-piece "melted" top).

Because his U.S.-made basses tend to hit the high end of the price range, Bill Conklin launched the Groove Tools by Conklin series in 1998. These moderately priced Sidewinder-style basses are built in Korea to Conklin's specs and marketed by the Westheimer Corporation. The line includes 34"-scale basses in 4-, 5-, and 7-string configurations; all have bolt-on necks except the Bill Dickens signature bass, a neck-through 7-string with custom Bartolini pickups and electronics. The most recent Groove Tools model is a Rocco Prestia signature bass—somewhat surprisingly for Conklin, it has only four strings.

Capping the Conklin line is the M.E.U. (Mobile Electric Upright), a hollow-bodied creation that looks like a shrunken acoustic bass but has a 34" scale length and is strapped on like a bass guitar. (A tripod stand is optional.) Made of ash with a cherry top, it's available in 4- and 5-string models, has both magnetic and piezo pickups, and can be bowed as well as plucked. As with all Conklin basses, an M.E.U. can be custom built to suit the needs (and imagination) of just about any player—all you have to do is ask.

CURBOW

Greg Curbow has been a pioneer in the use of composites other than graphite. Soon after he founded Curbow String Instruments in the mid 1990s, he began to build basses using a material he called "Rockwood." Developed during World War II as an alternative to metal, it's a composite made by impregnating birch plies with phenolic resin under heat and high pressure. The resulting material is very stiff and strong, yet workable like wood. Curbow at first used Rockwood to build entire instruments, but because of its weight he eventually limited it to necks and fingerboards. To offset the weight of the Rockwood necks, Greg designed the small "Petite" body shape, which he has built from a variety of woods, including mahogany and purpleheart, topped with a wide selection of domestic and imported hardwoods. The top is carved, which makes these basses both more attractive and more comfortable to play.

Along with the flagship Exotic Petite models, Curbow's U.S.-made line has grown to include the XT-33 (33-fret extended-range fingerboard, extra-deep lower cutaway), the M-Series (maple body), the Retro (maple or ash body, single or double pickups), and the Acoustic Electric (hand-carved hollowbody basses with 30" or 34" scale length). All have Rockwood necks. The International Exotic Petite and XT-33 models feature a brass tone block in the body beneath the bridge, for improved tone and sustain. Bartolini pickups and electronics are standard on most models.

In 1996 Greg signed a deal with Jack Westheimer of Cort to produce Curbow-designed instruments in Korea. These basses also feature composites: the bodies are made of Luthite (a petroleum-based plastic) and the fingerboards of Ebonol (a hard plastic used for bowling balls). The necks, in an interesting turnaround on Curbow's domestic models, are Canadian rock maple. Back at home, Curbow has continued to investigate composite materials, including "Rockwood-Lite," which is made from maple laminated under pressure with phenolic/epoxy-based glue. As the name implies, it's lighter than Rockwood while offering similar structural advantages. In addition to building 4-, 5-, 6-, and 7-string basses in his Morganton, Georgia, facility, Greg Curbow also operates the Curbow School of Lutherie.

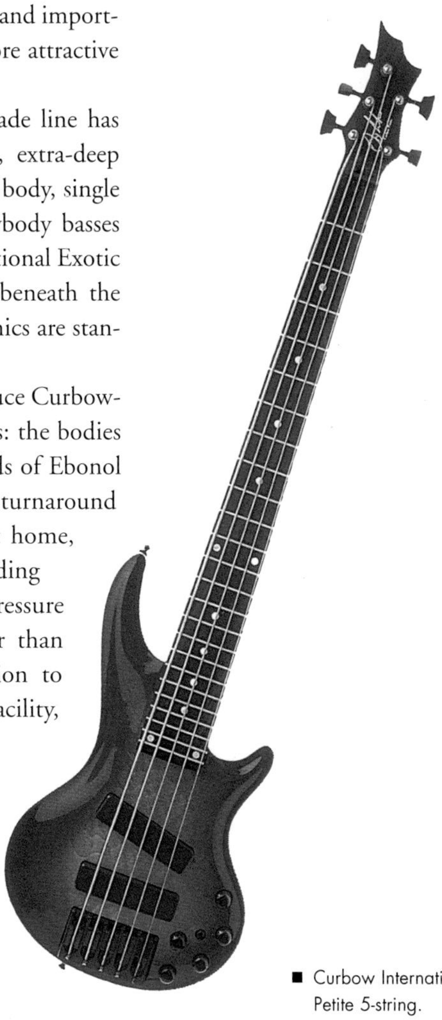

■ Curbow International Exotic Petite 5-string.

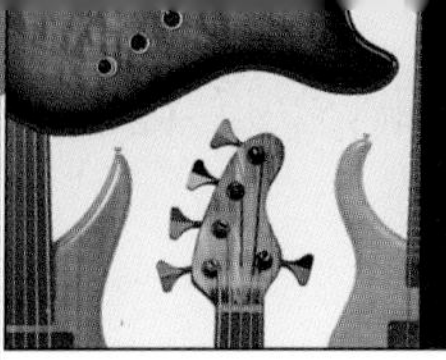

DAMMANN

"I don't conceive of the electric bass as a 4-string guitar tuned down an octave," says Ralph Dammann. "Bass players usually play with their fingers, not a pick, so there's no advantage to having the bass horizontal." In fact, Dammann believes, there are some major disadvantages—and when the instrument is reoriented to a vertical position, it's both easier and less tiring to play.

A university-trained composer and former rock & roll bassist, Dammann builds instruments part-time, as a sideline to running his construction company in Virginia. He conceived of a vertical electric bass in the 1970s, building a prototype that became his working instrument for seven years. He shelved the idea until the late 1990s, when he went into his woodshop and began to perfect the concept that became the Damman V^2 (V-squared). Ralph carves the bodies from mahogany, walnut, and cherry, attaching them to 24-fret through-body maple necks with ebony fingerboards, which he buys from Carvin and adapts to his design. The front of the body is shaped to provide a rest for the right hand, so the thumb isn't used as a pivot. Dammann has installed various electronic components, including EMG and Bartolini magnetic pickups, ABM piezos, LightWave optical pickups, and several custom preamps. He builds 4-, 5-, and 6-string versions of the V^2, fretted and fretless, all with 34" scales.

Having the bass upright facilitates a better left-hand position, similar to classical-guitar technique, providing better coverage of the fingerboard and less strain on the wrist. And with the right hand on the built-in "armrest," all of the fingers can be used more easily for plucking. While Dammann's design won't appeal to all electric bassists, he has high hopes that "it will, in the hands of a creative musician, lead to that rarest and most prized commodity among musicians: new styles of playing."

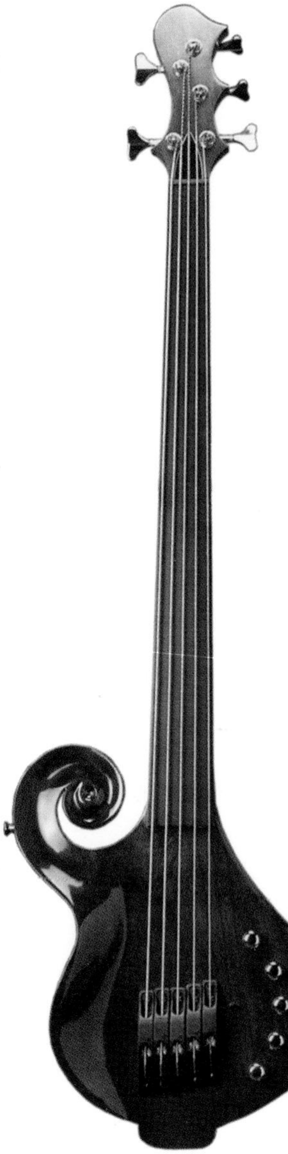

■ Dammann V^2 fretless 5-string.

DAN ARMSTRONG

SEE AMPEG, DANELECTRO

DANELECTRO

Sometimes cheaper is better—or at least more fun. As if to prove that very point, Nathan Daniel began to build basses and guitars in the mid 1950s that were inexpensive yet still credible as musical instruments. The bodies were made of Masonite, mounted on poplar frames that were stapled together, with decorative strips of pebbled vinyl glued around the edges. The necks had no trussrods, just square aluminum tubes down the middle. The single-saddle bridges couldn't be adjusted. The pickups were mounted in surplus lipstick tubes.

Daniel's company cranked out thousands of these cheap axes at its New Jersey factory, many of which were sold by Sears under the Silvertone name. The Danelectro label went on the rest. The earliest Dano basses, introduced in 1956, were the UB1 (one pickup) and UB2 (two pickups) models, single-cutaway 6-strings tuned *EADGBE*, like a guitar but down an octave. Scale length was 29½". These instruments played a vital role in the "tic-tac" style widely used in Nashville during the late '50s and early '60s, with the 6-string Dano bass, played with a pick, doubling the upright bass part.

Danelectro's true electric bass guitars (30" scale length) came in Long Horn and Short Horn models, the names being accurate descriptions of the body shapes.

The Long Horn was one of the most distinctive instrument designs of its era and remains a favorite of collectors. Both body styles came in standard 4- and 6-string (*EADGBE*) models. The standard finishes included a striking "bronze burst" effect.

Like many guitar manufacturers, Danelectro thrived in the early 1960s as the British Invasion fueled domestic sales. MCA bought the company in 1967 and introduced another brand name, Coral; the line included the Firefly semi-hollow bass. By 1969 the party was over, and the Danelectro factory closed. Dan Armstrong bought the name and some parts, which he used to build several hundred Dano-style single-cutaway instruments, including some basses. These are easy to spot: the pickguards are labeled "Dan Armstrong Modified Danelectro" in large letters.

Because so many musicians treasured their old Danelectros, Nashville's Jerry Jones began to build new Dano-style instruments in the late 1980s. His line includes both faithful reproductions and Neptune models incorporating sensible improvements like an adjustable trussrod. Nathan Daniel retired to Hawaii, where he died in 1994; a year later the Evets Corporation acquired the Danelectro name and began to market Korean-made knockoffs of the original basses and guitars, as well as some new models with similar features. Other than the name, these instruments have no connection to the original Danelectros.

■ Danelectro Long Horn 4.

SEE ALSO: JERRY JONES

DAVE MAIZE

The diminishing supply of traditional tonewoods concerns many builders, but Oregon's Dave Maize is doing something about it. Since 1990 he's been building a small number of acoustic bass guitars—five or six a year—using wood obtained with "minimum negative impact on the planet." Following the guidelines of the SmartWood program, Maize selects materials taken from trees harvested on a sustainable basis or salvaged from demolition projects, urban tree removal, and similar sources. Typical woods used in a Dave Maize bass include redwood, spruce, red cedar, walnut, black locust, pearwood, and madrone.

Maize strives to build ABGs that are loud enough to function as true acoustic instruments, without amplification, yet are still comfortable to play. "The traditional Mexican *guitarrón*, while having a huge acoustic sound, is ungainly for the majority of bass players," he says. "There's an inherent tradeoff in output for size, and this compromise is something that has kept me interested in design—how to make a louder instrument while keeping the body size fairly reasonable." That translates to standard body dimensions of 18⅛" x 21¼" with a depth of 5¾"—big, but not boat-like. Maize has further enhanced the volume of his instruments by paying careful attention to the bracing pattern, soundboard thickness, and bridge. "My bridge design borrowed an idea from classical guitarmaker Jeff Elliott," he explains. "Since bridge pins aren't needed, the bridge plate on the underside of the soundboard can be left off. This has the advantage of opening up the sound of the bass, because the soundboard responds more freely to the vibration of the strings." (For those who crave even more volume, Dave will install a Highlander integrated pickup/preamp.)

Maize builds 4-string and 5-string (*EADGC*) ABGs, fretted or fretless, with a 34" scale length. Cutaway bodies, binding, inlays, and many other custom options are available. He also sells SmartWood-certified guitar woods to other builders. "Translating wood into sound—it continues to be fascinating," says Dave. "And it beats pounding nails all day."

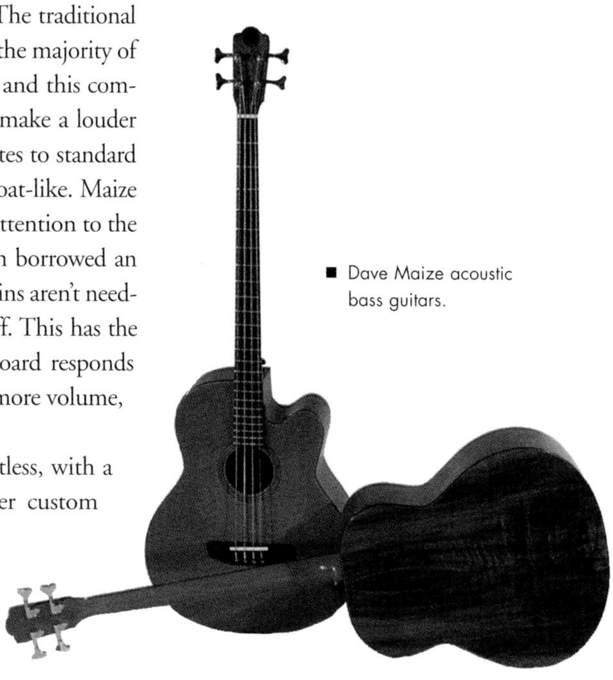

■ Dave Maize acoustic bass guitars.

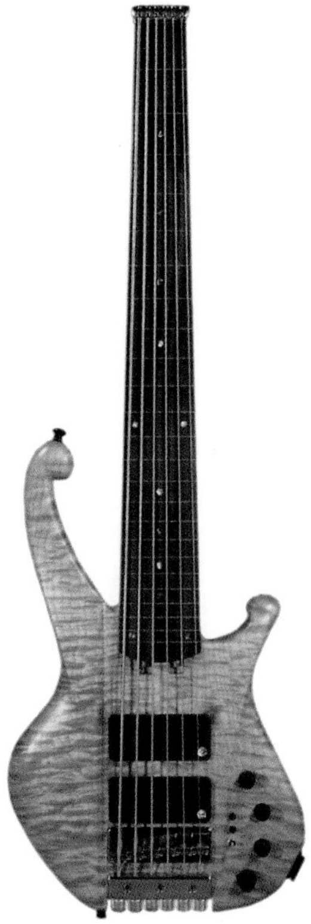

■ David J. King D Bass 6-string (above) and 32"-scale 7-string (below).

DAVID J. KING

After lugging an 11-pound '73 P-Bass around Europe, David King began to think about building a smaller, lighter bass guitar. "I wanted an instrument that preserved the feel and playability of my Fender," he says, "while eliminating as much of the bulk and weight as possible." He eventually drew up a headless bass with a pared-down body, which Danish luthier Johnny Mørch built for him.

Pleased with the results, King decided to build basses himself, making his first instruments while living with his parents in Amherst, Massachusetts, in the late 1980s. He moved to Portland, Oregon, in 1993, where he began to handcraft about ten instruments a year, working alone. Almost all of King's basses are headless, although he did offer the "traditional" Kappa model, with a 2+2 peghead, for a while. "I'm trying to focus on building a bass that sounds good, with no dead spots," he says. "I've spent years fussing over pickups and electronics, and I recently realized I was missing the point. Headless basses have their own set of challenges in this regard, and the physics involved is endlessly and delightfully complex."

King builds 4-, 5-, 6-, and 7-string basses in five body styles, which—in keeping with his low-key, no-hype style—he has named A, B, C, D, and E. The first two have minimal bodies—little more than a center block with an upper horn. (The A shape was derived from David's Mørch-built prototype.) The C, D, and E shapes have larger, double-cutaway outlines. King basses are available neck-through or bolt-on, and David has enhanced their functionality with a number of unique features. These include an integrated thumb rest running the full length of the body and a string-locking system that allows the use of conventional strings on a headless bass. His dovetailed wooden control-cavity cover requires no screws. King has even made headless basses with heads—ornamental headstocks without tuning keys.

Because King sells direct, his prices are lower than those of custom builders who sell through dealers. And since he builds to order, his customers can select just about any pickups and electronics on the market. The wood selection is equally wide, and King's instruments have featured everything from the usual maple and walnut to canary wood. "Wood is an amazing medium," he says, "and much of what I've learned about it recently is telling me to look at wood as a space-age material with unique and infinitely variable properties."

DE LACUGO

After one look at an Excelsior Bass, it's not hard to guess that Tony De Lacugo of Paso Robles, California, got his start in the custom car business. Available as either a 4- or 5-string, the Excelsior has the flowing lines and candy-colored metalflake paint of a hot rod—and it's not just for show. De Lacugo points out that the sculpted "acoustic loop" in the mahogany body enhances both the comfort and sound of the bass. (An earlier model, the Excalibur Bass, had a similar body shape but a flat headstock.) Tony has been building basses since 1993 and does all the work himself, including the painting. His instruments are available with natural wood finishes, too—but somchow that doesn't seem right.

■ De Lacugo Excelsior.

DINGWALL

On October 8, 1996, a fire engulfed the shop of Dingwall Designer Guitars in Saskatoon, Saskatchewan, Canada. Instruments, tools, wood, hardware, office equipment, and all of the company's business records were destroyed—"right down to the last pencil." Peering into the smoldering ruins, Sheldon Dingwall realized he had a choice: he could try to rebuild, or he could use the insurance money to pay off his debts and step away from the uncertainties of the musical-instrument business. Happily, he chose the former. Before the end of the decade, he was back to full production, building basses in a new shop equipped with the latest in computer-aided technology. And his strongest seller was a new model named the Afterburner.

Like many of his fellow luthiers, Dingwall started out as a player. His first instrument was the ukulele (which has four strings, of course), followed by piano, drums, and guitar. By the time he was a high school student in Saskatoon, he was teaching both drums and guitar. After graduation, Sheldon went on the road as a guitarist—and a budding instrument builder. "I had done my first guitar design in 1973, when I was 12," he recalls. "I guess it was something I always wanted to do."

Dingwall hadn't even taken wood shop in school, although he had studied machining and built a Floyd Rose–style locking guitar bridge. Thanks to an uncle who was an amateur guitar builder, he learned enough about woodworking to begin making instrument parts. "Also, when I was growing up, the Canadian equivalent of Leo Fender lived not far from me, and he had a son my age. His name is Glenn McDougall and his company is Fury Guitars [see Fury]. Because of him, I was always aware that small shops could manufacture electric guitars."

Sheldon got his start as a builder while he was still working as a player. "I built a couple of guitar necks that I'd scalloped on my hotel bed—a real mess, with ebony dust all over the place. My plan was to leave the road and build scalloped replacement necks, and that's what I did. The necks led to bodies, which led to assembling the parts, which led to complete guitars. As I was doing that, I got drawn into the repair business. That's college for guitar builders—it allows you to see every mistake that comes along and figure out a way of correcting it. At one point, I had a team of people working with me, and we were getting guitars from all over Canada. During my repair career, five or six thousand guitars went through my shop. I was trying to build at the same time. Eventually the guitars led to basses—I'd sell a guitar and then get a call from the guy's bass player, asking if I could build him a 5-string."

In 1992 Dingwall plunged into the bass business. He began—oddly enough—at the piano. "If you sit with your bass at a piano and compare the tone of the strings, it's pretty wild." That experiment led to discussions with piano builders, as Dingwall tried to figure out how to replicate the strong, clear tone of a grand piano's bass strings. "Then I opened up a *Guitar Player* magazine and saw a Klein guitar with the fanned-fret system invented by Ralph Novak [see Novax]. That just blew my mind—it was a 'Eureka!' moment. Within a month, I saw Ralph at a convention. I walked up to him and said, 'Boy, that sure would work well on basses.' He said, 'Well, I wouldn't mind if you took a crack at it.' After that, I went back and started on the design of the Voodoo." (He had roughed out the body shape earlier, while modifying a customer's damaged Yamaha BB300.)

Dingwall soon discovered that building a fanned-fret 5-string wasn't going to be easy. "I determined the scale length by installing a .130 *B* string, putting a sliding nut on a Fender headstock, moving it back and forth, and retuning until I had the tone I was looking for. When I measured, it was 37". I had found that string

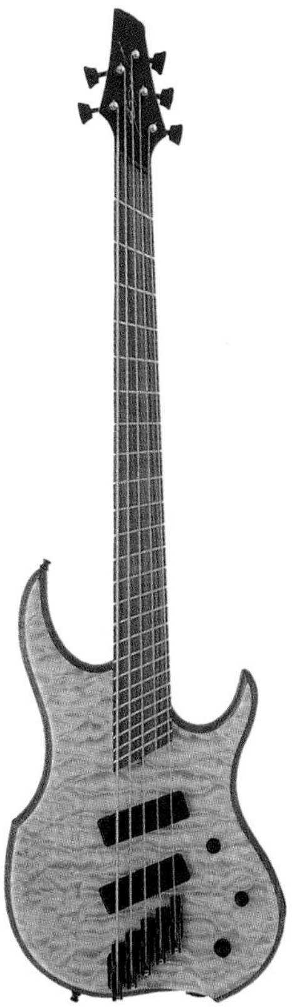

■ Dingwall Voodoo Prima 5-string.

■ Dingwall Voodoo Prima 6-string.

■ Dingwall Voodoo Z-Series 5-string.

in a box at a music store, with no package, so I had no idea what brand it was. I never even considered that it might be some crazy string I'd never be able to find again." That almost turned out to be true. Several major string manufacturers told Sheldon they couldn't make what he needed. Eventually, though, the Kaman factory agreed to supply 5-string sets ranging from a 34" *G* to a 37" *B*. (Dingwall 6-strings have a 33¼" *C*.)

The rest of Dingwall's design came together through trial and error, research, and observation. "For example," he says, "most of my understanding of wood resonance stems from a milkshake. I know it sounds funny, but when they serve one in a glass container and you tap it on a table, the whole thing has this resonant *thunk* to it. If you do that with a regular glass of milk, it has no resonance whatsoever. That led me to realize the importance of trapped air in the cells of the wood. There's more to it than that, but the trapped air is something I've never heard other luthiers talk about."

Sheldon unveiled his revolutionary 5-string at the 1993 NAMM show. The first Voodoo was red, and it had a sassafras body, a three-piece maple neck with a pau ferro fingerboard, and Bartolini pickups. Although some bassists found the fanned-fret neck scary, many were won over by the instrument's commanding sound. (In a 1997 *Bass Player* shootout, one tester described the Dingwall's *B* string as sounding like "the voice of God.")

Fanned-fret basses have been Dingwall's claim to fame ever since, although he did try—briefly—to build instruments with conventional frets. ("My heart just wasn't into it," he says.) By 2002, all Dingwall basses were equipped with fanned frets mounted on graphite-reinforced bolt-on maple necks. To accommodate the varying string lengths, Dingwall uses a specially designed Kahler bridge with individual units for each string; it's attached to an aircraft-aluminum plate countersunk in the body.

The Afterburner, available as a 4- or 5-string, has a soft-maple body and a pair of Bartolini passive single-coil pickups. The Voodoo Prima has a walnut or alder body with a quilted-, curly-, or flame-maple top and back, Bartolini split-coil soapbar pickups, and 2-band passive/active electronics; it's offered as a 4-, 5-, or 6-string. The vintage-inspired Super J is a 5- or 6-string with a soft maple or alder body and two Basslines passive pickups. Z Series basses are similar to Primas but have ash bodies treated with a black pre-stain for a distinctive "zebra" look. The Z2 has two pickups mounted side-by-side in the "sweet spot" near the bridge, for a punchier sound. Many options are available (but don't ask for parallel frets). Dingwall's latest R&D venture has been a partnership with Fury Guitars to develop a proprietary line of pickups. "They're designed to emulate vintage tones," says Sheldon Dingwall, "but with greater depth and clarity."

DON GROSH

In 1993, after eight years at Valley Arts Guitars in North Hollywood, Don Grosh started his own custom bass and guitar shop. His vintage-inspired line includes the Retro P4 and J4 (4-string) and Retro J5 (5-string; 21- or 24-fret) basses; all have alder or swamp ash bodies, maple necks, Lindy Fralin pickups, nitrocellulose-lacquer finishes, and a 34" scale length. A bent top of quilted or flame maple is optional, as are PJ pickups and 3-band active electronics. Grosh installs a heavy-duty trussrod of his own design, and each instrument gets a fret dressing and "Vintageizing" treatment to give the neck a broken-in feel.

■ Don Grosh Retro J5, 24 frets.

ELRICK

Rob Elrick of Chicago was one of the new breed of bass-only builders who emerged during the 1990s. He trained in crafts at Detroit's Center for Creative Studies, where he worked with clay, glass, and steel, and later studied bass at Berklee College of Music in Boston. Building basses turned out to be the perfect way for him to blend all of his creative interests—and to make the perfect bass for himself. Starting out as a 6-string specialist, he eventually developed a full line of 4-, 5-, 6-, and 7-string basses in neck-through, set-neck, and bolt-on configurations, as well as piccolo basses (including a piccolo 8-string). Elrick's recent models all have bodies made of swamp ash or alder; they're divided into Platinum Series and Gold Series instruments.

Platinum Series Thru-Neck basses feature exotic-wood tops and backs, with necks made of wenge or graphite-reinforced maple. The body shape can be either double- or single-cutaway; on the single-cut models, the upper bout extends to the 12th fret. Elrick also offers Platinum Series basses with a "hybrid" neck—a set neck with a carved heel that provides the feel of a neck-through. His hybrid-neck basses are available semi-hollow, with a top made of spruce, flame maple, or curly walnut; these basses have a piezo bridge and a single humbucker. The less-expensive Gold Series basses have "heel-less" bolt-on necks; they're made in Elrick's standard body style or in the vintage-inspired New Jazz Standard shape (4- and 5-string only). Some unusual fingerboard woods are available, including bubinga and pink ivorywood. All Elrick basses have a zero fret for a more balanced sound on the open strings. A 35" scale length is standard; 34" and 36" scales are optional. Bartolini pickups and electronics are standard on all models.

■ Elrick New Jazz Standard 5-string.

EPIPHONE

The Epiphone Company of New York was a major manufacturer of stringed instruments during the first half of the 20th century. It was best known for its fine-quality archtop guitars, but Epiphone also built large numbers of mandolins, banjos, and upright basses. Gibson president Ted McCarty acquired the company in 1957, and by 1960 he had moved all Epiphone production into the Gibson factory in Kalamazoo, Michigan. From 1961 to 1970, Gibson made thousands of Epiphone basses and guitars, many of which were simply rebranded Gibson models with minor cosmetic differences. This was a clever marketing move: it allowed Gibson to sell Epiphones to music stores competing with nearby Gibson dealers. Almost all of the Epiphone instruments made after 1970 have been manufactured in Japan, Taiwan, or (more recently) Korea.

The U.S.-made Epiphone line from the '60s included the solidbody Newport and Embassy Deluxe basses, but the best known Epiphone 4-string of that era was the semi-hollow, short-scale (30½") Rivoli. Only the shape of its headstock and the big "E" on the pickguard distinguished it from the Gibson EB-2. A Korean-made reproduction was offered in the 1990s.

■ Epiphone Rivoli.

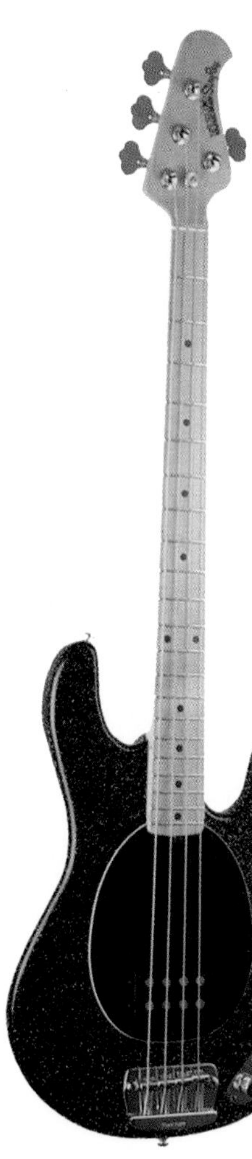

■ Ernie Ball Music Man StingRay Bass.

ERNIE BALL MUSIC MAN

Ernie Ball was a Southern California kid who learned how to play Hawaiian guitar from his dad and opened one of the first guitars-only music stores in the country. He pioneered the custom-gauge string business, selling sets to the Ventures and other recording artists. In the early 1970s Ball decided the world needed an acoustic bass guitar. "I always thought," he later explained, "that if there were electric bass guitars to go with electric guitars, then you ought to have acoustic basses to go with acoustic guitars." Ball bought a Mexican *guitarrón*, added frets to the neck, and tried to find a guitar manufacturer that would take on the project. No luck—so he decided to do it himself, introducing the Earthwood Bass in 1972. His friend George Fullerton, who worked at Fender, built the prototype.

The Earthwood was the first of its kind, a true ABG designed to produce enough sound to hold its own without amplification. It had a tilt-adjustable maple neck with a maple fingerboard, and it was . . . gigantic. The standard depth of the walnut body was 6⅝", and the Deluxe model was even bigger, with a depth of 8¼". This lifeboat-size bass was too big for most players (although John Entwistle of the Who was a notable supporter), and it was not very successful in the marketplace. Production was sporadic, ending in 1985.

In 1984 Ernie Ball acquired Music Man, the company Leo Fender had started in 1972. Along with the name came the rights to build the StingRay Bass, the most successful of Leo's post-Fender 4-strings. With its characteristic 3+1 headstock, 8-pole pickup, and 2-band active electronics, the StingRay has been a mainstay of the Ernie Ball line ever since. The original strings-through-body bridge was dropped, and a series of changes were made to Leo's design—six-bolt neck attachment, better truss rod, improved electronics (including 3-band EQ and piezo-bridge options)—but the StingRay remains one of the few electric basses that has been a classic from the moment of its introduction. Its bone-crushing sound has been much imitated but never matched, even by the most high-tech contemporary basses. Ernie Ball also produced the Sabre Bass, a two-pickup version of the StingRay, but it was never as popular as the StingRay and disappeared from the catalog in 1991.

Ernie Ball introduced a 5-string version of the StingRay in 1987, and the Sterling (named after one of Ernie's sons, a bassist and company executive) joined the line in 1993. The Sterling is, if you will, a "Jazz Bass" to the StingRay's "Precision": smaller, lighter, easier to play thanks to its slimmer neck, and equipped with more sophisticated electronics. Its single pickup has a hum-canceling "phantom coil," and the standard preamp has treble, midrange, and bass controls. Scale length of all StingRay and Sterling models is 34". Ernie Ball also makes the Silhouette 6-String Bass Guitar, tuned an octave below a standard guitar, like a Danelectro 6-string or Fender Bass VI; its scale length is 29⅝".

■ Ernie Ball Earthwood Bass, 1972.

SEE ALSO: MUSIC MAN

F BASS

O Canada—home and native land of fine extended-range basses. Why do so many great-sounding 5- and 6-strings come from way up north? Maybe it's the proximity to all those tall trees.

Some of the most-admired Canadian instruments are crafted in the Hamilton, Ontario, shop of George Furlanetto. He has refined his F Basses through more than 20 years of building experience and input from many pro bassists, most notably Alain Caron. George will build you a 4-string if you really want it, but he is renowned for his extended-range basses: 5-strings, 6-strings, and (recently) 7-strings.

Furlanetto has perfected his design over the years, focusing on a number of key features that make his basses unique. To name a few: 34½" scale length; hand-wound pickups covered with wood veneers that match the body; knobs hand-turned from African blackwood; active/passive circuitry with 3-band boost-only EQ; bolt-on necks with a handrubbed oil finish; striking "cerusé" finishes. His fretted basses are made with maple fingerboards for better attack; the fretless basses have ebony fingerboards with upper-register position markers between the top strings. The control-cavity covers on all instruments are made from wood that matches the body. And, in addition to his proprietary pickups, George also offers LightWave optical pickups on fretless basses.

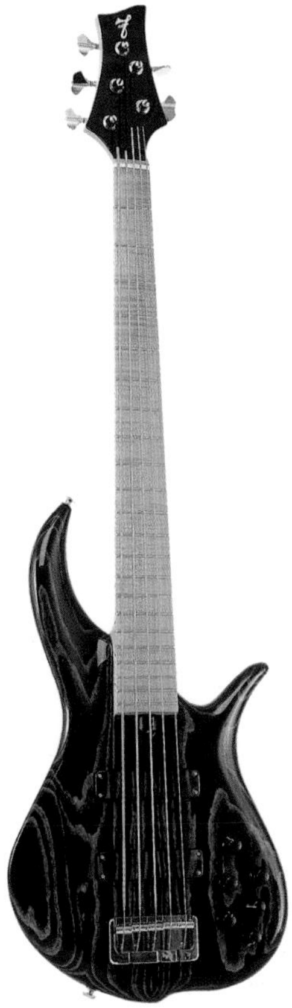

■ F Bass BN 5-string.

Furlanetto, a bassist himself, got into the guitar-repair trade in 1969, right after high school; by 1977 he had launched his own business, the Guitar Clinic, with American partner Froc Filipetti. Building instruments was a natural next step, and the two budding luthiers discovered that bassists were more receptive to their ideas than guitarists. The F Bass became their main product, and after Filipetti returned to the States, Furlanetto carried on alone. He builds 5- and 6-string basses in two basic versions: the 22-fret BN and the 20-fret Studio. The latter, he explains, has less wood in the neck and more in the body—"what this difference means functionally is that the Studio has more lower midrange." The Alain Caron signature model, available as a 5-, 6-, or 7-string fretless, has a chambered maple body with a spruce top, a bird's-eye maple neck topped with a 28-fret ebony fingerboard, and a combination of magnetic and piezo pickups. Furlanetto's latest venture is GFC, a secondary line featuring basses that are "more classically designed."

FARNELL

One night in 1985, Al Farnell dreamed he had made a guitar from plastic foam. Years of experiments with materials and techniques followed, until he came up with something that worked: a combination of foam and wood that made strong, resonant—and very light—instrument bodies. The Ultra-Lite body has a mahogany center block encased in closed-cell polyurethane foam; the middle of the wooden insert is scooped out and filled with more foam, creating a "sound reservoir" where the pickups are mounted. Farnell sheaths the whole thing in polyester for strength, and bolts on a wooden neck. The final product is sort of like the mutant offspring of a Parker Fly and a surfboard.

The Farnell bass line includes the USA Series EX 4-string and 5-strings, as well as lower-priced K Series and C Series basses built offshore. The USA models have Korean-made Ultra-Lite bodies with flame-maple tops, but they are assembled in California with American rock-maple necks and EMG pickups. Al Farnell says their sound is "thunderous."

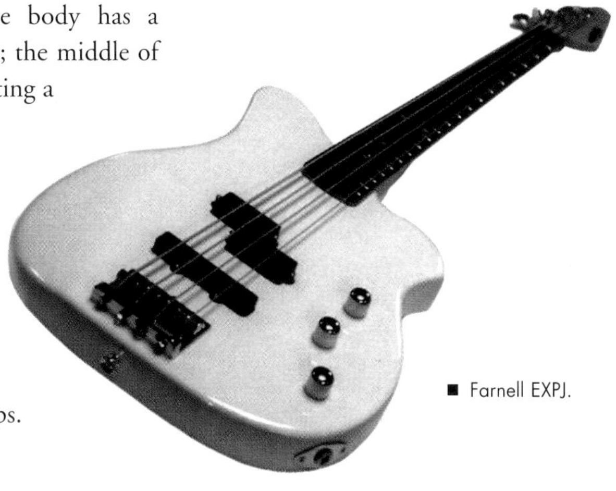

■ Farnell EXPJ.

■ 1951 Fender Precision Bass.

■ 1956 Fender Precision Bass.

FENDER

In the beginning Leo created the Precision Bass. The low end had been without tone or groove, and muddy sound was upon the face of the recordings. And Leo said, "Let there be frets." And the bass players saw that frets were good, and the out-of-tune notes were separated from the in-tune notes. And the world was transformed.

Actually, Leo Fender wasn't the first person who thought of using electricity to amplify a bass; credit for that goes to Gibson engineer Lloyd Loar, who created a crude electric upright in 1924. Leo didn't even invent the solidbody electric bass guitar, although he was usually given credit for doing so until the Audiovox Model 736 Electronic Bass, made by Seattle's Paul Tutmarc in 1936, resurfaced in the 1990s. (For more on the prehistory of the electric bass guitar, see my book *How the Fender Bass Changed the World*.)

But Leo Fender did create the first commercially viable electric bass guitar, and because of that he can rightly be considered the father of a new category of instruments—one that has flourished since the 1951 introduction of the Fender Precision Bass, as can be seen in the pages of this book. Why did he do it? What did Leo Fender have in mind when he began to sketch out his concept for an electric bass guitar? When Tom Wheeler asked him that question, Leo said: "We needed to free the bass player from the big doghouse, the acoustic bass. That thing was usually confined to the back of the band, and the bass player couldn't get up to the mike to sing. And besides, bands were getting a little smaller—combos—and sometimes guitar players would have an advantage if they could have an instrument with frets that would make doubling on bass easier for them." (From an interview published in *Guitar Player* and later reprinted in *American Guitars*.)

Leo worked on the prototype of the original Precision Bass in 1950 and early 1951. It was like a big Telecaster guitar, with a square-sided ash body (although it had two cutaways, for better balance) and a bolt-on maple neck. He experimented with various scale lengths, settling on 34" as a practical compromise between the 25½" scale of the Telecaster and the 40–42" scale of most uprights. Leo chose the name "Precision Bass" because the instrument was fretted and therefore produced more precise intonation than the fretless fingerboard of an upright. Its one pickup was a simple single-coil design, with a polepiece below each string. Chrome covers hid the pickup and bridge. Leo was, above all, a practical man, and these covers weren't just decorative: the pickup cover provided electronic shielding, and the bridge cover contained a rubber string mute, to keep the strings from sustaining too long. Leo figured that bass players would have the thump of an upright in mind, and he wanted his new instrument to make a familiar—but louder—sound.

The second part of the equation was an amplifier. Leo Fender discovered that his guitar amps couldn't handle the low frequencies the P-Bass generated, so he assembled a new amp, which became the first Fender Bassman. It had a single Jensen 15" speaker and a 26-watt tube amplifier with enough power to produce a reasonable bass sound at low to medium volumes.

The first batch of Precision Basses left the factory in October 1951 and went on sale the next month. They were introduced with little fanfare, but it wasn't long before Fender's advertising was touting them as the next big thing:

> PRECISION BASS — one of the greatest of modern instrument developments. Fast becoming the favorite of musicians in every field. Compact in size, but very large in performance. Requires only a fraction of the effort to play compared to old style acoustic basses.

> Extremely well suited for that fast delicate playing technique. When used with proper amplifier, it will produce considerably more volume than old style basses. The tone leaves nothing to be desired and the portability is the answer to every bass player's dream.

The Precision Bass remained much the same from its 1951 introduction until 1954. In addition to the slab body and bolt-on maple neck, it had a strings-through-body bridge with two adjustable saddles made of pressed fiber. The black pickguard was cut from Phenolite, the same vulcanized fiber used for the top and bottom of the pickup, and sprayed with glossy lacquer. The chrome volume and tone knobs were the same as the ones used on the Telecaster. A wooden finger rest, attached with a single screw, was mounted below the strings. While some Fender literature of the period says the Precision Bass could be played "in finger style, similar to classic guitar," the placement of the finger rest indicates that plucking with the thumb was considered more likely. (And indeed that's how its first notable user, Lionel Hampton bassist Monk Montgomery, played it.)

■ 1959 Fender Precision Bass.

Evolution

In 1954 Leo Fender made the first of a series of modifications that would radically transform the look and sound of the P-Bass over the next three years. The body was contoured, front and back, which gave it a sleeker look and (more important to Leo) made it more comfortable to play. The revised body shape was like that of the newly introduced Stratocaster guitar, and another Strat-inspired change soon followed: a white pickguard over a sunburst nitrocellulose-lacquer finish.

The bridge was upgraded, with steel replacing pressed fiber for the saddles, and the pickup's polepieces were set to staggered heights for better string-to-string balance. Custom colors became available in the mid 1950s, and P-Basses began to appear in such shades as Olympic White, Foam Green, and Fiesta Red. In 1957 the peghead caught up to the body, taking on a shape like a Strat's. The bridge was improved again, with four adjustable saddles; five screws, rather than the original three, attached it firmly to the body. Stringing was now top-loaded (from the rear of the bridge), rather than through the body. A plastic finger rest, mounted with two screws, became standard. The pickguard was reshaped and made of gold-anodized aluminum.

The most important change of all was the introduction of a new pickup. Leo Fender had never been happy with the P-Bass's pickup, and adjusting the height of the polepieces in 1955 hadn't solved the problems. It wasn't just a matter of tone. With a single polepiece directly beneath each string, the P-Bass had a strong attack transient that was hard on speakers. And, because of its single-coil construction, it was prone to hum. Leo solved all the problems at once by designing a split-coil pickup, with four polepieces on each half. Because the polepieces were on either side of the string, instead of below it, the attack was smoother and both tone and gain were improved. And by splitting the coils, wiring them out of phase, and orienting the two magnets with opposite polarities, Leo created a humbucking pickup. (At first some of the polepieces were staggered, but by 1959 they were all even with the cover.) The split-coil pickup was a brilliant solution, and the 1957 Precision Bass stands as one of Leo Fender's supreme achievements.

■ 1960 Fender Jazz Bass.

One of the smartest things that Leo did, as he perfected his bass guitar, was to leave its name alone. It would be hard to imagine a marketing department at a contemporary musical-instrument company that could resist the temptation to rename an instrument that had been modified as extensively as the P-Bass was from 1954 to 1957. In today's world, the '57 would surely have been christened the Precision II or the Precision Plus or the Super Precision—*something* to draw attention to all of those improvements. But Leo, wisely, left the name alone, emphasizing continuity.

Which is not to say that he was done tinkering with his invention. A rosewood fingerboard became standard in 1959. At first this was a so-called "slab" board, flat on the bottom, but these had a tendency to buckle because maple and rosewood respond differently to climatic changes. In the early '60s Leo altered the design, curving the bottom of the fingerboard and the top of the neck for better adhesion. The gold-anodized pickguard was another problem. It had excellent shielding properties but scratched easily—so Leo switched to a tortoiseshell plastic version. (It had a metal plate, so the shielding properties would not be lost.) The standard paint job got a little slicker, too, with a three-color sunburst replacing the earlier two-color finish. By 1962 the standard P-Bass had an alder body with a three-color sunburst finish, a tortoiseshell pickguard, a bolt-on maple neck with a rosewood fingerboard, and a split-coil pickup with polepieces mounted flush with the top. Many variations have appeared since then, but that classic P-Bass configuration has remained a constant. (You can still buy one today; Fender calls it the American Vintage '62 Precision Bass.)

■ 1965 Fender Jazz Bass.

Jazzing It Up

Leo Fender was born in 1909 on a farm in Orange County, California. He played the saxophone as a schoolboy, but never learned how to play guitar or bass. Fascinated by electronics since he was a teenager, Leo abandoned his early career as a bookkeeper to open Fender's Radio Service in Fullerton, California, in 1939. One of his customers was a local musician named Doc Kauffman, who shared Leo's interest in amplifiers. The two began to build lap-steel guitars and small amplifiers, selling them under the K&F brand name. Doc pulled out of the business in 1946, and it was renamed the Fender Electric Instrument Company.

The early Fender instruments were produced in a nondescript workshop on Santa Fe Avenue in Fullerton. The business struggled at first, but Leo's innovative amplifier designs and solidbody electric guitars soon caught the attention of musicians across the country. To keep up with the growing demand, another building was added in 1950. A large new facility, with three buildings, was built in 1953 at South Raymond Avenue and Valencia Drive in Fullerton. Before the end of the decade, the factory would expand to eight buildings.

Leo Fender said the Precision was "real popular" within two years of its introduction, but it's hard to determine what the early production numbers were because Fender did not keep accurate sales records. According to historian Richard R. Smith, it appears that fewer than 200 P-Basses were made annually in the early '50s, with production gradually increasing to about 1,000 a year by 1959. That was apparently enough to convince Leo that he needed another bass model, and in 1959 he began work on the instrument that would become the Jazz Bass.

In his *Guitar Player* interview, Tom Wheeler asked Leo Fender about the concept behind the Jazz Bass. "Well, it's like a car, you know," replied Leo. "You come out with a standard model, then you have a deluxe model, a Cadillac version. It had a narrower neck and the offset waist: it was fancier." It also had more elaborate electronics. Leo took a different approach to the split-coil concept this time, using two separate single-coil pickups, placed about 3" apart. On the 1959 prototype, these were large soapbar pickups like those on the Jazzmaster guitar; the neck pickup had five polepieces and the bridge pickup four. These were changed to narrower 8-pole pickups by the time the J-Bass went into production. As with the split-coil P-Bass pickup, a pair of polepieces flanked each string.

The control layout on the Jazz Bass prototype had two volume knobs, one for each pickup, and a single tone knob. For some reason, Leo altered this to a "stack knob" arrangement before the instrument went into production; with this system, there was a smaller tone knob above the volume knob for each pickup. In late 1961, Fender reverted to the original three-knob arrangement, although stack-knob J-Basses were made until sometime in 1962, as parts were used up. This was typical of Fender's "waste not, want not" production philosophy, and it's one reason why it's sometimes hard to gauge when an instrument was made. A neck might have been stamped with a date but not actually used on an instrument until many months later; a control assembly or set of tuning machines that lurked in the bottom of a bin could have been put on a bass long after it was supposedly obsolete.

The Jazz Bass's neck was, as Leo noted, narrower at the nut: 1½" rather than the 1¾" found on P-Basses at the time. It was also slimmer (although shapes varied considerably because of the handwork involved). This "speedy" neck undoubtedly contributed to the instrument's name, although it would be quite a few years before a jazz bassist of note—a guy named Jaco—played one.

Like the Precision, the Jazz Bass came equipped with chrome covers, one over the neck pickup and a second, larger one for the bridge pickup and bridge. The rear cover, adorned with a large F, also concealed the adjustable string mutes, one for each string. Most bassists took these off, and in 1963 Fender replaced them with a rubber mute glued to the inside of the chrome cover. The fingerboard was rosewood, with dot inlays made of clay until 1964, when pearl began to be used. The pickguard was tortoiseshell or, later, white. Many Jazz Basses sported custom colors—by 1961 Fender was offering 14 colors as well as the standard sunburst—and most custom-color J-Basses had headstocks painted to match their bodies. Leo Fender may have been thinking about Cadillacs, but these early-'60s Jazz Basses were more like Corvettes—sleek, fast, and flashy.

■ 1962 Fender Bass VI.

Acquisition & Transition

After noting the popularity of the Danelectro 6-string bass (tuned *EADGBE*, like a guitar, but an octave lower) in the Nashville studios, Leo decided to build his own version. He introduced the Fender Bass VI in 1961. The original version looked vaguely like a Jazz Bass but had a 30" scale length, three pickups, and three sliding switches that allowed seven different pickup combinations. That wasn't enough for Leo, apparently, so a year later he added a fourth switch—the so-called "strangle switch" that cut low frequencies. The pickups were also modified and a mute added. The Bass VI was never very popular, but it remained in the catalog until 1975 and was later revived, in a Japanese-made reissue, in 1995.

The popularity of rock & roll in the early 1960s gave Fender's business a huge boost. By 1964 the company had more than 500 employees working in 29 buildings, cranking out basses and guitars at a rate of 1,500 a week and making amps at a similarly feverish pace. But Leo Fender had a hard time enjoying his success. Plagued by illnesses both real and imagined, he decided it was time to sell his company. Executives at the Columbia Broadcasting System (CBS) were glad to oblige, figuring that their management expertise would drive Fender to new heights of profitability. The sale was concluded on January 5, 1965, with CBS paying $13 million for the company and securing Leo's services as a consultant (at $25,000 a year) for five years.

■ 1969 Fender Mustang Bass.

■ Late-'60s Fender Coronado Bass II.

Much has been written and said about the fate of Fender under CBS. One school of thought insists that the quality of Fender instruments immediately went downhill in 1965 and kept right on going; the contrary viewpoint says that this is false and Fender made many good instruments during the CBS years. The truth, as it often is, seems to be somewhere in the middle.

Many of Leo's trusted executives, including general manager Don Randall and plant manager Forrest White, remained with the company after January 1965. Business was carried on without many changes, at least at first, but CBS's desire to introduce "improved" procedures eventually caused problems. White, in *Fender: The Inside Story*, recalls an incident when a CBS-appointed purchasing agent decided he would show these Fender rubes how they could save money: "One day a salesman stopped by his office with an unusual bargain in a close-out on magnet wire. The man bought it at a bargain-basement price. There was a problem. It happened to be odds and ends of the wrong gauge and coating. I found out about it and said that we could not use that wire to wind our instrument pickups. I was told by one of the CBS marvels that I didn't have to tell him how to run the company."

Similar unfortunate decisions were made about purchasing other materials, and there was a noticeable decline in the quality of Fender instruments—although some of them were just as good as their pre-CBS counterparts. It was hit or miss—late-'60s Fender basses are notorious for their uneven quality. R&D also took an unfortunate turn. The decision to replace many of Fender's respected tube amps with "more modern" solid-state models was a disaster. And many of the new instruments created during the early CBS years weren't much better. A case in point is the Bass V, a 5-string introduced in 1965. It had a high *C* string and only 15 frets—adding the *C* string, it was assumed, would make it easier for bassists to play across the neck, rather than up and down it, so the bass would need fewer frets. It was a screwy idea; the Bass V was discontinued by 1970.

The Mustang Bass, designed by Leo Fender in his role as a consultant, was a much better instrument. Introduced in 1966, it was a competitively priced short-scale (30") bass that extended Fender's market reach. Its alder body, bolt-on maple neck, 4-in-line peghead, and split-coil pickup clearly said "Fender bass," and the body was later jazzed up with a racing stripe across the body. A staple of the Fender line into the 1980s, the Mustang Bass was reintroduced in 2002.

The other new models from the late '60s were less successful. The Coronado Bass, a partner to a similar guitar model, was a semi-hollow instrument similar to the Gibson EB-2, but with a 34" scale length and a 4-in-line peghead. It was created by Roger Rossmeisl, the German expatriate luthier who had designed the Rickenbacker 4000, the first neck-through electric bass [see Rickenbacker]. Rossmeisl had been working for Fender since 1962, mostly on acoustic guitars, and it must have seemed logical to the CBS masterminds to have him whip up an acoustic-electric hybrid—especially since that was one of Gibson's strongest market areas. Fender introduced the single-pickup Coronado Bass I in 1966; the double-pickup Bass II followed a year later. Some of them were made in the "Wildwood" finish (with bodies made from beechwood that had been colored by injecting dye into the growing trees), while others got the silver-to-black sunburst called "Antigua." Musicians reacted with a yawn, and the series died with a whimper in 1972.

A curious version of the Precision Bass appeared in 1966, apparently only for export to the U.K. It had a slab body and black pickguard, like the original P-Bass, but was otherwise the same as the contemporary models. The slab body returned again in 1968 on the Telecaster Bass, a new model patterned on the '51 Precision, right down to the strings-through-body bridge and single-coil pickup.

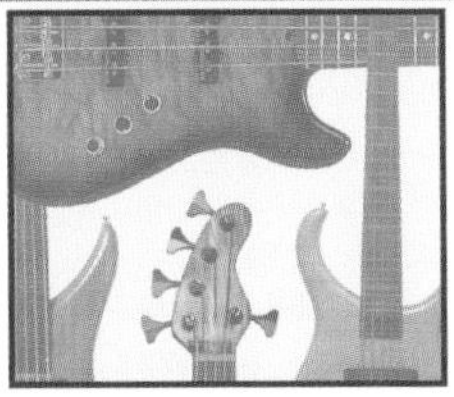

WHEN WAS IT MADE?

By Jim Roberts

In recent years, the frenzy over collecting vintage Fender basses has focused a great deal of attention on determining the manufacturing date of particular instruments. Dating them is not an exact science. Every bass has a number of clues, including its neck and/or body date, serial number, and construction details. Taken together, these can provide a good idea of when it was made—unless they've been forged, obscured, or altered.

Why is it so hard? Mostly because nobody who worked at Fender in the early days, including Leo himself, thought anyone would care when a particular bass was made. They didn't know they were building collector's items—and probably would have laughed if someone had suggested it. Their concerns were much more practical, focused on getting instruments out the door to fill orders.

The construction details of any Fender bass provide important clues about its age. If a Precision Bass has a slab body, large black pickguard, Tele-style headstock, and one single-coil pickup, it was probably made between 1951 and 1954 (unless it's a reproduction). A more precise guide to the instrument's age is the date on the neck heel. In the 1950s these were written in pencil, and some are very hard to make out. (Of course, checking the neck date requires removing the neck—which is usually impossible in a store or at a guitar show.) Even then, this is only a rough guide. A neck could have been completed and dated, then put on a rack and left there for months before it was attached to a body. The only thing an unaltered neck date tells you for sure is when the neck itself was made.

The same holds true for a body (many of which also have dates written on them, under the pickguard) or for just about any other part, including the control pots (which are stamped with a date code) or serial number plate. A plate might have been stamped with a number, tossed into a bin, and then covered up by more plates and left there for months before being used on an instrument. As Richard R. Smith has noted, "The key to understanding Fender serial numbers' limitations as date indicators is that the company made its own serial number plates, with no effort to keep the numbers consecutive during stamping, deburring, and plating. As a result, workers never applied serial numbers to guitars in order—there was no reason to (and no one ever imagined there ever would be). Serial numbers were simply used to identify instruments. Like neck dates, they were never intended to indicate a date of manufacture."

To assist in dating Fender instruments, collector James Werner spent years compiling an extensive list of serial numbers cross-referenced with neck dates. Most of this information was supplied to him by instrument owners, who swapped their information for a copy of the list. At first, this list (and a series of addendums) circulated as a stack of photocopied documents; in 1998 it was collected into a book called *Werner's List* (Louisa Publishing Company).

(Some of the product literature claimed that "the Telecaster Bass was originally introduced before 1950." Under CBS, Fender couldn't even get its own history right.) The choice of finishes included psychedelic Blue Flower and Paisley Red bodies. The single-coil pickup was replaced with a large chrome-covered humbucker in 1972; not many bassists found this to be an improvement. The Tele Bass was discontinued in 1979.

The look of the Jazz Bass began to change in 1966, as CBS tightened its grip. White neck binding was added, and then large pearl-block inlays replaced the fingerboard dots. (A maple fingerboard was added to the option list in 1969; this came with black binding and blocks.) The frets were also switched to a larger size. By 1970 the Jazz Bass had been significantly altered from its pre-CBS look, and its peghead also sported a new look. As the '60s drew to a close, Fender introduced a new decal on all models; it had the company name in black, outlined in gold, and the name of the model in large black letters. CBS executives undoubtedly saw this as a symbol of the company's advancement under their management. Many musicians took a different view.

■ Late-'60s Fender Telecaster Bass.

■ 1971 Fender Musicmaster Bass.

■ 1970 Fender Precision fretless.

Into the Depths—and Out

By 1970 both Forrest White and Don Randall had left the company. Fender basses still looked about the same, but the changes continued. Natural-finish instruments began to appear, with ash bodies that looked good but were often heavy—and not very resonant. Polyester "Thick Skin" finishes compounded the problem. The Jazz Bass's bridge pickup was moved back about ½", altering the tone. The most controversial change was the introduction of the three-bolt neck joint, which appeared on the Telecaster Bass in 1972 and on the Jazz Bass two years later. The Precision Bass was spared this "improvement," which degraded both the structural integrity and tone of the instruments.

Aside from the budget-priced Musicmaster Bass, most of the basses introduced during the '70s were cosmetic variations on the Precision and Jazz themes. The most important innovation was the 1970 debut of the Precision fretless—an ironic development, since the "Precision" name originally referred to the presence of frets. Fender offered maple fingerboards as options on both P- and J-Basses, and in 1974 began making some maple-neck Jazz Basses with white neck binding and inlay blocks rather than black. In 1972, perhaps because of the Jazz Bass's increasing popularity, the Precision Bass's neck width was trimmed to 1⅝". And, sometime in the mid '70s, the P-Bass's thumb rest migrated upward, above the *E* string, acknowledging that most bassists played with their fingers. The peghead logo was redesigned again in 1976, with the name of the instrument appearing in slightly smaller letters. The serial number was now included in the decal rather than being stamped on the neck plate.

While the '70s are often seen as the dark ages of Fender—and not without reason —the company made many good basses during the decade. For proof, you don't need to look farther than the '77 Jazz Bass that has been Marcus Miller's favorite instrument for many years. (Admittedly, it was upgraded considerably by Roger Sadowsky, who installed active electronics and made other improvements.) Jazz Basses with block-inlay necks have come back into favor with many players, a fact that Fender acknowledged in 1995 with the introduction of its Vintage '75 Jazz Bass. On the vintage market, prices for '70s Fender basses have edged upward (although they lag far behind the pre-CBS instruments), and some excellent basses from this era are still in circulation.

By the end of the '70s, sales of all Fender instruments had declined, and the company appeared to be in desperate straits. The introduction of such oddball models as the Lead Bass and the Bullet Bass (available in both 30" and 34" scale lengths) only heightened that impression. The Precision Special, with active electronics and a brass bridge, acknowledged changes that were sweeping through the bass world, but, tarted up with a white pickup and gold-plated hardware, it was more gaudy than good.

A new management team took over in 1981, led by industry veteran John McLaren. Bill Schultz was named president. Perhaps because McLaren and Schultz had worked previously for Yamaha, they looked to Japan for salvation. The Fuji-Gen Gakki factory, which had been making high-quality Fender copies, was selected to produce "the real thing"—instruments licensed by Fender USA. At the same time, the new management began to revamp U.S. operations, dumping the three-bolt neck and rewriting production standards.

The key to Fender's revival was the old Fender—the pre-CBS instruments revered by musicians around the world. McLaren's team decided to re-create these in a new line of Vintage models. To do this, they had to go out and buy old Fender basses, because the CBS management had disposed of many of the instruments it inherited. In 1982 Fender rolled out U.S.-made Vintage models of the '57 and '62 Precision Basses and '62 Jazz Bass. (The latter designation has never been quite right, since the reissue has the stack knobs more typical of 1960–61 J-Basses.) For bassists who couldn't afford these reproductions, there was the plain-vanilla Standard Precision. Fender Japan also began to crank out basses carrying both the Fender and Squier names.

Elite P-Basses appeared in 1983, sporting one or two split-coil "noise-canceling" pickups and active electronics. Most featured the traditional Fender recipe of a maple neck attached to an ash body, but an all-walnut Elite appeared, too. The neck width at the nut reverted to the original 1¾". At that time, the Precision Bass dominated Fender's bass manufacturing; only a single J-Bass model, the Standard Jazz Bass, was being made. It had a four-bolt neck and dot fingerboard inlays—just like the good old days—but the pickups were white.

Although Fender appeared to be headed in the right direction again, the parent company had lost interest. Product development slowed to a crawl, and "Frankenbasses" began to appear in stores, made from whatever parts were available. The Elite P-Basses disappeared almost as quickly as they had appeared. In 1984 CBS began to entertain offers for the purchase of Fender, but none of them was appealing. CBS eventually decided to sell the company to an investor group headed by Bill Schultz, and the deal was completed in March 1985. The purchase price was $12.5 million—half a million less than CBS had paid for the company 20 years before. Fender executive Dan Smith later told Tony Bacon that he believed the deal had saved Fender from oblivion. "To be honest," said Smith, "if nobody had come up with an offer better than liquidation, Fender would have gone under. That would have been it."

■ 1972 Fender Jazz Bass.

Rebirth

The Schultz group acquired the Fender name but not the Fullerton factories, which were sold separately. Production of instruments was limited to what could be assembled from existing inventory or made offshore. The number of employees dwindled to about 100. Headquarters were re-established in Brea, California, where Schultz's management team huddled to make plans for reinventing the company.

A modest new factory was established in Corona, California, and domestic production initially focused on guitars. The Fender Custom Shop was started nearby (see sidebar, page 64). To survive, Schultz had decided, Fender needed to build large numbers of its best-selling products: Strats and Teles. Basses would come later. Fender gradually ramped up U.S. production during the late '80s and opened a new factory in Ensenada, Mexico, in 1987. This facility works on a co-operative basis with the Corona factory; U.S.-made instruments often include components made in Mexico and vice versa. The final point of assembly determines whether the bass is marked "Made in USA" or "Made in Mexico." This has been a highly successful strategy for Fender, which can take advantage of lower labor costs and less-strict environmental regulations (especially with regard to lacquer spraying) south of the border.

Fender's bass offerings in the late '80s and early '90s emphasized tried-and-true Precision and Jazz models, with some twists. The Jazz Bass Plus had Lace Sensor pickups, active electronics, and a 22-fret fingerboard; it was offered as both a 4-string and 5-string. The P-Bass Plus followed, with a PJ pickup configuration.

■ 1982 Fender U.S. Vintage P-Bass.

■ Fender Stu Hamm Urge II.

■ Fender Roscoe Beck 5-string.

The Precision Acoustic/Electric, made in Japan, was a semi-hollow instrument with a spruce top and a piezo bridge pickup. The American Standard Jazz Bass was just what its name implied—a return to the classic look and feel of the J-Bass.

In 1991 Fender moved its corporate offices to Scottsdale, Arizona, celebrating the 40th anniversary of the Precision Bass that year with a limited-edition Custom Shop model that had a figured-maple top, an ebony fingerboard, and Lace Sensor PJ pickups. A small number of Japanese '51 Precision reproductions were also made, as well as U.S. limited-edition James Jamerson P-Bass and Jaco Pastorius J-Bass commemorative models created for the Bass Centre in Los Angeles.

To maintain a presence in the bass market, Fender assembled a collection of American-made and imported instruments that were sometimes hard to recognize as Fenders. The HM Bass Ultra, available from 1990 to '92, had a basswood body with a figured-maple top and an array of three J-style pickups; a 5-string version was also offered. Even more obscure was the Japanese-made HMT Bass, an acoustic/electric sort-of-P-Bass with a piezo bridge pickup and strangely shaped headstock; it came and went in 1992. The JP-90 was another short-lived model, with PJ pickups in a poplar body. A similar model with active electronics, the Prodigy Active, was in the catalog from 1992 to 1995. There were also Japanese Foto Flame models, with "simulated woodgrain" tops. The Precision Lyte, MB, and Prophecy models—all made in Japan—helped to fill out the line. So-called "Collectables," Japanese-made replicas tagged the '50s Precision, '60s Precision, and '60s Jazz, at least had the right look, but they did little to stir the hearts of Fender traditionalists.

In 1993 the Custom Shop collaborated with Stuart Hamm to develop a new model that blended classic Fender features with the playability and active electronics of the Kubicki basses Hamm had been playing [see Kubicki]. The new model, dubbed the Urge, had a 24-fret neck with a 32" scale length and specially designed Precision and Jazz pickups. The circuitry allowed active or passive operation, and the controls included two stack-knobs, a 4-way rotary switch, a 3-way toggle switch, and an internal trimpot. It was a long way from a '51 P-Bass, baby, although it shared one important characteristic with that seminal axe: a strings-through-body bridge. A Mexican-made Urge Standard, with simplified electronics, was also developed. The Urge worked well for Hamm, but commercial acceptance was limited because of the shorter scale length. In 1999 Fender remedied this problem with the Urge II, a new-and-improved version with a 34" scale.

Another artist-driven instrument was the Roscoe Beck 5-string, also developed in the early '90s. Like Hamm, he wanted an instrument that combined vintage appeal with modern electronic refinements. His vision produced a 5-string with a wide neck, to maintain the traditional string spacing, but an asymmetric profile for better playability. The two pickups are double-coil J-style models, wired for single- or dual-coil operation, and a 3-way switch selects neck, bridge, or both.

In 1994–95, with Strats flying out the door, Fender's R&D efforts finally zeroed in on basses. While the Vintage reissues and a few other models were selling well, the catalog was clogged with Prodigies and Prophecies and Foto Flame fakes. Led by Dan Smith, the marketing VP for guitars and basses at the time, a project team that included the Custom Shop's Mark Kendrick and John Suhr began to revamp the bass line from top to bottom. They concentrated their initial efforts on instruments that Smith characterized as "traditional" (standard Precision and Jazz models) and "tweaked traditional" (P- and J-style basses with active electronics and other contemporary features).

The new American Standard basses—"traditional" models—started to show up in stores late in 1995. There were two 4-strings—Precision (fretted or fretless) and Jazz—and the Jazz Bass V 5-string. At first glance these were garden-variety passive P- and J-Basses, but they incorporated such subtle improvements as graphite-reinforced necks, strings-through-body bridges, and lightweight Gotoh tuners on the 5-string.

The "tweaked traditional" Deluxe models represented more of a break with the past. Also available in Precision, Jazz, and Jazz 5-string models, these basses had 22-fret necks, downsized bodies, and active electronics. The alder bodies had ash veneers front and back, and the "convertible" bridge accommodated either top-loaded or through-body stringing. The P-Bass Deluxe, with a rosewood or maple fingerboard, was equipped with a second pickup placed near the bridge. Rather than go the familiar PJ route, John Suhr created a new dual-coil model that gave the bass the throaty punch of a Music Man StingRay. The Jazz Deluxe models also featured new pickups, with split coils for hum-free operation. The Suhr-designed 3-band EQ offered bass and treble shelving controls and midrange boost/cut centered at 950Hz.

The Deluxe basses were a creative response to the problems created by the company's legacy. "We're like an actor who's been typecast," explained Dan Smith, who became head of Fender R&D after leading the bass-redesign project. "Our products were the tools that the pioneers of pop and rock and country music used, and we became known for that. That's wonderful, because it has given us products that will endure regardless of the fashion trends in music. But when we want to go outside of that, to come up with something new, it can be extremely difficult."

■ Fender American Standard basses, 1995 (left to right): Precision, Precision fretless, Jazz, Jazz 5-string.

■ Fender Marcus Miller Jazz Bass.

Happy Anniversary

In 1996 Fender celebrated the company's 50th year with limited-edition Precision and Jazz basses sporting figured-maple tops and gold hardware. A number of Japanese-made signature-model basses were offered in the late '90s, such as a Duck Dunn P-Bass and Jazz Basses bearing the names of Marcus Miller and Geddy Lee. The American-made special-edition models included a Ventures Limited Jazz Bass, with an ash body finished in midnight black, offered in 1996, and a Noel Redding J-Bass, made to 1965 specs and sold only in 1997. For the surfer dudes, there was the California P-Bass Special of 1997, with a Jazz neck, PJ pickups, and a gold-anodized pickguard.

In 1998 Fender opened a large new factory (177,000 square feet) in Corona. The Ensenada facility was also expanded, and North American production began to increase dramatically. The U.S.-made Standard and Deluxe lines offered maple fingerboards and a fretless option became available for most models. New "Noiseless" pickups, designed by Bill Turner, became standard on the J-Bass models in 1998. They were also used on the Stu Hamm Urge II. In 1999 a Precision Deluxe 5-string appeared; the Hot Rod P-Bass, with PJ pickups, and a Jaco Pastorius signature J-Bass (fretted or fretless) also joined the party. In 2000 the American Standard models were upgraded and renamed the American Series.

■ Fender American Deluxe Jazz Bass.

■ Fender American Deluxe Precision Bass V.

(Fender now uses the Standard name for lower-priced P and J models made in Mexico.) Cosmetic changes on all late-'90s basses included abalone fingerboard dots and a new peghead decal that reprises the classic "spaghetti logo" of the '50s.

The year 2001 marked the 50th anniversary of the Precision Bass, and Fender celebrated in style. A special event at the Summer NAMM show in Nashville featured the unveiling of a limited-edition '51 P-Bass reissue, created by the Custom Shop. Every detail of the original, right down to the output jack, had been painstakingly reproduced. (Every detail except the price tag, that is: in contrast to the introductory price of $199.50, the replica retailed for a hefty $5,999.) Fender also introduced a 50th Anniversary American Series P-Bass, with the post-'57 configuration but the "butterscotch blond" look of the '51. Other new basses included the Victor Bailey signature Jazz Bass, with a koa top over mahogany, and the Zone Bass, a new Deluxe model with soapbar pickups and a choice of a walnut-over-mahogany or maple-over-alder body. Both of these basses have 18-volt active electronics.

By 2002 the hodgepodge of basses that was the Fender line in the early '90s had been transformed into seven series. The signature basses comprise the Artist series, including a Japanese-made Sting model based on his '55 P-Bass. The American Vintage series contains the trusty '57 and '62 Precisions and '62 and '75 Jazz Basses. The "tweaked traditional" basses introduced in 1995, as well as the more recent Zone Bass, fall into the American Deluxe series; the Mexican-made Deluxe series has lower-priced versions of these basses. The American Series, as noted, consists of back-to-basics P and J models. There's only one bass in the Classic series, a Mexican-made '60s-style Jazz Bass. The Standards, also made in Mexico, are budget-priced P and J models.

Fender continues to extend its bass line in both classic and contemporary directions, reintroducing old favorites like the Mustang Bass and rolling out such new models as the Reggie Hamilton 5-string, with PJ pickups and active/passive EQ. One interesting variant that appeared in 2002 is the Mark Hoppus Bass, created for the blink-182 bassist. In a twist on the many P-Basses that have been modified with Jazz necks and pickups, this 4-string has a Jazz body with a Precision neck and a Basslines Quarter-Pound P-style pickup. It's more proof, as if any were needed, of the endless possibilities offered by Leo Fender's dead-on designs for the Precision Bass and Jazz Bass.

■ Fender Jazz Bass fretless.

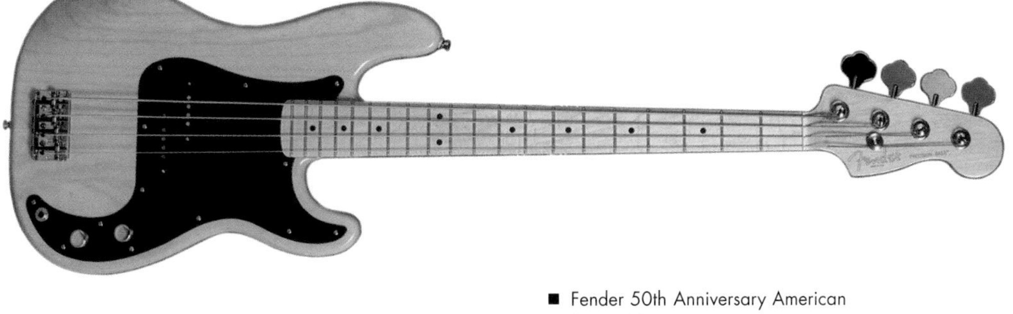

■ Fender 50th Anniversary American Series P-Bass.

BUILDING BERRY OAKLEY JR.'S "TRACTOR" REPLICA

By Todd Krause

The Fender Custom Shop in Corona, California, began operations in 1987. It was originally intended to be a small facility, with master builders John Page and Michael Stevens making five or six instruments a month. But word spread fast, and within three months there was a backlog of almost 600 orders. More luthiers were hired, the workspace was expanded, and production soared to more than 4,000 instruments a year. In addition to unique "dream instruments," the Fender Custom Shop also builds replicas of existing basses and guitars—one such job is described here by master builder Todd Krause.

I was brought into this project in a second-hand sort of way. Mark Ford of the Black Crowes has had a pretty good relationship with the Custom Shop over the years, and he was playing in a side band with Berry Oakley Jr. I'm not sure exactly how it came up—they might have been at the factory for a tour, or were talking to one of our artist-relations guys—but somebody mentioned to Berry that we make Relic instruments.

We can make new basses and guitars that look and feel as if they've been played for years: aged parts, rust on the screws, worn finishes and fingerboards, nicks in the right places, etc. These aren't just cosmetic creations; they really feel like vintage instruments. They have "mojo." In the past, our builders have made replicas of Muddy Waters's Telecaster and Rory Gallagher's Stratocaster, among others, and Berry liked the idea of having a replica of his father's bass—his dad, Berry Oakley Sr., had been the original bass player in the Allman Brothers Band. I think Berry realized that he was touring with a piece of history and didn't want anything bad to happen to it. He brought the bass into the shop one day to see if it was possible to reproduce it, and we started working on the specifics.

The original "Tractor" is a Frankenstein Jazz Bass. The neck was swapped out at some point, and the pickups are all over the place. You've got a Guild pickup in the middle, and instead of just tossing the J-Bass pickup he took out, Berry Sr. sandwiched it in between the existing bridge pickup and the bridge. Berry Jr. learned from someone in the band that his dad was always fooling around with the bass late at night, until he came up with what it looks like today. The rest of the band hated it because it was so ugly—that's why somebody called it "The Tractor." But the tone was incredible, and everybody loved it for that.

The first thing we realized was that we still make the Guild pickup at Fender, although it now looks a little bit different. At that point, we decided to approach the project with an emphasis on the unique tone of the bass, and not so much on trying to build an exact replica. Berry's thought was that he didn't need to fool anybody; he just wanted a bass he could take on the road.

■ Berry Oakley Jr. with "The Tractor" (right) and its Custom Shop replica.

Still, I wanted to get as close as possible, which meant trying to get all of the dents and worn areas to match up. We're talking about two different bass players: Berry Sr. put wear in different places than Berry Jr., so trying to replicate those areas was a challenge. But it turned out to be pretty close.

The body work was standard, and routing for the extra pickup was not a chore. I duplicated the neck profile as closely as possible by taking a piece of solder and wrapping it around the neck to get a rough fingerprint of its shape, then laying that on a piece of paper and tracing the edges. I took the specs of the thickness and the width, and from all of this we were able to closely replicate the neck profile. After adding the block inlays and brown shell binding on the fingerboard, we used our Relic process to give the neck a "worn in" feel.

We also used the Relic process on all of the hardware, including the tuning machines. The originals had the round "paddle" shape, but Fender doesn't make those anymore. You can find them on eBay for about $400, but, again, we were going for tone and not just cosmetics, so we decided on a set of vintage-style bass keys that we make.

The only aspect of the original I didn't try to replicate was something that, looking back, I almost wish I had. When Berry Sr. re-routed the body to accommodate the larger Guild pickup, he went in at the wrong angle and actually drilled through the back. He then filled in the hole with putty. Maybe I should have done that, because lots of folks who have tried to re-rout a pickup cavity have done the same thing. I don't think it would have affected the tone, but if I ever have to build another replica of "The Tractor" . . .

FLEISHMAN

Harry Fleishman is the Thomas Edison of luthiers. Since the early 1970s he has conceived and built a series of innovative basses in styles ranging from compact, headless 4-strings to full-scale electric uprights. He's also been a touring bassist, a design consultant, a Hollywood songwriter, a music journalist, and a lutherie instructor.

Fleishman doesn't really have standard models, since he builds his instruments, as he says, "one at a time"—and many are one-of-a-kind creations. One style that he has built over the years, in a number of variations, is a bass guitar he calls the Scroll Bass. It has an open, scroll-shaped headstock and a swooping double-cutaway body shape that manages to look both futuristic and classic at the same time. Harry built the first one in 1976; because conventional knobs would have interrupted the clean lines of the body, it had foot controls instead. That was a bit cumbersome, so he switched to roller-style knobs recessed into a slot in the body's upper edge. In the late '90s Fleishman made a matched pair of 5-string Scroll Basses, fretted and fretless, with ebony-covered Bartolini pickups; they were displayed at the Bartolini NAMM booth. The Scroll Basses use a fanned-fret system that Fleishman developed in the '70s while working with John Starrett on a tapping instrument. (This raises an interesting question: what do you call a fretless bass built this way—fanned fretless?)

■ Fleishman Scroll Bass 5-strings, fretless and fretted.

Another Fleishman eye-opener is the Bassic IV, which was one of the first headless basses. (Harry calls the concept "right-hand tuning.") A few hundred were produced in the late '70s and early '80s at Fleishman's Denver shop. They used conventional tuning machines mounted in an open "backstock" at the end of the body, behind the bridge. The synthetic fingerboard covered a full three octaves, and the electronics included both a magnetic pickup and a piezo bridge, which was unheard of at the time. "A small piezo-disc network picked up the vibrations of the strings through the body, adding a bright punch unlike the tone of any other bass before it," says Fleishman. "My intention in creating it was to make an economical, ultra-lightweight bass with a bright, full tone." The design was later licensed to the International Music Corporation (IMC). Fleishman designed a number of other "right-hand tuning" basses; the body shape of one, the Jayne, has been emulated by Kenneth Lawrence (with Harry's blessing).

Not long after Ernie Ball launched the acoustic bass guitar category with the gargantuan Earthwood bass, Fleishman applied his brain to the concept—and came up with something quite different: "I call my instruments 'Compact Acoustic Basses' because I think of them as small acoustic basses rather than big acoustic guitars." He started building them in 1978, using Indian rosewood, then Honduras rosewood, and finally curly claro walnut to get the tone he wanted. He employed an unusual bracing system and fanned frets, which Fleishman feels are especially well suited to acoustic basses. In 1990 he created the Asymmetric Compact Acoustic Bass, which had a larger bout on the bass side and an offset soundhole. Later versions had two soundholes. "That idea was based on research conducted by Heinrich Helmholtz showing that if one has two different-sized holes in a box, there will be a box resonance at the individual hole sizes and the sum of their sizes," says Harry. "This gives a lower, flatter response to the Compact Acoustic Bass." Fleishman has experimented extensively with graphite in the necks and bracing of his acoustic basses.

■ Fleishman Bassic IV series.

Leaving no low-frequency idea unexplored, Fleishman has also built an array of electric upright basses in scale lengths from 35" to 42". One of his most celebrated hybrids is the much-modified 36"-scale 5-string, known as "The Beast," which Nashville bassist Dave Pomeroy has used for more than 20 years. Its tone is so unmistakable that when Harry thought he heard it coming from a jukebox in a Denver cafe, he checked the selection—sure enough, it was a Don Williams song with Pomeroy on bass. Another of Fleishman's EUB creations is the Boulder Upright, which weighs only six pounds.

Lightweight instruments remain a subject of great interest to Fleishman; one of his recent designs is what he calls the Anti-Gravity Bass. Made of spruce with a mahogany/rosewood/graphite neck, it weighs only five pounds. It can be equipped with magnetic pickups, the LightWave optical-pickup system, or a "super-sensitive" proprietary system that Harry developed just for this instrument. Fleishman has licensed the design to Jackson, which is building a production version [see Jackson].

FODERA

In 1975 Vinnie Fodera was a student at New York's School of Visual Arts and an aspiring luthier who doodled sketches of guitars in the margins of his notebooks. He had played guitar since he was 14 and knew he wanted to build instruments, but he didn't know how to get started. And then he found the answer—in a bank window.

"I had taken a part-time job on Wall Street as a stock runner," Fodera recalls. "They would give me envelopes full of securities to take to a bank. One day I'm making a delivery at the World Trade Center and spot a sign in the window. I don't know what drew me to it—it was just a piece of paper about a hundred feet away. It was an advertisement for adult evening classes at the New School for Social Research in Manhattan. There was a listing for a class in classical guitar construction, taught by Thomas Humphrey. I knew I *had* to get into this class—this was what I'd been dreaming about."

■ Fodera Monarch Deluxe, 1983.

Fodera called just in time to reserve one of the last spots in the class, where he built his first guitar under Humphrey's tutelage. One of his classmates was an attorney named Alan Redner, who mentioned he had a friend who made guitars. "It turned out to be Stuart Spector," says Vinnie. "Alan arranged for me to visit Stuart's shop, which was in this woodworking co-op in Brooklyn. This was in early 1977, and Ned Steinberger was there, too. I was enchanted and amazed by this place—I *had* to work there."

Spector didn't need any help at the time, but he took Fodera's name and number. It wasn't long before he called, offering a job cutting out logo inlays from mother-of-pearl blanks. It wasn't much—but Vinnie leapt at the chance to work at Spector Guitars. He stayed for three-and-a-half years, learning about instrument design and woodworking from Stuart and his partner, Alan Charney.

In 1980 Ken Smith contracted with Spector to build the basses that Smith had designed. "The whole shop glued up the carcasses, but it fell to me to give them the finished carving," says Vinnie. Smith supervised the work, often sitting next to Fodera and directing him.

When it became difficult for Spector to keep up production on both lines, Smith hired Fodera to set up a woodworking shop for producing his basses. Vinnie found a suitable storefront in Brooklyn, and by early 1981 he was working full time on Ken Smith basses. "I was able to give him a bass a week. It would be carved and finished, and Ken would take it to his place in Manhattan, where he put in the electronics and set it up. He sold them out of the apartment, which doubled as a teaching studio. He gave lessons, and he got his start by selling these basses to his students."

Fodera says his working relationship with Smith was enjoyable at first, but he eventually grew restless. "I wanted to do my own thing. Then, about a year and a half into my stint with Ken Smith in that shop, a knock comes at the door. It's Joey Lauricella." Lauricella, a local bassist, had noticed someone leaving the unmarked storefront carrying a gig bag and wondered what was up. When Fodera explained that he was building Ken Smith basses, Joey was amazed. It turned out that he knew Smith, owned two of his basses, and had been selling them—never suspecting they were being built right in his neighborhood.

"Joey started hanging out, and we became fast friends," says Vinnie. "He asked if he could help, and he became more and more involved with building the basses. Eventually he asked me if I would consider forming a partnership." Eager to focus on his own designs, Fodera worked out a deal: he would continue to build Ken Smith basses while slowly building equity in the shop. This gave Smith the opportunity to set up an alternative manufacturing operation before Vinnie finally broke away—which he did in March 1983, forming Fodera Guitars with Lauricella. They made an ideal bass-building team: Fodera was a master luthier, and Lauricella had a pro bassist's perspective and ears to go along with his abilities as a builder, technician, and salesman.

The new partners soon had one of New York's leading bassists as a customer. Anthony Jackson had been pursuing his dream of a contrabass guitar since the early '70s, working first with Carl Thompson and then Ken Smith (and thus Fodera) on creating a usable 6-string. Impressed by Vinnie's dedication to the task, Jackson asked him to build another contrabass. In the ensuing years, they have collaborated on a series of cutting-edge 6-strings. "He's ruthless in his pursuit of perfection," says Vinnie, who has built a succession of ever-more-sophisticated instruments for Jackson.

Even before the founding of Fodera Guitars, Vinnie had designed the bass that became the basis of the neck-through Monarch Series. "The first one I built was a 4-string, but the next one was a 5-string that Tom Kennedy bought after he saw it at a guitar show," says Vinnie. That Monarch 5-string might have been the first of its kind; Jimmy Johnson had been using an Alembic 5-string, with a low *B*, since the mid-'70s, but it was a custom bass. The Fodera Monarch 5-string was a standard model. Monarchs have remained in the Fodera line ever since, available as 4- and 5-strings in Deluxe and Elite configurations.

In 1984 Fodera created the Emperor bass, which featured more sophisticated electronics than the Monarch. Because the Emperor circuit was larger, Vinnie designed a bigger body to accommodate it. The Emperor has since become an extensive series, available as bolt-on or neck-through 4-, 5-, 6-, or 7-string basses in single- or double-cutaway body styles. Scale length can be 34", 35", or 36"; 24 frets are standard, but the Emperor can be ordered "vintage style" with a 21-fret neck and JJ single-coil pickups.

The first Fodera/Anthony Jackson Contrabass Guitar, a double-cutaway 6-string, was built in 1984. It was originally a 34"-scale instrument, but it can also be made with a 35" or 36" scale. Its successor, the Fodera/Anthony Jackson Presentation Model Contrabass Guitar, is a single-cutaway 6-string that was built for Jackson in 1989. "The upper part of the body joins the neck at the 12th fret," notes Vinnie, "which allows the vibrations to flow more freely and excite more rapidly." It's made in whatever configuration Jackson himself is currently using—in 2002, that meant a bass with a chambered alder body and a quilted-mahogany top. Scale length is 36". The bass is an intriguing blend of design sophistication

■ Fodera Emperor.

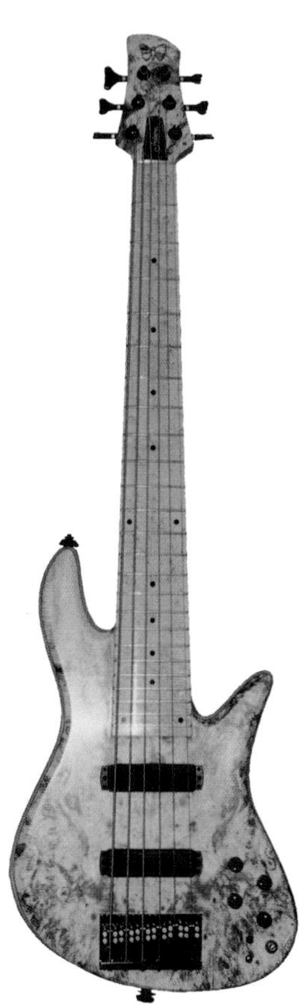

■ Fodera Emperor 6-string.

SOME THOUGHTS ON HARDWARE AND PICKUPS

By Vinnie Fodera

Designing and fabricating proprietary hardware is, even under ideal conditions, a daunting task. This challenge was especially difficult in 1981–82 when Joey Lauricella and I were imagining the components for our first 5- and 6-string bass guitars. Back in those days, when such components simply didn't exist as off-the-shelf parts, we had to design everything ourselves.

■ Vinnie Fodera (left) and Joey Lauricella.

The Bridge

To give you an idea of the thought process that goes into designing a custom bridge, I'll begin with what, in my opinion, is the most important aspect: the way the bridge affects the sound of the bass. First, you have to decide which type of material to use. In our case, it was extruded brass. Softer materials such as aluminum could dampen the string vibration to some less-than-optimal degree, whereas a much denser material such as steel would produce a brighter tone. We chose brass because it is sufficiently dense to efficiently transmit vibration, yet soft enough to contribute a more pleasing tonal character. Brass is also readily available and easy to machine, and it can be finished in a variety of ways. These are all important considerations. Equally important are the functions that will be incorporated into the final design. We wanted to have the advantage of a multi-directional bridge—that is, one in which the individual string saddles move back and forth to achieve accurate intonation, up and down for setting string height, and side to side to allow adjustable string spacing. We also wanted a lock-down for each saddle. (These details may seem ordinary now, but 20-plus years ago they were rather innovative.) It is also important, when designing proprietary hardware, to give it an original look that will be recognized as uniquely yours.

I should also note the difficulty we faced in trying to get our designs manufactured. In the early '80s, Fodera Guitars was a small, unknown, fledgling company with limited financial resources. Finding a machine shop that would work with us, given our budget, was probably as difficult as all the other considerations combined. Luckily, we were able to.

Tuners

We have, over the years, designed various types of tuning machines to complement our instruments, but the designs have proven either too complex, too delicate, or too expensive to justify their manufacture. We therefore decided to use some of the tuners readily available from parts companies. This was acceptable because we didn't feel the tuning machines played a significant role in the overall sound of the instrument, for two reasons: First, they are usually placed beyond the point where the string is stopped at the nut, so you don't really "hear" them. Second, their weight constitutes an insignificant fraction of the total weight of the instrument. When it comes to tuners, we're more concerned with their ergonomic comfort, mechanical reliability, and aesthetic appeal.

The Nut

You may not consider the humble nut an important piece of hardware, but there is one crucial aspect of its function. Most manufacturers fabricate the nut from some sort of plastic—a logical choice, since it can be produced cost-effectively. The drawback is that open-string notes, on a fretted neck, will sound different from fretted notes. When you play a fretted note, the string is resonating against hard-metal fretwire; when you play an open note, the string is resonating against much softer plastic. Different materials—different tones. We form each nut out of brass, which yields tonal response more like a fret's. A subtle detail, perhaps, but a significant one, in my opinion. Besides, a brass nut will never break and will last many years before the string slots wear down.

Pickups

Nowadays, the intrepid luthier has at his or her disposal such a bewildering array of pickups that the problem is

not one of availability but of choice. I wish this had been the case in the early '80s, but at that time the contrary was true. So when the designs for our first 5- and 6-string bass guitars were complete, we faced the problem of designing and fabricating custom pickups. We decided to leave the fabricating part to the experts, but at first the pickup makers were reluctant to help us, and understandably so—it was just too expensive to tool up to make completely new pickups that required new molds, bobbins, magnet configurations, etc.

For our 6-strings, the initial solution was to wire two EMG guitar humbuckers in series, creating something like a giant P-style pickup. It was an awkward solution, but it got us started. A more elegant solution was available for the 5-string. The Bill Lawrence company had been manufacturing an extra-long, dual-coil humbucking pickup for pedal-steel guitars, with blades instead of polepieces. The extra length of these pickups perfectly fit the wide spacing of our Monarch 5-string neck, so the problem was solved. Eventually Bill and Pat Bartolini came to the rescue and created for us the first true proprietary 5- and 6-string bass pickups. Later, Seymour Duncan, EMG, and (more recently) Aero were able to provide us with many fine exclusive pickups.

and electronic simplicity: it has one pickup, a custom Seymour Duncan humbucker, and no circuitry at all—not even a volume knob.

Imperial Series basses are 5- and 6-strings with single-cutaway bodies like those on the Anthony Jackson Presentation Model. They have dual pickups and can be made in any scale length from 33" to 36". Fodera also builds signature models based on instruments created for Lincoln Goines, Matthew Garrison, and Victor Wooten (two different models, including one that's a replica of Victor's '83 Monarch).

Most Fodera basses are made with bodies of mahogany or alder. "As for tops," says Vinnie, "we have a wide wood selection at the standard price. There are about 65 types or degrees of grain available, with the most in-demand being buckeye burl, koa, flame maple, quilted maple, figured walnut, figured redwood, maple burl, and spalted maple." A limited selection of even more rare and select woods is also available, for an additional charge. Fodera necks, whether through-body or bolt-on, are always hard maple and can be ordered in standard or narrow width. Fingerboards are made from rosewood (several varieties), bird's-eye maple, or ebony; fretless basses get a hard-rosewood (kingwood or Brazilian rosewood) or ebony 'board. Fodera selects pickups from the best brands on the market, including Aero, Bartolini, EMG, and Seymour Duncan; almost all are proprietary models tailored to Fodera's specs. The onboard electronics have evolved with the basses, and the current Emperor preamp is an 18-volt circuit designed by Mike Pope in 1999. The Fodera bridge is also a proprietary design—it had to be in 1983, because there were no off-the-shelf 5-string bridges around—and it's been continuously refined over the years.

One recent Fodera innovation is the "Extended-B Headstock." In 1999, because some customers were hesitant to order 36"-scale basses, Vinnie created a new headstock design that improves the *B*-string sound on basses with shorter scales. It places the *B*-string tuning key at the top, farther from the nut than the *E* or *A* strings.

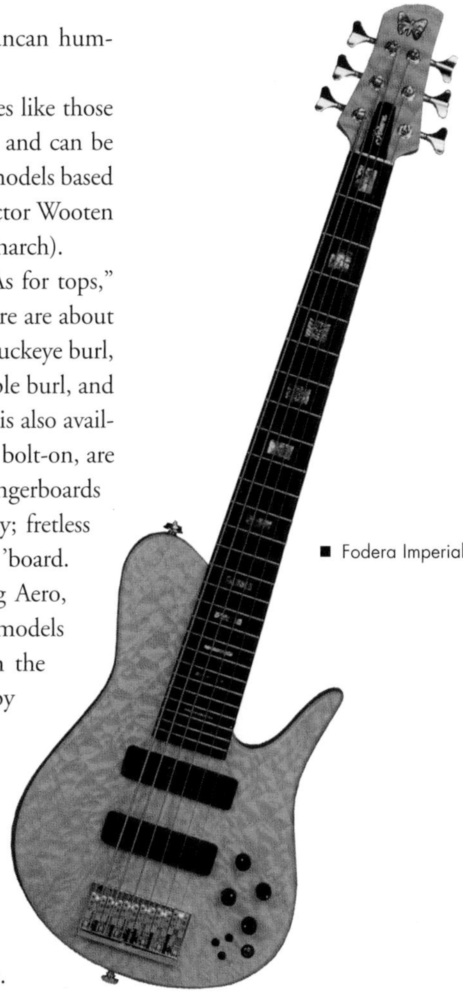

■ Fodera Imperial 6-string.

■ Fury Tornado.

"Extending the *B* makes the total string length a little longer," says Vinnie, "so it's tighter and therefore more responsive."

In the late '90s, Fodera experimented with a second line of lower-priced 4- and 5-string basses called the NYC Series. They had ash or alder J-style bodies with optional figured-maple tops, bolt-on 21-fret maple or Moses graphite necks, and Seymour Duncan vintage pickups. Only about 170 were made.

Even after 20 years, Fodera Guitars remains a small operation, producing about a dozen basses a month for a select customer list. Fodera and Lauricella stay focused on the "pursuit of perfection," whether it's locating a source for superior wood or evaluating the latest pickups and preamps. "We still build instruments the same way we've always done it," says Vinnie Fodera.

FURY

Glenn McDougall of Saskatoon, Saskatchewan, is the godfather of his country's electric guitar and bass industry. (Fellow Saskatooner Sheldon Dingwall calls him "the Leo Fender of Canada.") McDougall founded Fury Guitars in 1962 and has always made most of his own components, including pickups and bridges. He produced his first bass, the LS4, in 1967. Features included a double-cutaway mahogany body, bolt-on maple neck with 20-fret rosewood fingerboard, 4-in-line headstock with underslung tuning keys, and one single-coil pickup. Scale length was an unusual 31⅝". Fury unveiled a fretless fingerboard in late 1967, making the LS4 one of the first production fretless basses. Various improvements, including a dual-coil pickup and optional maple fingerboard, showed up over the next few years. In the late 1970s the company offered a two-pickup version with optional stereo wiring.

The LS4 was discontinued in 1987 and replaced by the Anthem, which had a soft-maple body, 24-fret neck, and improved electronics. In 1996 a "Drop D" bridge mechanism was offered, and it's remained a popular option on Fury basses since then. (Perhaps that's why Fury does not make a 5-string.) In 1997 the Tornado succeeded the Anthem. The main differences are an altered body shape for improved upper-fret access and a coil-split switch that allows full humbucking, modified humbucking, or single-coil operation of the two ZP pickups. Both the Anthem and Tornado have the same medium scale as the original LS4. Fury also produced a small number of Space Basses between 1983 and 1985. These featured a bat-shaped hard-maple body, the same underslung headstock as the LS4, and lots of shiny black paint. "Their styling," says Glenn McDougall, "appealed to heavy metal groups . . . and most have found their way into the hands of collectors."

■ Fury Space Bass.

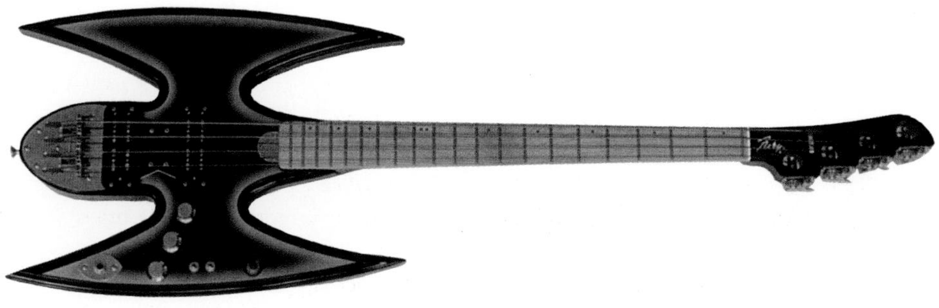

G&L

G&L was Leo Fender's last company, and he worked there, in his cluttered workshop, almost every day from the company's 1980 founding until his death in 1991. The name stands for "George and Leo," George being George Fullerton, an old friend from the pre-CBS Fender company. Dale Hyatt, another longtime associate, joined them to make up the management team; in 1984 he and Leo bought out Fullerton's share. (After that, people were told the name meant "Guitars by Leo.") Leo Fender funded G&L's start-up, and he made most of the important decisions. He wasn't too concerned about production numbers or profits, and many of his designs took years to get to market, if they got there at all.

Leo was adamant that G&L should not make instruments that copied his old designs. There was a certain degree of irony in this—the market for vintage Fenders was taking off, and many of G&L's competitors were selling instruments that were little more than Fender copies—but Leo insisted that he "owed it to musicians" to build *better* basses and guitars. G&L used traditional materials (ash and alder bodies, bolt-on maple necks with rosewood or maple fingerboards), but Leo insisted on finding ways to improve the instruments. He worked tirelessly, even in ill health, to do it.

■ G&L L-1000.

One of Leo's most important inventions during the G&L era was a new style of pickup, which was patented under the name "Magnetic Field Design." Leo's pickups for Fender instruments had alnico magnets and non-adjustable polepieces; these G&L pickups had a ceramic bar magnet under each coil, with adjustable soft-iron polepieces. This produced more output with less winding wire, and the pickups were also brighter-sounding—sometimes too much so; some of Leo's G&L instruments were considered harsh-sounding by musicians. (Although Leo's hearing had deteriorated, he still trusted his ears when testing his designs.)

Leo also had a better idea about installing trussrods. In most basses, the trussrod is installed either through a rout in the back of the neck (which is then covered by a "skunk stripe" of contrasting wood) or in a rout on the face of the neck, under the fingerboard. With Leo's "Bi-Cut" necks, the neck blank is sawed in half longitudinally and routed for the trussrod. After the rod has been installed, encased in a plastic sleeve, the halves are glued back together under pressure. Leo felt that the glue joint made the neck stronger and more resistant to twisting and warping. G&L basses still use both Magnetic Field Design pickups and Bi-Cut necks.

The first G&L bass was the L-1000, introduced in 1980. It may not have been a Fender copy, but its body shape, 34" scale length, and single-pickup design owed much to the Precision Bass (and perhaps a little to the Music Man StingRay). The pickup was, of course, one of Leo's new Magnetic Field Design models, and the die-cast bridge was considerably more substantial than anything Fender had ever installed on a P-Bass. There was also a two-pickup version, the L-2000, and this has proven to be G&L's most popular and enduring bass. (G&L dropped the L-1000 in 1993, but the L-2000 has been in continuous production since its debut.) The passive/active electronics allow a variety of operating modes, including series or parallel wiring of the pickups, giving the L-2000 loads of tonal flexibility—which is just what Leo had in mind.

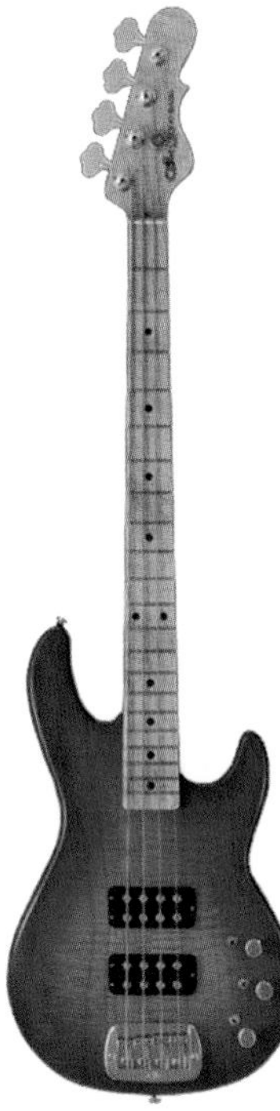
■ G&L L-2000, cherryburst.

Not content with that, Leo Fender created a half-dozen more G&L bass models during the 1980s. These included the Interceptor and El Toro—both of which used smaller humbucking pickups than the 8-pole models on the L-Series basses—and the Lynx Bass, with two single-coil pickups. The single-pickup SB-1 and two-pickup SB-2 offered some of Leo's innovations at a more affordable price. More important was the L-5000, a 5-string that Leo spent several years perfecting. It had a 4+1 headstock and a single split-humbucking pickup. Rounding out the catalog was the single-cutaway ASAT Bass, introduced in 1989. Its Tele-style body at least nodded in the direction of the old Fender designs. The ASAT Bass

■ G&L ASAT gold sparkle (left) and L-2500.

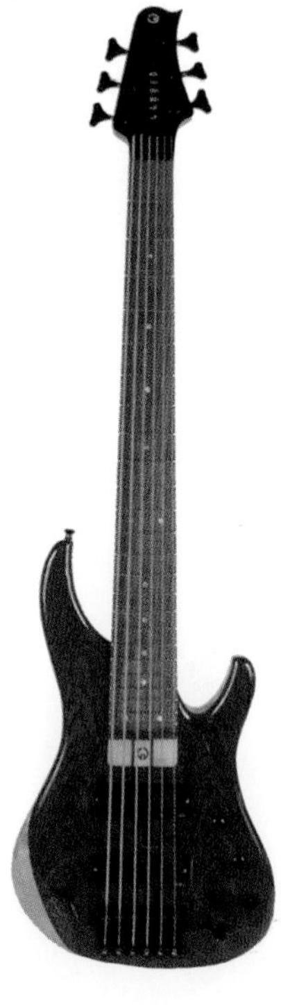

■ G. Gould GGi6.

has also proven to have lasting appeal and was still in the G&L catalog, in both solidbody and semi-hollow versions, in 2002.

After Leo Fender's death, G&L was acquired by BBE Sound, headed by John McLaren. McLaren, who had been in charge of Fender at the end of the CBS era, made a conscious effort to preserve Leo Fender's legacy—Leo's widow, Phyllis, was named honorary chairman of G&L—but he also reduced the number of models and made other changes to put the company's books in order. Some new (and more Fender-like) models were introduced, including the aptly named Legacy Bass, later known as the LB-100. Other BBE-era basses include the L-1500 4-string and L-1505 5-string, with single pickups and downsized bodies, and the JB-2, a Jazz-inspired model with a pair of alnico "vintage style" pickups.

Under BBE, much of G&L's bass R&D has focused on refining the 5-string. In 1994 the L-5000 was succeeded by a new model, the L-5500, with a pair of EMG-40DC active pickups. (EMGs? Leo must have been spinning in his grave.) The L-5500 was replaced, in turn, by the L-2500, a 5-string with the same electronics as the L-2000. That bass was updated in 1998 with a slimmer body and a 3+2 headstock; a Deluxe option—curly maple top, bird's-eye maple neck—was also offered.

One G&L bass that never made it into production was the Bass VI–style 6-string prototype Leo was working on in March 1991. It remains in his workshop, which has been preserved just as it was when Leo left work at G&L's Fullerton, California, factory for the last time.

SEE ALSO: FENDER, MUSIC MAN

G. GOULD

Geoff Gould was the founder of Modulus Graphite, where he helped to popularize high-tech, graphite-neck basses and pioneered the use of the 35" scale on 5- and 6-strings. Soon after selling his interest in Modulus in 1995, Gould started a new company whose instruments combine his knowledge of composite materials with his affection for vintage instruments, especially the Fender Jazz Bass. "I considered it an engineering challenge to make a bass that had that essence," says Geoff, "but was also an improvement on the original."

G. Gould basses have graphite-reinforced wood necks, but that's hardly unusual these days. What sets them apart is the *way* that Gould uses the graphite. "Most graphite reinforcements are placed near the center of the neck, close to the structural 'neutral axis,' where there are no stresses," he explains. "Being familiar with the work of James Rickard at Ovation in the '70s [see Ovation], I decided to utilize horizontal graphite strips, placed as far away from the neutral axis as possible. I inlay a flat strip measuring roughly 1" x ⅛" up into the fingerboard, in addition to two strips alongside a traditional trussrod. This creates an upside-down U-channel that's quite stiff. With the graphite hidden, it looks traditional—but it has the strength, stiffness, and tonal improvements of graphite."

G. Gould's initial product offerings were the J-style GGJ basses, available in 4-string (34" scale) and 5-string (35" scale) models. They have ash or alder bodies with optional maple tops, 24-fret necks with a graphite headstock laminate, and EMG pickups and electronics. ("Vintage style" basses with 21-fret necks are also available.) Geoff expanded his line with 5- and 6-string basses in the GGi body style, a more modern "streamlined" design. Many of these feature tops in such exotic woods as cocobolo, amboyna, and canarywood. The most recent addition to the G. Gould line is the GGi5 Pulse bass, a single-pickup model.

SEE ALSO: MODULUS

GIBSON

Gibson is one of the oldest and most venerated names in the stringed-instrument business, with a history that stretches back to Orville Gibson's shop in Kalamazoo, Michigan, in the 1890s. Gibson was also the first company to have the opportunity to market an electric bass, when legendary Gibson engineer Lloyd Loar created the prototype for an amplified "stick" bass in 1924. It had a small oval body, and the pickup was an electrostatic transducer mounted in a Bakelite box under the bridge. Company management thought Loar's bass was a crazy idea, and they refused to manufacture it. (Loar later left Gibson to found a company called Vivi-Tone, but his bass never made it into production.) During this period, Gibson also produced the Style J mando-bass, a gigantic 4-string, fretted acoustic instrument that provided the bass lines for the mandolin orchestras of the Roaring '20s. It was nearly as large as an acoustic bass viol and could be played in either a vertical or horizontal position, with the bassist seated behind it.

In the late 1930s Gibson took another foray into the low end with the Electric Bass Guitar—the name, if not the instrument itself, proving prophetic. An oversize, 4-string hollowbody guitar made of solid maple, it was equipped with an endpin for stand-up playing and had a magnetic pickup similar to the Charlie Christian–model guitar pickup. The curved fingerboard had 24 inlaid fret markers, making it the first "lined fretless." Scale length was an upright-like 42¾". According to Gibson historian Julius Bellson, only two Electric Bass Guitars were made between 1938 and 1940, before World War II shut down product development. It's interesting to speculate about what might have happened if Gibson had been able to follow this line of thought.

- Gibson Electric Bass (above); as seen in 1954 ad (left).
- Gibson EB-2 (below).

The EB Era

Gibson didn't re-enter the electric bass market until two years after the introduction of the Fender Precision Bass. The Gibson Electric Bass of 1953, like the Electric Bass Guitar of the late '30s, was equipped with a telescoping endpin for upright playing—but this time the instrument had a small, violin-shaped solid-mahogany body (with painted-on *f*-hole) and a scale length of only 30½". The short scale was intended, apparently, to make it more appealing to guitarists, an impression that would seem to be confirmed by the inclusion of frets and a pickguard. The large single pickup had a brown plastic cover and was mounted at the end of the neck. The tuners were banjo-style, with rear-facing knobs on the back of the peghead. The Electric Bass was renamed the EB-1 in 1958, when Gibson introduced another electric bass, but discontinued within the year. Only 546 were made between 1953 and 1958. Updated with a chrome-covered humbucking pickup and some cosmetic refinements, the EB-1 made a brief comeback in 1970 but was dropped again two years later.

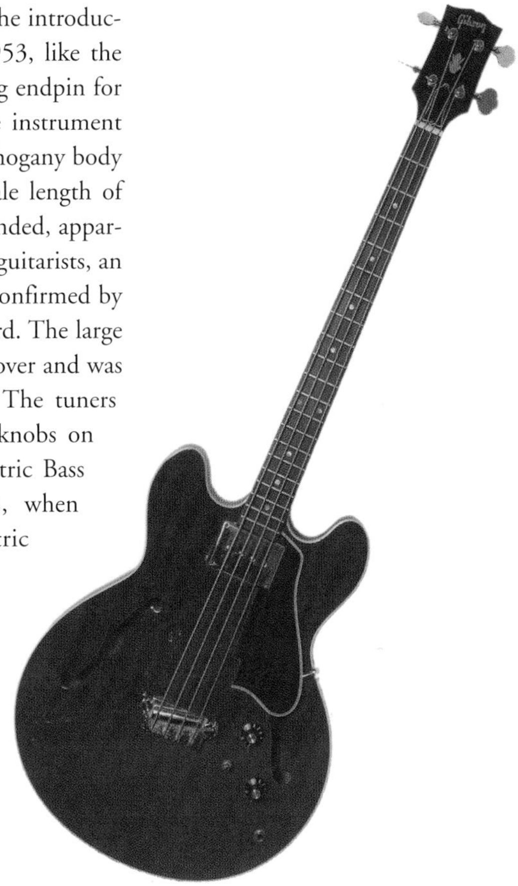

Gibson's second electric bass model established a pattern that would hold true for almost all of the company's basses from that date forward. The EB-2 of 1958 was a "partner" to a similar

■ 1962 Gibson EB-3.

guitar model—in this case, the semi-hollow ES-335. The EB-2 was, in effect, an Electric Bass neck (complete with banjo-style tuners) glued onto the double-cutaway, "thinline" body of the ES-335. The earliest models had a single-coil pickup with a brown-plastic cover, but this was soon replaced by a large humbucker with a black-plastic cover. It came in sunburst or natural (EB-2N); black was offered in 1959 and cherry red in 1960. A pushbutton "baritone" (i.e., bass-cut) control was added in 1959, and conventional right-angle tuners replaced the banjo tuners in 1960. The semi-hollow EB-6, with six strings tuned an octave below standard guitar, was available from 1960 to 1962, when it was replaced by a solidbody model with the same designation.

The original EB-2 was dropped in 1961 and reintroduced, with a metal pickup cover, in 1964. A double-pickup version, the EB-2D, joined the line in 1966. Several finish colors, including "Sparkling Burgundy," were offered before both models were discontinued in 1972. Although not commercially successful, Gibson's short-scale, semi-hollow basses—and such similar models as the Epiphone Rivoli and Guild Starfire Bass—were popular with many '60s rock bands because they were easy to play and offered different tonal possibilities than Fender basses.

Soon after the original EB-1 was dropped, Gibson introduced another solidbody model: the EB-0. Its double-cutaway mahogany body had the same shape as that of the recently revised Les Paul Jr. guitar, and the neck was the same one used on the EB-1 and EB-2. The pickup and other features were, unsurprisingly, the same as those found on Gibson's other basses. In 1961, the EB-0's body changed to the pointed-horn "SG-style" shape—once again, in lockstep with changes in the company's guitar line. This single-pickup 4-string and its double-pickup brother, the EB-3 (with 4-position "Varitone" switch), were Gibson's most popular models for the ensuing decade. A number of variations came and went, including the unique EB-0F, with built-in fuzztone (1962–65), and the solidbody EB-6, a double-pickup 6-string tuned *EADGBE* (1962–66). Gibson also incorporated EB-3–style basses in some of the doublenecks that the company made during this era. In 1969 the solid pegheads of the EB-0 and EB-3 were dropped in favor of a classical-guitar-like slotted peghead; the solid peghead returned in 1972. Long-scale versions of both basses, designated EB-0L and EB-3L, debuted in 1969 and remained available until 1979. The scale length was 34½"—although some sources say 34⅜"; either way, Gibson seems to have been trying to outdo Fender by just a bit.

Gibson's line during the late '60s and early '70s also included the "student model" Melody Maker Bass, a short-scale, single-pickup bass version of the Melody Maker guitar; introduced in 1967, it was succeeded by the maple-body

■ Gibson Melody Maker Bass.

■ Gibson SB-450.

EB in 1970, which quickly vanished. The EB-4L showed up in 1972; this long-scale 4-string was essentially an EB-0L with different electronics, including a pickup designed by Bill Lawrence. It was gone by 1979. The SB models, with their oval black-plastic pickup covers, were more variations on the theme. They were available with one pickup (long scale, SB-400; short scale, SB-300) or two (long scale, SB-450; short scale, SB-350)—but not for long. Introduced in 1971–72, they were discontinued before the decade was over. The SG-style bass returned, swathed in nostalgia, with the EB-Z model of 1998—but it came with a standard long scale of 34". It was later renamed the SG-Z.

Historical note: From time to time, Gibson has manufactured budget-priced instruments sold under other brand names, either by retailers like Montgomery Ward or its own dealers. One of the in-house labels was Kalamazoo, which was used off and on after 1933, including the years 1966–70. During that period the Kalamazoo KB bass appeared; its solid body was made of chipboard rather than wood. The KB had a 4-in-line headstock, one pickup, and came in red, white, or "Las Vegas Blue." (What's blue in Las Vegas? Poker chips?)

T-Birds & Turmoil

A second, and ultimately more important, line of Gibson basses emerged in 1963, with the debut of the Thunderbird. The partner of the Firebird guitar, it shared the same neck-through-body construction and reverse body shape, with the longer horn on the bottom. With their 4-in-line headstocks and 34"-scale necks, the Thunderbird II (one pickup) and Thunderbird IV (two pickups) were the closest thing to a Fender bass that Gibson had ever offered, and they produced a raw, powerful sound that was an immediate hit with rock bassists.

Within two years of their introduction, the bodies of the Thunderbirds had been shifted to non-reverse and the neck-through construction replaced by Gibson's more usual set (glued-on) necks. Both models were discontinued in 1969, but two-pickup T-birds returned in the form of special anniversary models (with reverse bodies) in 1976 and 1979, and as the Thunderbird III from 1979 to 1982. Another limited-edition version—confusingly called the Firebird II—was available in 1982; its reverse body had a curly maple top. Properly named the Thunderbird IV once again, this venerable two-pickup 4-string came back for good in 1987.

■ 1976 Gibson Thunderbird.

The 1970s and early '80s were a period of management turmoil at Gibson, which is reflected by the many models (and variations) introduced during this period, often to be quickly withdrawn or replaced by similar instruments with different names. This was in large part due to the company's 1969 takeover by Norlin. Gibson had enjoyed a fairly stable evolution before then, marked by gradual expansion of its

■ Gibson Ripper (left) and Victory Standard.

manufacturing facilities in Kalamazoo as Gibson instruments gained favor with musicians all over the world. The company overcame the problems caused by both World Wars and the Depression, and it continued to prosper after it was acquired in 1944 by the Chicago Musical Instrument Company (CMI).

In 1950 Ted McCarty took over as president, and under his able leadership Gibson reached new heights in terms of both product innovation and profitability. McCarty stepped down in 1966, and in 1969 CMI was swallowed by the Ecuadorian Company Limited (ECL), a multinational corporation. The resulting conglomerate was named Norlin. Under the new regime, many changes were made in the name of corporate "efficiency"—and, as was true of Fender during the CBS period, many faithful customers (and employees) became disenchanted with the instruments being produced. The sense of loss became more acute as production was gradually shifted to a new Nashville factory that opened in 1974. The historic Kalamazoo facility was closed in 1984, marking the end of an era in American musical-instrument production. (Three former Gibson employees, including plant manager Jim Deurloo, subsequently launched Heritage Guitars and reopened the Kalamazoo plant. Their line included some neck-through-body basses.)

A few of the Gibson basses issued during the Norlin years were serviceable instruments, others merely curiosities. One of the best was the bass originally called the L9-S (a partner to the L6-S guitar) but better known as the Ripper. This was a long-scale (34½") solidbody 4-string with two humbucking pickups. The original version, first offered in 1973, had a solid-maple body with a bolt-on neck; when it was renamed the Ripper a year later, the body wood was changed to alder and the neck was glued on. It was available fretted or fretless. A similar model called the Grabber (G-1) had a single movable pickup; the Grabber III (G-III) had three single-coil pickups wired in a humbucking configuration. By 1982 the Rippers and Grabbers were goners.

The Gibson bass catalogs from the late '70s and early '80s included the RD and Victory models, both of which have acquired minor cult status over the years. (They were, of course, partners to similar guitar models.) The RD Artist bass, made from 1977 to 1982, had an amoeba-shaped maple body, strings-through-body bridge, and active electronics that included compression and expansion circuitry; a few were made with curly maple tops. The Victory bass was Fender-like, with a double-cutaway body, 4-in-line headstock, and 34" scale length. The Victory Standard had a single humbucking pickup with a coil-tap switch; the Victory Artist upped the ante with a pair of humbuckers and active electronics. Gibson also offered bass versions of the Flying V and Explorer guitars in the early '80s.

■ Gibson RD Artist.

Lester P. & Henry J.

The Les Paul guitar had been the mainstay of the Gibson line since its 1952 debut, and in 1969—as Norlin was taking over—that famous name was applied to an electric bass. Les Paul had come to the company with the idea of building a version of his namesake guitar with low-impedance pickups, which would be superior for recording purposes. When the guitar was introduced, it had a companion bass model. The original Les Paul Bass had a walnut-finished mahogany body with a carved top, 30½" scale length, and a pair of low-impedance pickups with black-plastic covers. It weighed a ton—and to plug it into an amp, you had to use a special cord with an impedance-matching transformer. Gibson renamed the bass the Les Paul Triumph in 1971 after making a number of modifications, including mounting the pickups at an angle rather than straight across. This time, the transformer was onboard. That was an improvement, but sales were still slow, and the Triumph was discontinued in 1979. A semi-hollow, single-pickup version called the Les Paul Signature Bass, with an asymmetrical double-cutaway body finished in sunburst or gold, appeared in 1973. Scale length was 34½". In 1976 the pickup was switched to high impedance and gold became the standard finish. While fewer than 1,000 of these basses were made, they have proven to be more popular with working bassists than the solidbody Les Paul models. (A Korean-made Epiphone knockoff, the Jack Casady signature model, showed up in the late '90s.)

■ Gibson Les Paul Bass.

Gibson—and its basses—moved into a new era in 1986, when Henry Juszkiewicz and two partners bought the company from Norlin for a bargain-basement price reported to be $5 million. Massive reorganization followed. Some of Juszkiewicz's management decisions have been controversial, and more than a few ex-employees have said it was difficult working for him because of his propensity for changing his mind. (One well-known consultant told a reporter, "Working for Gibson was like hitting yourself with a hammer. It feels good when you stop.") Be that as it may, with Juszkiewicz at the helm Gibson returned from the brink of financial ruin. It also acquired a number of other musical-instrument companies, including bass builders Steinberger and Tobias.

Many of the Gibson basses made in the late '80s fell into the "curiosity" category. Consider, for example, the Gibson IV, another stab at out-Fendering Fender, and the Q-80, a dual-pickup model made from leftover Victory bodies and finished in bizarre colors like "Panther Pink." (Renamed the Q-90 in 1988, it was also available as a fretless with factory-installed nylon-tapewound strings.) Then there was the futuristic 20/20, designed for Gibson by Ned Steinberger after Juszkiewicz acquired his company. It was made for only a year. Most obscure of all was the WRC Bass, a model created by Wayne Charvel as a companion to his WRC guitar; it appeared in the 1988 catalog but was never actually produced.

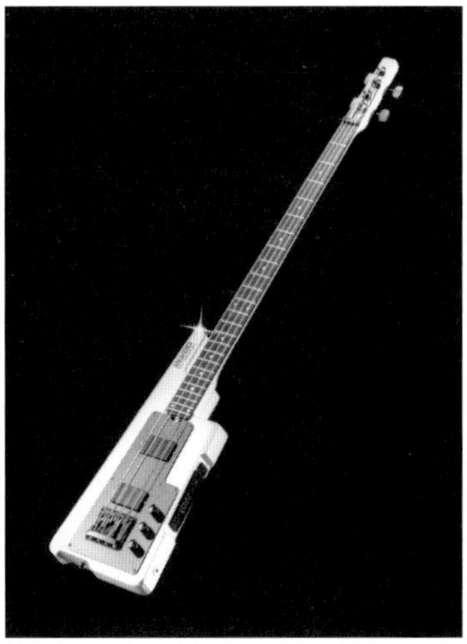

■ Gibson 20/20.

The Gibson bass line became more stable in 1991 with the decision to emphasize the Les Paul models. In one sense, these were classic Gibson basses: instruments made from guitar bodies with long necks attached. But they also offered more consistent manufacturing quality, and better sound, than most of the oddball Gibson basses of the '80s. They also signaled the end (perhaps) of Gibson's short-scale fascination: all of the post-'91 Les Paul basses have a 34" scale length.

The Les Paul Special Bass (LPB-1) had the familiar single-cutaway mahogany body with glued-on mahogany neck and ebony fingerboard. It was equipped with

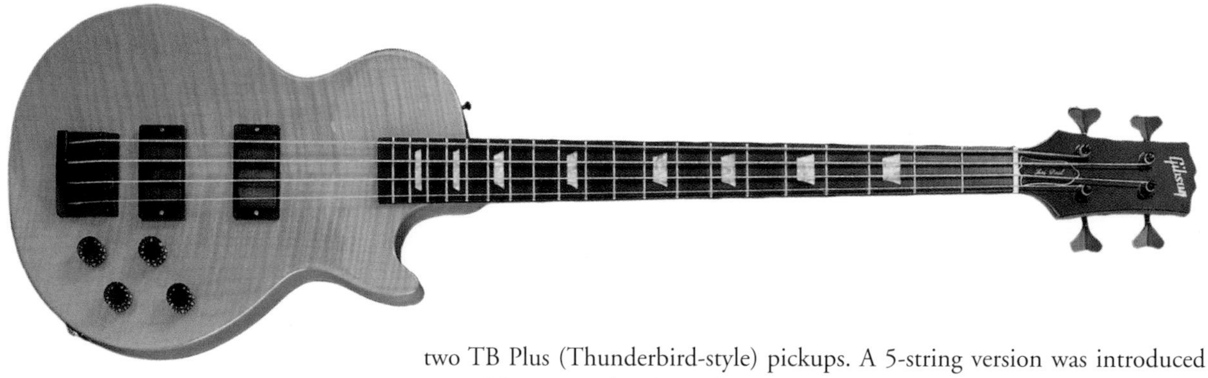

■ Gibson Les Paul Deluxe Premium Plus Bass.

two TB Plus (Thunderbird-style) pickups. A 5-string version was introduced in 1993. The Les Paul Deluxe Plus Bass (LPB-2) added a carved maple top and was equipped with Bartolini pickups and active electronics. The Premium Plus version had a figured-maple top and was also available as a 5-string. Gibson discontinued both the LPB-1 and LPB-2 in 1998.

The top-of-the-line Les Paul Standard Bass (LPB-3), still in production in 2002, is a gussied-up version of the LPB-1, with a carved maple top and trapezoid fingerboard inlays. It can be upgraded to Premium Plus status with the addition of a figured-maple top and is available as a 5-string. In 1998 Gibson introduced the Les Paul SmartWood Bass; as the name implies, it's made with wood certified by the Rainforest Alliance as environmentally friendly. The semi-hollow mahogany body has a flat maple top, and the fingerboard is made of chechen. TB Plus pickups and Bartolini electronics complete the package.

Hollowbody basses made a brief return to the Gibson line in 1991, with the introduction of the single-cutaway EB-650 and EB-750. Both had laminated-maple archtop bodies, maple necks with ebony fingerboards, and 34" scale length. The EB-650 was equipped with TB Plus pickups and chrome hardware; the EB-750 had Bartolinis, active electronics, and gold hardware. They were handsome instruments, but their $2,000-plus list prices didn't attract many buyers, and they vanished in 1993.

By 2001 the Gibson bass line had been boiled down to the Les Paul Standard, the Thunderbird, and the SG-Z (which was dropped in 2002). The only other U.S.-made Gibson 4-string was the Blackbird, a Nikki Sixx signature model of the T-Bird. All are mid- to high-priced models. Gibson covers the lower price points with Epiphone basses made in Korea; several of these are "Authorized by Gibson USA" knockoffs of classic Gibson models, including the EB-0, EB-3, Thunderbird, Les Paul Special, Les Paul Standard, and Ripper.

SEE ALSO: EPIPHONE, STEINBERGER, TOBIAS

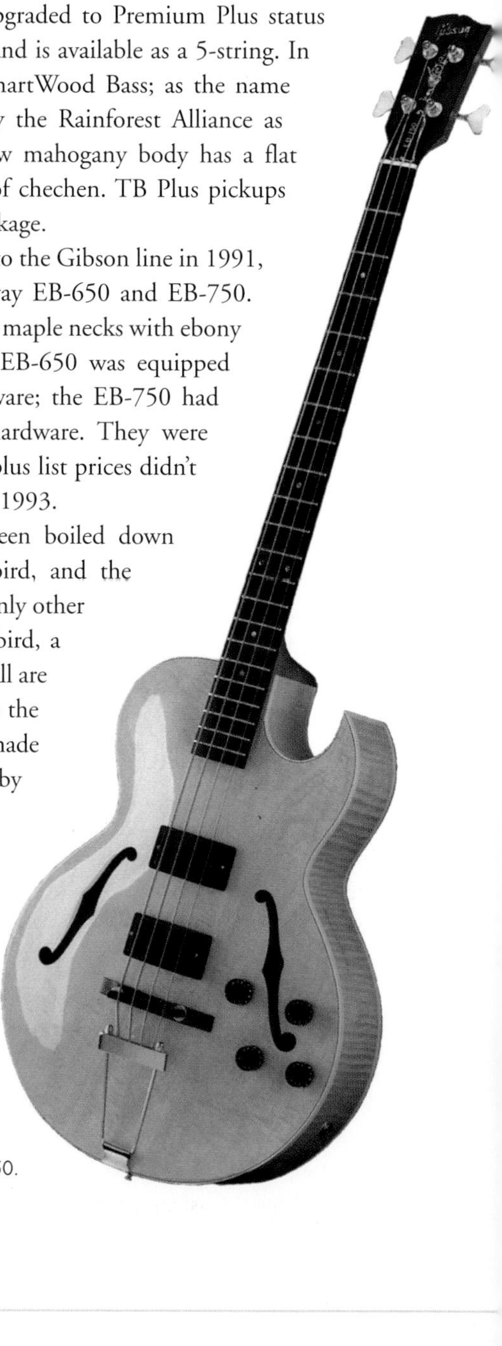

■ Gibson EB-750.

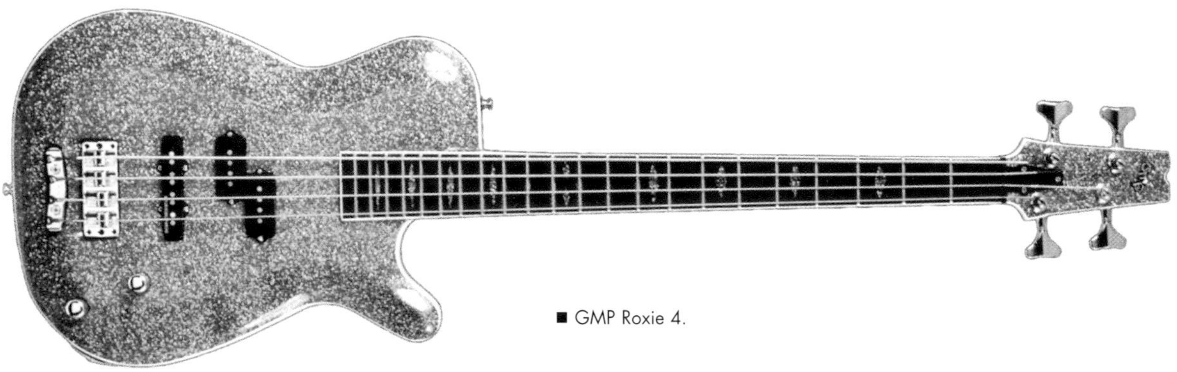

■ GMP Roxie 4.

GMP

GM Precision Products (GMP Guitars) of San Dimas, California, was founded by Gary Moline in 1989. Most of the builders he hired had learned their trade working at large musical-instrument companies such as Fender, Jackson, B.C. Rich, and G&L. Bass production has focused on neck-through-body instruments in three styles: Standard, Elite, and Roxie. All have 34" scale lengths. The Standard is a double-cutaway, dual-pickup bass with mahogany or alder body wings topped with quilted or flame maple; its maple neck has a 24-fret ebony fingerboard. The Elite is an upgraded version, with a carved top and multi-laminate neck. Both models are available as 4-, 5-, or 6-strings, fretted or fretless, in a wide variety of finishes including custom graphics. The Roxie is a retro-cool 4- or 5-string that screams "rock & roll!"—it's got a single-cutaway body shape, neck and body binding, and PJ pickups. An eye-catching metalflake finish is standard.

GODIN

Finding your niche can be the key to success in almost any endeavor, whether it's baking bread or building basses. For Godin, that niche has been defined by a unique acoustic/electric bass that falls right between conventional solidbody basses and acoustic bass guitars.

Godin is the brand name used for electric instruments made by LaSiDo. One of the world's largest manufacturers of acoustic guitars, LaSiDo operates three factories in Québec and one across the border in Berlin, New Hampshire. The company traces its origins back to a guitar-building shop operated by Norman Boucher in the tiny town of La Patrie, Québec, during the late 1960s. A chance meeting with Robert Godin of Montréal led to a partnership; when that fell apart, Godin took over the business, greatly expanding its production of both OEM components for other manufacturers and complete instruments. LaSiDo sells thousands of acoustics under the Seagull, Norman, LaPatrie, Simon & Patrick, and Art & Lutherie brand names, and also has an extensive line of Godin electrics.

The original Godin Acoustibass was conceived by pickup designer L.R. Baggs as a vehicle for his AB-4 piezo transducer and 3-band preamp with sliding controls. The preamp was mounted on the face of the instrument, with its metal top peeking out through a hole cut above the end of the neck. The double-cutaway hollow body was made of either limewood (for instruments with solid-color finishes) or mahogany (for those with natural or sunburst finishes). Alaskan spruce was used for the top, and an 8" thumb rest accommodated just about any plucking position.

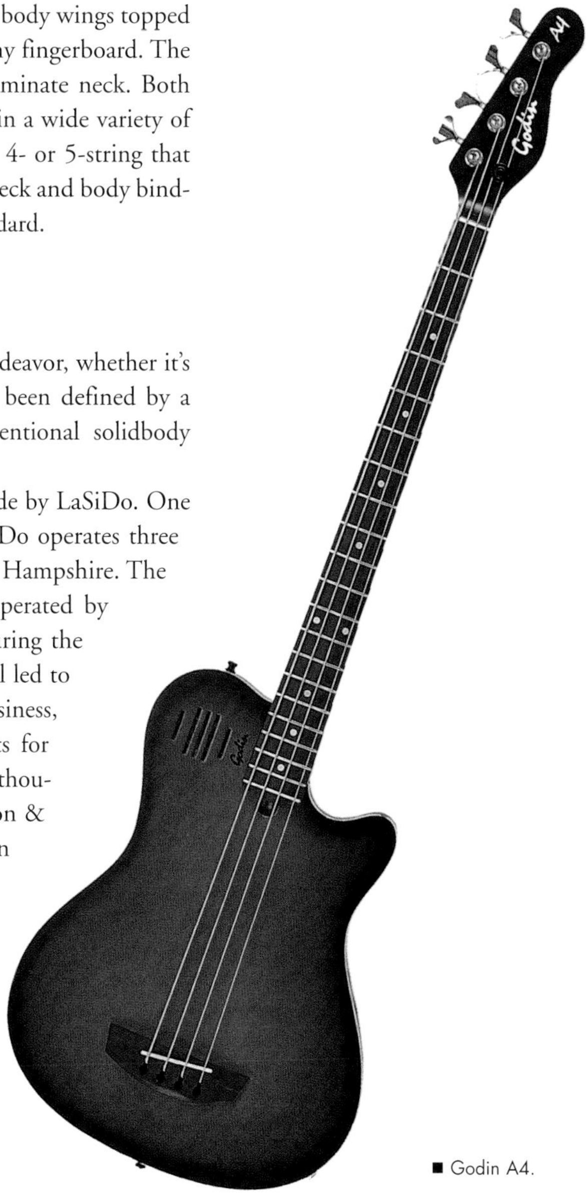

■ Godin A4.

■ Godin BG4 (left) and Freeway 4.

The bolt-on rock-maple neck was available in P and J shapes; fretted basses had rosewood fingerboards while fretlesses got ebony. Scale length was 34". One of the keys to the Acoustibass's unique tone was a patented "resonating harp" attached to the underside of the ebony bridge. This 12-tine harp enhanced the vibrations sensed by the bridge-mounted transducer, providing fatter, more upright-like tone than would be expected from an instrument only 1¾" deep.

In 1998 the Acoustibass was replaced by the single-cutaway A4, which has a deeper body (2⁹⁄₁₆") that's made of maple and completely hollow. Because of the increased body depth and the addition of "cello inspired" fan bracing, the resonating harp was eliminated. The L.R. Baggs electronics remain, but this time the slots for the preamp's sliders are cut right into the cedar top—a more elegant solution. The sound remains impressive; Gregory Isola, reviewing the A4 in *Bass Player*, raved about a "round, three-dimensional tone that outshines many of today's acoustic bass guitars." It's available fretted or fretless, 4-string or 5-string (A5).

Godin also builds solidbody basses. The BG4 and BG5 debuted in 1996; their double-cutaway bodies are made with a rock-maple center section and light-maple wings. There's more maple in the 22-fret bolt-on neck. Scale length is 34". The basses used EMG pickups at first; more recent models have a pair of Basslines soapbars. The Basslines active electronics include a "slap contour" circuit operated by the push/pull volume control. Figured-maple tops became standard in 2000. The SD4 and SD5 models, with their single-cutaway maple bodies, "duck head" pickguards, and PJ pickups offered a lower-cost alternative. They were replaced in 2002 by the Freeway basses, which feature more traditional styling. They're available as 4- and 5-strings, both with 34" scale length.

■ GR GRP 5-string.

GOULD

Despite some confusion on the subject, Mark Gould of Gould Guitars & Basses in Escondido, California, is not related to Geoff Gould, and there's no connection between his company and G. Gould of San Francisco. Mark founded his business in the late '90s and produces four or five "semi-headless" Rebel Basses a month. They're available in 4-, 5-, and 6-string models, fretted or fretless, all with a 34" scale length. Features include a contoured alder, ash, or lacewood body, a 24-fret laminated-maple neck, and Bartolini electronics.

■ Gould Rebel B440, fretted and fretless.

GR

Designed and built by Greg Rupp, GR basses appeared on the scene in 1998. The company is based in the San Diego area. Rupp says his goal is producing "high-end basses at reasonable prices," ones that fall between the mass-produced instruments from the big-name makers and the premium axes of the boutique builders. His flagship GRP bass has some familiar features—ash or alder body with large pickguard, bolt-on maple neck, early-'50s P-Bass body shape—but it's not just another vintage copy. The open headstock, "inspired by upright basses," is distinctive, as is the custom bridge with large-radius brass saddles. A single Basslines MM pickup is standard; two pickups and Basslines active electronics are optional. The GRP is available as a 4- or 5-string with 34" scale length. The other basses in GR's Classic Series are the GRT, with a Tele-like body, and the J-style GRJ. The lower-priced Road Series 4-string has a double-cutaway body with no pickguard, one MM-style pickup, and a less elaborate bridge. Scott Shiraki, reviewing it in *Bass Player*, pronounced it "a high-quality bass at a fair price," saying it was "a great alternative for Fender or Music Man players looking for a bass that will instantly appeal to their hands and ears while providing a tone somewhere in between."

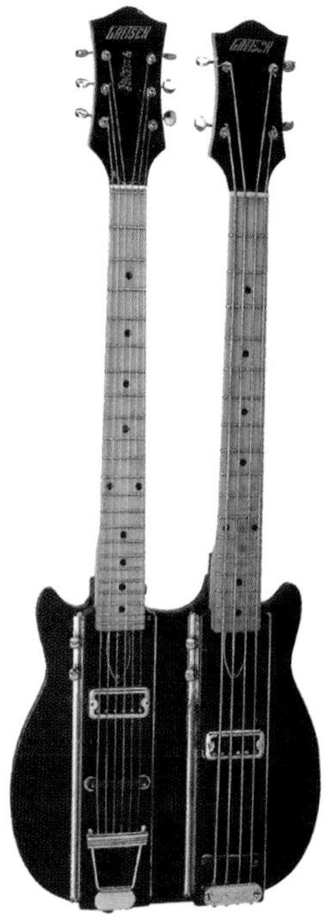

■ 1961 Gretsch Bikini.

GRETSCH

While much better known for its guitars (and drums), Gretsch is a venerable music-industry company that has produced some interesting basses over the years. The company got its start in a Brooklyn music shop opened by patriarch Friedrich Gretsch in 1883. Until late 2002, when it signed an agreement with Fender, the company had remained in family hands almost continually except for a period commencing in 1967, when it was owned by the Baldwin piano company. (Baldwin also marketed basses under its own name during this era; they were made by another acquisition, the Burns company of England.)

Manufacturing and sales were located in the ten-story Gretsch Building in Brooklyn for more than 50 years. Baldwin moved instrument production from Brooklyn to Arkansas in 1970, but quality (and sales) suffered. Manufacturing of Gretsch basses and guitars came to a halt in late 1980 or early 1981, although a few strays lingered on the price lists until 1983. Fred Gretsch, Friedrich's great-grandson, reasserted his family's ownership of the company two years later. Under his leadership, Gretsch began making instruments again in 1989, this time by offshore subcontractors using some U.S.-made components.

Like Gibson, Gretsch has created most of its electric basses by grafting a bass neck onto the body of a similar guitar model—although it started out with a considerably more radical concept in 1961. The Bikini, invented by Charles Savona, was a modular system consisting of guitar (Model 6023) and bass (Model 6024) "shafts"—each a maple neck bolted onto a rectangular slab with a bridge, tailpiece, and pickup. The necks could be interchanged in a hinged, folding body or mounted side-by-side in a double-slotted body, creating a doubleneck instrument. The Bikini bass had a 29½" scale length, 17 frets, and a single pickup. A little too weird even for the '60s, it quickly disappeared from the catalog.

Gretsch had more luck with its next bass offering, the Model 6070 double-cutaway hollowbody bass, which was used for a time by John Entwistle of the Who. The single-pickup 6070 had a 34" scale length and an extendable endpin that allowed an upright playing position (although it's doubtful anyone bothered to use it). A double-pickup version, the 6072, was also offered; a reissue of this model appeared in the late 1990s. The company offered a short-scale (29") hollowbody bass, with either one pickup (Model 6071) or two (Model 6073), from 1968 to 1972. All of these basses came with a round pad snapped to the back of the body, "to cushion pressure and eliminate fatigue."

In the 1970s Gretsch marketed a solidbody 4-string called the Broadkaster Bass.

■ 1963 Gretsch Model 6070.

■ Gretsch Broadkaster Bass. 1990s model.

■ Gretsch G6175 acoustic bass guitar.

The Broadkaster name has been associated with the company since the 1930s, when it first appeared on an acoustic guitar, and has been applied to a variety of instruments—including drums. (In 1950, when Leo Fender introduced a solidbody guitar called the Broadcaster, Gretsch objected; Leo obliged them by renaming his instrument the Telecaster.) Other Gretsch bass offerings from the '70s included the imaginatively named Solid Body Bass (Model 7615), the neck-through Committee Bass, and the bolt-on TK 300 Bass with its hockey-stick headstock.

In recent years, Gretsch has marketed Japanese- and Korean-made basses in both solidbody and hollowbody configurations, as well as an acoustic bass guitar with a triangular soundhole. The solidbody basses, such as the Jet and Junior Jet models, are inexpensive short-scale instruments with a vintage-like look that recalls the Gretsch Duo Jet guitar. The hollowbody model is called—here's that name again—the Broadkaster Bass; it's a partner to the Tennessee Rose guitar. It has two Bass Filter'Tron pickups and a 30¼" scale length, and it's available in a variety of finishes—including that famous Chet Atkins orange. In late 2001 the Spectra Sonic Bass debuted, alongside its Lead and C Melody guitar siblings. Designed by Tom Jones of TV Jones Guitars, this single-cutaway, black-and-white 4-string has a 33" scale length, two TV Jones alnico pickups, and a chambered alder body with a laminated-spruce top.

While they have not been especially influential or sought after by collectors, Gretsch basses are an interesting side-show attraction in the big bass circus, and the hollowbody models have some appeal for players looking for a thumpy, upright-like tone. As of January 1, 2003, Fender took over exclusive rights to develop, produce, market, and distribute Gretsch instruments worldwide. Fred Gretsch was to remain with the company in a consulting role.

GUILD

Guild started out as a small guitar-building shop in a New York City loft, grew rapidly, went through several relocations and ownership changes, and ended up—some 40-odd years later—as a division of Fender. Along the way, the company has produced a number of interesting and historically important bass guitars.

Guild was founded in 1952 by a guitarist named Alfred Dronge. Working with a five-man staff, he produced acoustic and electric archtop guitars that were readily accepted by the professional musicians working in the city's studios and nightclubs. By 1956 Guild had become successful enough to move to a larger facility across the river in Hoboken, New Jersey. (According to some accounts, this was also done to escape from union organizers in New York City.) Guild went public in 1960, issuing 325,000 shares of stock, and within a year had doubled the size of its factory. By then, the company was cranking out flat-top acoustic and solidbody electric guitars as well as archtops.

In 1966 Guild was acquired by Avnet Inc., a manufacturer of electronic components, and within a year production began to shift to a former furniture factory in Westerly, Rhode Island. By 1969 the transfer was complete, and the Hoboken factory was used only as a warehouse. Corporate headquarters remained in New Jersey, and Alfred Dronge commuted between his office and the Westerly factory by private plane.

Guild jumped into the electric bass market in 1964 with the short-scale (30½") Jet-Star Bass. Its mahogany body had the same strange shape as the Guild Thunderbird S-200 guitar, described by Tom Wheeler as being "somewhere between that of a Fender Jazzmaster and a Hershey bar left too long in the sun." Intended, no doubt, to compete with the Gibson EB-0, the Jet-Star Bass had a single pickup made by Hagstrom of Sweden. The original Jet-Star, made until 1966, had a 2+2 headstock; the revised version had a 4-in-line headstock and a different pickup, the small single-coil known to Guild aficionados as the "Mickey Mouse" pickup. It was replaced in 1970 by the JS Bass, which unabashedly copied the SG-style body of the Gibson EB-0 and EB-3. It came in one- and two-pickup models, the JS Bass I and JS Bass II (renamed the JS Bass 1 and JS Bass 2 in 1973). Guild introduced long-scale versions of the JS Basses in 1972, again following Gibson's lead, but had discontinued all the JS models by 1977.

■ Guild JS Bass 2 with carved top.

Swedish Fire

A more important Guild 4-string, the Starfire Bass, appeared in the 1965 catalog. It was the bass version of the Starfire IV guitar, introduced in 1963. The Starfire Bass was a double-cutaway, semi-hollow, short-scale (30½") bass much like the Gibson EB-2. The neck was mahogany, and the body was made of laminated maple or mahogany, depending on the finish. A single Hagstrom single-coil pickup, originally mounted near the bridge but later moved closer to the neck, contributed to its distinctive sound. A two-pickup version, the Starfire Bass II, was added in 1967. Many bassists, including the Jefferson Airplane's Jack Casady and the Grateful Dead's Phil Lesh, liked both the easy playability of the Starfire's neck and the sound of its Hagstrom pickups. In the late '60s, the Starfires of Casady and Lesh were used as platforms for Alembic's electronic experimentation, and their much-modified Guilds hold an important place in the history of the electric bass [see Alembic].

Guild stopped using the black-faced Hagstrom pickups in 1970, replacing them with chrome-covered humbuckers. The new pickups lacked the bite of the Hagstroms, and Starfires with these pickups are usually regarded as less desirable. Interest in the Starfire Bass, and short-scale basses in general, faded during the '70s; the single-pickup model was discontinued in 1975, and the Starfire II was dropped three years later. (The Starfire II was reintroduced in 1997, after Fender acquired Guild, but it had vanished from the Guild catalog by 2002.)

A second semi-hollow short-scale Guild bass, the M-85, debuted in 1967. Another partner instrument—it matched the BluesBird M-75 guitar—the M-85 had a 2¾"-deep single-cutaway body that resembled a Les Paul. Its arched top was made of laminated spruce or maple; the sides and back were laminated maple. The other components and specs matched those of the Starfire Bass, including the Hagstrom pickups—either one (M-85) or two (M-85 II). According to Mark Dronge, the son of Alfred Dronge, Guild made a custom M-85 for Phil Lesh in the late '60s; it had a hollow body and a three-piece neck that passed through the full length of the body cavity, making contact only under the tailpiece. The semi-hollow M-85 was dropped in favor of a solidbody version in 1972. Most of the

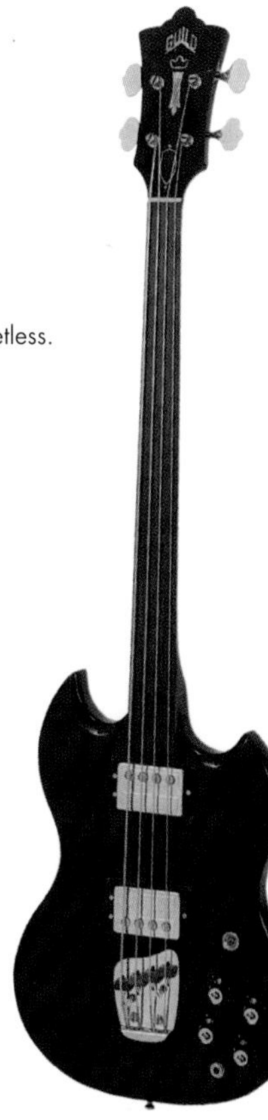

■ Guild JS Bass 2LB fretless.

solid M-85s made were two-pickup basses, with chrome-covered humbuckers, before the line was discontinued in 1976.

In 1972 Alfred Dronge was killed when his plane crashed near Westerly during a rainstorm. He was succeeded by Leon Tell, who had been a vice president since 1963. Guild continued on much as it had, until it was sold by Avnet in 1986 to an investment group headed by Jerre Haskew. Within two years, the company had declared bankruptcy and been sold to the Fass Corporation of Wisconsin (later known as U.S. Music), which made Randall amplifiers.

Into the Woods

Guild's bass line changed radically during the transition period of the late '70s and early '80s. The most significant introduction was the debut of the B-50 acoustic bass guitar in 1975. It was the first ABG offered by a major manufacturer—and one that was known for building good acoustic guitars—and it did much to establish the category. (The Ernie Ball Earthwood bass had preceded it by three years, but only a few were made and they were less appealing because of their size.) The B-50 was a musician-friendly instrument with a body large enough to produce a decent tone but small enough to be comfortable. And the scale length was an easy-to-play 30½"—although Guild historian Hans Moust says 30¾" and the catalog specified 31". It was short, however you measured it.

■ Guild Starfire Bass I (left), with original Hagstrom pickup, and Starfire Bass II, with later chrome-covered humbuckers.

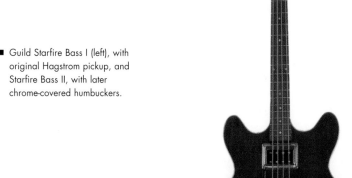

The B-50 was made from traditional materials, including a spruce top, solid-mahogany sides, and a laminated-mahogany back. The rosewood bridge had a split saddle, with the *E* and *A* strings set farther back for better intonation. Recognizing the need for more volume in many playing situations, Guild created the B-50E, with a bridge-mounted piezo pickup, in 1983. Both models remained in the line until 1987, when they were upgraded and renamed the B-30/B-30E. The changes included a slightly deeper body, for more volume. In 2002 they were still in production. (The B-30 was officially dropped in 1997, but the B-30E has a "no pickup" option.)

Guild's success with the B-50 led to additional ABGs, including the thinline FS-46CE Bass (or FB-46) of 1983, a partner to the FS-46CE guitar. More important is the B-4E, a single-cutaway short-scale bass with a shallow body (3" deep), oval soundhole, and bridge-mounted transducer. Introduced in 1993, it was still in production in 2002. A number of variations—including the "Crossroads" bass of 1993, with a magnetic pickup in addition to the bridge system—have been offered.

The solidbody B-Series basses of this era were less notable. Their double-cutaway "bell-bottom" body shape was original—no more Gibson copies—but it didn't quite work aesthetically. Mahogany was still used for bodies and necks; an ash body was optional (and indicated by an "A" at the end of the model designation). Scale length, in a nod to Fender's market dominance, was 34". The B-301 (one pickup) and B-302 (two pickups) were made from 1976 to 1981; the B-401 and B-402, with active electronics, were available from 1980 to 1982. Other here-today-and-gone-tomorrow Guild basses from the early '80s included the SB-201/202/203, the SB-502E, and the MB-801. The SB models were distinguished primarily by their array of knobs and switches, perhaps in an effort to emulate Alembic; the MB-801 took the high road with a carved maple top and ebony fingerboard.

■ Guild B-302A.

Take Me to Your Pilot

In 1983 Guild finally hit its stride again as a bassmaker, when the Pilot appeared. (The name was somewhat ironic, considering Alfred Dronge's unfortunate fate.) When introduced, these new 4-strings were known as the SB-600 Series, but the Pilot name was adopted in 1984 and has generally been applied to all Guild basses in this configuration. The Pilot looked something like a Fender Jazz Bass, although its body was more pinched in the waist and had longer horns. The body wood was poplar rather than alder, but scale length was 34" and the slim, bolt-on maple neck had a rosewood fingerboard.

One of the things that distinguished the Pilot—and made it very popular for a while—was the use of EMG active pickups. When introduced in 1983, the Pilot was available with either DiMarzio (SB-600) or EMG (SB-602) PJ pickups, but the EMG configuration was far more popular. At that time, EMGs were new on the market and bass players were captivated by their high-fidelity sound. Many were sold as replacement pickups for Fender basses. The Pilot was a reasonably priced, easy-to-play, lightweight bass that felt familiar to Fender players—and it came with EMGs already installed. It was a hit.

Guild produced more than 6,000 Pilot basses between 1983 and 1995, in a number of variations. According to accounts by factory workers, components were sometimes changed from day to day, so precise model descriptions are elusive. Adding to the confusion is the fact that Guild used at least five different headstock shapes on Pilots: the "foot," the "cakeknife," the Charvel-style "hockey stick" (two different versions), and the "Pro." The most common Pilots were the

■ Guild SB-602 Pilot.

■ Guild SB-605 Pilot.

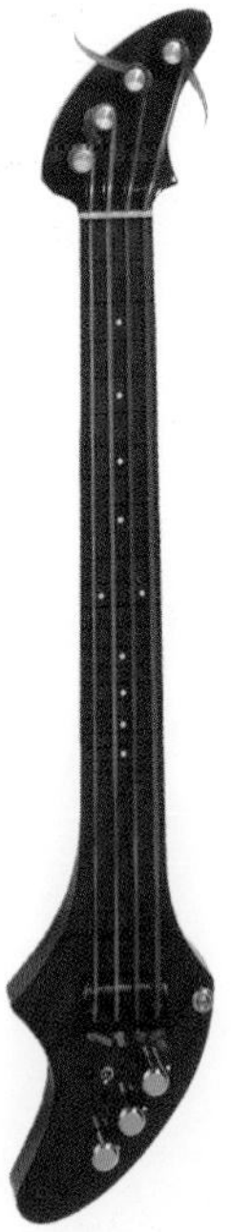

■ 1987 Guild Ashbory B-100.

SB-602 and SB-604, both with EMG-PJs; the SB-604 had a hockey-stick headstock but was otherwise the same as the SB-602. The SB-600 was the same bass with DiMarzio PJ pickups. A few Pilots were made with only one P-style pickup, either DiMarzio (SB-601) or EMG (SB-603).

Options included a solid-maple body, maple fingerboard, Kahler bass tremolo, and fretless. Sales of fretless Pilots jumped in 1985 when Jaco Pastorius signed on as an endorser and appeared in ads, although the image of Jaco with a Pilot in hand has not proved lasting. A 5-string Pilot, the SB-605, was introduced in 1986. It was one of the first inexpensive 5's on the market and helped to popularize the 5-string with club musicians. The SB-605 was usually set up in the standard *BEADG* tuning, but could be ordered in *EADGC* tuning with a Hipshot D-tuner on the *E*.

Guild tried to extend the Pilot's reach into the premium-bass market with the SB-902 Advanced Pilot, introduced in 1988. Features included a flame-maple body, ebony fingerboard, Bartolini PJ pickups, and slick finishes such as Amberburst and Transparent Charcoal. The SB-905 5-string also had Bartolinis, but in a JJ configuration (probably because there were no P-style 5-string pickups at that time). The Advanced Pilots were dropped after a year, but reappeared, with cosmetic changes, as the Pilot Pro4 and Pro5 of 1993 to 1995.

In the early '90s, the Pilot model numbers went through some mutations. The non-Pro version was called the Standard Pilot, available as the ST4 and ST5. By late 1992, those designations had changed to 402 and 405. Within a year they were gone, and only the Pros remained in the catalog. Production of all U.S.-made Pilot basses ended after Fender bought Guild in 1995; manufacturing was later moved to Korea, where the instruments are given the DeArmond brand name.

During the Pilot's heyday, Guild produced a few "radical" basses, apparently in an effort to appeal to heavy metal players who found the Pilot too staid. These included the X-701/702 (mutated B-Series; 1982–84), the SB-608 Flying Star (star-shaped body, EMG-PJ, optional Kahler vibrato; 1984–85), and the SB-666 Blade Runner (star-shaped body with cutouts, EMG-PJ; 1985–86). All of these were partners to similar X-Series guitars.

Last and perhaps least among the Guild basses of the '80s (in terms of size, anyway) was the Ashbory B-100. Designed in the U.K. by pickup maker Alun Jones of Ashworth Electronics and luthier Nigel Thornbory, this was a tiny, dogbone-shaped fretless with an 18" scale length, bridge-mounted piezo pickup, active electronics, and weird silicone-rubber strings. (Players were told to put talcum powder on the strings to make them feel less sticky.) Plugged in, it sounded surprisingly like an upright. Hard to tune, hard to finger, and hard to look at without snickering, the Ashbory was in the Guild line only from 1986 to 1988. It has lived on, though: a redesigned Ashbory Mk II model was introduced in the U.K. in 1990, and Fender has revived the original Guild version in a Korean-made knock-off, sold as the DeArmond Ashbory.

Soon after Fender acquired Guild from U.S. Music, several venerable models, including the Starfire Bass II, went back into production, and a Guild Custom Shop opened in Nashville. Hopes were high for a Guild renaissance, but they were dampened when the Westerly plant closed in August 2001. Fender transferred the manufacturing of some Guild models to its California factory, but as of late 2002, no Guild basses were being made in the U.S. A spokesman indicated the company was considering renewed production of some models, including the Starfire Bass II and M-85.

HAMER

When Cheap Trick's Tom Petersson asked him to build a 12-string bass in 1977, Hamer's Jol Dantzig didn't have to think for long. "My immediate response was, 'No way!'" recalls Dantzig. "I thought there would be too much tension on the neck." Petersson kept pushing, though, and Dantzig finally agreed to build a 10-string prototype. When that worked out, he moved on to a 12-string—which has since become Hamer's trademark bass.

Hamer was founded in 1975 by Dantzig and Paul Hamer, who played in a band together and later opened a guitar store in Palatine, Illinois. Their shop was a Gibson warranty-service center, so it was natural that their early designs showed a strong Gibson influence. Hamer's first production guitar, the Standard, had the zig-zag body shape of an Explorer; other Hamers resembled Les Pauls. But Hamer and Dantzig weren't just making copies: they used high-quality woods and premium parts, and their instruments quickly gained a reputation for excellent workmanship and good sound. They also found favor with players in search of unusual custom axes, like Petersson and his fellow Cheap Trickster, guitarist Rick Nielsen.

Hamer's earliest 4-strings were the Standard Bass (made from 1975 to 1984) and the bolt-on Blitz Bass (1982–90), both of which had Explorer-like bodies and were partners to similar guitars. The FBIV, with a reverse-Firebird shape and PJ pickups, was made from 1985 to 1987. But it was Petersson's 12-string that really turned heads. In addition to being an outrageous feat of lutherie, it had quadrophonic electronics, with an array of knobs and switches that made its double-cutaway body look like a mixing board.

Paul Hamer left his namesake company in 1987, and a year later it was acquired by the Kaman Corporation, makers of Ovation guitars. Hamer kept building 12-string (and 8-string) basses that had less elaborate electronics but incorporated a series of improvements in both hardware and construction. The scale length was 30½" because it was thought that a longer scale would put too much strain on the neck. Then, in 1991, Hamer began to offer a choice of either 30½" or 34". The long-scale model had the same body shape as Hamer's Chaparral Bass and was dubbed the Chaparral 12; its three-piece "stressed maple" neck had double trussrods. The short-scale 12 remained available, and another 12-string—a semi-acoustic, single-cutaway version with a figured-maple top—also joined the line.

The other notable Hamer basses of the '80s were the Chaparral Bass, the Impact Bass, and the CruiseBass. The Chaparral was the flagship model from 1987 to 1995; it was available as a 34"-scale 4-string, a slicked-up Max version (with figured-maple body and boomerang fingerboard inlays), and a 5-string. Later versions of the 5-string had a reverse 5-in-line peghead, to maximize the length of the *B* string "for a more defined piano-like tone." The Impact Bass had a compact mahogany body and unique 1+3 peghead. In its original incarnation, the CruiseBass was a set-neck double-cutaway 4- or 5-string with pointy horns and PJ pickups. It disappeared from the catalog in 1990 and returned five years later, with a more traditional body shape, two J-style pickups, and a bolt-on neck.

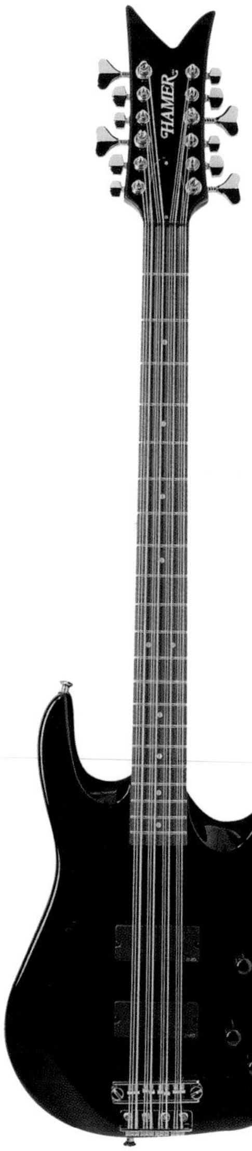

■ Hamer Chaparral 12.

■ Hamer CruiseBass with 2TEK bridge.

■ Hamer Acoustic 12.

While the CruiseBass 4-string of the mid '90s was more retro than the original version had been, it was offered with an optional 2TEK bridge. (The 2TEK was standard equipment on the 5-string.) This unusual piece of hardware had separate "tonal fingers" for each string that went through the body and attached to a rear-mounted resonator plate. Made of chrome-plated brass, it weighed more than a pound—but the payoff was outstanding clarity and sustain. The music industry never embraced it, though, and the Seattle-area company that produced it went out of business in the late '90s.

Bass production continued in Hamer's Arlington Heights, Illinois, plant until 1997, when it was shifted to the Ovation factory in Connecticut. As of 2002, co-founder Jol Dantzig was still keeping an eye on things—and the Chapparal 12-string bass was still in production, along with import versions of the CruiseBass and other models.

HARMONY

The Harmony Company of Chicago once billed itself as "The World's Largest Manufacturers of Stringed Musical Instruments," and much of its success in the early 20th century was based on 4-strings . . . but they were ukuleles. Purchased by Sears, Roebuck & Co. in 1916, Harmony manufactured many of the instruments sold in Sears stores under the Silvertone brand name, as well as dozens more "private labels" for other retailers.

By the 1960s guitars dominated Harmony's production, but very few of them were basses. The company waited until 1962 to offer an electric bass—is this thing just a fad?—and took the usual conservative approach, sticking a bass neck on a guitar body. Harmony's first electric bass was the H-22 "Hi-Value Bass," a single-cutaway, semi-hollow 4-string with a bolt-on neck and one pickup. The scale length was 30". Its most interesting feature was an oddly shaped "angelfish" pickguard. A double-cutaway version, the H-22/1, was added to the catalog in 1969. By 1972 the market preference for Fender-style basses led to the introduction of models like the H-426, a solid-body 4-string with a 4-in-line headstock.

As late as 1965, the Harmony factory was still cranking out a thousand guitars a day—but the handwriting was on the wall. Japanese imports had begun to pour into the country and take over the low end of the market. Too slow to adapt, Harmony went under in 1975. Since then, the brand name has been bought and sold several times by instrument importers.

■ 1963 Harmony H-22.

HERITAGE

SEE GIBSON

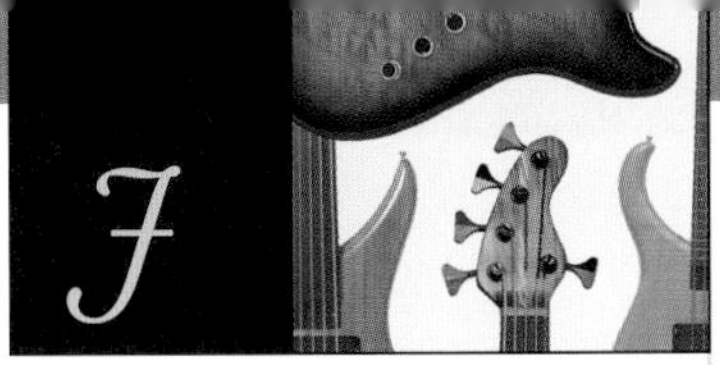

JACKSON/CHARVEL

The saga of the guitar company most folks simply call "Jackson," which sells instruments under the Jackson and Charvel brand names, is extraordinarily convoluted—even for the music industry. Consider this: The company got its start as the Charvel Repair Shop, which was operated by Wayne Charvel in Azusa, California, in the mid 1970s. Grover Jackson, a guitarist from Tennessee, became Charvel's partner in 1977. A year later, Jackson bought out Charvel and began to build his own guitars, which he introduced at the 1980 NAMM show. Made in San Dimas, California, they carried the Charvel name, even though Wayne Charvel was no longer associated with the business. Thanks to a kid from Pasadena named Eddie Van Halen, they became very popular. Then, late in 1980, another hot young guitarist, Randy Rhoads, came to Grover Jackson and asked him to build a special guitar. Jackson cooked up a flying-V neck-through design—but because Charvels were bolt-ons, he decided to put the Jackson name on his neck-through creations.

In 1985 the International Music Corporation (IMC) of Fort Worth, Texas, signed a manufacturing and distribution deal with Grover Jackson. After that, the Charvel name was used on guitars made in Japan and the Jackson name appeared on guitars made in the U.S., regardless of neck style. (Korean-made instruments carried the Charvette label.) That same year, Wayne Charvel signed a deal with Gibson to design instruments; no problem there, but when Gibson tried to use Charvel's name, Jackson sued. And won—so Charvel's Gibson designs, which vanished almost as soon as they'd been announced, carried the mysterious WRC designation. All of this corporate maneuvering must have been too much for Grover Jackson, because by 1990 he'd turned over management of Jackson/Charvel to IMC. Shortly after his departure, the factory was moved from San Dimas to Ontario, California. IMC continued to market instruments under the Charvel and Jackson names, but post-Grover Jacksons were made in both the U.S. and Japan. In 1997, the Japanese company Akai acquired Jackson/Charvel—and then in 2002 Fender acquired it from Akai. Since leaving his namesake company, Grover Jackson has designed instruments for other companies, including Washburn.

So there are American-made and Japanese-made Charvel guitars, none of which actually have anything to do with Wayne Charvel. And there are pre-IMC, IMC, and post-IMC Jackson guitars, some (but not all) of which were designed by Grover Jackson and/or were made in the U.S. And there are also Charvel-designed Gibsons and Jackson-designed Washburns. And some other Charvel-designed instruments, none of which carry the Charvel name, because that belongs to Jackson, which used to belong to IMC, which used to belong to Akai, but as of October 2002 belongs to Fender. Got it?

It's perhaps fortunate that basses have never been a big part of Jackson's business, simply because we might never have been able to figure out which ones came from where and were made by whom. Many Jackson and

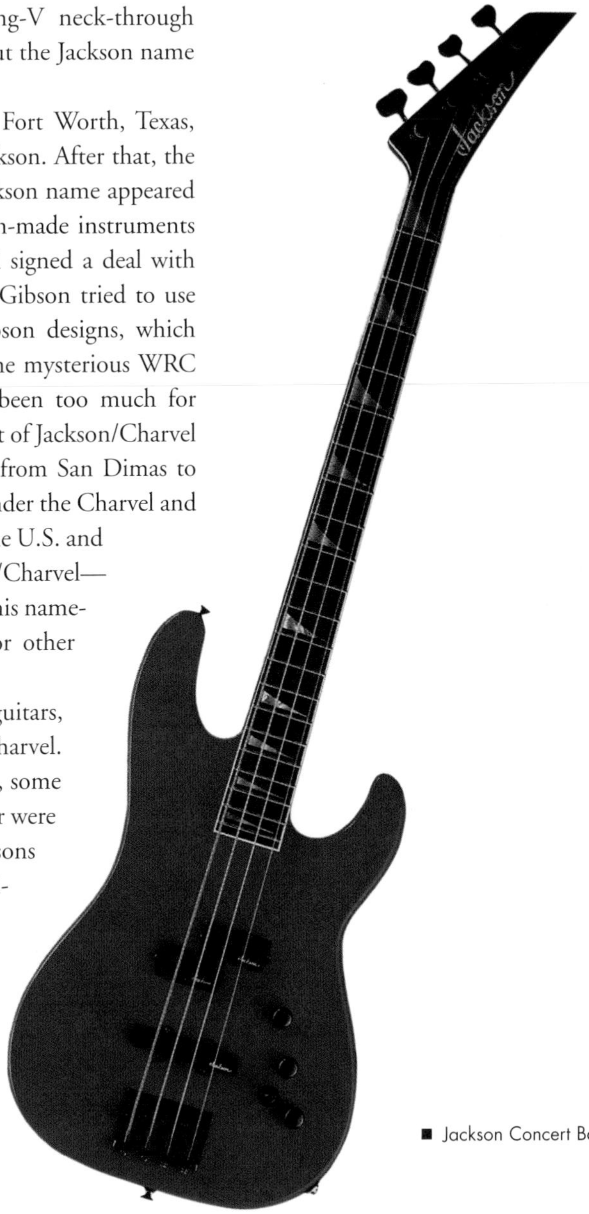

■ Jackson Concert Bass.

Charvel basses have been partner instruments that shared the body shapes (and pointy headstocks) of the company's guitars. The most notable models are the Jackson Concert Series basses, which date back to a 1980 Grover Jackson design and were still in production more than 20 years later. These are neck-through-body instruments with P-style bodies, PJ pickups, active electronics, and fast rock & roll necks, often with binding and sharktooth inlays. In the mid '80s Jackson built a few Concert-style fretless basses equipped with piezo bridges and no magnetic pickups—an idea that was well ahead of its time. Even after most bass production was moved to Japan (and, later, India), Jackson continued to build the Concert Bass Custom, with EMG pickups, in the States. Jackson also has a U.S. custom shop that creates unique basses (often with wild paint jobs) for endorsers and paying customers. Charvel basses disappeared in the mid '90s, after the Akai acquisition.

Somewhat surprisingly, given the company's metal-head image, Jackson began to offer the Harry Fleishman-designed Anti-Gravity Basses in 2002 [see Fleishman]. These expensive, high-tech instruments have lightweight, ergonomic bodies and are equipped with either Basslines pickups or the LightWave optical-pickup system. Initial production was in Ontario, California, although Fleishman has indicated that it might be moved to Japan.

■ James Trussart Steelcaster Bass.

JAMES TRUSSART

Wielding an oxyacetylene torch instead of a bandsaw, James Trussart fabricates metal bodies for his instruments. He began to build his industrial-strength basses and guitars in France during the 1980s and relocated to Los Angeles in 2001. "I have the most beautiful workshop a luthier could dream of," he says, "kind of an old log cabin with great light and trees and a view of the Hollywood sign." Trussart's Steelcaster Bass has a hollow body made of contoured steel plates. Its one-piece P- or J-style neck is maple, stained deep red and topped with a rosewood fingerboard. A variety of Seymour Duncan pickups is available, including P, JJ, PJ, MM, and MM+J configurations. The bass can be ordered with passive or active (2-band or 3-band) circuitry. When plated with satin-brushed nickel, its body gleams softly; allowed to oxidize, it has a left-out-in-the-rain look that ZZ Top's Billy Gibbons has dubbed "rust-o-matic."

JERRY JONES

"One day a customer brought an old single-cutaway, one-pickup Silvertone guitar into my shop," says Nashville's Jerry Jones. "Right away, I admired its simplicity—and the tone was incredible. It was the kind of instrument that fit me personally, so I built myself a copy." Before long, Jones was making more reproductions of the classic Danelectro instruments of the 1950s (which were sold under the Silvertone name at Sears). He launched the Jerry Jones line in 1988, offering lovingly updated versions of Dano's Masonite basses and guitars. His Longhorn Bass6 was an immediate hit with Music City's studio players, many of whom were looking for a modern instrument that could produce the great sound of the classic Danelectro 6-string basses.

■ Jerry Jones Longhorn Bass4 (left) and Longhorn Bass6 (below).

Jones worked as a repairman at the Old Time Pickin' Parlor in Nashville before opening his own business in 1981. Along with repairs and modifications, he built a few custom instruments—but after seeing that Silvertone, he decided it was time to focus on building. Jerry's first 24 instruments carried the Silver Jones label, before he decided that was a little goofy and switched to Jerry Jones Guitars. In 1993, he created a second line called Neptune (named after the New Jersey hometown of Danelectro); these instruments had adjustable trussrods and could be ordered with intonation-adjustable bridges, making them more useful to working musicians.

By 1990 Jones was producing a full line of Danelectro-style basses, including the Longhorn Bass4 and Bass6, the Shorthorn Bass4 and Bass6, and the Single-cutaway Bass4 and Bass6, all with 30" scale length and lipstick-tube pickups. They came in more than a dozen colors, including such classics as Copperburst and Turquoise. In 2001, because of increased demand for his electric sitars, Jones cut back bass production to just the Longhorn Bass4. A year later, he decided to focus on the Neptune brand, making some modifications to the bass that included a reshaped neck, revamped controls, and a Gotoh bridge. "By the end of 2001, demand started to creep back up on the basses," says Jerry, "so I added the Longhorn Bass6, the Shorthorn Bass4, and the new Single-cutaway Bass4 L/S—with a 34" scale—to the catalog. All of these instruments have Neptune features."

SEE ALSO: DANELECTRO

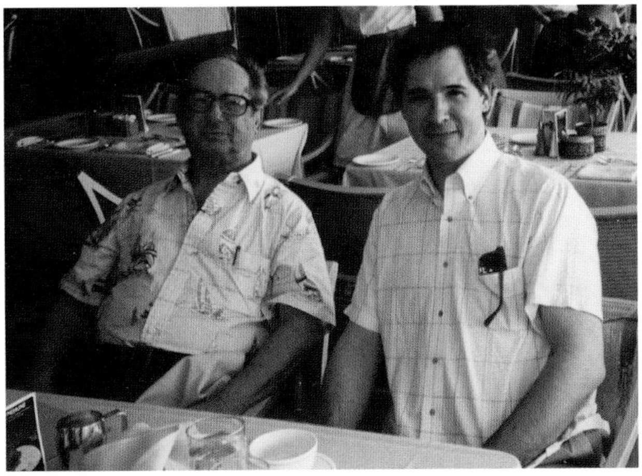

■ Jerry Jones (right) with Nathan Daniel in 1991. Daniel created the original Danelectro instruments that inspired the Jerry Jones line.

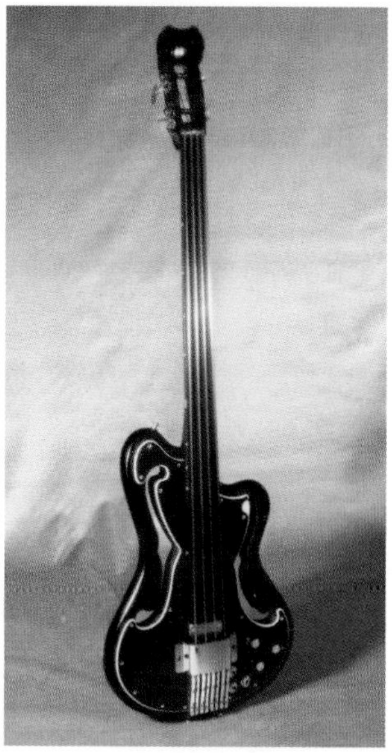

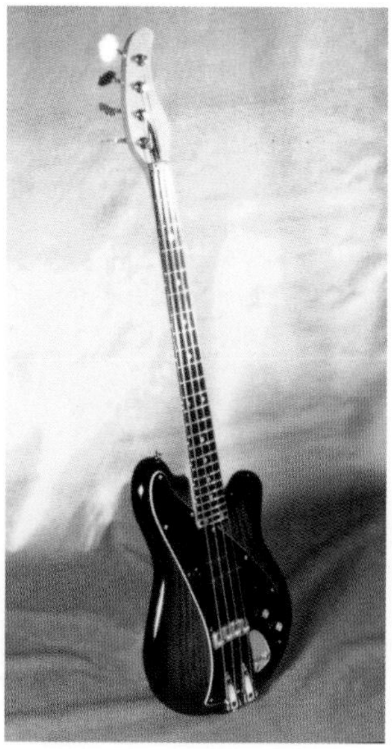

JOHNSON'S EXTREMELY STRANGE MUSICAL INSTRUMENT COMPANY

Bruce Johnson is a mechanical engineer by trade and a bass nut by preference. He collects Ampeg "scroll basses" and is probably the world's leading authority on these instruments. So it wasn't surprising when Ampeg hired him, in 1996, to create updated versions of these unusual 4-strings, which parent company St. Louis Music (SLM) would distribute. Johnson retained the look of the original AEB-1 (fretted) and AUB-1 (fretless) but made a number of improvements, including a 35" scale length, a headstock carved completely from maple (the originals had plastic parts), a stronger and more comfortable neck, and modern electronics. He also employed an Alembic-like brass block in the body, under the bridge, for better clarity and sustain. Prototypes of these basses—tagged AEB-2/AUB-2— were shown at the Ampeg booth at the 1997 NAMM show, and dealer orders were booked. Production proved to be difficult, however, and Johnson ran into some real problems with painting. He was able to build only a handful of basses in 1997, so he ended his distribution agreement with SLM.

Johnson continued to work on these instruments, eventually solving the production problems and adding further refinements. These include a chambered body, for more warmth and sustain, and better pickups and electronics. He builds the AEB-2/AUB-2 on a limited basis, producing 10 to 15 per year at his Burbank, California, shop, most of which he sells direct. He also does restoration and repair work on the original Ampeg basses.

As striking as these instruments are, Bruce is quick to point out that the aesthetics are only part of the story. "The cool headstock and the strange-looking body aren't the important features," he says. "It's the unusual relationship between the strings and the structure that makes it different from other basses. The AEB-2, like the original AEB-1, uses strings that are about 4" longer than normal, because the tailpiece is separate from the bridge and mounted at the very back edge of the body. This allows the strings to be plucked more aggressively. Because there's more length of string to be stretched, it can be pulled farther to the side with the same amount of force, while keeping the string's overall tension high to get the best tone."

Johnson has also created a modern update of the Ampeg SSB short-scale (30½") bass. Available fretted or fretless, it's larger than the original and has a chambered ash body. As with his AEB-2/AUB-2 models, Bruce has created new electronics that offer a much wider range of tones than the original. He also intends to build new versions of the Ampeg ASB-1/AUSB-1 "Devil Basses"—these are "not for the squeamish," he says.

While the reinvented Ampegs have been the main thrust of Johnson's building, he has also worked on several other bass projects. One was a prototype of a new bass guitar, dubbed the Workingman's Bass, that he built for the SWR amp company in 1995. It was never put into production. Even more unusual was "Banjozilla," the huge upright bass banjo he created in 1991–92. A fretted 6-string

■ Johnson's AEB-2 Scroll Bass (top) in red/black sunburst, AUB-2 Scroll Bass (middle) in satin black, and SSB (bottom) in red/black sunburst.

tuned *BEADGC*, it has a 34" scale length, roundwound strings, and a pair of bridge-mounted Fishman pickups. "I've had a lot of fun terrorizing bluegrass festivals with it," Bruce says. Although the instrument was not as loud as Johnson had hoped it would be, he feels he can improve the design by extending the scale length and making other changes. "Over the years I've refined the design in my head," he says, "and I plan to develop it into a production instrument." Now that's a scary thought.

SEE ALSO: AMPEG

J.T. HARGREAVES

"I started out as a player," says Jay Hargreaves, "first on cello and then upright bass in the high school orchestra, before I got my first electric bass, a Univox with a semi-hollow body like a Gibson ES-335. This gave me years of experience hearing rich bass sounds in ensembles, and when I started building bass guitars those sounds were always in my head."

Hargreaves, a native of the Seattle area, made his first bass guitar, a solidbody 4-string, in 1974. He plunged deeper into lutherie with studies at the Northwest School of Instrument Design and a job at Boogie Body Guitars in Puyallup, Washington. Exposure to the revolutionary guitar-design concepts of Dr. Michael Kasha and Richard Schneider piqued Jay's interest in building an acoustic bass guitar, and he spent several years formulating the ideas that would be expressed in his Bluejay bass. He completed the first one in 1995.

The Bluejay is a single-cutaway ABG with an off-center soundhole. Both the top and back are made of Sitka spruce with bracing that follows the precepts of the Kasha/Schneider system, which has long bars on the bass side and short bars on the treble side. "Using tonewood for the back and bracing it similar to the top gives my bass a back that moves with the top, without impeding the top's motion," explains Hargreaves. "That gives it longer sustain, warmer sound, and more volume." The Bluejay's body measures 24" x 18" x 5" deep—large, but not unmanageable. The sides are made of flame maple finished in "Oriental blue" (thus the name), and the maple neck is topped with an ebony fingerboard, fretted or fretless. The bridge is a unique "fish skeleton" design that further enhances tone. Scale length can be either 30½" or 34". The Jayhawk, a double-cutaway bass with body depth of 3½", is also available. "These are not easy instruments to build," says Hargreaves, "but the results speak for themselves. And I'll continue to experiment with the design, always looking for improvements in sound and playability."

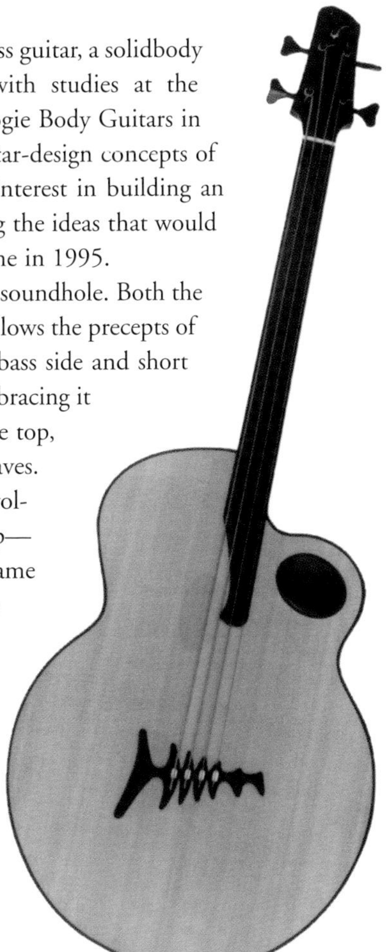

■ J.T. Hargreaves Bluejay acoustic bass guitar.

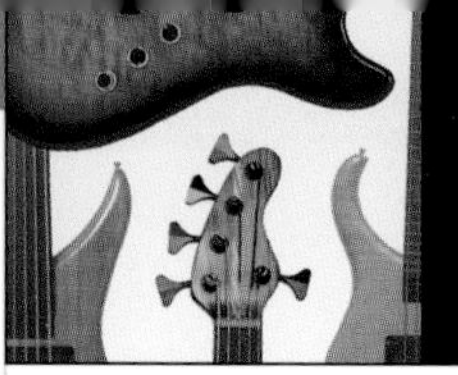

KAY

■ 1953 ad for "the new Kay electronic bass."

With a little luck—and maybe a better sense of where music was heading in the 1950s—the Kay Musical Instrument Company could have been a major player in the story of the electric bass. As it turned out, though, it's little more than a footnote.

In 1951, when Leo Fender introduced his Precision Bass, Kay was one of the largest musical-instrument manufacturers in the world. Not only did the Kay factory in Chicago churn out as many as 300 guitars a *day,* it was the leading U.S. builder of laminated string basses (many of which became vintage collectibles). Given this expertise in both guitar and bass building, and the marketing muscle of a major company, Kay was perfectly positioned to jump into the electric bass market. Which it did—although less than enthusiastically.

Within a year of the P-Bass's debut, Kay had rolled out its K-162 "Electronic Bass." It was a reworked version of the company's popular single-cutaway archtop guitars, with a short-scale neck and a single pickup. Priced at $150, it undercut the Fender bass by almost $50. The idea had actually been "prototyped" ten years earlier, when James Thompson (the father of Carl Thompson) created a crude electric bass by attaching a homemade neck and crude pickup to a Kay guitar body. Thompson used this instrument on his home recordings, but there's no evidence that the folks at Kay ever heard about it [see Carl Thompson]. Too bad for them.

The advertising campaign for the K-162 featured Chubby Jackson, a well-known jazz bassist whose signature-model 5-string upright (tuned *EADGC*) was one of Kay's featured bass products. You have to wonder what might have happened if Kay had decided to apply the 5-string concept to the electric bass at that time. And the speculation gets even more interesting when you consider the K-160 electric bass, which came along a few years later. It had a curious "baritone" tuning of *DGBE*, an octave below the top four strings of a guitar—and not that far from *DGCF*, the top four strings of a 6-string bass. Someone at Kay clearly was thinking about different ways of building and tuning a bass.

Be that as it may, Kay soon fell into the ranks of purveyors of cheap, unimaginative 4-strings, and they never challenged Fender for market leadership. The company prospered during the Beatles-driven guitar boom of the '60s and was acquired by jukebox manufacturer Seeburg in 1965. Another sale, to Valco, took place in 1967, but Kay was already on a fatal downward spiral. The factory closed in 1969. The brand name itself lived on (as so often happens in the music industry), and Korean-made Kay electric basses were available long after the original company had ceased to exist.

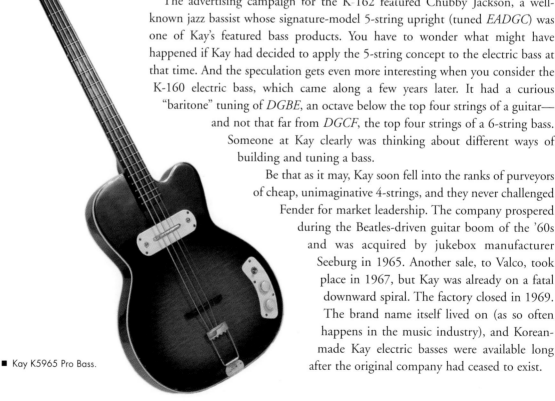

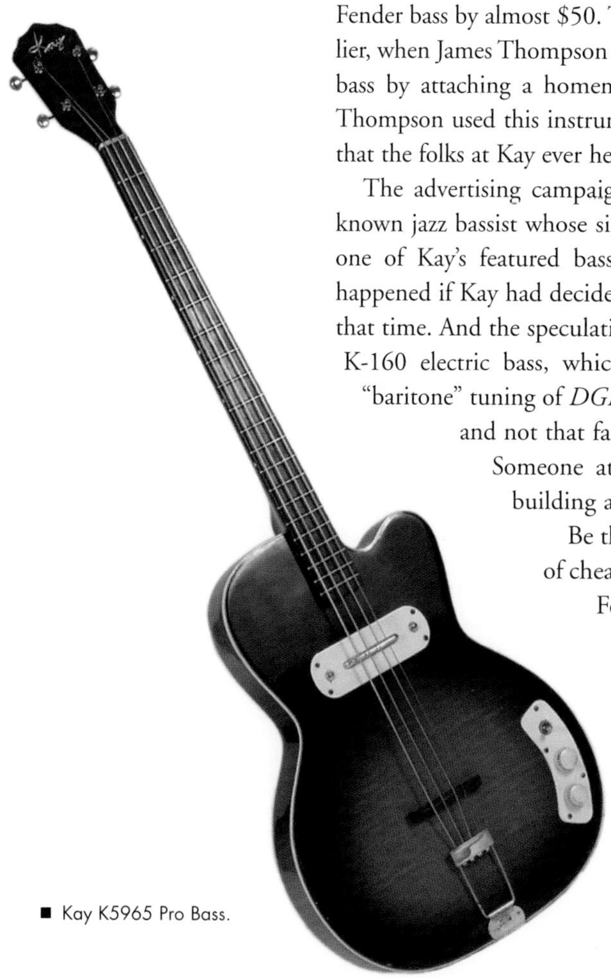

■ Kay K5965 Pro Bass.

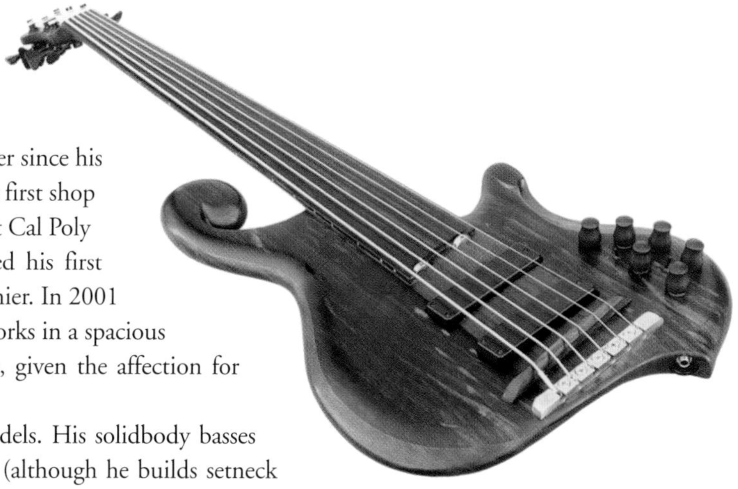

KEN BEBENSEE

Aside from a two-year tour of duty as an army cook, Ken Bebensee has been building instruments ever since his high school days in Redding, California. He set up his first shop in 1989 in San Luis Obispo, while attending college at Cal Poly State. Within a couple of years, Bebensee had issued his first catalog and embarked on a career as a professional luthier. In 2001 he relocated to rural Northern California, where he works in a spacious shop surrounded by trees—which seems appropriate, given the affection for wood displayed in his handcrafted basses.

Bebensee builds to order and has no standard models. His solidbody basses usually have graphite-reinforced through-body necks (although he builds setneck and bolt-on instruments, too) and "ergonomically designed" bodies with beautiful tops made of burl wood, purpleheart, koa, and other exotics. He also makes hollow and semi-hollow fretless basses with carved tops and piezo bridges. His Sereph II bass (every Bebensee instrument has a name) is a single-cutaway 6-string with a 36" scale length and an adjustable "picking board" mounted between the wood-covered pickups. Many of Ken's instruments feature intricate carving and inlay work. He will build a bass with any number of strings from four to ten, and it can be electric, acoustic/electric, or acoustic (including archtop). Many different pickups and onboard circuits are available, including the LightWave optical-pickup system and the RMC MIDI system. In short: if you want it, Ken can make it.

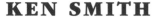

■ Ken Bebensee fretless 6-string.

KEN SMITH

Ken Smith says if you really want to understand what sets him apart as a builder, you have to go back to when he was an eight-year-old fishing off the South Beach pier in Miami Beach. "The old-timers there taught me how to tell the difference in the nibble between a snapper and a mackerel. You learn how to feel the tug. It's the same when you're playing bass—different gauges of strings, different woods. You just feel it."

Trained on upright bass from age 13, Smith had a successful career as a New York studio musician before he started to make instruments. He joined the AFM in 1968 and played both acoustic and electric bass for jingle sessions, Broadway shows, pop concerts, and jazz gigs. He also did most of the maintenance and repair work on his instruments. "In the eighth grade I was taught that you care for the bass like it's your child," he says. "In New York I would see people banging instruments around, and I would almost have a heart attack. I had learned that if you cleaned the instrument and set it up again, it sounds better. I would do anything I could to improve my instruments."

■ Ken Smith BT Custom VI.

■ Ken Smith BMT Elite G.

■ Ken Smith CR Custom Six G.

Ken emphasizes that his interest in bass building was motivated by his practical playing experience. He was always asking, "What can I do to make things better? I might make a recording with my Fender Jazz Bass and get a nice ring and growl on the *E* string, but then I'd play in a club with an amplifier and it wouldn't sound like that. I'd wonder: how can I get that sound out of an amp?"

In the early 1970s Smith shared a practice studio in a building on Seventh Avenue in Manhattan. The instrument maker Carl Thompson had a studio one floor above him, and the two eventually got together [see Carl Thompson]. Thompson built his first basses using Smith's Jazz Bass as a reference. Smith bought Carl's third instrument. "That was my bass for a while," Ken recalls. "I remember playing Broadway shows with that bass."

For Smith, the next step was creating his own design. He started—literally—with a clean sheet of paper. "I took out graph paper and drew something that looked right. A friend of mine had a cabinet shop, and we made a prototype out of pine, just to get a dummy shape. It was two pieces, with a glued-in neck. And then we made it in Carl's shop. Carl did the glue-up, he gave me the blank, and I took it home and carved it. The body was bird's-eye maple, and the neck was made from a hard-maple block I got from the widow of a former student of mine. It was sliced down the center and routed for the trussrod, and then we put in a rosewood strip and glued it together. The fingerboard was rosewood."

For electronics Ken turned to a local repairman. "There was a Japanese guy named Ichi who worked at Alex Music. He was an electronics whiz, and he made a circuit for me. For the pickups, we used a Schaller humbucker—whatever they were making back in '76—in the neck position, and two Jazz Bass pickups wired together in the bridge position. We just cut off the tabs, put the two pickups together, and wired them in parallel. The bridge was a Badass II. We put on Schaller tuners, and then I took some StrapLoks, ground them down, and inlaid them in the body. That was the first bass I know of with inlaid StrapLoks, which was one of the proprietary designs."

The instrument sounded great, says Smith, so he began to gear up to build more basses. In 1979 Ken struck a deal with Stuart Spector, who was making instruments in Brooklyn [see Spector]. At the time, Vinnie Fodera was one of Spector's employees. Fodera did the woodwork on the early Ken Smith basses, turning them over to Ken to install hardware and electronics and do the final setup. In 1980 Smith opened his own shop, which Vinnie ran. Fodera bought the shop three years later, but he continued to do the woodwork for Ken Smith basses [see Fodera].

In 1985 Smith shifted his woodworking operation to a subcontractor in Pennsylvania, and soon he was shuttling back and forth regularly from New York. He eventually bought out his subcontractor, and then in 1995 moved to Perkasie, Pennsylvania, where he personally oversees all aspects of production—"right down to going out and picking the trees." In 2002, his shop was producing 30 to 40 instruments a month as well as doing repair and restoration work for Ken Smith owners.

The mainstay of the Ken Smith line is the neck-through BT model, which has been offered since 1981. (The name was derived from the original Smith preamp, which provided bass and treble boost.) Smith's experience as a player is evident in such BT design features as the heel-less cutaway, which is not only elegant but makes upper-register playing far easier. Smith later expanded his line with the BMT and BSR neck-through basses, as well as the bolt-on CR series, inspired by Chuck Rainey.

Over the years, the Smith catalog has listed a bewildering array of models, but Ken's approach is easiest to understand by viewing it as an "à la carte" system: he offers a wide range of options on a few basic configurations. The top-of-the-line BSR and BT Elite G models have five-piece through-body necks reinforced with graphite bars, Macassar ebony fingerboards, gold hardware, the Smith BMT 3-band EQ system, and Smith custom pickups—but the real key to their flexible sound is the wide range of woods available (see chart, page 98). These basses are offered in 4-, 5-, and 6-string models, as well as a Melvin Davis signature 7-string. Lower-priced neck-through models, such as the BSRMS, have a three-piece neck, a morado (pau ferro) fingerboard, and fewer wood options. The bolt-on instruments are available in BSR and CR shapes; all have three-piece necks and, once again, many possible wood combinations. The Jazz Bass craze of the 1990s inspired the BSRJ model, which has Smith stacked-coil J-style pickups and a center block that gives this bolt-on instrument a neck-through look. While the majority of Ken Smith basses have been made entirely in his shop, whether in New York or Pennsylvania, he has offered some lower-priced models—originally known as the Burner Series and later designated BSRB—with components manufactured offshore and final assembly done in the U.S.

In addition to being one of the first bass builders to offer high-end "connoisseur" instruments, Ken Smith played an important role in the development of the modern 6-string bass. Anthony Jackson conceived of this extended-range instrument in the 1970s, inspired by organ-pedal notes that went below the range of his Fender bass. Jackson believed the proper configuration of what he called a "contrabass guitar" would be an instrument with six strings, adding a *B* string below and a *C* string above the *EADG* of a 4-string electric bass. Carl Thompson built an instrument like this for Jackson in 1975, but Anthony was not entirely happy with the way it played or sounded [see Carl Thompson]. He then turned to Ken Smith, who made him two 6-strings. The first was delivered in 1981 and the second in 1984. The second instrument was ridiculed for its wide neck, but it offered the Fender-like string spacing that Jackson wanted—and his masterful use of this bass encouraged other players to take the plunge. One was John Patitucci, who ordered a Smith/Jackson 6-string in 1985; he played this BT Custom-style bass on three albums with Chick Corea's Elektric Band and on his first two solo albums, *John Patitucci* and *On the Corner*.

Ken Smith remains committed to innovation, and his product line offers new models and wood selections almost every year. "Every single day, some little thing might change," he says. "We'll get an idea and try it out. Anything we can do to improve the instrument, we'll do it."

■ Ken Smith BSR5J.

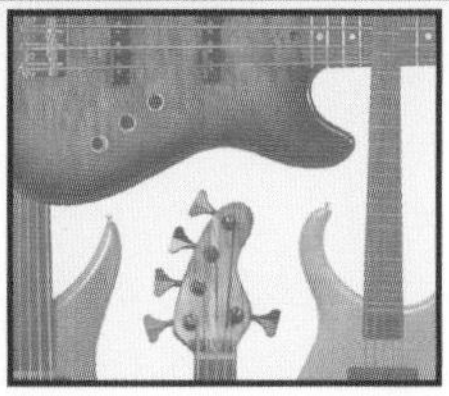

THE WOODS OF KEN SMITH BASSES

Ken Smith has one of the largest and most varied inventories of wood of any bass-maker. By carefully selecting and combining different types, he can offer "tone recipes" that meet the requirements of a wide range of players, whether the desired instrument is a 4-string with the thump of a vintage P-Bass or a high-fidelity 6-string with exceptional clarity and brilliance. To assist his customers, Smith offers a guide to wood species at his website (www.kensmithbasses.com); this chart was adapted from that guide—which also has photographs of Ken Smith basses made from the different woods and information about their current availability.

■ Ken Smith, 2003

All average weights are per board-foot at 6–8 percent moisture

ASH
Other common names: swamp ash, light ash, southern ash, southern white ash, lightweight ash, guitar ash, soft ash
Note: Northern white ash (hard ash) is too heavy and dense to produce guitar-grade tone wood.
Origin: Southeast US
Average weight: 3 pounds
Weight classification: light
Where used on Smith basses: solid body wings (BSR only)
Tone produced on Smith basses: bright, punchy

AVODIRÉ
Other common names: African white mahogany, blond mahogany (US), apaya (Nigeria), esu (Congo), lusamba (Zaire)
Note: For many exotic woods the common name (or trade name) varies from country to country.
Origin: tropical West Africa
Average weight: 3 pounds
Weight classification: light
Where used on Smith basses: solid or laminated body wings and heel blocks
Tone produced on Smith basses: smooth and bright

BUBINGA
Other common names: African rosewood, kevazingo, essingang
Note: Bubinga ranges in color from light pinkish/reddish brown to deep vivid reddish brown. Bubinga is occasionally figured.
Origin: equatorial West Africa
Average weight: 4.8 pounds
Weight classification: heavy
Where used on Smith basses: tops and backs, features, and fingerboards
Tone produced on Smith basses: deep pronounced lows, articulate high mids

CHERRY
Other common names: black cherry, American cherry
Note: Smith uses cherry as a mahogany core substitute.
Origin: mainly Pennsylvania and New York state
Average weight: 3.1 pounds
Weight classification: medium light
Where used on Smith basses: cores and veneers for five-piece body wings
Tone produced on Smith basses: sounds like a mix of maple and mahogany

COCOBOLO
Other common names: granadillo (Mexico)
Note: This dense rosewood is heavier than ebony. Colors range from yellow brown to orange brown to reddish brown with colored streaks running through the grain.
Origin: Mexico, Nicaragua (Pacific Central America)
Average weight: 5.6 pounds
Weight classification: very heavy
Where used on Smith basses: top and back sets with matching headstocks
Tone produced on Smith basses: strong low end with notched high-end bite

EBONY (MACASSAR)
Other common names: striped ebony, Indian ebony
Note: This ebony's elasticity makes it less prone to cracking in the wider widths needed for bookmatched tops and 5-, 6-, and 7-string fingerboards.
Origin: Celebes Islands, Indonesia
Average weight: 5.5 pounds
Weight classification: very heavy
Where used on Smith basses: fingerboards, tops, headcaps
Tone produced on Smith basses: smooth, strong low end with definitive highs

IMBUIA
Other common names: Brazilian walnut, imbuya, canela imbuia, amerela
Note: Imbuia is not a true walnut, but its similar color earned it the trade name of Brazilian walnut.
Origin: Brazil
Average weight: 4.2 pounds
Weight classification: medium heavy
Where used on Smith basses: tops and backs, cores, and features
Tone produced on Smith basses: bright high mids with strong, clear bass

KOA
Other common names: Hawaiian koa, acacia
Note: Due to excessive use, this wood has become very scarce, driving the price sky high in recent years.
Origin: Hawaiian Islands
Average weight: 3.4 pounds
Weight classification: medium
Where used on Smith basses: laminated top and back sets and center block
Tone produced on Smith basses: smooth lows with warm mids

LACEWOOD
Other common names: London plane, European plane (UK), Australian silky oak, Australian lacewood (Australia), leopard wood, Amazon leopard wood (Brazil)
Note: Australia, Europe, and South America produce many varieties of lacewood. They are all different species with a similar pattern, but not directly related.

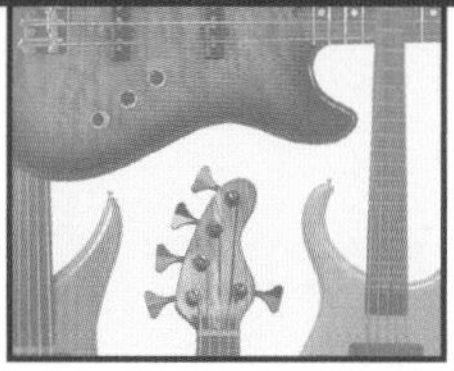

Origin: Brazil
Average weight: 3.1 pounds
Weight classification: light
Where used on Smith basses: body wings (solid or laminated) and center blocks
Tone produced on Smith basses: low-mid growl with attractive highs

MAHOGANY
Other common names: Honduran mahogany, caoba, South American mahogany; Brazilian—, Nicaraguan—, Peruvian—, etc., depending on country of origin.
Note: Mahogany from the tropical Americas is still called Honduran mahogany in the trade but is no longer imported from Honduras.
Origin: Central and South America
Average weight: 3.1 pounds
Weight classification: light
Where used on Smith basses: laminated core stock only
Tone produced on Smith basses: true, even tone that complements its laminates

MAPLE (HARD ROCK MAPLE)
Other common names: hard maple, rock maple, white maple, sugar maple
Note: Smith finds this species the best overall material for neck wood. On occasion, figured pieces are used for body materials.
Origin: Northeast US and Canada
Average weight: 3.8 pounds
Weight classification: medium heavy
Where used on Smith basses: laminated necks
Tone produced on Smith basses: N/A (mainly used as neck wood)

MAPLE, QUILTED
Other common names: big leaf maple, blister maple, figured maple, West Coast curly maple, quilted flame maple, cigar quilt, scalloped maple
Origin: Pacific Northwest
Average weight: 3.2 pounds
Weight classification: medium light
Where used on Smith basses: tops, solid wings, center blocks
Tone produced on Smith basses: warm and bright

MAPLE, TIGER (EASTERN CURLY)
Other common names: curly maple, flame maple, figured maple, fiddleback maple
Note: Most of Smith's tiger maple is from soft (red) maple. On occasion Smith also uses figured hard (sugar) maple for top and back sets.
Origin: Northeast US
Average weight: 3.3 pounds
Weight classification: medium
Where used on Smith basses: tops, backs, wings, centers, and cores
Tone produced on Smith basses: strong, round, and punchy

MAPLE, TIGER (WESTERN FLAME)
Other common names: flame maple, big leaf maple, figured maple, western tiger maple
Origin: Pacific Northwest
Average weight: 3.2 pounds
Weight classification: medium light
Where used on Smith basses: tops, backs, and heel caps
Tone produced on Smith basses: even, punchy

MORADO
Other common names: pau ferro, Bolivian rosewood, ironwood, jacaranda pardo, caviuna
Note: Morado and pau ferro are trade names for the same wood. Morado is not a true rosewood.
Origin: Bolivia and Brazil
Average weight: 4.9 pounds
Weight classification: heavy
Where used on Smith basses: tops, backs, fingerboards, and features
Tone produced on Smith basses: smooth low end with high-end clarity

SHEDUA
Other common names: ovankol, amazakoué, amazoue, ehie, Mozambique
Note: Shedua ranges in color from light yellowish brown to dark grayish brown. Shedua is in the same family as bubinga.
Origin: western Equatorial Africa
Average weight: 4.4 pounds
Weight classification: heavy
Where used on Smith basses: bookmatched tops and backs
Tone produced on Smith basses: tight, high mids with deep lows

WALNUT
Other common names: black walnut, American walnut, American black walnut, Virginia walnut
Note: For figured walnut, see claro walnut and crotch walnut
Origin: Eastern US (mostly Pennsylvania and New York state)
Average weight: 3.3 pounds
Weight classification: medium
Where used on Smith basses: tops, backs, cores, and heel blocks
Tone produced on Smith basses: articulate high end with clear lows

WALNUT, CLARO
Other common names: flamed walnut, figured walnut, California walnut, California black walnut, Oregon walnut, Oregon black walnut, West Coast walnut
Note: West Coast walnut includes a smorgasbord of species and cross-breeds sometimes difficult to classify. Claro (from the spanish word for "clear") is the common name for this group of walnuts.
Origin: Pacific Northwest (California/Oregon)
Average weight: 3.1 pounds
Weight classification: medium light
Where used on Smith basses: tops and backs (mainly Elite series)
Tone produced on Smith basses: punchy bass with clear mids and highs

WALNUT, CROTCH
Other common names: figured black walnut, feathered crotch walnut, curly walnut, figured walnut
Note: Figured walnut is one of the most beautiful woods in the world.
Origin: Eastern US (mostly Pennsylvania and New York state)
Average weight: 3.3–3.5 pounds
Weight classification: medium
Where used on Smith basses: bookmatched tops; Black Tiger models
Tone produced on Smith basses: articulate high end with clear lows

ZEBRAWOOD
Other common names: zebrano, zebra
Note: Although not classified as a figured wood, this highly attractive wood is a favorite for neck-through buyers.
Origin: western Equatorial Africa
Average weight: 3.8 pounds
Weight classification: medium heavy
Where used on Smith basses: bookmatched tops and backs
Tone produced on Smith basses: clear mids with defined lows

■ Kenneth Lawrence Chambered Brase 6 with figured-myrtle top and fretless katalox fingerboard.

KENNETH LAWRENCE

Like Roy Hobbs, the hayseed hero of Bernard Malamud's *The Natural*, Kenneth Lawrence discovered early in life that he had an innate gift. For Hobbs, it was playing baseball; for Lawrence, it was playing—and then building—basses. "It all started when I was 14," Ken recalls, "and it came out of the blue. Some of my friends said, 'Go buy a bass,' and without any deliberation I said, 'Okay.' Instantly I was a bass player—and it seemed to be the right thing for me."

That bass was a Raven, one of the barely playable Japanese 4-strings that were about the only low-budget option in the early '70s—especially if you lived in Edmonton, Alberta, where there were a lot more hockey sticks than musical instruments. "After that," Ken says, "I had a Framus bass, which was nice but kind of funny. And then I got a brand-new Jazz Bass. A drummer friend had bought a P-Bass, and I was incensed. He was a *drummer*, and he had a better bass than me. So, without any money in my pocket, I ordered a J-Bass. By the time it came, I had the money. It was supposed to happen, I guess."

Lawrence later swapped his Fender for a Rickenbacker, in emulation of Yes bass man Chris Squire. And then he saw a new kind of 4-string that stirred the artist within. "Around 1975 Alembics started to show up. It was really something to see those instruments. They struck me as beautiful." Inspired, Ken began to sketch bass designs and hang them on his bedroom wall. "I was thinking that someday I would have these instruments built for me. But I wondered, How am I ever going to afford that? And then I thought, Wait a minute—I think I can do this. I didn't know any luthiers to study with, so to get some woodworking skills I signed up for the Alberta apprenticeship program and learned to be a cabinetmaker. I worked in European shops for about five years, building Scandinavian-style furniture."

But Lawrence never wavered from his original intention: he wanted to build basses. "I started modifying the instruments I had. I took everything made of metal and plastic off my Rickenbacker and did it all in wood. And in the late '70s I started doing repair work for friends of mine." Ken also found inspiration in the instruments of Harry Fleishman [see Fleishman]. "That had a powerful impact on me because I really liked his designs. When I started building, my basses had a Fleishman look. I sent letters to him, asking if I could use some of his ideas, and he was great about it."

■ Kenneth Lawrence neck-through 5-string with curly purpleheart top and extensive carving and inlays. Built in 1994.

In the fall of 1980, an invitation to play took Lawrence to the idyllic Northern California town of Arcata, where he found compatible musicians and the shop of Moonstone Guitars, one of the first builders to use radically figured woods [see Moonstone]. "I knew I had to get a job there. It took a little convincing, but they finally took me on. I worked there for four-and-a-half years and stayed on for another three or so building under my own name."

The first Kenneth Lawrence bass was built in Arcata and based on one of the designs he had drawn in Edmonton. "It was supposed to be a doubleneck with a real Alembic look. It would have been huge, and I hadn't figured out how I was going to muscle it around. Fortunately, one of the necks twisted while I was building it, so I just left it off and finished it as an 8-string."

Starting with an 8-string was ambitious enough—but this one had many unusual features, including a padauk body, a maple-and-padauk neck, body and neck inlays, custom-made Bartolini pickups, and "way too many knobs and switches." Lawrence still has the bass (although it's been modified many times), and he's still in Arcata. Since 1989, he has shared space with the Wildwoods Company, which makes OEM bodies and necks for several well-known bass builders. "Mark Platin of Wildwoods has been great. On his side of the wall, it's full production; on my side, it's handmade stuff. He's given me a wonderful situation to work in, because I have the run of his machinery. I don't have the high overhead of running my own shop, and that has given me the time to develop my own stuff."

That includes such innovative instruments as the semi-hollow Chamberbass, a 35"-scale fretless 5-string with graceful, wave-shaped soundholes and an extended wooden tailpiece. And the Brase, a single-cutaway 35"-scale 5-string (or 6-string) with an extended upper horn that connects to the neck between the 11th and 15th frets. Lawrence is quick to credit the single-cutaway Fodera basses as inspiration for the Brase [see Fodera]. "I really liked the idea of connecting more of the body to the neck, so I came up with that design. I built two and sent photos to Vinnie and Joey at Fodera, saying, 'I got the idea from you guys. Is it okay?' They gave me their blessing, and off I went." Ken also builds a more moderately priced bass he calls the Associate, a 34"-scale bolt-on 4-string with an "updated vintage" look. It has an ash or alder body, 24-fret rosewood fingerboard, and a pair of Basslines J-style pickups. (A 35"-scale 5- or 6-string Associate is also available.) The Sonority is a neck-through version of the Associate. All Kenneth Lawrence basses can be ordered with a wide range of wood, electronics, hardware, and finish options.

Ken builds only 25 to 30 basses a year, doing almost all of the work himself. "I'm always trying to make instruments that appeal to me—that get the player in me excited," he says. "That was the reason I started to do this. I wanted to make an instrument I would be totally in love with, and it's great that I've been able to do that for other people—to make their dream instrument."

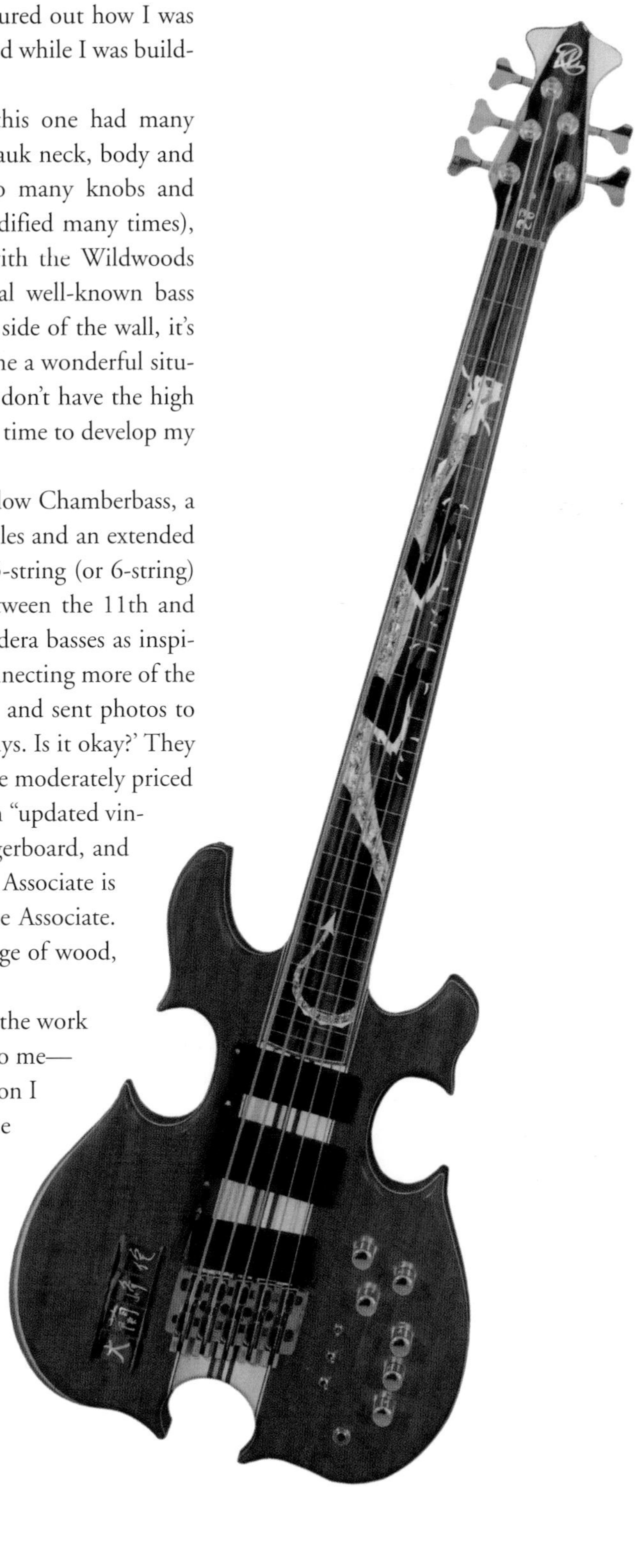

■ Kenneth Lawrence neck-through 5-string with curly purpleheart top and Macassar ebony lined-fretless fingerboard with dragon inlay. Built in 1993.

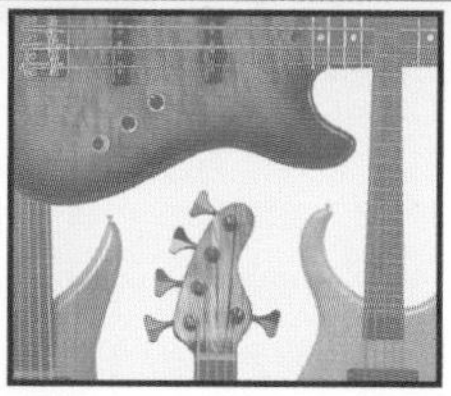

THE ART AND SCIENCE OF INLAY

By Kenneth Lawrence

■ Kenneth Lawrence in his shop holding Brase II with "Quetzalcoatl" inlay.

Inlay can transform an instrument in much the same way dramatic woods or a touch of color can. Inlays are also a great way to make a statement that reflects the sensibilities of the builder or the customer, or both. Inlay designs can be geometric, traditional, highly personal, or humorous—they're reflections of who you are at a certain point in your life. They could reflect spiritual influences (I Ching, yin-yang, and cultural/spiritual icons), or they can just be something that catches your eye. They needn't be large and dramatic; a single gecko or bumblebee or pair of frogs on the body could be enough to personalize your instrument. The possibilities are endless; inlays can make your instrument into a "one of a kind" creation.

The subtle nuance and individuality of a hand-done inlay immediately set it apart from machine-done pieces, much like the difference between a print and an original painting. It's like owning any truly good piece of art. And when you have the opportunity to participate in the design, it's all the more magical.

■ Brase II 5-string with "Quetzalcoatl" and "Mayan Sun" inlays in white, gold, and black mother-of-pearl and red abalone on a Macassar ebony top.

Once you've decided on the subject of the design, the artwork begins. Having a tendency to use the eraser more than the pointy end of the pencil, I often seek help from artists whose work I like, commissioning them to create drawings that I will use to do the inlays. I like this method because I get perspectives from these artists that I might not have thought of myself, and the interaction is often inspiring. Artists who draw for stained glass, tattoos, rubber stamps, children's books, and the like are good people to approach. (Be sure to obtain permission when considering any copyrighted drawings or designs.)

Once the design is complete, the choice of materials is as important to the overall effect as any other factor. This is where the choice of woods for the fretboard or body—the "canvas" for your artwork—comes into play. Ultimately your choice has already been determined by your sonic needs and not the other way around. (You want your bass to sound as good as it looks!)

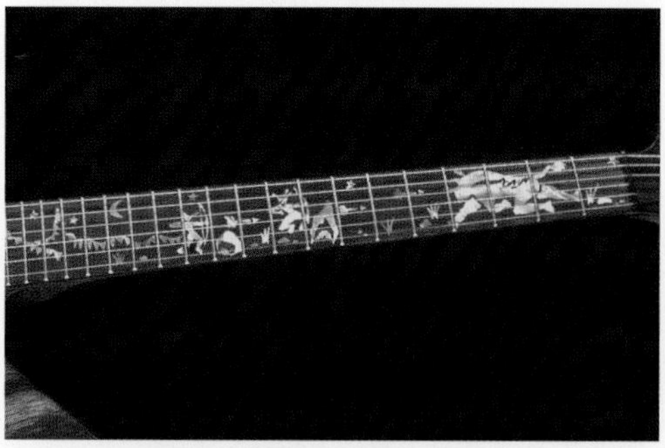

■ "Petroglyph" inlay in white mother-of-pearl on a grenadillo fingerboard.

I prefer to work with shells and abalone, with details in wood, metal (silver, brass, copper), and fossil or recycled ivory. What appeals to me most about using white, black, and gold mother-of-pearl is the depth that can be created by the combination of figure, reflection, and color. I've done entire designs using either gold or black mother-of-pearl, creating wonderfully dramatic pieces. There are, however, myriad other materials and techniques that can and are being used for inlays. Look at the

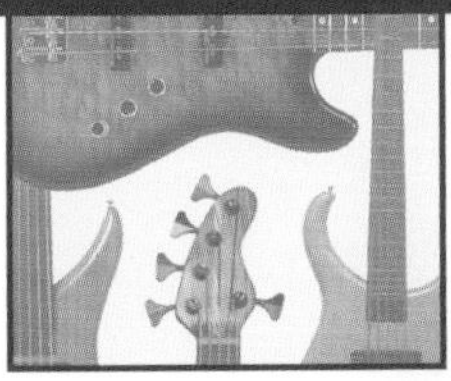

astonishing work of Larry Robinson, Grit Laskin, Steve Klein, Ren Ferguson, Jean Larrivée—to name just a few of my inlay heroes.

I've been asked if inlays affect the sound of an instrument, and I have to say that I have not encountered any inlays that have. Consider that an inlay, after leveling and sanding, is only .040"–.050" thick—there's really not enough material to affect the resonance of either the fretboard or the body. A possible exception would be inlays on a fretless fingerboard. Inlays of some materials might need the protection of a hard coating like polyester, and that would most definitely affect the sound. Inlays of wood can be used if careful placement keeps them out of "heavy traffic" spots, and if the woods used are compatible.

As luthiers, we must be problem solvers. We're always asking how we can do things more easily, efficiently, and consistently. Here are a couple of inlaying tricks I've stumbled across that have helped make my life a little more pleasant:

• I have an adjustable air nozzle that I use to blow away chips and dust as I'm routing the pockets for the inlays. (I also have a recirculating air filter, so I'm not just launching the dust into the air to breathe it later.) This keeps my view of the work clear, so I can better control the cutter. I also have separate Dremel rotary tools with different-size cutters, so I don't have to stop to change cutters or backtrack later.

• I like to glue large, flowing patterns together on wax paper over a copy of the pattern that is, in turn, taped over a block radiused to match the fretboard, so everything fits together the way it will on the board itself. I've experimented with taking the wax paper, with all the shell on it, and taping that to the fretboard, and then using a scribe and an X-Acto knife to cut into the board through the wax paper. It usually works like a dream, saving me the time of having to set up the shell on the board all over again. (Important note: Be sure to use thick Super Glue, because thin glue will saturate the wax paper and you'll have a nightmare on your hands.) A variation of this technique is gluing the pattern upside down on the wax paper and then tacking it down to the face of the body or fretboard with Duco cement, in one large section. The wax paper peels off quite easily, and you're ready to start scribing.

If you'd like to try your hand at inlay, I recommend reading Larry Robinson's book, *The Art of Inlay*. His work is awe inspiring, and he offers a great deal of information and insight into what it takes to create good inlay. Good luck!

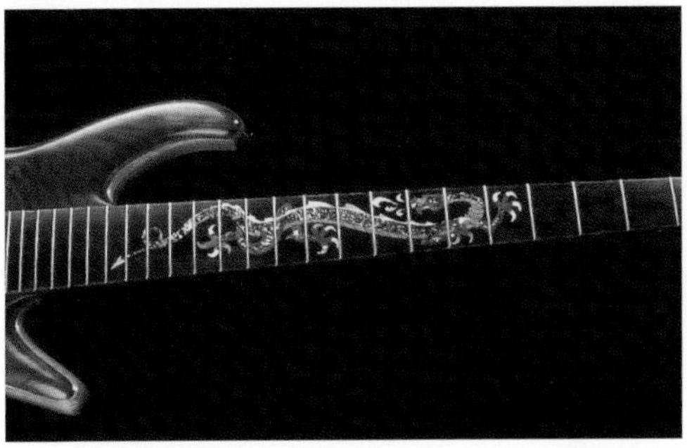

■ "Chinese Dragon" inlay in green abalone, purpleheart, Osage orange, and white mother-of-pearl on a ziricote fingerboard. This bass has red fiber-optic side dots.

■ Chambered Brase 5-string with "Dragonfly" inlay in white, gold, and black mother-of-pearl and purpleheart, set into ebony first and then inlaid into a spruce top.

■ Chambered Brase 5-string (tuned *EADGC*) with "Hummingbird and Fuchsias" inlay in white, gold, and black mother-of-pearl, sea snail, purpleheart, and copper.

KINAL

Mike Kinal marches to the beat of a different drummer—himself, which in itself makes him unusual in the bassmaking world. (He also plays bass, but drums were his first instrument.) Kinal got his start in lutherie as a Vancouver high school student, when he made a guitar. After graduation, he worked as a cabinetmaker but still repaired and built basses and guitars in his spare time. He also studied with archtop-guitar builder Atilla Balough, who schooled Mike in the finer points of finish work.

Kinal's designs have traced the evolution of the electric bass. His early models borrowed from Fender, Gibson, and Rickenbacker models from the '50s and '60s; he then moved on to Alembic-inspired and Steinberger-like instruments. In the early 1990s Mike took another look at the Jazz Bass, but he gave it an update with high-quality woods, 24 frets, a 3+1 headstock, state-of-the-art pickups, and other refinements. The Kinal MK4-B was born.

The MK4-B soon became a series, with 5-string (MK5-B) and 6-string (MK6-B) models. Kinal tops their alder, swamp ash, or korina bodies with a wide variety of tonewoods, including figured maple, figured walnut, bubinga, and koa. Originally neck-throughs, Kinal's basses later became bolt-ons—but their graphite-reinforced multi-piece necks are attached with six bolts, for extra strength and better sustain. The fretted or fretless fingerboards are made from rosewood, ebony, maple, or pau ferro. Pickups come from Lindy Fralin, Bartolini, EMG, Basslines, and other makers, with 9- or 18-volt active electronics available. Scale length can be 34", 34½", or 35". With so many choices, Kinal basses are all essentially custom instruments—yet Mike keeps his prices surprisingly low. "I wanted to design a bass for the working musician on a limited budget," he told *Bass Player*'s Scott Malandrone, "but one that offers high-end features and options."

One of the things that sets a Kinal bass apart is the way Mike uses wood where others might have plastic or metal. The control-cavity cover is made from wood that matches the body, as is the trussrod cover. The front and back of the headstock have wooden laminates, for both appearance and extra strength. The jack plate is carved from ebony. An optional finger platform—matching the body wood—can be placed between the pickups; this keeps the right-hand fingers from "digging in" too far, and its top edge makes a handy thumb rest. All of this detailed woodwork gives Kinal's instruments an air of Old World craftsmanship that's missing in most mass-produced basses.

In the late '90s Mike expanded his line with the SK Series basses, which have more rounded, symmetrical bodies, and the DK Series, with chambered, semi-

■ Kinal MK5-B, early neck-through model.

■ Kinal SK4-21.

■ Kinal MK5-B.

acoustic bodies. The most recent addition to the Kinal line is the MK21, a 21-fret version of the MK models that has standard active electronics. Although he builds many more basses than he did in his early days, Kinal emphasizes that he still does most of the major work himself—and he likes it that way. "Will I ever get into mass production? I doubt it," he says. "I'd like to keep the operation small and the quality in, which is why I started making instruments in the first place."

KLEIN ELECTRIC

Everything about the Klein Electric Bass seems a bit odd—until you pick it up. Suddenly, the strange shape and headless construction make perfect sense. The sculptured alder body fits comfortably against you, every note on the 24-fret neck is easily accessible, and the instrument balances perfectly whether you're sitting or standing. It's an ergonomic marvel.

Inspired by the work of Ned Steinberger, luthier Steve Klein created the K-Bass in 1992. The early models were equipped with bolt-on Moses Graphite necks and EMG pickups; more recent instruments have maple necks and Bartolini pickups. Scale length is 34", and the K-Bass is available as a 4- or 5-string, fretted or fretless. A Steinberger bridge is standard equipment, with the DB drop-tuner optional. In 1994 Steve sold Klein Electric Guitars to Lorenzo German, who continues to produce K-Basses in his Discovery Bay, California, shop. Steve Klein has had no connection to Klein Electric since October 2001. Focusing instead on acoustic instruments, he has designed such creations as the Taylor acoustic bass guitar [see Taylor].

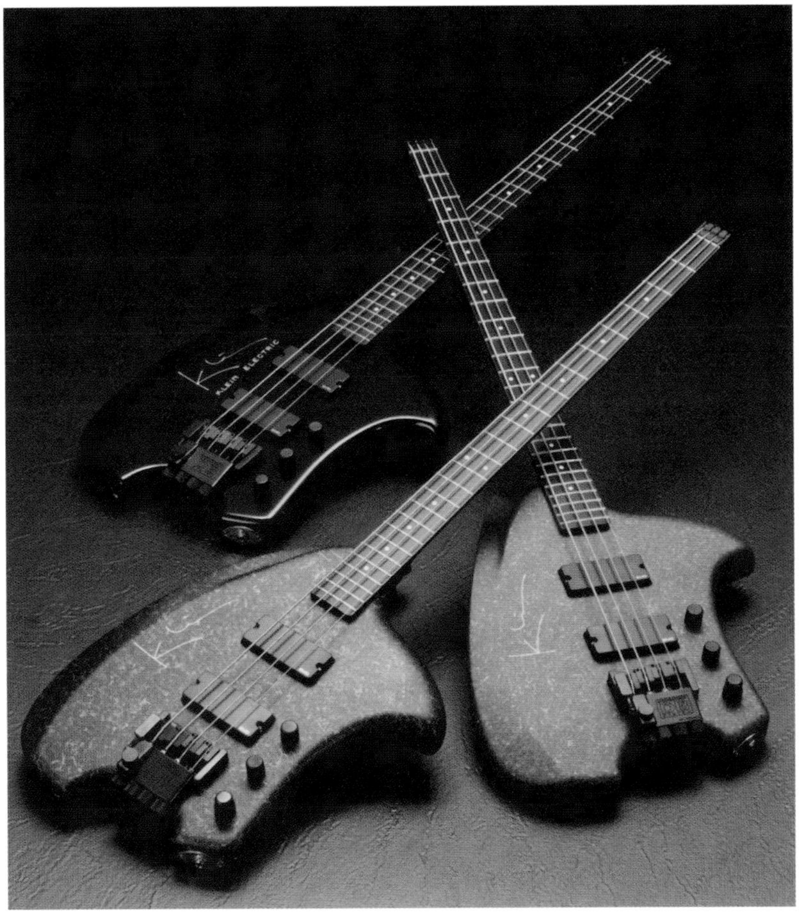

■ Klein Electric K-Basses.

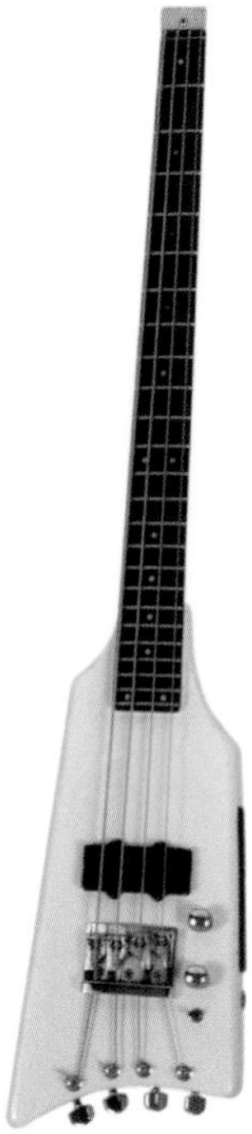

■ Kramer Duke Deluxe.

KRAMER

In the musical-instrument business, brand names often have a life of their own, moving from one owner to another and sometimes ending up on products that bear no resemblance to the ones on which they started. In the case of Kramer, the brand has been around almost continuously since the mid 1970s, although its namesake—Gary Kramer—was with the company for only about a year.

Kramer, who had backed Travis Bean in his venture to build aluminum-neck instruments [see Travis Bean], joined with Dennis Berardi and Peter LaPlaca in 1975 to form BKL International. Kramer helped to design the company's first instruments, and with financial help from real-estate magnate Henry Vaccaro, they began to roll off a production line in Neptune, New Jersey, late in 1976. Kramer left the company only a few months later, reportedly in a management dispute, but the instruments continued to carry his name.

While Travis Bean instruments had an aluminum "receiver" that extended the neck into the body all the way to the bridge, Kramer's aluminum necks, with their "tuning fork" pegheads, were bolted on. And they weren't solid hunks of aluminum—they were T-shaped structures with wooden inserts on the back, so the player's hand would rest on wood rather than metal. This helped to overcome the two primary objections to Travis Bean basses: that they were neck heavy and the necks felt cold to the touch. The early Kramers had bodies of walnut, maple, or koa, but the fingerboards were Ebanol, a synthetic used to make bowling balls. The initial bass offerings were the 350B and 450B, both of which were double-cutaway instruments that looked like the Travis Bean basses. The 350B had two single-coil pickups while the 450B sported a pair of humbuckers.

In the late 1970s Kramer expanded the line with several new bass models, including the DMZ series, which featured DiMarzio pickups. As the company's guitars became more popular with heavy metal bands, the instruments became more outrageous in design. The XL series, which included an 8-string bass, had a shark-fin look, while one member of the XK family was the wedge-shaped XKB-10 bass. The real eye-catcher, though, was the limited-edition Gene Simmons Axe, available only in 1980. It perfectly embodied its name.

By the time Kramer introduced its Duke models in 1981, the days of aluminum necks were numbered. Obviously influenced by Steinberger's success, the short-scale Duke bass had a rectangular body with a sort of tail-fin curve at the butt end and a headless, bolt-on aluminum neck. The Duke came in Standard and Deluxe versions; the latter had a Schaller Double-J pickup and a Schaller bridge/tailpiece.

Another headless aluminum-neck bass, the star-shaped Voyager, joined the line in 1982, but over the next three years Kramer gradually shifted its production to wooden necks.

During the 1980s Kramer guitars were hugely popular because of their association with Eddie Van Halen, and bass production took a back seat. One exception was the Ferrington Bass, an acoustic/electric model designed by California custom builder Danny Ferrington. This Korean-made 4-string had a thin hollow body, an asymmetric soundhole, and an electric-style neck complete with pointy headstock. It wasn't a great instrument, although Gene Simmons did play one on MTV's "Kiss Unplugged"—proving that it could take a licking and keep on ticking.

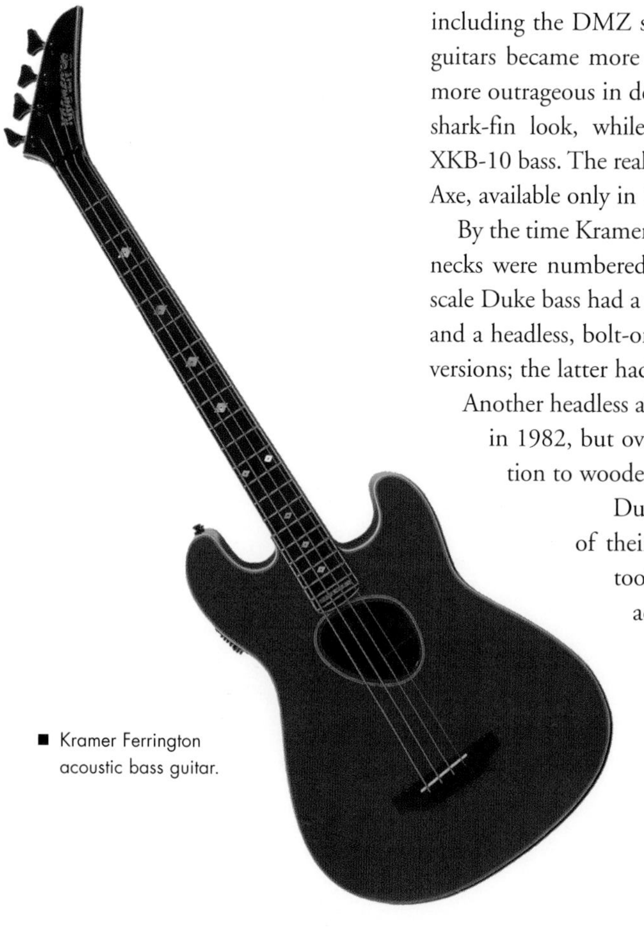

■ Kramer Ferrington acoustic bass guitar.

In 1986, apparently rolling in cash from sales of its trendy guitars, Kramer acquired Spector [see Spector]. For the next five years, Spector's U.S.-made basses were built at Kramer's New Jersey factory, with Stuart Spector serving as a consultant. There was also offshore production of some Spector models, like the NS-2A. Kramer boasted of $15 million in sales and looked like an industry powerhouse—but the truth was that the company was financially overextended. By the end of 1989 it was bankrupt.

Kramer managed to stagger along for a while selling imported guitars but eventually succumbed. It was briefly revived in the mid 1990s by Henry Vaccaro, who displayed a line of new aluminum-neck Kramer prototypes at trade shows. That operation never got off the ground, though, and late in 1996 the Kramer name was sold to Gibson. Vaccaro subsequently launched a new company under his own name, featuring many of the same aluminum-neck designs he had developed for the "new" Kramer. Gibson kept the Kramer brand dormant for a while, and then capitalized on it with a line of inexpensive imported knockoffs, including several basses, sold directly to customers on the Internet.

■ Kramer Stagemaster.

KUBICKI

Philip Kubicki didn't intend to make his mark as a bass builder. "I'm really an acoustic guitar maker," he says—but his best-known creation is the Ex Factor bass. Introduced in 1985, it offered an innovative approach to extended range: an extra-long bottom string with a spring-loaded string clasp at the nut. Leave the clasp down, and you've got a standard 4-string with an open *E*. Flip it, and you've added *E*♭ and *D*, without a change in string tension or any of the mental gymnastics required with a detuned string.

The route leading to the Ex Factor's creation took some interesting twists and turns. It began at the home of Kubicki's grandparents, back in the 1950s. "For some reason my grandfather had a guitar in the closet," recalls Philip. "And that's where I'd head: to play with that guitar. It had one string that was a mile off the fingerboard. I think all of us instrument makers have had that kind of fascination—some little spark, back at the very beginning."

A few years later, while Kubicki was in high school in Whittier, California, a friend introduced him to Ernie Drumheller. "His hobby was making guitars. He invited me and my friend to come to his shop on Saturdays, and he taught us how to make guitars. I took off with it and built a half-dozen classical guitars during my high school years."

■ Kubicki Ex Factor.

■ Kubicki Custom 4 with redwood top.

After graduating in 1961, Kubicki enrolled at Fullerton Junior College—which happened to be about a mile from the Fender factory. Curious, he dropped by and took a tour led by production manager Babe Simoni. "I told him I'd built some guitars and was interested in employment. Babe told me they were building a new facility to make acoustic guitars, and he suggested that I go over there and meet Roger Rossmeisl."

Rossmeisl was a German luthier who had worked previously for Gibson and Rickenbacker, where he designed the Rick 4000 bass [see Rickenbacker]. Leo Fender had hired him to design a new line of acoustic guitars. Rossmeisl sized up Kubicki and then gave him some wood. "He asked me to come back in nine months, so I built another classical guitar over that period. I really wanted to impress him with it." After scrutinizing the guitar, Rossmeisl offered Kubicki a job building acoustics.

In 1966 Rossmeisl moved to Fender's R&D department, and Kubicki followed two years later. In addition to working on limited-edition projects like the LTD archtop guitar, he helped build bass and guitar prototypes and contributed to one-of-a-kind instruments, such as the rosewood Telecaster that went to George Harrison and a rosewood Strat made for Jimi Hendrix (who died before it could be delivered).

After Rossmeisl left Fender, Kubicki stayed on for a couple of years. Then, in 1973, he opened his own shop in Santa Barbara, where he made instruments for customers like Joni Mitchell and John Fogerty. Now and then, he built a bass—usually a Fender copy, like the P-style bass he made for Fogerty. The operation slowly expanded, and in the late '70s he teamed up with Carla Collins to form Collins-Kubicki, Inc. Jeff Richardson come onboard a little later, to handle marketing. "Around 1983 the three of us began to have meetings, with the idea of designing our own line of basses and guitars," explains Philip. "We started by developing a set of criteria based on human factors, and a little later Jeff suggested the name 'Factor' for the bass."

The new Kubicki instruments were to be totally original designs—"we wanted to make everything ourselves: pickups, circuit boards, knobs"—and the Factor, their first creation, was an immediate hit. Rick Turner, reviewing it in *Guitar Player,* called it "an engineering tour de force." Available as both the Ex Factor (32" scale, with string clasp) and Factor 4 (34" scale, no clamp), it emphasized ergonomics in a way that was both beautiful and practical. The bolt-on neck was made of 34-laminate maple for stability and anchored by machine screws threaded into metal inserts. The electronics could be run in either active or passive mode, with preset cut, boost, and flat positions. The body-mounted bridge-tuner assembly provided excellent balance and was sufficiently original to be awarded a patent, as were the string clasp and the overall design.

The Ex Factor was such a striking invention that the company's electric guitar never made it off the drawing board. The new bass was embraced by players like Stuart Hamm, Vail Johnson, and Duran Duran's John Taylor, who gave it a big boost when he played one on *Saturday Night Live.* Sales took off—so much so that in 1988 Kubicki signed a licensing deal with Fender to build instruments for him, because he couldn't keep up with the demand. Over the next three years, Fender produced about 1,800 Factors, some of which have different electronics than the Kubicki-made models. The contract was not renewed in 1991, and Philip went back to making the basses in his own shop.

Since then, Kubicki has added a couple of models to the line: the Key Factor 4 and 5, 34"-scale basses with headstock-mounted tuners. He's offered some aesthetic refinements, including exotic-wood tops and a wider range of colors, but his original concept has remained essentially the same. "Gibson and Fender came up with designs that never really changed, and they're still popular. I knew that if I wanted to design a classic, it had to be done right and not altered. I still make them the same way, and I hope that long-term commitment will make it a classic instrument eventually."

■ The Kubicki Ex Factor peghead has a spring-loaded clasp at the nut, allowing the *E* string to be dropped to *D* without changing the pitch of the fretted notes.

■ Kubicki Key Factor 4 and 5.

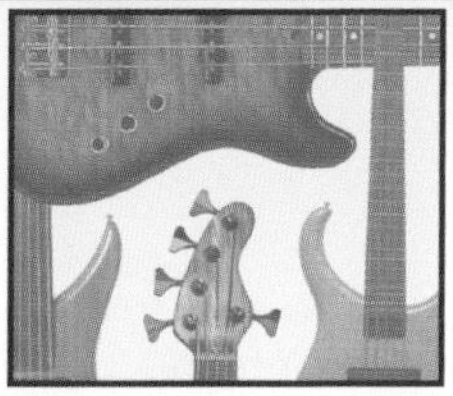

NECK WOOD AND TONE

By Philip Kubicki

When I'm asked, "What's the best wood to use for the body of a bass?" people are surprised to hear me say that the neck wood actually contributes more to the sound of a solidbody instrument than the body wood does—although, to be honest, I think the pickups and electronics probably play the largest role in determining the plugged-in sound of an electric bass.

The neck conforms to the strings much more than the body does. The body is much thicker, wider, and heavier than the neck (not to mention usually being asymmetric as well). The neck is more of an acoustically engineered shape; it gradually gets thinner and narrower—and therefore weaker, not unlike a fishing rod or a ship's mast—as it extends out from the body toward the headstock. Since the neck is a lot less massive than the body, it can vibrate more easily and freely in response to string motion than the body can. This means the neck effectively acts as an exposed acoustical brace that wants to vibrate in sympathy with the strings (much like the tines of a tuning fork).

If you'd like proof of the way the neck contributes to the acoustic resonance of an instrument, try this simple experiment: Strike a string on a solidbody bass and (carefully!) press the headstock against a wall—you will hear the note get louder as the neck's vibrations couple with the wall and use it as a sounding board. Then flip the bass around, strike the same string, and press the end of the body against the wall. You will not hear nearly as much of a difference, because less of the string's vibration is being transmitted through the body.

The tuning keys on the headstock of a conventional bass act as a kind of ballast to counteract the moving weight/ inertia of the vibrating string and dampen some of the neck's vibrations, which consequently reduces the neck's absorption of the strings' energy. A headless neck must therefore be built more stiffly to raise the acoustic frequency so the neck's sympathetic vibrations don't absorb an unacceptable amount of the strings' energy. (That's why Kubicki Factors have very stiff multi-laminate necks.)

■ Philip Kubicki, 2003.

By now you're probably thinking, Okay, what's the best wood for a bass neck? There are many choices, the most common being maple (typically eastern rock maple) laminated to a maple, rosewood, or ebony fingerboard and usually bolted to the body, or mahogany with a rosewood or ebony fingerboard, which is typically glued into the body. There are also laminated through-body necks made from many different species of wood, non-wood necks made of metal and various composites, and necks that combine wood and non-wood materials.

Which is best? It depends. It depends on the type of instrument being built; it depends on the style(s) of music to be played; it depends on the desired appearance of the finished instrument. Most important, it depends on the particular sound and feel you want. As with so many other things in music, the answer to the question really depends on the player's tastes and opinions. For this reason, I recommend that my customers use their ears and then tell me what sounds best to them.

KYDD

The KYDD bass is a hybrid: an instrument that looks like an electric upright yet features the shorter scale length—and easy playability—of a bass guitar. Its creator, Bruce Kaminsky of Philadelphia, explains: "Other than my family, my two great passions are basses and motorcycles. I wanted to be able to combine the two by creating an upright electric bass that I could take to gigs on a bike, and get off the bandstand before the horn players."

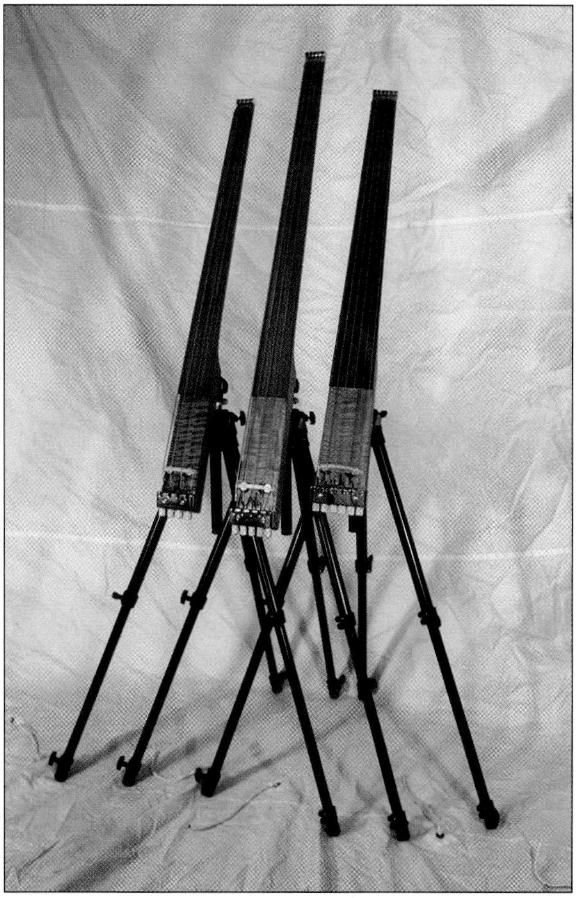

■ KYDD basses: Carry-On 4- and 6-string models flank a Big KYDD 5-string.

Kaminsky conceived of the KYDD Carry-On, with its 30" scale length and ultra-compact dimensions, in the early 1980s, combining what he'd learned from experiments with piezo pickups on a Guild Starfire Bass with the minimal size of a Steinberger L-series instrument. He made his instrument from curly maple, attached a cello fingerboard and maple bridge, wired up a Fishman pickup, and strung it with a set of bass guitar flatwounds. And then he stood it on its end, attaching it to a tripod and playing it in an upright position. Not only did it work, it had a surprisingly big sound, both plucked and bowed. Kaminsky notes that when he first demonstrated the Carry-On, many listeners assumed it was some kind of MIDI controller and the sound was coming from an acoustic bass sample.

The Carry-On 4-string went into production in 1994, and Kaminsky later added 5- and 6-strings, as well as an *8va* model (the same instrument in cello tuning). In 2000 he introduced the Big KYDD, a slightly larger version with a 35" scale length; it's available as a 4- or 5-string. The big sound these small instruments produce remains something of a mystery, although Kaminsky is willing to decipher his company's acronymic name. "KYDD stands for Kaminsky's Yukon Deli & Drygoods," he says. "But that's another story."

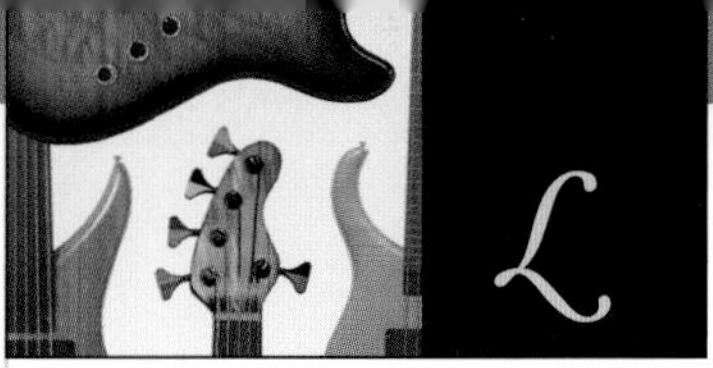

LAKLAND

■ Lakland 4-76 Standard 4.

Dan Lakin (LAY-kin) did an unusual kind of market survey before founding Lakland Musical Instruments; the Chicagoan's first music-business venture was buying and selling used basses. "In 1990 or '91," he says, "I started looking for basses in the trading papers. I would buy them and then resell them, more as a hobby than a business. Because of that, I got to see just about everything on the market. There were aspects of certain instruments that I liked, but nothing seemed to have it all in one package. I liked Fender basses, and I also liked Music Man and some other top brands, but I thought the ultimate instrument was not on the market."

Dan would sometimes buy an instrument that needed to be repaired, and he often turned to luthier Hugh McFarland. "Anytime Hugh refretted something, it would play amazingly well. Eventually, I talked with him about putting together an instrument. He had production experience at Dean Guitars, so he knew what to do. We began designing the instrument in January 1994. We put together a prototype and took it to the NAMM show that July. I brought the player's point of view to the project, and Hugh brought the builder's point of view.

Dan says the first Lakland (LAKin + McFarLAND) was "sort of Leo Fender's greatest hits—a Jazz Bass and an early Music Man StingRay put together." The body shape was similar to a StingRay's, but the treble side featured a deeper cutaway for better upper-fret access. It was made of lightweight ash with a quilted-maple top, a recipe like the one Roger Sadowsky was using for his respected Fender-style instruments. Quartersawn rock maple was the choice for the neck, which was capped with a bird's-eye maple fingerboard. A stickler for playability, Lakin worked with McFarland to come up with a slim neck shape. McFarland's excellent fretwork was the finishing touch.

The flexible electronics of the Lakland prototype were inspired by something Lakin read in a product review. "The coils in the Music Man-style bridge pickup are splittable," Dan explains. "I got that idea from a review of the Warwick Dolphin bass [in the Jan/Feb 1992 issue of *Bass Player*]. I remember reading that the Dolphin's rear pickup was splittable, so you could have one or both coils on, and I thought, Wow, that's a really good idea!" Bartolini supplied the pickups and preamp. "The preamp was an NTMB model. After we got it in, we asked Bill Bartolini to make some minor changes in the EQ points. So that became our preamp, the NTMB-L. We also changed the pickups after we had made the first 20 basses, because I wasn't happy with my first choice."

The prototype had a clunky-looking oval bridge plate based on the early StingRay design. McFarland had decided to use aluminum, believing it offered better sound, but it proved to be hard to work with. "And we couldn't find anyone who could chrome-plate it," says Dan. The bridge plate was eventually streamlined, and chrome-plated steel took the place of aluminum.

■ Lakland Bob Glaub Signature Model.

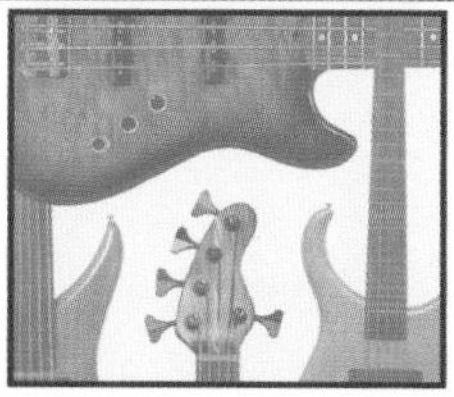

CREATING SIGNATURE MODELS

By Dan Lakin

There's more to creating a signature-model bass than just slapping a famous player's name on something you already make—or there should be, anyway. The instrument should reflect the player and be something he or she likes and wants to play.

I got the idea for the first Lakland signature model in 1997. I had just reread Chris Jisi's *Bass Player* article on Joe Osborn (May/June 1992), and I realized Joe was probably my favorite bass player. His tone killed me, and his lines were perfect. I had to meet this guy. I didn't think I had a shot to make him a bass because his connection with his '60 Jazz Bass was so strong, but I was willing to give it a try. I called Chris and got Joe's phone number. I decided to call it, just to see if it was still good. I dialed the number and when someone answered, I hung up. Mission accomplished—Joe still lived there. About a minute later my phone rang; it was Joe, saying, "Who are you? You called me. What do you want?" I was caught. (He had dialed *69, which calls back the last person who called you.) I quickly apologized and explained why I called. Joe soon warmed up to the idea and, to my surprise, was interested in trying one of our basses.

I sent Joe a 4-63 model, which is our original body style with two single-coil J-style pickups. Joe liked a lot about it, especially the neck, but he had some issues with balance. I asked Joe to come to Chicago, so we could work things out face to face. He brought along his famous Jazz Bass, and I also invited some area friends who have pre-CBS J-Basses. All the necks were a little different, but Joe's was the best—except for one thing: his *E* string sounded dead. We tried everything we could think of, including switching pickups. Still dead. In talking with Joe and listening to his playing, we realized this had affected his playing style—he almost never played on the *E* string.

That night at dinner, Joe and I agreed that we would bring a J-style Lakland bass, with his name on it, to the market. Some aspects were easy. For example, we were able to copy the neck shape with the current generation of CNC machines; these machines can probe an existing shape and create a program to cut that shape. We had our tuning gears custom made to go in the reverse direction, as they did on the old Fenders, but with smoother operation. We also incorporated some Lakland design features, like a strings-through-body bridge and graphite-reinforced neck.

Chasing the sound of an old bass can be daunting. We focused on two major variables: body finish and pickups. Since Joe's bass had very little finish left, we made two bodies to test, one with a light oil finish (done by Mike Tobias) and the other with our standard polyester. Both bodies were alder of a similar weight. We could tell no difference between the finishes. We then focused on pickup selection. We tested with Joe playing to a bass-less track on a Roland VS-880, using one bass and swapping pickups in and out. In addition to the recorded test, we listened to the sound live while Joe played though an amp. It was amazing how different they all sounded. In the end, we selected pickups made by Lindy Fralin.

■ Joe Osborn (left) with Dan Lakin and signature bass.

We began production and marketing of the Joe Osborn Signature Model later that year. It was great hanging out with Joe for the photos and interviews that went along with the introduction, and Joe has attended every NAMM show for Lakland since we met. It's been a real honor to work with him, and we were very pleased when *Bass Player* gave Joe a lifetime achievement award in 2000.

In contrast to Joe's model, which is an updated replica of an existing instrument, our Jerry Scheff Signature Model is something completely new. To make it, we combined our 4-94 body and neck, Danelectro-style pickups, and a modern preamp. After I met Jerry in 1998, I sent him one of our 4-94 models. He liked it, but the producer he was working with liked the sound of his Jerry Jones Longhorn bass plugged into a Sadowsky preamp. Jerry liked that sound, too, but he hated playing the short-scale bass. So he asked if we could make him a custom bass with the physical characteristics of the 4-94 but two "lipstick tube" pickups placed as they are on the Longhorn. We were happy with the way it turned out, and so was Jerry, so we decided to put that bass into production and name it for him.

■ Lakland Joe Osborn Signature Model.

In addition to visiting trade shows, the first Lakland bass spent a fair amount of time on the bandstand. "I was playing in a Grateful Dead cover band," notes Dan, "and we were gigging fairly often. Right from the start, I was pleased with the way it sounded. It was versatile and had a wide range of usable sounds. It could get close to both a Jazz Bass and a StingRay, but it also had a sound of its own."

Lakland basses went into production in 1995, and annual output had risen to about 500 instruments a year by the end of the decade. The mainstay is the Standard, based on the original prototype, available in both 4-string and 5-string models. The Standard has a swamp-ash or alder body (a quilted-maple top is optional), a graphite-reinforced bolt-on 22-fret neck, Bartolini or Basslines pickups, and active electronics. The line also includes signature models inspired by studio bassists Joe Osborn (a J-style instrument available in active and passive configurations), Bob Glaub (a P-style bass with either P or J string spacing at the nut), and Jerry Scheff (featuring Kent Armstrong "lipstick tube" pickups), as well as a thinline hollowbody that was co-designed by Michael Tobias. In 2001, Lakland introduced the Skyline Series; these mid-priced 5-strings are built in Korea to Lakin's specifications.

■ Lakland Hollowbody Deluxe (left) and 55-94 5-string.

LANDING

"My company was founded around the concept of a high-quality short-scale bass with the best in pickups and hardware," says Jimmy Wilson of Landing Guitars. His first realization of that concept was the L1, an elegantly simple 4-string with an ash body, one EMG-HB pickup, and scale length of 30½". It has been succeeded by the L1+1, with a pair of EMG-HBs. Wilson also makes the short-scale two-pickup L2 (originally with EMG-35 DCs, upgraded to EMG-40 DCs). For those preferring a 34" scale, there are the L4 and L5, both equipped with EMG-40 DC pickups. A short-scale 5-string and long-scale 6-string were on the drawing board in 2002. All Landing basses have Strat-style bodies and bolt-on necks; their rosewood fingerboards can be fretted or fretless. Basslines pickups are optional. Wilson assembles the instruments in his western Pennsylvania shop and sells them directly to his customers.

■ Landing L1+1.

LIEBER

Reading a 1972 *Guitar Player* article about the first Alembic bass inspired a young bassist named Thomas Lieber to consider becoming a builder. He was serious enough to pack up and head west, in search of the instrument's creators. When he arrived at Alembic's door, he offered his services as an apprentice—only to be told there were no positions available. Fortunately, Lieber was referred to Doug Irwin, a former Alembic associate who had recently set out on his own. Thomas secured a job as Irwin's assistant, helping him to design and build instruments for Jerry Garcia, Phil Lesh, and other San Francisco notables. After further studies with Steve Klein, focusing on acoustic instruments, Lieber returned to the East and established his own business.

Lieber first gained notice for his Spider Grinder acoustic bass guitar, which was based on concepts he developed while working with Irwin. This large, single-cutaway instrument has a dual-bowl synthetic back, a hand-carved top, and a mahogany neck. The body design was sufficiently unique to be awarded a patent—and to get the attention of Stanley Clarke, who bought one in 1979. Impressed by Thomas's work, he suggested they collaborate on an all-composite solidbody bass guitar. Lieber and Clarke went into business together in 1980 as the Spellbinder Corporation, producing 50 Spellbinder basses (plus one custom left-handed model, as a gift for Paul McCartney) and then destroying the molds, thus guaranteeing "limited edition" status for the instruments.

During the late '80s and '90s, Lieber built custom instruments and continued to develop his ideas in several areas, including neck designs, molding processes, and the EQ-4 bass pickup, with sliding polepieces, which he incorporated into a new acoustic/electric version of the Spider Grinder. Lieber, who has been awarded nearly a dozen patents for his innovations, joined forces with Clarke again in 2001 to revive the Spellbinder Corporation. According to their mission statement, they intend to "design and produce benchmark instruments, which will set the standard for the next 50 years."

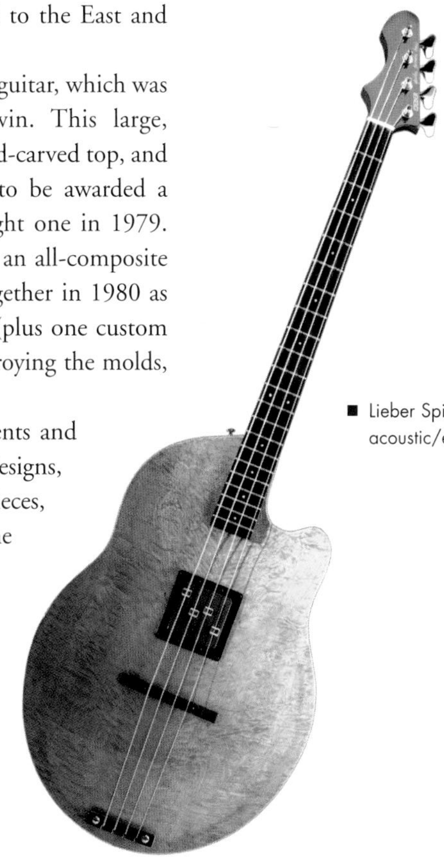

■ Lieber Spider Grinder acoustic/electric bass.

■ Linc Luthier Zebra G-6.

LINC LUTHIER

His real name is Lincoln Hoke, and he's been building basses in Upland, California, since the early 1990s. Linc Luthier basses are instantly recognizable, thanks to their upswept horns, small pegheads, and gleaming exotic-wood bodies. There's nothing else quite like them—and Linc has the patents to prove it.

Linc's first design, now called the Luthier Bass, is a semi-acoustic, neck-through-body instrument. The neck has an asymmetric triangular shape and is made of horizontally oriented laminations—a unique approach to solving the problems caused by the tension of bass strings. Linc selects the woods from some two dozen varieties, from the familiar maples to such rarities as platymiscium and ziricote. The design of the instrument minimizes non-wood materials, and there's virtually no plastic to be seen, except for the pickup covers. The Luthier Bass is available as a 4-, 5-, 6-, or 8-string, fretted or fretless, with a 34" scale length. Bartolini pickups are standard, and the circuit is passive. ("Why put a transistor radio in a Faberge egg?" Linc asks.)

The Impression Bass is a hollowbody with a central bracing system, which, Linc says, "transfers sound more efficiently between the instrument's vibration plates and bridge . . . [for] increased frequency response, clarity, and articulation." Linc's latest creation is something he calls the Danger Bass, which has a 28" scale length and can be strung with either standard or piccolo bass strings, in a variety of tunings. It's equipped with a magnetic + piezo pickup combination, producing a percussive tone that makes it "the ultimate close-quarters audio assault vehicle." Linc also builds guitars, doublenecks in various configurations, and the Impression Upright Bass, a 42"-scale EUB.

■ Little Torzal 434.

LITTLE

Playing bass is gratifying, but it can also be painful. Bassists suffering from such playing-related disorders as carpal tunnel syndrome are faced with a difficult dilemma: find an instrument that eases the strain—or quit playing.

One choice is a bass that's smaller, lighter, and has a shorter scale length. But that can mean a hard-to-accept sacrifice in sound. Another choice is an instrument like the Torzal bass, designed and built by Jerome Little. With its patented "Natural Twist" design, the Torzal reduces hand and wrist strain—yet it's a full-size, long-scale electric bass. "After studying different techniques and body positions, I realized there were compromises to be made between good physiological movement and normal bass technique," Little says. "This gave me ideas about a truly comfortable instrument that would help both prevention of and recovery from repetitive-strain injuries. My goal is to create basses that are attractive to the eye, ear, and touch—so pleasing that they become a part of the player, allowing the bassist to transcend the instrument and focus complete attention on the music."

Little learned his trade at the Guitar Building Institute on the Spanish island of Formentera. He has a degree in music and acoustics from Hampshire College in Amherst, Massachusetts; while studying there he received a Lemelson Foundation grant that supported the research, design, and construction of the first Torzal bass. Little worked for Parker Guitars from 1996 to 2000 before moving to California and setting up his own shop.

The Torzal is a neck-through-body instrument available with either a 34" or 35" scale in 4- and 5-string versions. It can also be ordered as the extended-range Big Easy, which has a 36" scale length created by adding an extra fret to a

34"-scale neck. Many wood and electronics options are available. For those who prefer conventional bass design, Little custom builds instruments in a variety of styles, including the J-Bird, which features Japanese-inspired joinery.

LIUTAIO MOTTOLA

"I began building custom-made stringed instruments in 1994," says R.M. Mottola of Newton, Massachusetts. "I'm a bass player, woodworker, and engineer, and my goal from the start has been to mix creativity, craftsmanship, science, and engineering, and to apply that combination to the design and development of one-of-a-kind handcrafted musical instruments." Mottola describes his approach as "challenge based," explaining that he considers both the requirements (the qualities an instrument must have) and the wish list (the qualities it should have) for every project.

One look at some of the basses created at Liutaio Mottola (*liutaio* is the Italian form of *luthier*) confirms that R.M. is serious about taking on challenges. His Mezzaluna is a solidbody electric bass designed to keep the neck at a 45-degree angle, whether the player is sitting or standing, which is easier on the wrist than a more horizontal playing position. It weighs only eight pounds and is quite beautiful, with graceful, flowing curves and elegant proportions. Mottola also makes a hollowbody acoustic/electric version of the Mezzaluna, with a braced top of spruce or cedar; the piezo bridge and onboard preamp are his proprietary designs. Even more radical is the Bassola, an archtop acoustic bass guitar that Mottola built with the goal of coming as close as possible to the sound of an upright bass. It looks like a huge mandolin (a Gibson F-series mandolin was used as the template) with a 34"-scale fretless neck grafted on, and it makes a big sound indeed. In blind tests, listeners have identified it as an upright. Another unusual Mottola creation is the Elastico, a small acoustic bass guitar (18" scale length) that uses the silicone-rubber strings of the Ashbory bass [see Guild].

In the midst of the many production builders, whose R&D often focuses on better ways of doing more of the same, it's "mad scientists" like R.M. Mottola who are advancing the art of bass building by constantly pushing the envelope and asking, "Why not?" And he's more than willing to share his knowledge, frequently writing about his projects for the journals *GuitarMaker* and *American Lutherie*. "I started building instruments when an illness forced me to quit work as an engineer," says Mottola. "It was [fellow Boston-area luthier] Jim Mouradian who suggested that building an instrument might be a good project for a person in my position, for its therapeutic value if for no other reason. He's always been forthcoming with tips and ideas, and not just to me. With Jim's high standards for giving back clearly in mind, I feel sharing what I've found out to be the least I can do."

■ Liutaio Mottola Elastico Ashbory-style acoustic bass guitar.

MARTIN

By the time the first Fender Precision Bass went on sale, the Martin company had been building guitars for 118 years. It began in 1833, when Christian Frederick Martin immigrated to the United States from Saxony and opened a shop in New York City. Twenty-one years later, he moved his family to Nazareth in eastern Pennsylvania, an area that strongly resembled his German homeland. C.F. Martin & Company has remained there ever since, and in 2002 the CEO was C.F. Martin IV, a direct descendant of the founder.

Although Martin is a hugely important name in the history of the American guitar, it has played only a peripheral role as a bassmaker. The famous Martin dreadnought guitar—the company's mainstay instrument—was developed in response to "bass guitars" offered by its competitors, but these were simply large-bodied 6-string guitars that had stronger bass than smaller instruments. Martin also built 4-string flat-top instruments, but these were tenor guitars.

The first real Martin bass, oddly enough, was a solidbody instrument. Introduced in 1979, the single-pickup EB-18 was a partner to Martin's E Series electric guitars. Its scroll-shaped headstock echoed the Stauffer-style pegheads of early Martins, but it was otherwise a modern instrument that at least nodded in the direction of Alembic with its natural-finish laminated-hardwood construction. The EB-28 was added to the line a year later; it had a mahogany body and PJ pickups. Both models were discontinued in 1983.

Martin didn't get back into the bass business until 1989, and this time the approach was more consistent with the company's history: acoustic bass guitars that were big flat-tops with 34"-scale mahogany necks. Designed by Dick Boak, these new ABGs used the same bodies as Martin's Jumbo guitars; measuring 16" wide with a depth of 4⅞", they were large enough to produce decent acoustic volume without being ungainly. The top was solid spruce, the fingerboard was ebony, and the body could be made of either solid Indian rosewood (B-40) or solid flame maple (B-65). For plugged-in playing, a Fishman bridge-pickup system was available. In 1992, two more models were added, the single-cutaway BC-40 and the 5-string B-540.

Although these Martin basses were widely admired, they proved to have limited appeal because of their $2,000-plus list prices. By 1997 they had all been dropped in favor of the B-1, a lower-priced ABG with laminated-mahogany sides. The BM Jumbo, an even less-expensive model in Martin's Road Series, followed; it has laminated-mahogany sides and a solid-mahogany back. The most recent additions are the BC-15, a single-cutaway version with a mahogany top, and the SWB Sting Signature Model, made with woods certified by the Rainforest Alliance's SmartWood program. The SWB's top is made with Sitka spruce reclaimed from pulp logs, the body is solid certified cherry, and the fingerboard is certified katalox. Sting's signature is inlaid between the 18th and 19th frets, and a sticker inside the body states that a portion of the sale price is donated to the Rainforest Foundation International. In addition to these U.S.-made instruments, Martin also markets Sigma ABGs made in Korea.

■ Martin B-540 (top), 1995, and BC-15 acoustic bass guitars.

■ Matt Pulcinella Level 5.

MATT PULCINELLA

When a graphic designer takes up the bass, it won't be long before he begins to design instruments. That's how Pennsylvania's Matt Pulcinella got started. In 1996 he sketched out his ideas for two basses, a 4-string and a 5-string, and built them. He was going to play them for a while himself, but they were purchased by local bassists. So he built two more—and those sold quickly, too. Matt Pulcinella Guitars (MPG) was born.

Pulcinella builds instruments one at a time, working by himself and selling directly to players. His Level 4JJ is a 34"-scale J-style 4-string that can be made with or without a pickguard; it's available in active or passive configurations. A "punchy and growly" 5-string version, also with a 34" scale, debuted in May 2002. The 35"-scale Level 5 and Level 6 basses reflect Matt's original design concept. Their alder or swamp ash bodies have a deep lower cutaway that provides easy access all the way to the 24th fret. Originally conceived as bolt-ons, they can be ordered as neck-through-body instruments. The fingerboards—rosewood, maple, or ebony (on fretless basses)—have distinctive off-center abalone dot inlays. One of Pulcinella's clever ideas is a "semi-fretless" that's fretted in the lower positions (for better intonation of low notes) but fretless above the 5th or 7th fret. MPG basses feature pickups and electronics from EMG, Bartolini, Basslines, Aero, Aguilar, and Demeter. Matt queries his customers extensively about their technique and the music they play to find the right combination of wood, electronics, and hardware for each bass he builds.

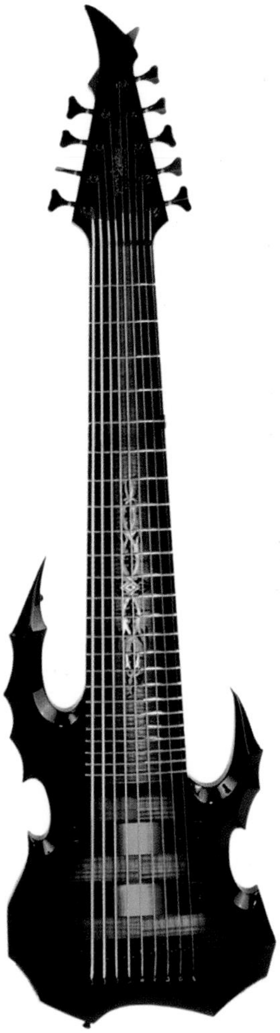

■ Michael Dolan 9-string in figured flame maple, green-to-black sunburst.

MICHAEL DOLAN

After graduating from Sonoma State College with a Fine Arts degree, Michael Dolan worked at Alembic for two years before establishing his own business in 1977. He offers no standard models and builds every bass to order; stylistically, they range from vintage-inspired models to custom creations in "every imaginable configuration . . . including, but not limited to, solidbody, archtop, acoustic, neck-through, bolt-on, set-neck, and headless instruments." Working with two assistants, Dolan produces about 30 instruments a year in his Santa Rosa, California, shop. He also does repair work and makes custom necks and bodies. "What's different about our approach is that you get what you want, rather than what we want to sell you," he says. "It's a unique way to go about this as a business, and as a result we get to produce many exotic and interesting instruments."

■ Mike Lull Modern 4.

MIKE LULL

Mike Lull owes it all to his parents. "In 1967 I was in eighth grade and wanted to learn how to play bass guitar," he recalls. "My parents said, 'No, the bass guitar is a fad. You can learn to play guitar—that's a *real* instrument.' So I got a Harmony guitar and took lessons. I drove my instructor insane making him teach me the bass lines to all the songs he had in his little book. After three months he told my parents, 'Hey, the kid wants to play bass. Get him a bass guitar.' They had that same conversation with him, about it not being a real instrument. He said, 'I've had a bass guitar player in my band since 1953. Where have you guys been?' So they finally said, 'Okay, but you're going to have to buy it yourself.'"

Despite lots of lawn mowing, Mike couldn't come up with the funds. While most of us would have kept working or tried to find a clever way to cajole our parents, Lull had a different idea. "I decided to build a bass in shop class. I traced the outline of the drawing on a Mel Bay bass method book and enlarged it until it was about the right size. It was kind of like the body of a Fender Jazz Bass."

Mike selected a piece of cherry wood, cut it to match his drawing, shaped and sanded it, and had the body. He just needed the rest of the parts. Fortune intervened, in the form of an accident. "A friend of mine had a Kingston bass that his parents had run over with a car. He gave me what was left. The neck and pickup were still good, so I put those onto the body I had made in shop class. It didn't sound very good, but it worked."

Mike admits he didn't know what he was doing. "When I put on the neck, I routed it about an inch-and-half farther back than I should have. And then I said, 'Well, all the pictures show the bridge back *here*, so there you go.' It had a single Harmony-style pickup that I put right in the center between the neck and the bridge. I made my own pickguard from some plastic at shop. I lifted the volume and tone controls and output jack from the Kingston, because I didn't know anything about soldering."

Lull played his shop-class special for two-and-a-half years, until he had saved enough to buy a '66 Jazz Bass. (He passed along the homemade bass to his younger brother, who later gave it to a neighbor.) Mike immediately began to tinker with his new bass, trying to improve the setup and make it easier to play. "At that point I was totally enamored with the idea of working on my own instrument."

While attending high school in Bellevue, Washington, Lull steadily improved his repair skills. Pretty soon his friends were bringing him their instruments for setup and fretwork. This continued after he enrolled at Central Washington State College, where he spent more time playing gigs and doing repairs than going to class. After a year, he quit school to go on the road. "That was in 1972. I was doing more and more repairs—learning how to solder, how to fix electronics, how

■ Mike Lull Vintage 4.

to change tuners. On the road I was doing repairs for the other bands. After a couple years of that, I went back home, got a job in a music store, and did repairs as well as selling."

In 1976 Lull opened his own shop. Word got around about the quality of his work, and over the years his client list expanded to include just about every notable Seattle-area act, from Heart to Soundgarden. For a time he also did a booming business in vintage instruments ("I had a three-bedroom apartment, and two of the bedrooms were filled with guitars and amps"), but he eventually sold most of his collection to support his business.

While working in his shop during the mid '80s, Lull got a shock. "A woman came in and said, 'My son has this bass, and he wants to fix it up.' She opened the case, and there it was: the bass I had built in shop class. I almost had a coronary. I started looking at it, and that was when I discovered all the things I hadn't done right. I took the bass in, said, 'This is on me,' and fixed it up."

Lull continued to expand his repair business while making the occasional custom instrument. In 1995 he got more serious about being a builder and introduced his own line of basses. They reflect both Mike's affection for vintage Fenders and his own high standards for fretwork, electronics, and shielding. "Leo Fender was a genius at ergonomics," he says. "You may not like the sound of the instruments, but you cannot argue with the ergonomics and the function of Fender instruments. They work so well. So we've stayed with that idea and made them even more comfortable by doing things like sculpting the body so you have better access to the upper frets. And we've paid more attention to some of the details, like having better fretwork and stiffer necks with graphite reinforcing rods."

Lull's first bass model was an updated version of the Jazz Bass, dubbed the Modern 4 (M4 for short). It has a "compact" J-style body, like the trimmed-down body of a Sadowsky bass, that's just a bit smaller than the original. It's available in alder or swamp ash, with an optional figured-maple top. (If you like the smaller body but prefer the vintage look of a pickguard and cover plate, that's the Modern 4V.) The M4's bolt-on 21-fret maple neck is topped with a rosewood or maple fingerboard, and the scale length is 34". A pair of Lindy Fralin vintage-style single-coil pickups and a Bartolini preamp are standard; other electronics are available—Mike has offered different pickups and preamps over the years, reflecting his assessment of the best options at the time. For traditionalists, Lull offers the Vintage 4 (V4), which has a full-size Jazz-style body with pickguard and cover plate.

The 24-fret 5-string version of the M4 is called the Modern 5 (M5). Originally offered with a 34" scale length, it became even *more* modern when it stretched to 35" in 1998. An intermediate model, the Custom 535, was available for a short time; when the longer scale length became standard for all Mike Lull 5-strings, the Custom 535 simply became the new version of the Modern 5. (The Post-Modern 5?) For

■ Mike Lull P4.

■ Mike Lull Modern 5V.

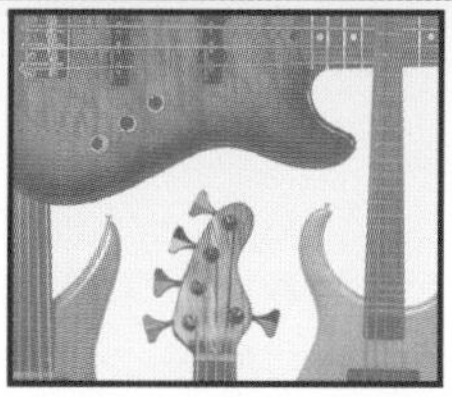

GOOD FRETWORK – THE KEY TO A GREAT BASS

By Mike Lull

If working in the instrument-repair field for more than 25 years has taught me anything, it's that frets are the single most important factor on a bass (unless it's a fretless bass, of course). Without good fretwork, a bass is likely to have fret buzz, feel inconsistent, lack sustain, and may not even play in tune.

The problems I see most often are:

- No glue was used in the fret slots.
- The frets are not the same radius as the fretboard.
- The frets are not seated correctly.
- The fingerboard is not trued correctly.

We take great care in our fretting process, whether we're building a new bass or refretting an old one, and the extra steps help make our customers confident their basses will play the way they expect them to play.

There are several factors that contribute to a good fret job. The fingerboard must be trued with a consistent radius, and each fret arced to the same radius as the fingerboard. The same rule applies to compound-radius fingerboards. This ensures that each fret will be properly seated. We also use glue to make sure the frets will not work their way out of the slots. Many manufacturers don't do this—so we often see basses with "high frets" caused by the frets being pushed up because changes in temperature and humidity have made the wood contract and expand.

■ Mike Lull releveling a fingerboard for a refret job.

Another thing to consider is string tension, which pulls the neck upward and creates "peaks and valleys" in a fingerboard. We always simulate string tension during fretting, so that when our necks are brought up to pitch, they have the proper amount of relief and a small amount of "fall away" at the end of the fingerboard. This allows for very low action with no fret buzz.

Once the neck is fretted, we begin the process of cutting the fret ends, leveling the tops of the frets so they're all the same height, and then going back to crown each fret. How many basses have you seen with flat fret tops? The intonation point of each fret should be dead center. If a fret is flat on top, that fretted note is likely to be ever-so-slightly out of tune. But if the frets are crowned properly, the instrument will play in tune, or as close to it as a fretted instrument can. (That's another subject altogether—just ask Buzz Feiten.)

■ Mike Lull P5.

those who prefer the vintage look, even in a 5-string, Mike offers the Modern 5V, with a 21-fret neck, pickguard, and cover plate.

Lull's most recent creations are the Precision-style P4 and P5. "The P4's neck is a reproduction of a '59 P-Bass," says Mike. "Those are some of the finest necks Fender ever made." He added graphite reinforcement for stability and flattened the fingerboard radius for better action. The full-size body is available in alder or swamp ash. Lindy Fralin custom-winds the standard P-style pickup; other pickups and a PJ configuration are available. The P5 has a custom-wound Seymour Duncan pickup created to give the "1964 sound" to a modern 5-string bass with a 35" scale length.

Lull builds most of his basses to order, so personal preferences such as neck shape, finish, pickup/preamp combination, and setup are always considered. Mike brings a musician's sensibility to the instruments he builds, so it's no surprise that he likes to give his own basses a workout on weekend gigs.

"I can't put it down," Lull says with a smile. "As much a hassle as it might be getting to the gig, when you're onstage and the first note comes out, you think: This is why I do it."

MOBIUS MEGATAR

A Möbius strip is a one-sided surface that was discovered by German mathematician August Möbius in 1858. A Mobius Megatar is a 12-string instrument that was conceived by musician Henri DuPont in 1997 and put into production by a team that included Colonel Reg Thompson (RAF, retired), Bruce Sexauer, and Traktor Topaz. It has six bass and six melody strings; the bass strings can be tuned as a standard 6-string bass (*BEADGC*) or in the inverted-fifths system used on the Stick, for players familiar with that system [see Stick]. The melody strings are usually tuned in fourths.

Unlike the Stick, the Mobius Megatar is modular, with a small body in which a variety of pickups and bridges can be mounted, and a separate neck. It incorporates the Buzz Feiten intonation system, which uses nut and saddle offsets to create a compensated, or "stretch" tuning that sounds better than conventional tuning. Instruments in the TrueTapper series are made of alder and maple; MaxTapper models have a mahogany neck with rosewood fingerboard and a sapele body. The ToneWeaver series features the Ralph Novak fanned-fret system, with scale lengths ranging from 35½" for the lowest string to 31" for the highest [see Novax]. On the MidiTapper model, an optical pickup provides MIDI-interface capabilities. All models are equipped with the patented MegStrap, which holds the instrument in the preferred near-vertical playing position. Whether or not the recent proliferation of two-handed tapping instruments signals the "Touch-Style Revolution" proclaimed by the Mobius Megatar company remains to be seen, but these instruments do open up new creative vistas for some bassists.

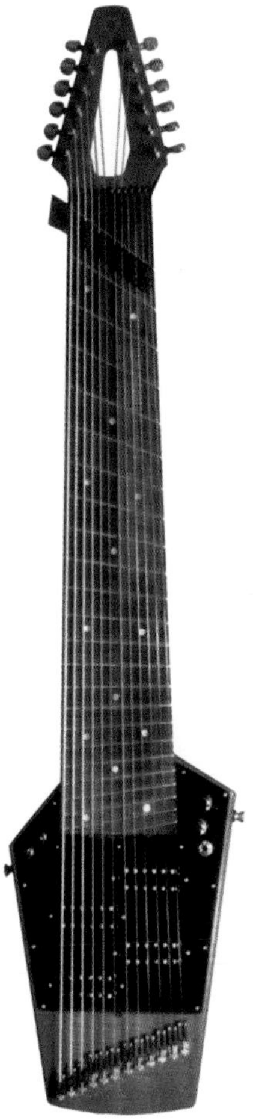

■ Mobius ToneWeaver.

MODULUS

The company now known as Modulus Guitars was founded in 1978 by Geoff Gould as Modulus Graphite. The name reflected Gould's pioneering use of graphite (carbon fiber) to build bass necks. He chose "modulus" because one of the most attractive qualities of carbon fiber is its high modulus of elasticity; that is, it's very stiff for its weight, making it an ideal material for a long, thin structure like a bass neck. A neck made of carbon fiber also has high internal damping, which gives it even response and good sustain. And it's very stable, making it impervious to the climatic changes that can wreak havoc with wooden necks—so stable, in fact, that it requires no trussrod. (Some graphite necks do have a "fine-tuning" rod.) Building a graphite neck in the Modulus manner is a time-consuming process that involves hand-laying sheets of the raw material, a carbon fiber and epoxy resin composite, in a mold and then curing it in an autoclave. It's

■ Modulus Quantum 4.

■ Modulus Flea Bass 4.

expensive—but the musical result is well worth it, at least in the opinion of many Modulus customers.

In the '70s Gould was an engineer at Ford Aerospace—and a fan of the Grateful Dead. "I was at a Dead concert at [San Francisco's] Winterland in October 1974," he says, "and I noticed that Phil Lesh had this thick lamb's-wool strap to hold his bass. I assumed the bass was really heavy. I was working on the Voyager project at the time, and many of the parts we were using were made from composites, to save weight. It seemed to me that you ought to be able to do the same thing with a bass." Gould got in touch with Ron Armstrong and Rick Turner of Alembic, and he showed them samples of the composite used on the space probe. After some deliberation, they collaborated on building a bass with a graphite neck, completing their first prototype in the spring of 1976 [see Alembic]. "Stanley Clarke tried it during the soundcheck before a Return to Forever concert," Gould says. "It was an ideal situation, because he was using an Alembic bass that was virtually the same in every respect except the neck. The difference in sound was striking."

Alembic built a short-scale bass with a graphite neck and presented it at the January 1977 NAMM show. John McVie of Fleetwood Mac bought the bass, and word began to spread about this new way to build an instrument. Turner obtained a design patent, which was assigned to Modulus Graphite. Alembic was Gould's only customer at first, and a handful of Alembic/Modulus basses were made in 1977–78. Over the next few years, Gould began to produce Fender replacement necks and build OEM graphite necks for several customers, including Music Man, as well as offering his own designs under the Modulus Graphite name. The early Modulus line included Fender-style Bassstar 4-strings as well as basses with the distinctive Quantum body shape, in both bolt-on (SPi) and through-body (TBX) configurations. Modulus also built some unusual custom creations, the strangest probably being an 18-string bass (a 6-string tuned *EADGBE* with triple courses) that was ordered by Cheap Trick's Tom Petersson in 1981.

Modulus was one of the first builders to offer a 35" scale length, and the combination of the longer scale with a graphite neck proved to be an effective way to improve the *B*-string sound on 5- and 6-string basses. Early company literature described the sound achieved with the longer scale length as "punchier, more defined, and piano-like," and reviewers agreed: Dan Erlewine's 1992 *Bass Player* review noted the "excellent pitch focus" of the *B* string on a Quantum 5 TBX.

Gould continually reworked the Modulus line throughout the 1980s and early '90s, seeking both to respond to industry trends and to satisfy his own engineering muse. By 1992 the Bassstars were long gone, but the catalog included the new M92, a bolt-on 4- or 5-string that was sort of a high-tech/vintage hybrid. It was equipped with a single EMG-DC 18-volt pickup, an EMG-BTS active circuit, and an alder or poplar body with a multi-layered pickguard. The Prime offered a different look for a single-pickup bass, with a cocobolo fingerboard and a swamp ash body with no pickguard. The Quantum models were still available, in 4-, 5-, and 6-string versions, either bolt-on or through-body. By 1994 Quantum "SweetSpot" basses were available, featuring a

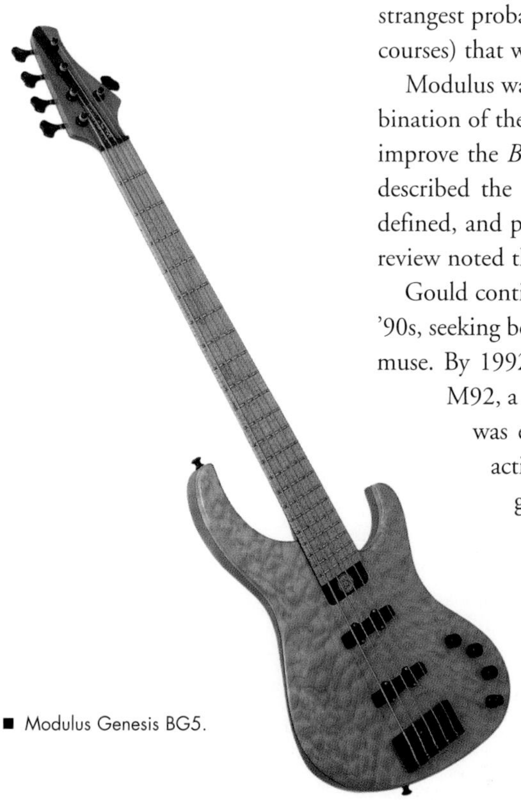

■ Modulus Genesis BG5.

single EMG-DC pickup rather than the usual pair of EMG or Bartolini pickups. Fender-style models re-emerged as the J Series, 4-strings with 34" scales.

In 1995 Gould sold his interest in Modulus Graphite, and the new owner hired Rich Lasner to run the company, which was renamed Modulus Guitars. Lasner had worked previously for Ibanez, Yamaha, and Peavey, and he immediately took steps to improve both production efficiency and the instruments themselves. (Among other things, he introduced a relief-adjustment system to the necks.) The bass line also took on more of a rock & roll look with the debut of the SonicHammer, which had a 34" scale length and a single Bartolini MME 3-coil pickup mounted back on the body, near the bridge. It was, in effect, a high-tech reinterpretation of the Music Man StingRay Bass, so it wasn't surprising that the SonicHammer appealed to Flea of the Red Hot Chili Peppers, one of the most visible StingRay players. When Flea signed on as an endorser in 1996, the SonicHammer morphed into the Flea Bass, complete with flashy metalflake finishes. By 2002, the Flea line included both FB4 and FB5 basses (4- and 5-string, respectively, now equipped with a standard Basslines MM pickup) and FBJ4 and FBJ5 models, with Bartolini J-style pickups.

Even as the Flea Bass was taking shape, Lasner was contemplating another way to use graphite in Modulus instruments. He explains: "I sat down and thought, What do we have? Well, carbon fiber is strong, it sounds good, and it lasts forever. What else is there? Well, wood . . . duh. It sounds incredible, and there are lots of versions of it. I found that by not simply reinforcing a wooden neck but by allowing the wood to do whatever it wanted, I could create a whole new kind of neck."

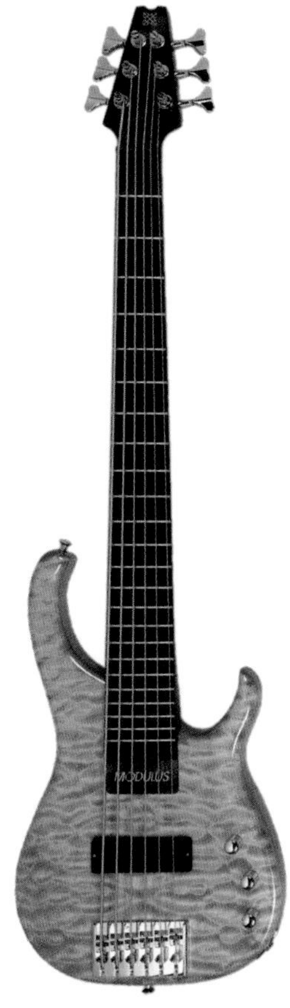

■ Modulus Quantum 6 SweetSpot.

That "whole new kind of neck" became the centerpiece of the Modulus Genesis Basses. Designed in conjunction with Michael Tobias, these instruments have a hybrid design that combines a graphite load-bearing structure with selected tonewoods (certified as "earth-friendly and properly harvested" as much as possible). The graphite is used to create a "spine" that runs from the tip of the peghead, down the neck beneath the fingerboard, and into the neck joint. Because this structure bears the string tension, unusual tonewoods like red cedar can be selected for the neck and body. Genesis Basses are available in 4-string (34" scale, 24 frets) and 5-string (35" scale, 22 frets) models, with Bartolini J-style pickups standard. In 2002 the Modulus line comprised the original Quantum design (in a variety of 4-, 5-, and 6-string models, all with bolt-on necks and a 35" scale), the Flea Bass, the Genesis Bass, and the Fender-style VJ (available with either a Quantum or Genesis neck).

Rich Lasner left Modulus Guitars in March 2002, handing the reins to CFO Chris Hill. If the idea of building basses with carbon-fiber necks seemed outlandish when Geoff Gould proposed it in the '70s, the increasing importance of composites in instrument building—and the large number of companies now using non-wood materials in one way or another—testifies to the growing importance of this innovation.

SEE ALSO: G. GOULD

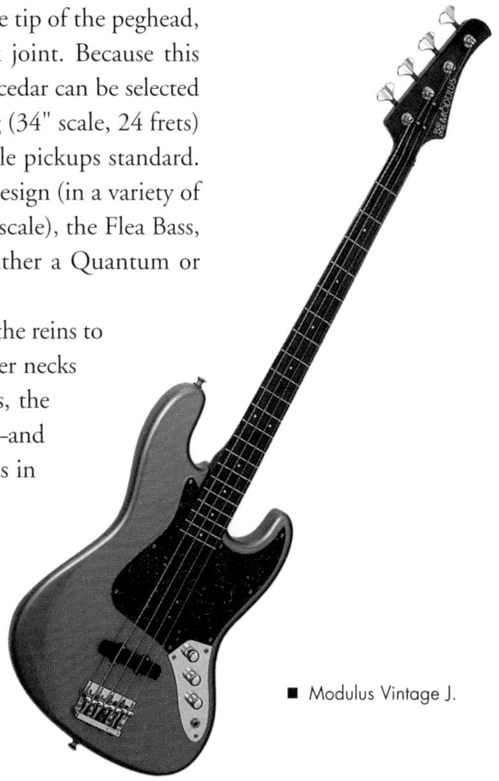

■ Modulus Vintage J.

■ Moonstone Eclipse.

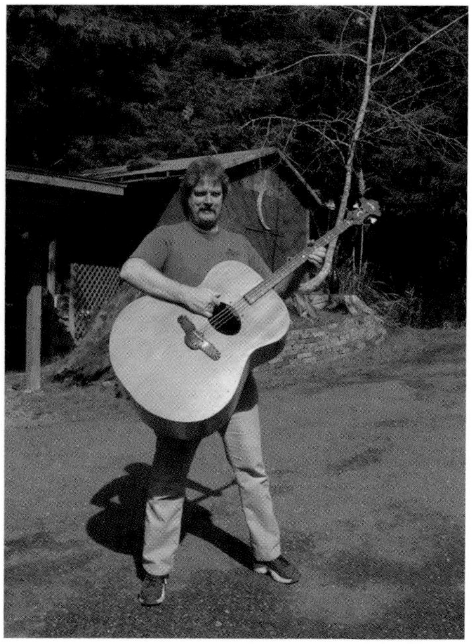

■ Steve Helgeson (right) in 1976 with an early—and very large—Moonstone acoustic bass guitar.

■ These eagle-head carvings were created for a Moonstone custom doubleneck built for Leland Sklar in 1978.

MOONSTONE

Like the legendary phoenix, Moonstone arose from its ashes to fly again. The company was founded in 1972 by Steve Helgeson, whose first lutherie project was an unusual acoustic bass guitar. It had a triangular body, like a balalaika, and a neck scrounged from a Japanese-made Kent bass—but it worked. At the time, Helgeson was living in Humboldt County, California, and studying wildlife management. "I wanted an acoustic bass," he later told Richard Riis Jr. in *Vintage Guitar*, "because I would go to Yosemite and there would be 50 guitar players out in a meadow, and no bass players." Making one instrument whetted Helgeson's appetite for more, and it wasn't long before he had dumped his academic pursuits and set up shop in Moonstone Heights, overlooking the Pacific. In his early years, he made several more acoustic basses, including a birch plywood mando-bass and a mammoth ABG that measured 24" across and was 8½" deep.

Helgeson pioneered the use of exotic woods in solidbody electric instruments, quickly gaining fame for the unique look of his maple-burl basses and guitars. During a 1978 visit to Los Angeles, Steve met Leland Sklar, who asked him to build "something outrageous." The result was a doubleneck bass (the upper neck was a 30"-scale fretless piccolo bass; the lower was a 33½"-scale fretted bass) featuring elaborate eagle-head carvings with red-opal eyes that lit up. Sklar used the Eagle Bass while on tour with Jackson Browne, and photos of it appeared in the liner booklet for Browne's *Running on Empty*. Orders for Moonstone instruments poured in, and Helgeson hired several assistants, including Kenneth Lawrence, to assist him in a larger shop in Arcata, California [see Kenneth Lawrence].

Moonstone's business boomed during the 1980s, as more and more musicians discovered the pleasure of playing a handcrafted custom instrument. The bass line was headed by the double-cutaway Vulcan Bass and the Eclipse Bass, a neck-through model with Bartolini pickups and a graphite-reinforced neck—a revolutionary idea at the time. The Exploder and Flaming-V 4-strings paid tribute to the Gibson Explorer and Flying-V shapes, respectively, and the M-80 Bass was a beautiful semi-hollow neck-through-body instrument with a carved top and back. All were partners to Moonstone guitar models; all had a standard 33½" scale length; all were made from premium woods complemented by high-grade electronics and hardware. And soon after Helgeson met Geoff Gould of Modulus

Graphite, Moonstone began to offer Modulus-made graphite necks on its Vulcan and Eclipse basses.

A distribution deal with Morley further boosted Moonstone's business—and then disaster struck. A 1988 arson fire wiped out much of the production machinery, although the wood supply was spared. Helgeson shut down operations for two years, eventually re-opening on a smaller scale in Eureka, California. Since then, he has gradually expanded his product list, introducing new models such as the neck-through Neptune bass and creating updated versions of the M-80 Bass and the Flaming-V Bass.

In 1995, perhaps recalling those Yosemite jam sessions of yore, Helgeson created the B-95 acoustic bass guitar. It has a 20"-wide body with a single cutaway that can be either Florentine (pointed) or Venetian (rounded) style. A variety of premium woods, including wenge and quilted maple, are available for the body. The top is Engelmann or Sitka spruce, and the fingerboard is made from ebony with oval abalone inlays. The B-95 is available as a 4-string (34" scale) or 5-string (35" scale). "The large body allows the volume of this bass to be heard when accompanied by two or more acoustic guitars without being drowned out," says Helgeson, although a Fishman pickup is available, just in case.

■ Moses Vertical Jump Bass.

MOSES

One night in 1979, unhappy with the sound of his bass guitar, Steve Mosher began to think about the materials he'd been using for boating and aquatic-sports projects. What if he used some of those high-tech composites to make a bass neck?

Eleven years later, Mosher was building and selling his own line of carbon-fiber bass necks. The bulk of his business has been as an OEM neck supplier to other builders, and to musicians who want to install graphite replacement necks on Fender or Music Man basses, but Mosher has also developed several instrument models. The best known is his Vertical Jump Bass, a 35"-scale "hybrid" 5-string that can be played in a vertical or horizontal position. (For upright players, there's a 42"-scale 4-string version, as well as the KP Series of 4-, 5-, and 6-string all-graphite electric uprights.) Moses also builds such custom models as the Key Bass 5, a neck-through-body instrument that doesn't really have a body—just a metal frame that can be quickly removed for travel. (Mosher licensed the concept from Wright Guitar Technology, creators of the SoloEtte body-frame system.) For those looking for something a bit more traditional, there's the Starhawk, a neck-through 5-string with wooden body wings and back.

Mosher has his own patented recipe for constructing one-piece graphite necks, and he says the materials he uses produce a "warmth" not offered by other composites. Moses necks are equipped with trussrods and can be made with either graphite or Diamondwood fingerboards; the latter is a stabilized-wood product that provides more of the feel and sound of a conventional wooden fingerboard without warping or shrinkage problems. "In many ways, our graphite necks are as good as the very finest wood necks that are being made," says Mosher. "There is an advantage to the evenness of the graphite necks we produce . . . and there is also a clarity that is far greater than one would experience with many wood necks."

■ Moses Key Bass 5.

■ Mosrite Ventures bass. This is an unusual example, with two pickups and the company name on the pickguard.

■ Mosrite Joe Maphis Mark X.

MOSRITE

The rags-to-riches-to-rags saga of Semie Moseley and his Mosrite company is outlandish even for the music industry, where weird deals and crazy marketing schemes are the usual order of business. "I left school when I was in the seventh grade, traveling with an evangelistic group and playing guitar with them," Moseley told Tom Wheeler in 1980. "Traveling with the evangelists didn't work out financially, so I decided I needed to get a job. I thought maybe it would be possible for me to make guitars."

With financial help from preacher Ray Boatright, Moseley set out to do just that. In 1953, after doing some design work for Rickenbacker at $1 an hour, he founded Mosrite. (The name was derived from Moseley and Boatright; the correct pronunciation is MOZE-rite.) Semie set up shop in Los Angeles and drew attention to himself by building a triple-neck instrument with guitar, mandolin, and octave guitar (one octave above standard tuning) necks. His big break came in the early '60s, when he sold a guitar to Nokie Edwards of the Ventures—and let's not forget that Edwards was originally the group's bass player, later switching to lead guitar. By 1963 the Ventures were not only using Mosrite guitars and basses exclusively but had set up a deal that made the band Mosrite's worldwide distributors. They even sold Mosrite instruments at their concerts—one of the earliest examples of direct marketing in the music business.

The Ventures models were by far the most successful Mosrite instruments. The body shape, as Semie Moseley freely admitted, was simply the outline of a Fender Stratocaster flipped over, with the longer horn on the bottom. The peghead had three notches sawed into the top, to form an M—and the name of the band was displayed as prominently as that of the manufacturer. The Ventures bass was a short-scale (30¼"), set-neck instrument with a single pickup mounted on a slant at the end of the fingerboard, with the polepiece for the *G* string closest to the last (21st) fret. Like many Mosrite models, it featured a zero fret.

By 1968, when the Ventures deal ended, Mosrite was building about 1,000 instruments a month. In addition to the Ventures models, there were several other lines, each including a short-scale bass. For a short time, a bass player might consider the Joe Maphis Mark X (semi-hollow), the Celebrity CE I or CE II Mark X (double-cutaway, semi-hollow with a deeper body than the Joe Maphis), or the Gospel Guitar Mark X (similar to the Celebrity but apparently "sanctified"). All of these basses were introduced in 1968, and it's uncertain how many were made because Mosrite kept notoriously poor records. Not many, probably. And a year later the company was out of business—for the first time, anyway.

Undaunted, Semie Moseley bought a motor home and went on the road again doing gospel concerts. By 1972 he was back in the guitar business, building V Series instruments that looked an awful lot like the original Ventures models. The line included one- and two-pickup short-scale basses. The born-again Mosrite line also included Celebrity I and II double-cutaway semi-hollow basses and solidbody 300 and 350 Stereo basses. During this period, Mosrite also manufactured some Black Widow basses (double cutaway, semi-hollow) for the Acoustic amplifier company. Not for long, though, as Mosrite went under again in 1974.

After one more tour of the evangelical circuit, Moseley hit paydirt . . . briefly. Operating out of Bakersfield, California, he began to build Ventures model instruments that were shipped to Japan by the owner of Hollywood Music. The Japanese were crazy for the Ventures (still are), and there was strong demand for real Mosrite instruments. Actually, there was strong demand for fake Mosrite instruments as well, and copies of Ventures guitars and basses are still a staple of the Japanese market.

Semie Moseley continued to make instruments in several locations during the '80s and early '90s, but he was plagued by a series of misfortunes including a factory fire, serious injuries suffered in a traffic accident, and cancer. After his death in 1992, his widow continued to operate the company for two more years. Copies of Mosrite instruments, including Ventures model basses, are still being produced in the Far East, many of them exact (though unauthorized) replicas of the original instruments.

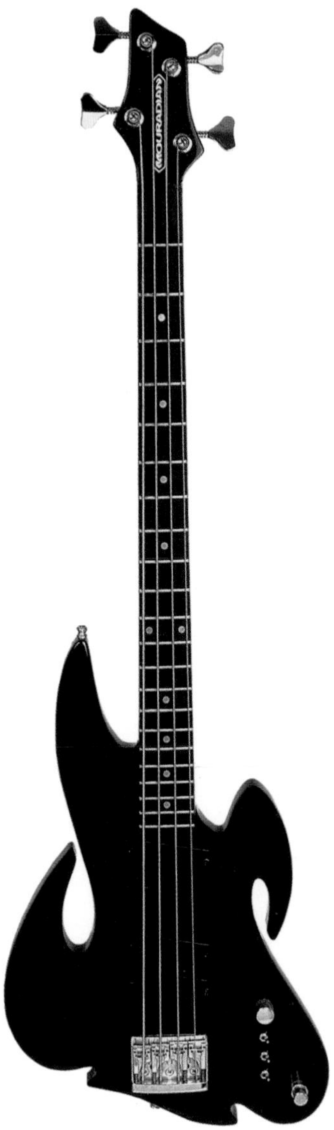

■ Mouradian CS-74.

MOURADIAN

Like many of the musicians of his generation, Jim Mouradian picked up an electric instrument—a Danelectro Short Horn Bass, in his case—after seeing the Beatles on the *Ed Sullivan Show*. But it was his affinity for Yes that launched his career as a builder. "I had played in bands around New England during my teens," says Mouradian, "but after college I went into the family oriental-rug business. Then, in 1972, a buddy turned me on to Yes. They changed my life. Here was a band with all the majesty and power of the great classical music I grew up with, but playing it with electric instruments." Convinced he should do something to express his appreciation, Mouradian created a rug with the Yes logo and presented it to the band. They liked it so much that they brought him in to make more rugs for use onstage during the Relayer tour. "Then, at dinner one night, I showed Chris Squire a drawing of a bass I had designed," says Jim. "He said, 'Great! Build me one, make it green, and put my initials on it.'"

Mouradian had never made an instrument from scratch before, but he spent the next three months creating what would be the first CS-74 bass, which Squire enthusiastically accepted. A 21-fret neck-through-body 4-string, it had swooping body wings inspired by Squire's initials, custom Joe Barden pickups, and onboard EQ. Mouradian went into limited production of the CS-74, perfecting the components and incorporating a "double expanding" trussrod for which he received a patent. He found his repair work more satisfying, though, and stopped building basses in 1986.

"Ten years and many experiences later," he says, "I had a bass design pop into my head during Sunday dinner. I drew it out right then and there and called it the Reality, because I had learned that less is really more." The Reality is sort of a "super vintage" bass, with a stylish double-cutaway alder body, maple neck attached with six bolts, 21-fret rosewood or maple fingerboard, strings-through-body bridge, 34" scale length, and EMG P4 and 35J pickups. Jim also updated the CS-74, adding another fret and making EMG pickups standard. Various options are available for both Mouradian basses, including 5-string, fretless, exotic woods, and different electronics.

■ Mouradian Reality.

MTD (MICHAEL TOBIAS DESIGN)

Michael Tobias never intended to become a bassmaker. "I'm a guitar player," he explains. "I started building acoustic guitars in Washington, D.C., in 1973, when I was working at a place called the Guitar Shop. I was mostly interested in archtops and concert-quality classical guitars."

■ The first Tobias Signature bass, built in 1980.

In 1978, Tobias moved to Orlando, Florida, where he opened a guitar repair shop. Between fret jobs, he built acoustic guitars. "And then one of my customers decided that if I could build acoustic guitars, I could make him an electric bass. He was a little guy, and he had always wanted a bass with a little neck, like a broomstick. So I built one, not really knowing what I was doing. It had a set-in maple neck that was 1½" wide at the nut and 2" wide at the last fret. The fingerboard was ebony, and the body had a flamed, highly figured koa top. [Luthier] Michael Gurian had sent me a chunk of figured koa that was 14" wide, 2" thick, and 22" long. I took it to a local mill, because I didn't have a surface planer, and I told them I wanted to plane it down to 1¾". The idiot who ran the planer said, 'No problem.' He set the planer at 1¾" and fed that piece of koa through all at once. It just exploded."

Tobias was able to salvage enough wood to build a bass that had a 1"-thick koa top joined to a two-piece koa back. "In the top," he says, "I carved a horn of plenty, running from the treble-side cutaway down between the pickups and out around the bridge." But when Mike mounted standard P- and J-style pickups, he realized he had a problem. Because the string spacing was so narrow, the strings did not align properly with the polepieces. Consequently, the inner strings (*A* and *D*) overwhelmed the outer strings. A call to Bill Bartolini solved the problem. Bill custom-built P- and J-style pickups that looked proportionally correct and fit the spacing. A bridge from Stars Guitars (a San Francisco custom guitar shop) was the last piece of the puzzle.

"Strangely enough, the guy didn't like it," Tobias says. "I had made exactly what he asked for, but he said it didn't feel enough like a Fender!" After that Mike built three more 4-strings, including a "dragon bass" ordered by the bassist for Root Boy Slim & the Sex Change Band. Then in 1980 he made "something that people who know me would recognize." The neck-through-body 4-string set the pattern for Tobias basses to come. "It's essentially the first Tobias Signature bass. It has a maple, mahogany, and koa neck, with visible graphite stringers that run the entire length of the neck-through. The fingerboard is ebony with a graphite underlay, and the body wings are koa. Bill Bartolini did the pickups, and the electronics came from Stars Guitars. The oil finish was a mixture of three chemicals. It was an alchemist's nightmare but it's held up really well. I built that bass for a customer who used it until 1989, when he decided he wanted a 5-string and traded it in. I've still got it, and it's still a pretty cool bass. I pull it out every now and then."

■ MTD 535.

■ MTD 435, maple burl.

Tobias headed west in 1980, stopping in San Francisco for a few months before settling in Southern California. By 1984 he had abandoned guitars to focus on basses. ("I never could sell guitars. People would come in, say, 'What a cool bass,' and buy the bass.") His reputation for building basses that played and sounded as great as they looked spread quickly, and by 1988 his small Hollywood shop was hopelessly backordered. Faced with the prospect of expanding to a size he was not comfortable with, Mike sold Tobias Guitars to Gibson in 1990. The operation was moved to Nashville in 1992, with Mike functioning as a consultant until the end of 1994.

After moving to Kingston, New York, Tobias began to hand-build basses that were initially sold under the Eclipse name; about 50 Eclipse basses were built before the name was changed to MTD (Michael Tobias Design). The MTD line includes 4-, 5-, and 6-string electric basses, all with 35" scale lengths, as well as acoustic bass guitars. Working with one part-time assistant, Mike makes about 130 basses a year. He also has done design work for several other companies, including Modulus (the Genesis bass), Brian Moore, Lakland, and Alvarez. Tobias-designed basses made in Czechoslovakia are sold under the Grendel name, and in 2001 MTD introduced the Kingston series, manufactured in Korea.

SEE ALSO: TOBIAS

MUDGE

Bill Mudge is one member of the ever-growing corps of bassists who have become luthiers simply because of their love for the instrument. He started building basses in 1997 and has produced about ten a year since then, making them only for "special" people. Most of his instruments are 4-strings with mahogany bodies, exotic-wood tops, EMG pickups, and satin-polyurethane finishes. "I'm not crazy about making 5-string basses," says Mudge, "but I will make you one if I like you."

■ Mudge Robert Jacob bass.

MUSIC MAN

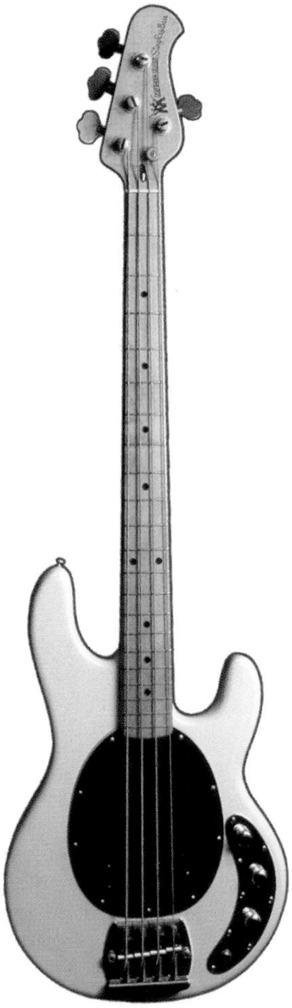

■ 1979 Music Man StingRay Bass.

In 1971 Leo Fender was restless after six years of relative inactivity since selling his company to CBS. Along with his former general manager, Forrest White, he began to hatch plans for a new music-products company called Musitek. After they were joined by Tom Walker, another former Fender executive, Leo decided to call the company Music Man. He had to keep a low profile until 1975—when his non-compete agreement with CBS expired—but customers soon figured out who the "music man" really was.

The company's first product offerings were amplifiers, but it wasn't long before Leo was drawing up a new line of instruments. Always eager to improve on his old designs, he came up with a new single-pickup 4-string called the StingRay Bass. Its 3+1 headstock was White's idea, but Leo was responsible for the rest of the innovations, including the powerful pickup with eight large polepieces, the massive bridge, and the active electronics. The rest of the ingredients were traditional—ash or alder body, bolt-on maple neck, maple or rosewood fingerboard—but the sound was revolutionary.

The StingRay, introduced in 1976, was an immediate hit. In typical Leo Fender fashion an "improved" model, the two-pickup Sabre, came out two years later. It never approached the StingRay's popularity and eventually became something of a guitar-show curiosity. Much more important (although largely overlooked at the time) was the Cutlass, which had a graphite neck made by Modulus. There were single-pickup Cutlass I and two-pickup Cutlass II models, but production lasted only about a year.

Disagreements among the founders drove Leo Fender to leave Music Man in 1979. He started over once more at G&L, where he worked until his death in 1991. Music Man was sold to Ernie Ball in 1984, and production of StingRay basses has continued to the present day.

SEE ALSO: ERNIE BALL MUSIC MAN

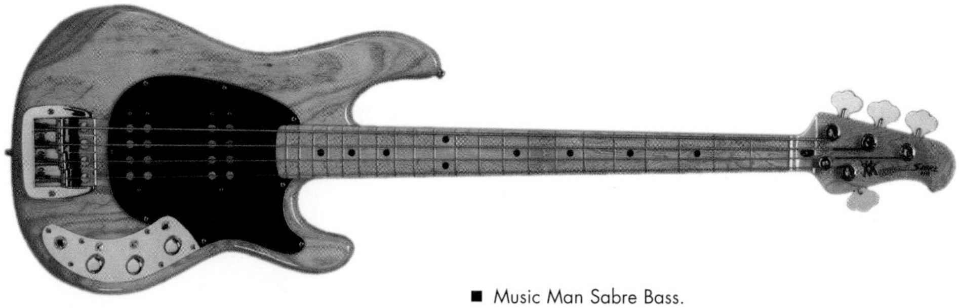

■ Music Man Sabre Bass.

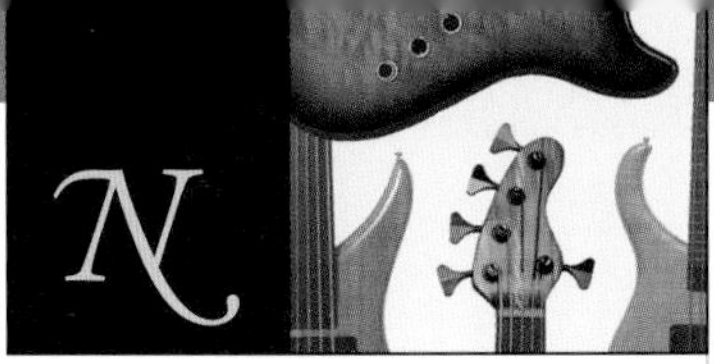

NATIONAL/DOBRO

Before electric amplification was acknowledged as the right way to solve the volume problem, designers applied various mechanical amplification systems to stringed instruments. Early in the 20th century, a German inventor named Augustus Stroh created a solidbody upright bass with a bridge that rested on a flexible diaphragm. A large horn, similar to the ones on early Victrola record players, was attached to the bridge; the horn amplified the sound coming from the bridge. Another approach surfaced in the 1920s, when the resonator guitar was invented. These instruments have one or more spun-metal cones housed in a metal or wood guitar body; the cones amplify the sound of the plucked or strummed strings. They tend to be sort of harsh, although they have a certain twangy charm—especially for the blues.

The first resonator guitars were built by the National Stringed Instrument Company of Los Angeles, founded in 1926 by John Dopyera and George Beauchamp—both of whom took credit for the idea. (Whether the resonator guitar was his idea or not, Beauchamp was a true crusader for amplification. He later invented the Rickenbacker Electro Bass-Viol, one of the first electric uprights; see Rickenbacker.) Less than three years after the company was founded, Dopyera left National to launch another company, Dobro, whose name become synonymous with the resonator instruments it built. A 1935 merger brought the two companies together as National-Dobro.

The most notable resophonic experiment, from the low-end perspective, was the massive Dobro stand-up bass of the 1930s. In *American Guitars*, Tom Wheeler described this as "a huge, guitar-shaped contraption with three circular soundholes on each upper bout and a resonator as big as a manhole cover." It was probably created as a publicity stunt, and it's doubtful that many were made.

The idea of building a resophonic bass lay dormant for more than 60 years, until the Original Musical Instrument Company (OMI), a resurrected version of Dobro acquired by Gibson in 1993, introduced its Dobro basses in 1995. These 34"-scale instruments were built like regular Dobros, with 3¼"-deep maple bodies and three-ply maple tops. They were available with either *f*-hole bodies (F Bass) or in the "classic" Dobro style with screen holes (D Bass). For plugged-in playing—pretty much essential with an acoustic bass guitar this small—there was an optional McIntyre bridge transducer. Fretless and 5-string versions were also offered. They were around for only a couple of years, although Korean-made copies were still on the market in 2002.

During World War II, National evolved into a new company called Valco, which made a wide range of instruments and amps. In 1961 Valco introduced a line of National electric guitars with molded bodies made of "Res-O-Glas," a mixture of polyester resin and fiberglass. (At the time, Ned Steinberger was 13 years old.) Some of these instruments had so-called "map-shaped" bodies that looked vaguely like an outline of the contiguous United States. The Valco line included one of the weirdest short-scale basses ever made, the Val-Pro 85 (later called the National 85). It had two pickups—one mounted *on* the bridge—and a scale length of 25". Vintage enthusiast Willie Moseley commented in *Bass Player*: "It appears that the company simply installed different tuners, nuts, bridges, and tailpieces on the same bodies and necks used for its guitars." Valco also offered some wood-body basses, including one known simply as the National Electric Bass (also with a 25" scale) and the semi-hollow National N-850 with its "modernistic" soundholes.

■ 1965 National 85.

■ OMI Dobro F Bass (left) and D Bass.

■ National Reso-phonic WB Bass, fretless.

Valco merged with Kay in 1967 and went bankrupt a year later. The National brand name was slapped on imported instruments in the 1970s, and in 1988 a new company called National Reso-phonic Guitars set up shop in California. In 2002 the new National introduced a line of single-resonator bass guitars, all with maple necks and 32" scale length. The WB Bass and the single-cutaway RTB Bass have maple bodies; the body of the Style "N" Bass is made of nickel-plated brass. They are available fretted or fretless, and a Highlander piezo pickup is optional. Resonator basses are also being made by builders such as Mark Taylor of Crafters of Tennessee, and some bluegrass players have found them a good-sounding (and more portable) alternative to the upright.

NEW YORK BASS WORKS

David Segal, the sole proprietor of New York Bass Works, is a professional bassist first and a professional bass builder second. Segal's playing career began in 1973, when he bought a new P-Bass and practiced until he had blisters on his fingers. He was soon gigging in Fort Lauderdale, Florida, where he met another up-and-coming bass player named Jaco Pastorius. Hearing Jaco in 1975, says Segal, "was the single paradigm that changed my approach to bass playing and the tonal possibilities of the instrument." So it's not surprising that when Segal launched New York Bass Works some 20 years later, his flagship instrument was a fretless bass he calls the Deep Jazz. It's not a Jazz Bass copy, though—Segal's Deep Jazz represents the evolution of the Jaco sound into the modern bass era: it's a 6-string with a 35½" scale length and a pair of custom J-style pickups mounted close together in the center of the alder body, in the harmonic "sweet spot." It's also available with a semi-hollow body, for a more acoustic-like sound.

Segal builds instruments in two other configurations. Studio Series basses are "updated vintage" models offered as a 21-fret, 34"-scale 4-string and a 22-fret, 35"-scale 5-string. Concert Series 5- and 6-string basses have a more contemporary look and are available with a scale length of 35", 35½", or 36". All New York Bass Works instruments have graphite-reinforced bolt-on maple necks. Bodies are made from alder, swamp ash, mahogany, or walnut; customers can select from many types of exotic wood for the tops, including zebrawood and quilted mahogany. Fingerboards are rosewood (Madagascar, East Indian, or Brazilian), bird's-eye maple, or ebony. Segal builds to order, so many custom options are available. "I've learned over the years that the 'perfect sound,' whether it's traditional or modern, varies from one player to the next," he says. "Listening to my customers and understanding what they're trying to achieve is the key to building them the perfect instrument."

■ New York Bass Works Deep Jazz 6-string (above) and Concert Series 5-string (right).

NOVAX

Ralph Novak is the inventor of the multiple-scale fretboard system (U.S. patent 4,852,450), better known as "fanned frets." In this system, the scale length of a string gets longer as it gets lower in pitch, as on a grand piano. Novak states that this yields stronger, clearer tone from each string; he has backed this assertion with considerable research into the properties of vibrating strings and has received the endorsement of notable musicians and music journalists. The fanned-fret system is particularly effective on 5- and 6-string basses, as demonstrated by the instruments built by Sheldon Dingwall and Novak himself. On the Dingwall Voodoo, a fanned-fret 5-string, the string length starts at 37" for the *B* string and steps down to 34" for the *G*; Scott Malandrone, reviewing it in *Bass Player*, praised the "amazing depth and clarity" of its *B* string and named it one of the ten most important gear ideas of the 1990s [see Dingwall].

Novak worked as a repair technician and built conventional parallel-fret basses and guitars before he invented the fanned-fret system. His dissatisfaction with the sound of many of the instruments he worked on led him to look into scale length's effect on tone. The more he studied it, the more convinced he became that it was the single most important factor. "Scale length comes first because the harmonic content of the final tone produced by the instrument begins with the string," he explains. "Structure and materials act only as 'filters' to tone—they can't add anything, they only modify output."

Since 1993 Novak has custom-built instruments using his fanned-fret system. His initial offerings included Tribute basses, with P- or J-style bodies and bolt-on necks, including some made by Moses Graphite. He also made the Mo'B bass, an original design available as a 4-, 5-, or 6-string, as well as one-of-a-kind instruments in a variety of configurations. His best-known creation is probably the Charlie Hunter 8-string guitar, which has five guitar strings (*ADGBE*) and three bass strings (*EAD*). In 2002 Novak announced production of a retrofittable fanned-fret neck for Fender Precision and Jazz basses; the scale length ranges from 35" for the *E* string to 33½" for the *G*. The neck also works for *BEAD* tuning. A new Novax production bass using this neck is on the drawing board, as is an updated version of the Mo'B. While fanned-fret basses have gained only limited acceptance so far, with increased production from Novax and licensees like Dingwall, these instruments are likely to become more common.

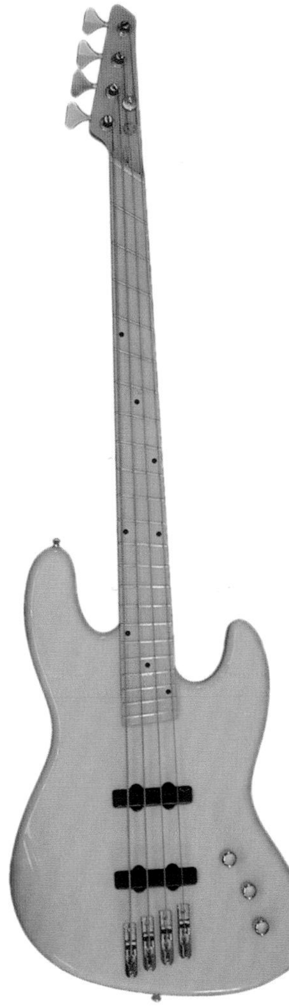

■ Novax Tribute, J-style.

■ Novax Mo'B 5-string.

■ Ned and his friend Billy Thomas with a 1977 version of his headless bass.

NS DESIGN

Ned Steinberger is unique. He didn't become an instrument builder because he was a musician—in fact, he admits he has no musical talent. He didn't learn about basses by doing repair work or serving as an apprentice. And he was not driven by the "romantic notion" (as Roger Sadowsky put it) that if he learned to build guitars and basses he could become self-supporting; for Ned, starting a company to produce instruments was something he did with great reluctance.

Ned Steinberger is a designer. "My design career started when I was 13," he explains. "I had a little shop in the basement. My father had some hand tools, and he helped me get a table saw. I was interested in making things, and I always designed the stuff. If I wanted to make a chair or a table, I would sit down and figure it out."

After graduating from art school, Steinberger worked as a cabinetmaker in Brooklyn. "In the mid '70s I was involved with someone who went out of business," he says, "and the equipment had to be sold. Some guys from the Brooklyn Woodworking Co-op showed up, and I got to talking with them. I realized that this was where I wanted to be—I would be able to work as a cabinetmaker and develop my design ideas."

Steinberger soon became friends with co-op member Stuart Spector. Curious about Spector's work, Ned began to investigate solidbody instrument construction. He then volunteered to design a bass—which became the influential Spector NS (for Ned Steinberger). While relatively conventional in appearance, the NS was radical in design. It was built by attaching both body *and* peghead "wings" to a neck blank that ran the instrument's full length, greatly simplifying construction. And the body was curved to make it more comfortable to play. It was quickly acclaimed a great bass [see Spector].

■ Bolin NS Design Bass 4.

Ned saw room for improvement, though. "Everybody seemed to accept that bass guitars were neck heavy, but I wanted to optimize the product." He improved the NS's balance by adding body weights, an inelegant solution. And then it hit him: "One day I thought, Wait a minute—what am I doing? Why don't I put the tuners on the body? Then it will balance the way I want it to balance."

That epiphany led to the birth of the Steinberger headless bass, which Ned first drew up in 1977. The headless concept had been floating around for a while—Fender's Gene Fields had built a headless prototype in 1975—but Ned's concept was more radical than anything ever tried before. "I had this idea that I was going to make a lightweight wooden structure, kind of like a bow, that would pump vibration back into the strings. That was a complete disaster. It sounded as wimpy as you can get."

After more thought, Ned tried again. "I had this heavy workbench, so I clamped that sucker down to the bench—and it took off. It sounded big, bright, deep; it had sustain. It was everything I wanted. I did another experiment where I added a lot of weight to the bass. That also improved the tone, but it was the rigidity that really put it over the top, so I covered the whole thing with a stiffening layer of fiberglass."

Fiberglass made the bass heavy, so Steinberger considered other materials. Graphite looked promising, but it was a new technology fraught with difficulties. Eventually he was able to mold a one-piece graphite/epoxy resin instrument that was lightweight and rigid, with impressive sonic clarity. Its rectangular shape was unusual but made perfect design sense: Steinberger had reduced the bass guitar to its essence. He figured it would be easy to sell his idea to a big instrument company and move on to other projects. Wrong.

"The music business people didn't get it at all," says Ned. Some musicians did, though. Encouraged by positive feedback from such players as Stanley Clarke and Tony Levin, Steinberger began to look for other ways to get his basses on the market. Steinberger Sound was founded in 1979, and by 1985 it was producing more than 200 instruments a month at a Newburgh, New York, factory. Gibson acquired the company in 1986. U.S. production later moved to Nashville and was shut down in 1998.

Ned Steinberger now operates NS Design, which is renowned for its NS Double Bass, available in both a handmade U.S. model and a less expensive Czech-made version. He continues to design innovative music products, including a new electric bass guitar being built by John Bolin of Boise, Idaho. This single-cutaway instrument, available as either a 4-string (34" scale) or 5-string (35" scale), has an alder body with a carved flame- or quilted-maple top and a bolt-on maple neck with a 24-fret (or fretless) ebony fingerboard. Its slotted headstock is reminiscent of the NS Double Bass; in typical Steinberger fashion, this not only looks good but is a functional improvement, reducing weight and making it easier to access the trussrod adjuster. The fold-away strap arm, another clever Steinberger touch, improves balance when you're playing while standing. The Bolin's electronics include an 18-volt onboard preamp with midrange frequency and gain controls, one or two EMG dual-coil pickups, and a Hipshot bridge with optional Fishman piezo transducers, one for each string. Sperzel locking tuners and a graphite nut are the final touches. The total package is elegant in both form and function—just what you'd expect in a Ned Steinberger design.

SEE ALSO: STEINBERGER

■ Bolin NS Design Bass 5.

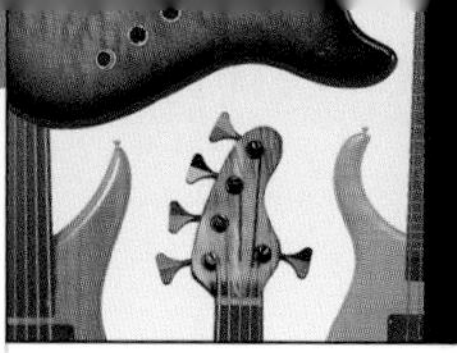

OVATION

■ Ovation Elite 5.

■ 1971 Ovation Typhoon V.

While Ovation is best known for its pioneering use of synthetics in building acoustic guitars—including acoustic/electric basses—it was also ahead of the market with such ideas as fretless fingerboards and graphite-reinforced necks. Ovation was founded by Charles Kaman, a guitar player who happened to own a large firm that manufactured helicopter rotor blades made from a sophisticated synthetic material. In 1964 Kaman decided to see if he could apply the kind of scientific testing he used in his aeronautical business to building a better guitar. After extensive experimentation, his engineers developed an instrument with a one-piece roundback (or bowlback) body made from "Lyrachord," a fiberglass composite similar to the material used for the rotor blades. After a limited production run at Kaman's headquarters in Bloomfield, Connecticut, an Ovation guitar factory was established in New Hartford, Connecticut.

Although Ovation has produced roundback guitars since 1967, roundback basses did not enter the line until 1990, with the introduction of the Elite Bass (B768). This 34"-scale instrument has a deep-bowl Lyrachord body and a spruce top with multiple "sound ports" rather than a single soundhole. The neck is bolted to the body and features the "Kaman bar" system designed by Bill Kaman, Charles Kaman's son and his successor as president of Kaman Music. An aluminum bar surrounds the trussrod, bearing most of the string-tension stress and making the instrument more roadworthy and resistant to climatic changes. The combination of a synthetic body and a reinforced neck makes this Ovation ABG sturdier than many solidbody 4-strings. For amplification, there are individual piezoelectric crystals in the bridge saddles connected to an onboard preamp with 3-band EQ. Ovation introduced a 5-string version in 1994 but dropped it four years later. Ovation has also offered acoustic/electric basses in its Viper series (EAB68, with an "acoustically carved" mahogany body) and Korean-made Celebrity series.

The solidbody and semi-hollow instruments built early in Ovation's history are less renowned, but they included several forward-looking bass models. The double-cutaway, semi-hollow Typhoon I (one pickup) and Typhoon II (two pickups) basses were made from 1968 to 1972. Ovation also offered fretless versions—the Typhoon III (1969) and IV (1970–72)—and this was several years before Jaco Pastorius kicked off the fretless frenzy with his 1976 solo album. That innovation wasn't enough to assure the success of the model, apparently, and the series blew itself out with the Typhoon V (1971–72).

Even more interesting was the solidbody Magnum Bass, with its weird off-center body and radical electronics. Introduced in 1974, the Magnum models offered such unusual features as a humbucking pickup with separate volume controls for each polepiece and an onboard 3-band equalizer. Not as obvious, but more important, was the incorporation of graphite reinforcing strips in the neck—common practice today, but unheard of in 1978 when Ovation's James Rickard patented the concept. "Ovation used his approach on the Magnum Bass and the Deacon 12-string guitar," says Geoff Gould. "It's still the most intelligent use of graphite and wood together that I know of." Strong words from the man who founded Modulus Graphite and has pioneered many graphite-and-wood combinations himself [see Modulus and G. Gould].

Intelligent or not, the Magnum was a goner by 1982. Kaman Music later re-entered the solidbody bass market after purchasing Hamer Guitars in 1988 [see Hamer], but the legacy of the Ovation Magnum lives on in every graphite-reinforced bass neck now on the market.

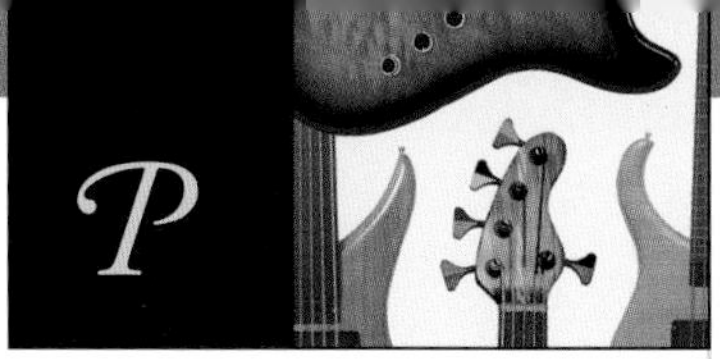

PARKER

Ken Parker created a buzz when he introduced his Fly guitar in 1992. A radical new design, the Fly was made from lightweight woods like cedar and spruce, with structural strength provided by a composite "exoskeleton"—sort of like the thin candy shell on an M&M. It was unlike anything on the market, although Ken was quick to point out that the concept was actually an old one, dating back to medieval lutes built from softwoods reinforced with thin hardwood veneers. He got the idea, he said, while searching for ways to build a stronger instrument after Anthony Jackson had approached him about making a 6-string bass.

In 1992 Parker created a prototype Fly Bass 5-string using the same materials and construction techniques as his Fly guitars. (In 1989 he had built a similar custom 5-string, tuned *EADGC*, for jazz bassist Steve Swallow.) The bass prototype was equipped with both a magnetic pickup and a Fishman piezo bridge, and it weighed only about five pounds. At the time, it was slated to go into production within a year, but the project was shelved because of financial and manufacturing considerations.

Ten years later, at the January 2002 NAMM show, Parker finally unveiled a production Fly Bass in 4- and 5-string models. The original concept had been modified: the body shape was altered, and a different construction method was used—the new Fly's mahogany neck is reinforced by woven-carbon cloth on the back. It has a composite fingerboard with 24 stainless-steel frets. The neck is glued to a laminated Sitka spruce body with a quilted-maple top and back. Parker retained the magnetic/piezo combination, with two DiMarzio Ultra-Jazz pickups, a Fishman piezo bridge, and a Fishman onboard preamp/mixer. Scale length is 34" for both models. While heavier than the '93 prototype (it weighs about seven pounds), the new Parker bass is still a flyweight, and it displays the admirable playability and unique tone qualities that made the prototype so stunning.

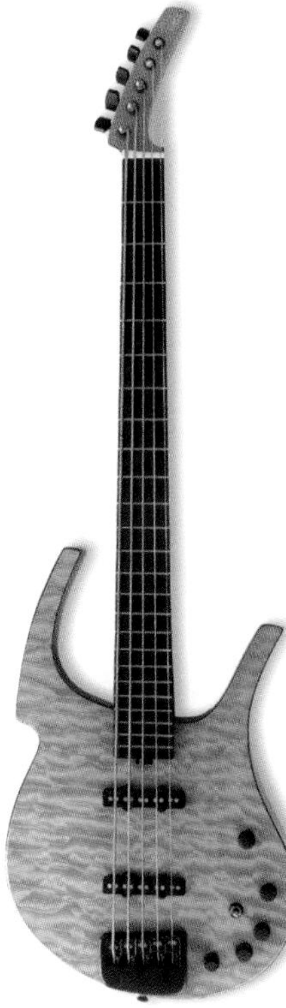

■ Parker Fly Bass 5-string.

PEAVEY

Hartley Peavey didn't intend to become an instrument maker. When he founded his company in 1965, he just wanted to make amps. But he soon found out that he had to build basses and guitars, too, if he wanted to compete—and Hartley loves to compete. He explained the situation in a 1994 *Bass Player* interview:

> Back in the mid '70s our amplifiers had gotten very popular, and some of the so-called big-name companies were coming in and telling their dealers, "Now look, if you want to buy our guitars, you're going to have to buy our amps, too." I said, "Well, if these turkeys are gonna do *that*, I'll fight fire with fire. I'll get into the guitar business."
>
> But I wasn't going to do it by using their methods, which were outdated. Frankly, making a guitar by slapping a Masonite pattern on a neck blank, sawing it out with a bandsaw, and then sanding the back with a belt sander—that's crazy. I know a little about guns, and I've always been impressed by the way a rifle stock fits the metal. You can't even take a sheet of paper and slide it between the metal and the wood. So I said, "Boy, if we could do it like that, it would eliminate all of these people sanding and fitting the joints. If we could make a guitar neck that precise, we could build it for a fraction of

■ Peavey T-40.

■ Peavey Foundation.

■ Peavey Fury Bass.

> what it costs to have all these people correcting sloppy work. And instead of using a bandsaw to cut out a body and then coming back with a router to do all the cutouts, if we used a computer-controlled router/profiler, we could carve it all at once.
>
> So we did a design program, working with a guy named Chip Todd, who is a mechanical genius. We started this thing with an open mind. What's the best way to build a guitar? Forget what this company's doing and what that company's doing. What's the best way to build a guitar? We went over to Germany and found a copy lathe that could make four necks at once—and they came out very close to the final shape. We did a little sanding, put the frets in, and the neck was finished. And everybody said, "Oh, you can't make guitars with computers that way. Peavey's crazy."

In 1978 Peavey Electronics rolled out its first bass, the T-40, a partner to the T-60 guitar introduced at the same time. It had a double-cutaway ash body, a bolt-on maple neck, and a pair of Peavey dual-coil pickups. The "bi-laminated" two-piece neck was made in a process that installed the trussrod before shaping, to keep it from warping. The tone circuitry was unique (and patented). Manufactured with computer-controlled machinery originally designed for building aircraft, it was made far more precisely than other production basses of its era—just as Hartley had intended. While it did not spawn many imitators, as an instrument, it did signal the dawn of a new era in American instrument production. Today many companies have adopted Hartley Peavey's "crazy" idea, using computer-controlled machinery to make basses.

In Leo's Footsteps

Hartley has often said that Leo Fender is his idol, and in operating Peavey Electronics he has tried to emulate Leo's tireless pursuit of better instruments and more efficient manufacturing processes. This has led to an amazing profusion of products—no other musical-instrument manufacturer has made as many products at as many price points, from guitar straps to recording-studio consoles, as Peavey. And the vast majority of them have been built, from the bottom up, in the Peavey factories in Meridian, Mississippi. (In recent years Peavey has begun to use some offshore manufacturing facilities, a move that Hartley resisted for many years.)

Peavey has come close to offering something for every musician at every level, from beginner to seasoned professional. And all have been sold, according to Hartley's philosophy, at a "fair and reasonable price." Product development has proceeded at an often feverish pace, and there has been a tremendous amount of product churn, with new or updated models rapidly replacing older ones. Since the 1978 introduction of the T-40, Peavey has offered more than 20 other bass guitar models, most of them available in an array of configurations (4-, 5-, and sometimes 6-string; fretless; left-handed; pickup and hardware options; many different woods and finishes). While this has meant that Peavey always has an up-to-date choice for a bassist shopping for a new instrument, at times it's also made it hard to know what's what. One lesson Hartley might have learned from his idol is that sometimes you can change almost everything about an instrument while still retaining its familiar (and beloved) name: the Fender Precision Bass is a perfect example.

While there may be no Peavey equivalent to the Precision, the Foundation came close. Introduced in 1983, it remained in the Peavey catalog for almost 20 years. The Foundation was designed by Mike Powers, who's had a hand in designing every Peavey bass since he came to the company in 1981, and he was still at in 2002, as this book was being written. In its original configuration the Foundation had a J-Bass flavor, with a slim 21-fret maple neck (1½" at the nut) bolted to a double-cutaway maple or ash body sporting a pair of single-coil pickups controlled by two pickup-volume knobs and a single master tone. The Foundation Custom, with a phenolic fingerboard, and Foundation S, with PJ pickups and an active-pickup option, followed. A 5-string version was added in the early '90s, and a completely updated model tagged the Foundation 2000 appeared at the turn of the century. The Foundation was discontinued just short of its 20th anniversary, although its replacement, the U.S.-made Millennium Standard, will carry on many of the characteristics of the Foundation S.

After the T-40 and before the Foundation, Peavey had offered a couple of other 4-strings. The T-20 debuted in 1982 but was around only for a couple of years. It looked much like a P-Bass, but its one single-coil pickup was mounted at an angle, and the mounting ring was wider at the top, creating an integrated thumb rest. The original Fury Bass looked much the same, although it had different neck dimensions. It was discontinued in 1986, but the Fury returned in 1993 with a P-style split-coil humbucker. The imported Fury II, with an improved pickup, replaced it a few years later. Korean-made Fury 4, 5, and 6 basses, with quilted-maple tops, appeared in the Peavey catalog in 2000.

Other Peavey bass models from the '80s included the short-lived Patriot Bass, with its thin "Naturalite" body, and the Dyna-Bass. No dinosaur, the Dyna-Bass had active electronics with 3-band EQ and was available in a bolt-on version with "Super Ferrite" soapbar pickups or as the neck-through Dyna-Bass Unity, with PJs. The Dyna-Bass Unity Ltd. was a deluxe neck-through model with a flame-maple top, large fingerboard inlays, and gold hardware. Like all the Peavey basses that had preceded it, the Dyna-Bass had a traditional double-cutaway body, 34" scale length, and 4-in-line headstock (4+1 on the 5-string). Hartley Peavey wanted his basses to be different, but he knew what the market demanded, too.

■ Peavey Dyna-Bass 5-string.

Signatures & Cyber Sounds

The Rudy Sarzo Signature Bass, developed in collaboration with the Whitesnake bassist, was introduced in 1989. It was a souped-up version of the Dyna-Bass Unity, with extra-deep cutaways and special "wide aperture" pickups. The body was ash, and the through-body neck was made of flame maple and purpleheart, topped with an ebony fingerboard sporting oval inlays. A lower-priced bolt-on version, the RSB Bass, took its place in 1994 but was dropped a couple of years later.

A more important artist relationship was formed with Tim Landers in the late '80s. Landers, an accomplished L.A. studio player, brought Peavey specific ideas about building extended-range basses. The resulting R&D effort yielded Peavey's first premium basses, the TL-Five and TL-Six. They had graphite-reinforced through-body necks, 24-fret ebony fingerboards, flame-maple bodies, and advanced active electronics.

Some of the lessons learned in the development of the TL basses influenced the production models of the 1990s. The bolt-on B-Ninety (introduced in '90, of course) had scooped cutaways in its poplar body for easy access all the way to the 21st fret, and its PJ pickups were available in passive and active versions. The Unity Bass, which replaced the Dyna-Bass Unity, was similar to the B-Ninety but had neck-through construction. An upgraded version, built to Randy Jackson's specifications, was called the RJ4; it had a maple body, ebony fingerboard, and 3-band EQ with variable midrange controls.

■ Peavey Rudy Sarzo Signature Bass.

■ Peavey TL-Six (top), B-Quad 4 (middle), and CyberBass (bottom).

Bass virtuoso Jeff Berlin worked with Peavey to develop a model that incorporated the features of his heavily modified Fender. Berlin was reluctant to put his name on the bass, so it was called the Palaedium. It had a three-piece alder body, graphite-reinforced bolt-on maple neck, 21-fret ebony fingerboard, and a pair of quad-coil humbucking pickups. Available from 1992 to 1996, it was introduced at a list price of $799.99—"fair and reasonable" by anyone's standards.

Peavey's reputation for value has sometimes obscured the sheer quality, regardless of price, of some of its basses. That was probably true for the Palaedium, and it was unquestionably true for the B-Quad 4 (34" scale) and B-Quad 5 (35" scale). Designed in collaboration with Brian Bromberg, they were state-of-the-art instruments when introduced in the mid '90s. Equipped with Modulus Graphite necks with 24-fret phenolic fingerboards and a magnetic + piezo pickup array wired for stereo (with string panning) or mono operation, the B-Quads offered both playing ease and a tremendous range of sounds, from the deepest bass to glass-shattering highs. They were unquestionably an engineering achievement, but that didn't translate to commercial success. They were made only for about three years. In 1998 the G-Bass appeared; the simpler graphite-neck model offered some of the B-Quad's advantages without the elaborate electronics—or the $2,000 price tag.

As a bass builder, Peavey has an advantage because it also makes amplifiers, signal-processing gear, and recording equipment. That means it has access to a level of electronics R&D that most other instrument manufacturers can only dream about. That capability was never more evident than when Peavey took the wraps off the Midibase in 1992. Although it was not the first bass synth-controller to be offered, it was way ahead of its predecessors in most respects—and it was affordable.

The idea of using basses and guitars to control synthesizers had appeared in the 1970s, when Roland began to offer systems based on pitch-to-voltage conversion. The tracking (the translation from pitch to voltage) was slow, especially for lower bass notes, and these systems were little more than interesting novelties. The 1983 advent of MIDI solved some of the problems, but it was the wired-fret system developed by Australian engineer Steve Chick that really made it practical to use a bass guitar as a MIDI controller. Peavey adopted Chick's system for their Midibase. Its combination of wired frets (to detect pitch) and bridge-mounted pickups (to detect the timing and intensity of string plucks) yielded impressive performance as a controller, with none of the annoying glitches of earlier systems. The Midibase also functioned well as a standard 4-string, and its analog and digital sounds could be blended together.

Not content with that, Peavey introduced an improved version, the CyberBass, in 1994. It had better capabilities both as a MIDI controller and a standard bass—and a cool-looking "mother-of-toilet-seat" pickguard, too. The CyberBass 5, with a 35" scale length, followed two years later, but both models had been discontinued by 1997.

As much as Peavey's engineers were enjoying these high-tech adventures, they hadn't forgotten their regular customers. For those looking for a good old meat-and-potatoes bass in 1993, there was the Forum. Another variation on the J-style template, it was equipped with a slim bolt-on neck and passive PJ pickups mounted in a poplar body. An active version was called the Forum Plus. By 1995, Peavey had tinkered with the formula, giving the Forum a single passive pickup and creating the Forum AX, with a pair of active humbuckers and an 18-volt circuit. A 35"-scale 5-string with an ash or alder body also joined the series.

The Axcelerator, which also debuted in '93, had a similar look, but active pickups were standard. In its base configuration, it had a poplar body and a maple neck with rosewood fingerboard; in the center of the body, a "well" was routed out, beneath the pickguard, to reduce weight. With the addition of a 2TEK bridge, it became the Axcelerator 2-T. Upgraded with a swamp ash body and pau ferro fingerboard, it was called the Axcelerator Plus. The Axcelerator 5-string had a 35" scale length and 3+2 headstock—unusual for Peavey at the time, although a sign of things to come.

Next Generation

Beginning in 1996, Peavey's bass catalog got a major overhaul. Many models were either dropped or extensively redesigned. (The victims included the B-Quads, the B-Ninety, the Axcelerators, the Palaedium, and the last of the Dyna-Basses.) Peavey also began to have its lower-priced models made offshore. On the low end, Peavey introduced the Korean-made Milestone models, plain-vanilla basses with laminated-wood bodies and two J-style (Milestone I) pickups or one P-style (Milestone II) pickup. These were later updated and renamed the Milestone III and Milestone IV, respectively. There's also a 5-string called the Milestone V. All Milestones have a 34" scale length.

In 1997 the new Cirrus basses, made in Mississippi, moved into the top slot of the Peavey bass catalog, offering multi-laminate neck-through-body construction and a selection of exotic woods including bubinga, wenge, walnut, and quilted redwood. Scale length on all models—4-, 5-, and 6-string—is 35", and they're equipped with VFL active pickups and 3-band EQ. An abalone "C" is inlaid at the 12th fret of every Cirrus bass. A 1999 *Bass Player* review described the sound of a Cirrus 4-string as "bright and snappy with a boatload of punch."

Introduced in 2000, the bolt-on Millennium basses have alder bodies, graphite-reinforced maple necks, JJ or MM+J pickups, active electronics, and Hipshot bridges that offer either top-loaded or through-body stringing. Scale length for both 4- and 5-string models is 35", and they attain Millennium Plus status with the addition of a flame-maple top. Models tagged BN have a bird's-eye maple fingerboard. The most recent Peaveys are the Grind Basses, available in American-made (USA) and offshore (BXP) versions. The USA models have alder bodies, 24-fret maple necks with pau ferro fingerboards, and 18-volt active electronics with a passive option. The 4-string has PJ pickups; the 5-string has a JJ configuration. Scale length is 35" for both. The BXP imports have a 34" scale, and the electronics are 9-volt.

Hartley Peavey is rankled by those who say Peavey products are "good—for the money." He's got a point. While it's true that many of the less-expensive Peavey basses have been notable primarily for their utility, a review of Peavey's history as a bassmaker shows both market savvy and an impressive capability for pushing the envelope. No other manufacturer has developed an instrument as revolutionary as the Midibase/CyberBass, and none has shown the ability to consistently improve both instrument technology and manufacturing processes for as long as Peavey has done it. And Hartley's not done yet. "I want to know all I can about technology and electronics," he says. "I want to know all about metalworking; I want to know all about marketing and personal relations and so on. . . . That's just the way I am—but it's crazy guys like me who change things and make 'em better."

■ Peavey Forum (top), Cirrus 6-string (middle), and Grind Bass 5-string (bottom).

■ Pedulla Pentabuzz (right).

PEDULLA

Clarkson University in Potsdam, New York, has turned out some terrific hockey players—and one terrific bassmaker. "I went to Clarkson to study engineering," says Michael Pedulla, "but after the first year I switched to the Crane School of Music. I had played violin since I was about eight or nine, so I auditioned there. I don't remember exactly what happened, but I decided I didn't like engineering. So I got my music degree instead."

Although Pedulla didn't finish his engineering studies, the lessons he learned about design and production stayed with him. He soon found another way to apply them. "I'd always made things, and my dad had done some woodworking, just puttering around. That was an influence. I had started to play guitar when I was a freshman, and the two interests came together in making instruments. It was also like engineering—figuring it out and putting it all together. I had made a banjo neck while I was in school, and later I tried to make a guitar."

After graduating from Crane, Pedulla moved to Massachusetts, where in 1975 he set up shop as a luthier. "I started making acoustic guitars and then some electrics, and I also did repair work. Then I got the great idea to sell the instruments to stores. At that time it was Martin for acoustics and Fender and Gibson for electrics—that was it. Guitar players wouldn't touch anything that didn't have one of those names; they were very close-minded. Then I made a bass, and I learned that bass players were a different breed. I went up to Wurlitzer Music in Boston, the store took a couple of basses, and they sold them right away. So I thought, Well, it's a matter of logic to make what you can sell."

■ Pedulla MVP5 Signature.

Michael's recollection of his first bass is a bit fuzzy, but he says his initial concept wasn't that far from the instruments he's still building. "It was basically the same kind of materials—it was maple, and we started right out with a neck-through. It was a slab neck at first; later we decided to cut it up and use a two-piece quartersawn neck, and then a three-piece. Things evolved." The first Pedulla bass featured DiMarzio pickups, Grover tuners, and a Badass bridge—largely because those were the only parts Michael could find. "And it had a brass nut, of course," he laughs. "That was the day of brass nuts." The early Pedulla basses were the EL and EMS models, most of which were sold at Wurlitzer Music.

Pedulla's skills got a big boost from doing repair work for Mark Egan and Tim Landers. "They were very coherent—they could come back and tell me something specific. It wasn't just, 'Oh, man, it doesn't do it for me.' They could tell me to move the bridge back, get the horn out, do this, do that." Landers requested Bartolini Hi-A pickups, which led to a meeting with Bill and Pat Bartolini at the 1979 NAMM show. Pedulla basses have featured Bartolini pickups ever since, including many proprietary models.

■ Pedulla ETB5 Thunderbass.

"Mark and Tim really helped me get the fretless Buzz Bass going," says Pedulla, recalling the 1980 introduction of one of his best-known models. "In those days, everybody was getting frets yanked and having lines put in. So I thought, Why not make a fretless bass? I built a couple of fretless basses and gave them to Mark and Tim to check out. And away it went."

Thanks to the Jaco sound (the landmark album *Jaco Pastorius* was released in 1976), Pedulla found a ready market for high-quality fretless basses that were fun to play and delivered warm, singing sustain—what *Bass Player* calls the *mwah* factor. At a time when Fender and other major manufacturers were building only a handful of fretlesses, Pedulla was soon devoting about half of his production to Buzz models. These neck-through basses feature an ebony fingerboard with a polyester coating that greatly enhances their sound. The fretted version is called the MVP.

In the mid 1980s Pedulla's line also included the Interceptor and XJ basses, models that had relatively short lifespans. The Series II bass—a bolt-on version of the Buzz/MVP—was available from 1988 until 1993. The Mark Egan Signature models debuted in 1992; these are Buzz/MVP-style basses with deeper cutaways and an ebony thumb rest. The series includes a doubleneck available in a variety of configurations—Egan often plays one with a fretless 4-string above a fretted 8-string.

In 1992 Pedulla created an entirely new neck-through model, briefly tagged the Exotic Bass but soon renamed the Thunderbass. It has a strikingly different look from the Buzz/MVP models; the body is longer and sleeker, with more-pointed horns, and the headstock has a distinctive asymmetric shape. Available in 4-, 5-, and 6-string models, all with 34" scale length, the Thunderbass comes in two different flavors: the Custom (later dubbed the T), with a solid flame-maple body and a polyester finish, and the ET, which features a body top of zebrawood, bubinga, or quilted maple and an oil/urethane finish. Within a year, a "Thunderguts" switch was added to the onboard electronics; a 1993 *Bass Player* review noted that this "adds a thicker texture to the tone without sacrificing clarity." The fretless version is known, logically enough, as the Thunderbuzz. A bolt-on model, the Thunderbolt, debuted in 1994. At first it was offered only with a maple-on-maple

■ Pedulla Rapture Bass 5-string (left) and 4-string.

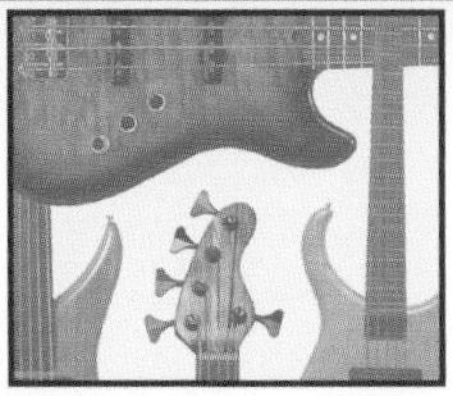

FINGERBOARD FACTORS

By Michael Pedulla

Bass design begins with the consideration of many factors, all of which have an effect on the instrument's sound, comfort, and feel. The first and most defining choice is which of three basic design categories to use: bolt-on, neck-through, or fixed (set-in) neck. This choice will determine the inherent properties of the sound, setting the basic parameters for the voice: attack, sustain, decay, and fundamental-to-overtone ratios. After we make this choice, we then look at all the possibilities for shaping a unique voice within that category. Next we choose wood types. This involves understanding combinations of woods and how they affect each other acoustically as well as structurally. In my opinion there is not much science to this process. Most builders accumulate knowledge from trial and error, refined with a healthy dose of the "voodoo" factor—more commonly known as experience.

Fingerboard material, an often overlooked component of the mix, affects the sound and feel of a bass. For our neck-through basses, we chose ebony for its glassy feel, great sustain, medium attack, and the sweet and supple low-mid grind it produces. We selected rosewood for our more "classic" bolt-on designs, as it delivers the vintage sound we're all familiar with: a softer attack, rich overtones, and less sustain. We also use a coated bird's-eye maple fingerboard on our Rapture series. The hard, bright maple offsets the bolt-on properties somewhat by delivering increased attack and sustain, giving the sound high end and a definite "snap."

The fretless Buzz Bass fingerboard is ebony, finished with a thin coating of polyester. Too much coating would diminish the effect of the fingerboard on the sound; the thinner coat allows the ebony's normal low-mid response to remain an acoustic factor. The coated surface is smoother and harder than the wood, and it sends more energy back into the string, complementing the low-mid growl of a fretless bass. The result is increased sustain, a defined attack, a wider swell, and a mega-growl in the low mids. The coating also protects the fingerboard from the wear and tear of roundwound strings. (Not all basses with coated fingerboards produce a sound like that of our Buzz Bass—there are many other factors of design and construction that give the Buzz its unique voice.) Ebony works in much the same way on our fretted basses and is responsible for the low-mid grind that rounds out the high end of a maple neck-through bass.

■ Michael Pedulla in his shop, mid 1970s.

Fingerboard radius (the arc of the fingerboard) affects the neck's comfort and is adjusted depending on fingerboard width and neck shape. The higher the number, the flatter the fingerboard. We use a 12" radius on our 4- and 5-string basses, and a 15" radius on our wider (19mm) 5- and 6-strings. Doing it right is important, because correct fingerboard radius facilitates technique. Most players are sensitive to the action (the height of the individual strings above the frets), but they often ignore the across-the-strings setup. Both the left and right hand pivot in a slight arc with most bass techniques, and the most comfortable fingerboard radius is one that mimics that arc. Too much arc requires excess motion in both hands, while too little arc becomes awkward. Both contribute to fatigue.

Bass design is a subjective endeavor, as is music itself. But to create a great instrument, or a great piece of music, there are guidelines and techniques the designer has to master. Timeless instruments, like ageless music, can be created only by following these guidelines.

body (flame maple topped with AA flame or bird's-eye maple), but an "exotic top" option was added in 1998.

In 1995 Pedulla made an aggressive entry into the mid-priced market (list prices around $1,500 at the time) with the Rapture Bass. Smaller and lighter than the other Pedulla models, this 4- or 5-string bass comes in candy and sunburst finishes and has a pickguard, for a "modern retro" look. Its single-pickup configuration, Michael Pedulla notes, allowed him to place the Bartolini humbucker "right where it should be to get the sound you're after, without the frequency cancellation and other problems that are inherent with a two-pickup bass." The Rapture's oversize control cavity reduces body mass, and the 5-string weighs in at less than nine pounds. The Bartolini electronics offer bass and treble boost/cut and a mini-toggle switch for midrange cut.

A year later Pedulla added the Rapture J2 to the line, offering two Bartolini J-style pickups rather than the single humbucker. Another variation, the Rapture PJ, joined the party in 2000—as the name indicates, this one has Bartolinis in a PJ configuration. The premium JJ or PJ version, featuring higher-grade maple and more finish options, is called the Rapture 2000.

Although Michael Pedulla has continually expanded his bass catalog, he actually reduced the size of his company in recent years. "When I started out I decided I didn't want to make one at a time—that's where the engineering came in," he explains. "The niche I was looking for was handmade, but *production* handmade, so I was between the big guys and the really little guys. But we started doing more and more production, and pretty soon I had too many people working for me. So I decided to cut that down, and now I'm more involved in making what we have. I've come full circle back to being personally involved in production, design, and marketing. I'm a lot happier that way. I'm fine as long as I know the basses we put out the door are top notch."

■ Pedulla Mark Egan Signature doubleneck: fretless 4-string + fretted 8-string.

■ Pedulla ETB4 Thunderbass, quilted-maple top.

■ Pedulla Rapture Bass J2-5.

PENSA-SUHR

SEE SUHR

PRS (PAUL REED SMITH)

Although he's widely admired for his beautiful and great-sounding electric guitars, Paul Reed Smith actually began his musical career as a bass player. The first instrument he built was a homemade bass that he assembled using the neck from a Japanese "Beatle Bass" copy. By 1976 Smith had opened a workshop in Annapolis, Maryland, where he built custom instruments for local musicians. His reputation for high-quality work grew quickly, and the first PRS factory opened in 1985.

In 1986 PRS offered its first production basses, the 34"-scale Bass-4 and Bass-5. They had mahogany bodies, set-in maple necks with rosewood fingerboards, and an unusual electronics configuration with three single-coil pickups and a rear-mounted humcanceling coil. Bolt-on CE models were added in 1990. The original PRS basses produced a tone heavy on low-end thump, winning favor with reggae players like Robbie Shakespeare, if not widespread acceptance. Sales were modest. Because of the way the factory was set up, building basses meant stopping guitar production—and this became less and less desirable as demand for PRS guitars mounted. Not surprisingly, production of the original PRS basses ended in 1992.

The second chapter in the PRS bass saga began in 1998, after the company had moved to a larger and more flexible facility in Stevensville, Maryland. An all-new bass design was prototyped and tested, leading to its introduction in 2000. Dubbed simply the Electric Bass, it's a 34"-scale 4-string with an alder body and a bolt-on 21-fret maple neck with a rosewood or maple fingerboard. A swamp ash body is also available. (A premium version, with a curly maple top over alder, is called the Electric Bass Maple Top.) A pair of PRS "high inductance" passive pickups is standard, and a PRS/L.R. Baggs piezo-bridge system with 3-band EQ can be added. Customers can order the fingerboard with the distinctive bird inlays seen on many PRS instruments. The electronics were upgraded in 2002 with the addition of a switchable 18-volt preamp.

■ PRS Bass-4, 1986.

■ PRS Electric Bass.

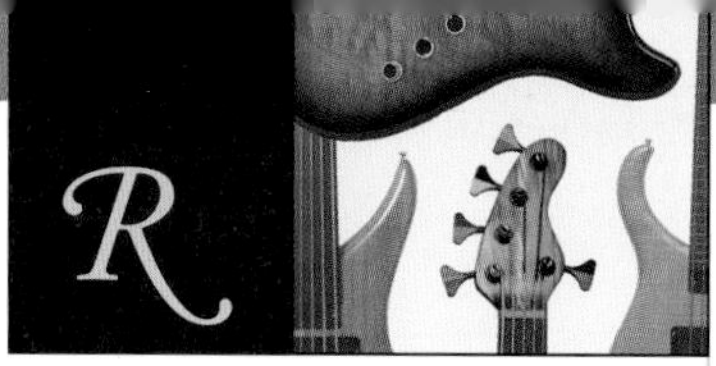

RAINSONG

If a graphite neck is stronger and more stable than a wood neck, then why not make a graphite body as well? That was the question RainSong Graphite Guitars of Hawaii answered with the all-composite acoustic bass guitars they introduced in 1996. The bodies were made from a special blend of graphite, Kevlar, and resin; the necks and fingerboards were graphite. Several models were offered, including the Acoustic Bass Guitar, PowerSong, and StageSong. While never commercially successful, the RainSong basses were ahead of their time in the utilization of composite technology to build acoustic instruments that were just about indestructible. And they didn't sound bad, either—in a 1997 *Bass Player* review, Scott Malandrone said an amplified RainSong Acoustic Bass Guitar produced "huge, bellowing lows bolstered with razor-sharp highs." Options included a racy "Maui Girl" peghead inlay. RainSong discontinued bass production in 1998, shortly before the company relocated to Woodinville, Washington. Such builders as CA Guitars have kept alive the idea of an all-composite ABG.

■ RainSong Acoustic Bass Guitar.

■ Ray Ramirez neck-through 6-string with zebrawood body.

RAY RAMIREZ

While he's better known for his Baby Bass–style electric uprights, Ray Ramirez of Humacao, Puerto Rico, also custom-builds solidbody bass guitars. His instruments are available as double-cutaway 4-, 5-, 6-, and 7-strings; scale length is 34" for 4-strings and 35" for extended-range basses. Thanks to the deep treble-side cutaway, there's full access to all 24 frets. (Fretless is also available.) Ramirez offers both bolt-on and neck-through construction, and he tailors the wood combination and electronics to suit each customer's playing style. An instrument builder since 1995, Ramirez produces about nine bass guitars a year.

READ

"I've been playing bass and repairing instruments for more than 20 years," says Jack Read. "In the early '90s I set out on a quest to find my perfect bass. There were great instruments to choose from—some had the look, the sound, or the feel I wanted, but none had all three. And none had the price tag I was looking for, either! I decided to make an attempt at designing and building my own bass. I made a list of all the features I wanted, such as playing comfort, balance, great tone, beauty, and versatility, and I designed a bass around that list. With some luck, some studying, and help from the very welcoming bass luthiers' community, I was able to create the perfect (for me) bass. Another player saw it, commissioned me to build one, and he told two friends, and so on. It wasn't long before I left my job as a design engineer and began building custom basses full time.

"I base my business on the fact that no two players necessarily have the same dream bass in mind, so each customer is afforded lots of individual attention when it comes time to put together a spec list for his or her bass. Unless a customer knows exactly what he or she wants, I ask them to describe their ideal bass

■ Read Step-Neck Bass, built for Victor Wooten.

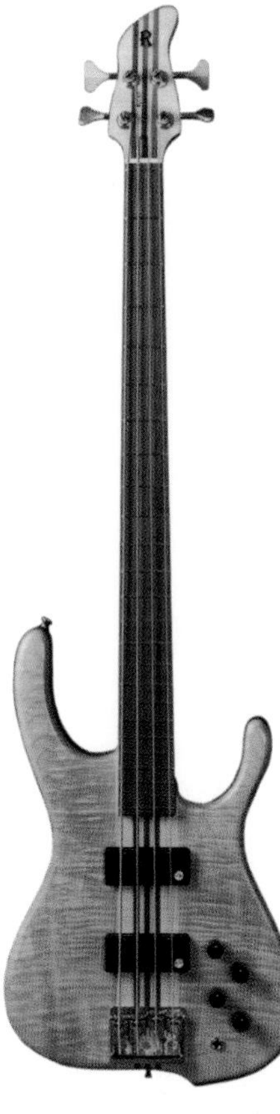

■ Read Custom with 7-piece neck.

tone as well as they can (recorded examples are helpful, too), and I use that as the foundation for the bass design. I offer basses in any configuration: neck-through, bolt-on, multi-laminate necks, single-piece necks, solidbody, hollowbody, active, passive, piezo, LightWave-equipped, any number of strings, any scale length . . . you get the idea."

Read's creations have covered just about all of bass-dom, from vintage-style 4-strings to 32-position fretlesses to 25-fret 8-strings tuned *F♯BEADGCF.* He also builds electric uprights in both full-scale and short-scale "hybrid" configurations. One of his most innovative creations is the Step-Neck Bass, one version of which has four strings in the lower positions, five in the middle of the neck (frets 6 to 10), and six in the upper register (frets 11 to 24). The shorter fifth and sixth strings are fed through ferrules in the back of the neck and tuned at the bridge. (The step-neck concept was created by Michael Hulsey and licensed to Read.)

"I started off as a one-man shop and haven't changed much since then," says Jack. "My wife, Carolyn, joined the business when we incorporated, and I have one part-time helper. This helps keep the overhead down and prices at what I would consider to be a fair level."

REVEREND

The cheap-but-cool vibe of 1950s Danelectros collides head-on with modern composite technology in Reverend Rumblefish basses. They were created by Joe Naylor, who had a successful guitar-amp company, Naylor Engineering, before he enrolled in the Roberto-Venn School of Luthiery and redirected his energy to building basses and guitars. Joe launched Reverend Musical Instruments in 1996, setting up shop in southern Michigan. (The name came to him, he says, while flipping through a blues magazine and seeing an article on Rev. Gary Davis.)

Naylor fondly recalls the Silvertone amp-in-case guitar he had as a kid, and that Masonite axe inspired his design for the Reverend instruments. They have patented "high resonance" semi-hollow bodies, with tops and backs made of a wood-and-phenolic composite. Inside, there's a 6"-wide mahogany center block with a steel "sustain bar." The one-piece molded side rim has a chrome-plated "forearm rest" on the upper edge, to prevent the instrument's square edge from digging into your flesh. The bolt-on maple neck has a rosewood fingerboard (maple is optional) and a graphite nut. In 2000, Naylor offered a "Metal Top" option: a thin sheet of aluminum bonded to the top, which contributes to both the look and sound. It was so popular it became a standard feature.

With the addition of upgraded electronics and a metal top, the original Rumblefish 4-string (34" scale) became the Rumblefish XL. The Rumblefish 5L 5-string (35" scale) was introduced in 1999. Both models are equipped with an angled pair of Reverend J-style pickups, but they're placed closer together, in the harmonic "sweet spot," on the 5-string. A 3-position voicing switch on the XL and 5L allows parallel, single-coil, or series operation. The Brad Houser 5 features two double-J pickups, better hardware, and wider string spacing. All Rumblefish basses are lightweight (eight or nine pounds), and they're finished in such tongue-in-cheek colors as Lake Superior Blue and Space Race Silver.

■ Reverend Rumblefish.

RICK TURNER/RENAISSANCE

In a career that stretches back to the 1960s, Rick Turner has been a professional bassist and guitarist, an instrument repairman, a record producer, an architect of PA systems, a recording technician, an artist relations man, a corporate consultant, and a writer for several music magazines. Most of all, though, he's been a luthier.

Turner grew up in the seacoast town of Marblehead, Massachusetts, where many of the antique shops sold guitars and banjos. Rick—whose father often played recordings of guitar music at home—became entranced with the look and feel of the old instruments. "When I was a senior in high school, I went to a party at a friend's house and found a Martin 2-17 guitar in a closet," he recalls. "It belonged to his mom, and I induced her to sell it to me for 25 bucks. Because it needed some work, I took it to the Vega company in Boston, which was the only guitar-repair place I could find. I was totally in awe."

Turner enrolled at Boston University in 1962, but he spent more time hanging out in coffeehouses than going to class. "I had started making woven-leather guitar straps, and this guitar shop hired me as a strap maker," he says. "After a week I'd made more straps than they could sell in a year, so they said, 'Hey, kid, you're pretty good with your hands. Here's a load of Mexican guitars that got dropped on the floor—see what you can do with them.' So I started taking things apart and putting them back together."

It wasn't long before Turner dropped out of BU to focus on fixing guitars by day and playing them at night. He gigged around Boston with a group that included Lowell Levinger, a.k.a. Banana, who later became the lead guitarist in the Youngbloods. In 1965 Rick was hired as guitar accompanist for the folk duo Ian & Sylvia, which he says was "one of the top three or four jobs of its kind you could get." The gig got even better when Felix Pappalardi signed on as the bassist. "Felix and I were road roommates for six or seven months," says Turner, who played on the duo's 1966 album *Play One More*. "Felix was a phenomenal musician, very versatile, and he was also getting into record production." (Pappalardi would go on to produce Cream, among others.) Turner credits Pappalardi—who was playing a Danelectro Long Horn Bass at the time—with opening his ears to the expressive capabilities of the electric bass.

After a stint in New York, where he played in a psychedelic rock band called Autosalvage and did repair work in Dan Armstrong's shop, Turner moved to Northern California. "I got there in 1968, and one of the things I decided to do was become an electric luthier. I knew people back East who were building acoustic guitars and autoharps, and I realized the one area where I didn't see any of this kind of craft being applied was *electric* instruments."

■ Rick Turner Model 1 bass.

In the late '60s Rick played bass on several studio projects led by Jerry Corbitt, another Youngblood, and he built his first bass for the group's leader, Jesse Colin Young. "I made it in '69," recalls Turner. "It was a set-neck, double-cutaway bass with a solid-mahogany body, like a Long Horn but with shorter horns, and a laminated mahogany and walnut neck." Needing pickups, Rick decided to make his own—something he has continued to do throughout his career. He bought ceramic magnets at Radio Shack and wound the wire by hand. "I jumped right into the sliding-pickup thing," he says. "I put brass tubing on the ends of the pickups, and they rode on brass rods supported at each end by screws on springs, so you could raise and lower the pickups and tilt them as well as slide them. I wasn't wild about dangling wire, so I ran the lead wire through telescoping brass tubing, which dropped down into the control cavity."

The sliding-pickup design proved prophetic. It appeared two years later in the first Alembic bass, which Turner built for Jack Casady. Rick had hooked up with the Grateful Dead's "sound wizards" thanks to his connection with the Youngbloods. "Their secretary was Phil Lesh's girlfriend," he explains. "After she saw the bass I'd made for Jesse, she introduced me to Phil. He invited me to the pink warehouse in Novato, which Owsley [Stanley] called 'Alembic'—the distillation vessel for all things musical and technical."

Turner's luthiery skills meshed well with the electronic know-how of Ron Wickersham, and they were soon collaborating on the groundbreaking instrument modification and design projects that would launch the custom-bass industry. Rick remained with Alembic until 1978, working on increasingly sophisticated bass-building projects and also contributing to the company's innovative work in PA-system design and live recording.

Since leaving Alembic, Turner has pushed the frontiers of instrument design in a variety of settings, from one-of-a-kind custom projects to consultations for corporate mass-producer Gibson. He launched Turner Guitars in 1978, focusing his attention on the Model 1 guitar, which proved to be a design success but a commercial failure. (Turner has also built a few medium-scale Model 1 basses over the years.) Turner Guitars went out of business in 1981, and for a while Rick supported himself as a cabinetmaker. He re-entered the music business as a consultant, creating pickup designs for several manufacturers. In 1988 Gibson hired him to work as both an instrument designer and an artist-relations representative in the company's Los Angeles office.

Five years later, frustrated by corporate politics, Turner left Gibson and returned to repair work at Westwood Music in L.A. In 1990 he set up shop in Topanga Canyon and began to build guitars and basses again. One of the instruments he developed was the Electroline, a solidbody 4-string he had designed for Gibson, although the company never put it into production. As introduced, the Electroline 1 was a 34"-scale fretless with a swamp ash body, graphite-reinforced bird's-eye maple neck, and 18-volt Highlander preamp. Equipped with Turner's piezo bridge system and strung with Turner-designed nylon-core strings, it delivered sounds ranging from a thick, upright-like thump to crystal-clear highs. The fretted Electroline 2 added a Turner Diamond magnetic pickup for even more tonal possibilities.

■ Renaissance Bass prototype.

In 1997 Turner moved up the coast to Santa Cruz, California. He also updated and expanded the Electrolines, adding a 35"-scale 5-string to the series. The 4-string EL-434 and 5-string EL-535 are available fretted or fretless with only the Turner "Reference" piezo bridge system or in Piezo/Magnetic versions with either a single Diamond pickup or two soapbars. A variety of woods and finishes can be ordered, and the basses are distinguished by such unusual touches as fingerboard dots made of New Zealand Paua shell.

While perfecting the Electrolines, Turner developed an entirely different low-end creature, the semi-acoustic instrument that he called the Renaissance Bass. He described its genesis in a series of *Bass Player* columns in 1996. When a customer asked him to build a bass lighter than the 13-pound 6-string he was playing, Turner wrote, "that got me thinking about how to eliminate as much weight as possible from an instrument without ruining its sound or balance." To keep the weight down, he assembled a semi-acoustic body with a through-body neck in the style of a Spanish classical guitar. The electronics were right at hand: the piezo bridge system he was using on the Electrolines plus a Diamond magnetic pickup. When it was done, Turner said he was generally pleased with the instrument's playability and sound—and especially satisfied that it weighed only six pounds. "In the end," he wrote, "I do feel this is a fundamentally good way to build a light-weight, good-sounding instrument."

That prototype became the basis for Turner's "Ampli-Coustic" basses, which he went on to offer in 4-string (34" scale) and 5-string (35" scale) versions, fretted or fretless. The production models have a single-cutaway acoustic-guitar-like body made of walnut or cherry, with a cedar top. Equipped with the piezo bridge system, Thomastik-Infeld Acousticore strings, and a Highlander 18-volt preamp, they weigh even less than the first Renaissance Bass—barely more than five pounds. "It's a total design concept," Rick says, "which includes the construction, pickup, electronics, and strings."

The "Ampli-Coustic" basses merge Turner's love for acoustic tone with his Alembic-bred electronic sophistication, embodying the full range of his career as a luthier. Perhaps in recognition of that, he changed the name of his company to Renaissance Guitars, although some older models, such as the Model 1 guitar, still carry the Rick Turner label.

SEE ALSO: ALEMBIC

■ Rick Turner Electroline 1.

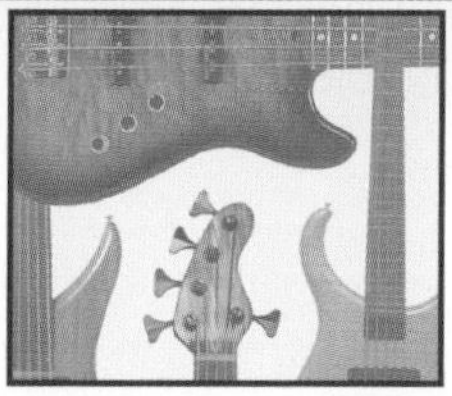

HOW TO DEFEAT HUM & BUZZ

By Rick Turner

There are two main sources of electrical hum and buzz, and both enter through your bass's pickups and electronics. The sources are AC electrostatic fields and the alternating electromagnetic fields radiating from electrical wires, lighting dimmers, fluorescent-light transformers, power transformers in amplifiers, etc. Pickup coils and unshielded wiring often act as antennas that capture these fields, passing the unwanted hum along with the instrument's signal.

With powerful modern amplifiers, multiple gain stages for distortion, and external effects, the noise problem really gets out of hand. If you're playing at 115dB onstage, the hum can easily be at 85dB, giving you only a 30dB signal-to-noise ratio—not exactly studio specs! Many musicians try to control hum and buzz by using noise gates; unfortunately, these units sometimes create as many problems as they solve. The best solution is to fix the problem as early in the signal chain as possible: in the instrument.

Electromagnetic noise shows up as a 60Hz hum (annoyingly close to *B♭*), and its intensity changes as you turn the instrument toward or away from hum sources such as amplifiers. Electrostatic noise is a buzzing sound, occurring somewhat at 60Hz but more at the 120Hz and 180Hz harmonics. This is the buzz you hear when you take your hands off the strings (assuming that the strings are grounded). Each type of noise has its own cure.

■ Rick Turner with Renaissance Bass, 2003.

Electromagnetic Noise, Single-Coils, and Humbucking

There's only one way to get rid of electromagnetic noise, and that's by using humcanceling or humbucking pickups, which were perfected and patented by Seth Lover of Gibson and introduced in 1957 as the famous "Patent Applied For" (PAF) guitar humbucker. Humcanceling pickups had been done before on Supro lap steels and in the obscure National bridge pickup, but it was Lover who developed the high-output pickup with dual coils covering all strings, wired in opposite polarity with one coil having a north magnetic pole and the other having a south magnetic pole.

A single-coil pickup intercepts radiated magnetic fields effectively and cannot differentiate between the string signal (picked up as a magnetic-field oscillation) and hum. In a humbucking pickup, two matched coils are connected out of phase; since the hum fields are picked up out of phase, they cancel each other out. The external fields do not interact with the pickup's own permanent magnetic field, so to pick up the string signal in phase, the polarity of each coil's permanent magnetic field is reversed. This results in two 180-degree phase shifts that add up to 360 degrees, thus putting the string signal back in phase.

In addition to doing a great job getting rid of noise, the humbucking configuration is also an inherently efficient pickup design, with a powerful and fat sound. But there are sounds you just can't get from a humbucker. To a large degree, the shape of a pickup's magnetic field determines its sound, and no changes to the coils or magnet types will give a single-coil sound to a double-coil humbucker. There are, however, some tricks that have been used to get hum cancellation and the single-coil sound. Fender Jazz Bass pickups cancel hum when you have both turned up full; the two single-coil pickups are polarized opposite and coil-phased opposite, so they act as one giant humbucker when combined. The Precision pickup is actually

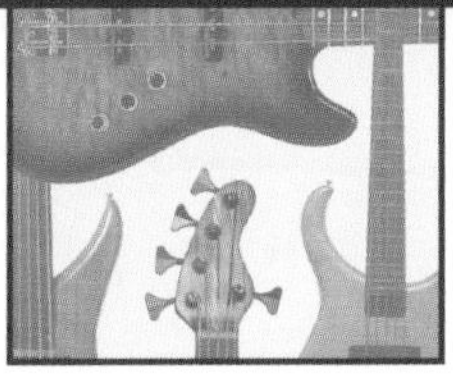

two out-of-phase single-coil pickups, one for the *E* and *A* strings and another for the *D* and *G*. The Alembic system uses a dummy coil, electronically combined out of phase with the two pickup signals. The dummy coil has no magnet, so it does not sense string vibration; it does, however, respond to external hum fields just like a pickup.

On a two-pickup instrument, one pickup can be flipped, giving a humbucking middle position. I often flip the polarity of the center pickup on Strat-style guitars, so the two combination settings of the 5-way switch (neck + middle and middle + bridge) become humbucking positions. There's no discernable change in tone—and the hum is gone.

There are some modern variations on the humbucking theme used to cancel at least some hum, including stacked coils and elaborately shielded pickups like the Lace Sensors, which attempt to shield most of the coil from outside hum while opening a "window" to the strings.

Electrostatic Noise and Shielding

Electrostatic noise can be eliminated with complete shielding of the pickups and control cavity. Usually, somewhat less than 100 percent will do an adequate job on instruments that are inherently hard to shield, but the more complete the job, the better the result. The idea behind shielding is to surround all "hot" circuit leads with a low-resistance conductive cage, which intercepts electrostatic fields and grounds them out. Just as you wouldn't use an unshielded speaker wire as an instrument cable, you shouldn't play a bass with unshielded electronics.

I use a combination of conductive paint and adhesive copper foil to shield pickups and control cavities, making sure there's a minimum resistance path to ground for all the shielding. I've encountered "shielding jobs" in which the shield is not connected to ground. This turns the shielding into a big hum antenna, which actually makes the noise problem worse!

When shielding an instrument, you should carefully insulate any signal points that could short out to ground. Unfortunately, many basses are not designed to be shielded, and "hot" points of the circuitry are too close to cavity walls. When in doubt, use heat shrink over connections. There is a material called "fish paper" that's useful in insulating tight spots; it's very tough, so sharp solder points won't poke through eventually, as can happen with ordinary electrical tape.

Star Grounding, Ground Loops, and Ground Lifting

My latest war against hum has been in instruments' internal wiring. For various reasons, including inherently wide bandwidth and gain stages, active instruments seem to be more susceptible to picking up stray noise in wiring. I've found that by adhering as strictly as possible to the "star grounding" practice, I minimize ground loops, which act like big turns of a coil picking up nothing but hum. I also carry signal ground separately from shield ground as far through the instrument as possible.

In star grounding, all component ground connections go to one point that is as close to the output-jack ground as practical. You never allow grounds to loop around and around inside the instrument, even inside a shielded cavity (which you really should have). I also don't tie signal grounds to the shells of potentiometers, and if I'm going to solder shield-ground wires to the pots, I use a separate wire for each pot and tie them together at the center of the star with all the other ground wires.

It's amazing how quiet an instrument can be if all these details are done just right—until you get to that nightmare gig where there's a 400-amp electrical room on the opposite side of the rear stage wall. And that isn't theoretical—there was a club in the San Fernando Valley where that was the case. When that happens, it's time for that *unplugged* gig.

RICKENBACKER

With their thin necks, lacquered fingerboards, horseshoe pickups, and Rick-O-Sound stereo wiring, Rickenbacker basses have a feel and sound unlike that of any other bass guitar. Some bass players find them a bit too unusual, but others swear by them—and the long list of Rick devotees includes Chris Squire, Geddy Lee, and Sir Paul McCartney. From a building perspective, Rickenbacker is of great importance as the first company to offer a neck-through-body electric bass, an innovation that would have lasting importance.

The first Rickenbacker bass guitar appeared in 1957, but the company's history stretches back to the 1930s, when it pioneered the manufacturing of electric instruments. The name is derived from Adolph Rickenbacker (who originally spelled it Rickenbacher), a Swiss immigrant who came to the U.S. as a young boy. His family lived in Ohio and Illinois before settling in Los Angeles in 1918.

In the 1920s Adolph established a tool and die business, and the National Stringed Instrument Company was one of his best customers. Rickenbacker became a stockholder in National, which was producing "ampliphonic" guitars with aluminum resonating cones mounted inside steel bodies [see National]. George Beauchamp, the general manager at National, was intrigued by the challenge of making stringed instruments louder. National's resonator guitars were a step in the right direction, but Beauchamp thought electronic amplification might work even better. One of his early experiments involved attaching a phonograph needle to a block of wood, running a guitar string above the needle, and plucking it. The sound of the string came out of the phonograph—amplified.

■ 1957 Rickenbacker 4000.

Beauchamp's experiments led to the development of the magnetic pickup. He put two horseshoe magnets side by side to create a strong magnetic field, below which he placed a coil of wire he had wound using a sewing-machine motor. When Beauchamp ran metal guitar strings through the aperture created by the magnets and then plucked them, their vibration disturbed the magnetic field and generated a varying electrical current in the coil. Sound waves had been converted into electrical energy, which ran through wires to an amplifier and speaker.

The next step was building an instrument, a job accomplished by Harry Watson of National. He made a crude one-piece lap-steel guitar from wood; because of its round body and long neck, it was dubbed the "Frying Pan." In 1931, with Beauchamp's horseshoe magnet attached, it became the first electric guitar. (Maybe—others were conducting similar experiments at the time, but the Frying Pan became the first commercially available instrument that could be called an electric guitar.)

Hot Frying Pans

Rickenbacker, Beauchamp, and another National employee named Paul Barth formed a company to sell these new guitars. Originally called Ro-Pat-In, it later became the Electro String Instrument Company. Ro-Pat-In began to sell cast-aluminum lap-steel electric guitars in 1932, but musicians were hesitant to try this newfangled gizmo. (Some things never change.) The line was soon expanded to include electric instruments made of Bakelite as well as wooden "Spanish style" acoustic guitars, with pickups attached. In 1936, Electro introduced a Beauchamp-designed electric upright "stick" bass with companion amplifier—one of the first commercial electric basses of any kind. The Electro Bass-Viol was gone by 1940, but the horseshoe pickup has endured. A modernized version is still used on Rickenbacker 4003 electric basses.

In 1940 Beauchamp sold his interest in Electro. He intended to found a new business making fishing lures, but died before he could get started. Adolph Rickenbacker continued to run the company until 1953, when it was purchased by F.C. Hall.

Hall was the owner of an Orange County wholesale electronics-parts outfit called Radio-Tel (short for the Radio & Television Equipment Company). One of his customers was a radio repair-shop owner named Leo Fender. In 1946, when Leo began to make his own line of lap-steel electric guitars and amplifiers, Radio-Tel became his distributor. This arrangement continued until 1955.

The use of the Electro name faded out under Hall's management, and the company was usually referred to as Rickenbacker, the brand name that had appeared on most of its instruments since the 1930s. (In a peculiar arrangement typical of the music industry, Electro was technically the name of the manufacturing division and Rickenbacker was the sales company.) At first the company continued to crank out lap-steel guitars and amplifiers, but the success of Fender's solidbody Telecaster signaled a major change in the guitar industry. In 1954 Rickenbacker hired German luthier Roger Rossmeisl, who had come to the U.S. a few years earlier to work for Gibson. Collaborating with Hall and Barth, Rossmeisl created the instrument designs that ushered Rickenbacker into the rock & roll era.

■ 1964 Rickenbacker 4001.

Neck-Through Breakthrough

Rossmeisl's creations included both hollowbody instruments inspired by the jazz guitars he had learned to build in Germany and solidbodies that would compete with the latest Fender and Gibson models. In 1956 Rickenbacker introduced his Combo 400, a neck-through guitar. A year later, Rossmeisl created the Model 4000 electric bass, which used the same method of construction.

The idea of building a guitar with a neck that ran the full length of the body did not originate with Rossmeisl. Lap-steel guitars—including the original Frying Pan—had been made that way for years, and Slingerland offered a "Spanish neck" version of one of its neck-through Hawaiian guitars as early as 1939. The best-known pre-1950 example of a neck-through guitar is probably the instrument that California luthier Paul Bigsby built for Merle Travis in 1947 or '48. But Rossmeisl applied the concept to production models of the modern electric guitar and bass.

Rossmeisl was proud of his status as a *gitarrenbaumeister* (master guitar builder), and one of the things he liked about neck-through construction was the high degree of craftsmanship it required. With separate necks and bodies, production problems are easy to correct—but the unified structure of a neck-through has less margin for error. Rossmeisl also saw practical advantages. The 1957 Rickenbacker catalog touts the 4000's "full-length neck with two double metal adjusting rods" and notes that "the fact that the tailpiece, bridge, nut, and patent [tuning] heads are mounted on the same piece of wood assures the player of maintaining a straight neck."

There's no mention of sustain, clarity, or other sonic advantages in the early product literature. This isn't surprising; sustain was not a design goal in an era when the *thud* of a gut-string upright was still considered the ideal bass tone—thus the string mutes found on many early electric basses. And the crude amplifiers of the '50s were not yet ready for the demands of high-fidelity bass instruments. It would be years before all the advantages of Rossmeisl's design could be fully appreciated.

■ Paul McCartney's Rickenbacker 4001S—left-handed, of course.

The 4000 had the "cresting wave" body shape that quickly became a Rickenbacker trademark. (In 1958, Rick introduced its series 425 and 450 guitars with the same shape—one of the few examples of a "reverse partner" relationship, where a guitar design copied an existing bass instead of the other way around.) The 4000's neck was made of mahogany, with maple body wings. The unbound rosewood fingerboard had dot inlays, and the scale length was 33¼", which would be the standard scale for all future Rickenbacker basses except for the short-scale 3000 of 1975.

A two-pickup "deluxe" model, the 4001, was added to the Rickenbacker line in 1961; it had checkered body binding and a bound fingerboard with triangular inlays. The two Ricks were the only neck-through basses on the market until 1963, when Gibson introduced the Thunderbird. (The T-Bird's design was soon altered, however, and by 1965 it had a glued-on neck.) It wasn't until the first Alembic bass appeared in 1971 that Rossmeisl's forward-looking design concept was fully vindicated—and since then many bassmakers have chosen this method of construction for their instruments.

Paul & Chris

In 1962 Rickenbacker moved its factory from L.A. to a facility on Kilson Drive in Santa Ana, California. Rossmeisl left the company soon afterward, accepting an offer from Fender to develop a new line of acoustic guitars. He later returned to Germany, where he died in 1979 at the age of 52.

The popularity of Rickenbacker instruments soared during the mid '60s because of their association with the Beatles. John Lennon had been playing a Rickenbacker 325 guitar since 1960, and in 1965 F.C. Hall presented a left-handed 4001S (the "export version" of the 4001) to Paul McCartney. It was heard to good effect on many subsequent Beatles recordings, especially *Sgt. Pepper's Lonely Hearts Club Band.*

The hollowbody 4005 bass, introduced in 1965, never achieved the popularity of the 4001. Even so, it remained in the Rickenbacker catalog for almost 20 years and was offered in a number of variations, including the 4005WB (white body binding), the 4005-6 (6-string tuned *EADGBE*), and the 4005-8 (8-string). The most bizarre version was the early-'70s 4005L "light show" bass, which had a translucent plastic top and colored lights inside the body that lit according to the frequency of the note being played: blue for bass, green for midrange, and red for treble. Far out, man!

The 4001 was Rickenbacker's mainstay during the 1960s and '70s. The limited-edition 4002, with a curly maple top and two humbuckers, appeared in 1967, but most bassists wanted the classic model with the horseshoe pickup. Sales got a boost in the '70s because of Chris Squire's high-profile work with Yes, which made

■ Rickenbacker 4005L "light show" bass.

the twangy sound of a Rick bass with roundwounds hugely popular. In 1979 Rickenbacker created a new model, the 4003, similar to the 4001 in most respects but "specially engineered to accommodate roundwound strings." (The main difference was a new truss-rod system.)

Rickenbacker also offered an 8-string version of the 4001, the 4008. From 1975 until the early '90s the catalog included doubleneck 4080 models that joined a 4001 to a 6- or 12-string guitar. During the '70s, Rickenbacker's designers also created a different double-cutaway solidbody 4-string, with a more "standard" (i.e., Fender-like) body shape. It was called the 3000 in its short-scale (30") version and the 3001 with the 33¼" scale length. Both models had been discontinued by the mid '80s.

Back to the Future

In 1984 F.C. Hall transferred ownership of the company to his son John and John's wife, Cindalee, who combined the Electro and Rickenbacker assets into Rickenbacker International Corporation (RIC). Under John Hall, Rickenbacker has mined its history judiciously, offering such models as the 4001V63 (a vintage reissue of the '63 4001) and the 4001CS (a limited-edition Chris Squire signature model). Several variations on the 4003 have appeared, including the 4003FL fretless, the 4003S5 5-string, the 4003S8 8-string, the 4003S Tuxedo (with a white body and black pickguard and hardware), and the 4003S/SPC Blackstar, a signature model created for Mike Mesaros of the Smithereens.

In 1989 RIC combined its offices and factory in a new Santa Ana location, at South Main and Stevens. The more spacious facility houses modern CNC machines, but Rickenbacker basses are still made slowly with a great deal of handwork.

Rickenbacker introduced a series of basses with model numbers beginning with 20 in the late '80s and early '90s. The 2030 and 2020 (which succeeded it, despite the lower number) were double-cutaway 4-strings based on the Hamburg guitar model. The 2030GF was a similar model with appointments that matched the 230 Glenn Frey signature guitar. The 2050 El Dorado (later the 2060) was a deluxe model, with a bound top and gold hardware, once again in lockstep with a similar guitar model. None of them achieved much popularity, and they had all been discontinued by 1997.

A new model featuring the "cresting wave" shape, the 4004, debuted in 1993; it had a pair of high-output humbuckers and was available in an oiled-walnut (Cheyenne) or gloss-black (Laredo) finish. In 2000 the Cheyenne was updated as the Cheyenne II, with a maple body and bubinga fingerboard; it's available as a 4-string (4004Cii) or 5-string (4004/5Cii).

The Rickenbacker line of 2002–03 focuses on the 4000 series: the classic Rickenbacker bass in 4003 and 4004 configurations, a limited-edition 4004LK Lemmy Kilmister signature model with a carved-walnut body and three humbuckers, and the 4001C64, a vintage reissue patterned on Paul McCartney's 4001S. Production remains slow and meticulous, with 15 days devoted to the finish process alone. "We're a healthy company with no debt, and we aren't beholden to shareholders," John Hall told *Bass Player*'s Bill Leigh in 2002. "I have no interest in building overseas or having copies of my products built overseas. . . . We've tried to increase production a bit, but I won't trade quality for quantity."

■ Rickenbacker 4004 Cheyenne.

■ Rob Allen MB-2f 5-string.

ROB ALLEN

"Tone is everything!" says Rob Allen—and who can argue with him? Rob, who logged time in Rick Turner's shop, has been building instruments under his own name since 1997, specializing in semi-acoustic basses with tone chambers in their double-cutaway ash or alder bodies. This produces a warmer tone and also reduces the weight: a Rob Allen MB-2 weighs only about 6½ pounds.

Allen says the key to building a great electric bass is choosing the right woods to create an instrument "that sounds outstanding acoustically first, and then amplifying it." The MB-2 has a ¼" curly maple top (other woods, including koa, walnut, and myrtle, are available) with ivoroid binding. There are no visible electronics: the Fishman piezo pickup is mounted in the strings-through-body cocobolo bridge, and a cocobolo volume knob sits right on the lower part of the bridge. A trim pot in the control cavity, accessible through a hole in the cover, adjusts high-frequency output. The bolt-on neck is made of bird's-eye maple, topped with a cocobolo fingerboard. A tung-oil finish is standard. (A gloss-finish version, the MB-1, was available for a short time.) The bridge and fingerboard can be upgraded to Macassar ebony; other options include headstock binding and a wooden thumb rest. Almost 90 percent of the basses Allen builds are fretless; they're available with lined or unlined fingerboards and equipped with LaBella nylon-tapewound strings. The fretted MB-2f has a walnut neck, ash body with walnut top, and mandolin frets. Rob Allen basses are available as 34"-scale 4-strings and 35"-scale 5- and 6-strings. (His early 5-strings were 34" scale.)

ROBIN

Classic designs with a twist—that seems to be the guiding principle of Houston's Robin Guitars, founded in 1982 by David Wintz. The company grew out of the Rockin' Robin music store that Wintz started with partner Bart Wittrock in 1972. Deciding they wanted a house brand, they drew up original bass and guitar designs and had them built by Tokai of Japan. Looking for something that would immediately distinguish the Robin line, they gave their instruments reverse headstocks, with the tuning keys on the bottom. "There wasn't any deep marketing concept behind the reverse headstock," Wintz later told Willie Moseley. "We just thought it looked cool."

The early import line included the Ranger Bass, which had the look of an early-'50s P-Bass but with a medium-scale (32") neck and a 2+2 headstock—later changed to reverse 4-in-line, in keeping with the company's preferred look. The other 4-string was the 34"-scale Freedom Bass, available in single- or double-pickup versions. The pickups were large "Double Jazz" humbuckers, and the active electronics were "so powerful you could plug a set of headphones right into the instrument—you didn't even need a preamp," according to Wintz.

■ Robin Ranger Bass.

In the late 1980s quality-control problems and the declining value of the dollar against the yen spelled an end to the relationship with Tokai. David decided it was time to handle production himself, so he sold his share of the retail business and set up a factory. By 1988 Robin was building Ranger Basses domestically, and a new 4-string, the Medley Bass, appeared in the catalog. A partner to the company's Medley guitar, it had a reverse 4-in-line headstock and an electronics array that included two J-style pickups and a soapbar near the bridge. In 1990 it was revamped with a V-shaped headstock and PJ pickups; that same year the Machete Bass, with its unusual "stair-step" body, debuted.

Robin's bass line expanded in 1993 with the addition of the Ranger Jaybird and Jaywalker J-style models; the latter sported a "custom vintage" look with a figured-maple top and no pickguard. In 1994 Robin added the Ranger Bass VI—tuned *EADGBE,* like a Fender Bass VI—and redesigned the Ranger Bass with a 34" scale length, a conventional 4-in-line headstock, and PJ pickups from Robin's sister company Rio Grande. The Jaybird, Jaywalker, Medley Bass, and Machete Bass V (a 5-string with a pointy 3+2 headstock) were also in production. A new domestic version of the Freedom Two (equipped with Rio Grande "Powerbucker" Pickups) showed up in 1996, and the Avalon and Savoy Basses, partners to Robin guitars, made an appearance a year later. In 1998 the Freedom Five and Super Freedom Five (with Bartolini pickups) were added. Robin backed away from making basses after that, but the lull was temporary, says Wintz; by late 2002 the company was completing plans for resumed production of most models.

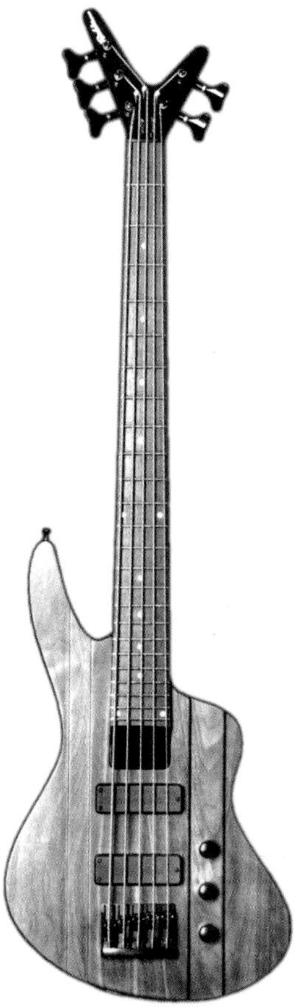

■ Robin Machete Bass V.

ROSCOE

Roscoe Guitars started out in a Greensboro, North Carolina, guitar shop founded by Keith Roscoe in 1971. Annual production increased from a handful of instruments to several hundred by the late 1990s. Originally known for its heavy-metal guitars—many with custom air-brushed paint jobs—Roscoe has evolved into a builder of premium basses.

Roscoe basses are made in two double-cutaway body styles, LG (4-, 5-, and 6-strings) and SKB (5-, 6-, and 7-strings). The LG style is more compact. Standard features include a figured-maple top over mahogany, swamp ash, or Spanish cedar; a graphite-reinforced neck; and Bartolini pickups and electronics. Fingerboards are cut from rosewood, maple, ebony, spalted purpleheart, or Diamondwood (birch veneers impregnated with phenolic resin). Scale length is 34" on 4-strings and 35" on all other models. Options include a selection of premium top woods, including quilted maple, burl myrtle, and cocobolo; 18-volt Bartolini or Aguilar electronics; and LED fingerboard inlays. Roscoe also builds a limited number of "totally over-the-top" Icon Series custom basses each year. Strong lower-register performance is a Roscoe hallmark; a 1997 *Bass Player* review praised an LG-3005 for its "room-shaking tone," saying that "the great sound of the Roscoe's 35"-scale *B* string is undeniable."

■ Roscoe LG-3005.

SADOWSKY

When Roger Sadowsky approached luthier Augie LoPrinzi about an apprenticeship, he had an unusual pitch. "I said to him," recalls Roger, "'If I can implant an electrode in the lateral hypothalamus of a rat's brain, I think I can build a guitar.' I'm sure he didn't have a clue about what I said, but he took me on."

At the time, Sadowsky was pursuing a Ph.D. at Rutgers University's Institute of Animal Behavior. But he wasn't having much fun—and lutherie looked a lot more appealing. "I started playing acoustic guitar in 1968, after going to a folk festival. Later on, as I was getting more and more miserable in grad school, I developed this romantic notion that if I learned to build guitars, I could have my cabin in the woods and musicians would beat a path to my door. So I quit school in '72 and went to work for a music store in Union, New Jersey. We were selling acoustic guitars built by a local guy named Augie LoPrinzi, and one day I said to his sales rep, 'Look, man, I don't want to be working here. I want to be building guitars. Can you hook me up with Augie?'"

■ Sadowsky Standard PJ4.

That led to Roger's "rat brain" interview and a $65-a-week job in LoPrinzi's shop. Sadowsky soon realized it would take years to establish himself as a luthier —and there wasn't much of a market for handmade acoustic guitars to begin with. Feeling the economic pressure, he took a repair job at Medley Music in Bryn Mawr, Pennsylvania, near Philadelphia. "I spent five years there getting good at being a repairman. I had a client who moved to New York, a guitarist named Craig Snyder who was a busy session player in the late '70s. He kept bringing me instruments, and he said, 'There's no one as good as you in New York.' I found that hard to believe, but I started commuting to New York every weekend and using his apartment as a base. His friends brought their instruments to me; I did simple repairs there and took the bigger jobs back to Philly. After six months I had established contact with enough players and developed enough confidence to open my own shop, so I moved to New York in September 1979."

Sadowsky's business flourished in the Big Apple, and many of his customers were bass players looking for better sound. After meeting Ron Armstrong of Stars Guitars, Roger began to install active electronics in basses—and his customers loved the immediate improvement in their tone. "The scenario in those days was usually like this: I would tell a bass player to go out to 48th Street and pick up the best early-'60s Jazz Bass he could find. In those days you could get one for $800. I would do a fret job, put in an active circuit, shield it, and maybe put on a better bridge. By the time we were done, he had a great workingman's instrument for $1,400 or $1,500 total. But by the mid '80s the vintage market had taken off, and that $800 Jazz Bass was now a $1,500 Jazz Bass—and everything I was doing was devaluing it as a vintage instrument. So I began to realize that this was not a fruitful way to continue, and I felt that with my experience modifying these instruments I could build a bass from scratch that would be even better than these modified Fenders."

■ Sadowsky Vintage PJ4.

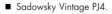

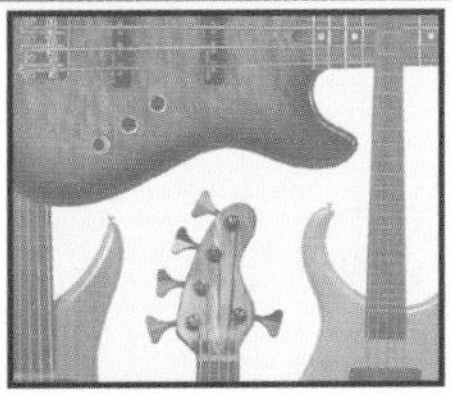

ACTIVE ELECTRONICS

By Roger Sadowsky

My introduction to active electronics took place in the late 1970s, when I met Ron Armstrong of Stars Guitars at a Gibson service seminar in Kalamazoo, Michigan. Ron came out of the Alembic school and had developed a line of retrofit active circuits for bass and guitar. I began to experiment with these circuits, and in 1979, shortly after I set up shop in New York City, a session bassist named Tony Coniff asked my advice about improving his tone. I suggested he try the Stars bass preamp, which offered independent treble and bass boost controls. I installed the circuit, and he reported back that many people were commenting on how good his sound was. Shortly thereafter, a young bassist named Marcus Miller came into the shop. I installed the same circuit in his Fender Jazz Bass (along with doing a fret job and putting on a new bridge)—and the rest is history.

Active electronics for bass run the gamut from active pickups like EMGs (a small preamp is built into each pickup) to active tone circuits consisting of either treble and bass (2-band EQ) or treble, midrange, and bass (3-band EQ). These controls can be either cut and boost or boost only. More complicated circuits have frequency sweeps that allow you to select the frequency range of your cut or boost, or "shelving switches" that preset the frequency at which the controls operate. Active electronics require battery power, and they make the bass's output low impedance instead of the high-impedance output that passive electronics produce.

In simple terms, some of the advantages of a low-impedance output are:

- No signal loss, especially high-end loss, when using long instrument cables.
- "Hotter" signal coming from the bass, which drives amplifiers and effects more efficiently.
- The opportunity to boost frequencies rather than just cut them, as with passive circuits.

The disadvantages of active circuits are:

- Dependence on a battery.
- The perception by some people that active electronics sound "colder" and "more sterile" than passive electronics.

■ Roger Sadowsky with Sadowsky 5-string, quilted-maple top.

Although active circuits for basses and guitars appeared at about the same time, these circuits have achieved much greater popularity among bassists than guitarists. One reason is that the Holy Grail of guitar tone is achieved with a good passive guitar and a good (usually tube) amplifier. It just doesn't get any better than that. Bassists, however, have historically struggled to be heard, and active electronics seem to benefit them more. On older recordings (1970s and earlier), electric bass often sounds very muddy compared to what's heard on newer recordings. Active electronics make the bass track sit much better in the mix, so the bass has clarity and can actually be heard separate from the kick drum and other instruments. A similar situation occurs in live performance —active basses tend to cut through better than passive instruments.

There will always be players who get a great sound with a passive bass and prefer that kind of tone. But for many electric bassists, the advent of active electronics has done much to give them the opportunity to be heard.

■ Sadowsky Vintage 5.

■ Sadowsky Standard 4.

Roger built his first Sadowsky Bass in 1982. "It was a PJ instrument, candy apple red, that went to Will Lee. Then I built one for Marcus Miller that had a slightly smaller body—it was reduced in the area where the arm contour is. The craftsman in me wanted to make a more original instrument, but the reality of Manhattan was that nobody was interested in anything but a Fender-style bass. That's what led me down that path—some people have said my instruments are like a Fender on steroids."

Sadowsky Basses were known, right from the start, for their consistently rich tone, which Roger attributes to both his training as an acoustic guitar builder and his intelligent use of active electronics. "Even in the early '80s I believed solidbody basses and guitars were, first and foremost, acoustic instruments—and the better they sounded acoustically, the better they sounded through an amp. Nobody else believed that in those days. The philosophy was: it's a plank of wood, and it's all about the pickups and bridge mass. People were making basses using all these exotic hardwoods—they were wonderful for building coffee tables, but they made horrible instruments. I focused on the acoustic qualities of the wood, and I think that point of view is recognized as correct today. The other thing that helped was that active electronics were a much greater asset to bass players than guitar players. Active electronics really helped bass players to be heard, in terms of how their instruments cut through in live situations and how well they sat in a studio track."

Sadowsky has never wavered from his belief in those concepts, or from his original vision of building a limited number of premium basses and guitars, most of which he sells directly to musicians. The close contact between builder and player means he can help his customers find the right instruments—and they can help him create new models.

The Sadowsky Bass has a J-style body that's slightly smaller than the Fender original, for player comfort and lighter weight. The 21-fret bolt-on maple neck is available in either J or P dimensions and can be ordered with a fingerboard of maple, morado, or other premium woods. The standard pickups are humcanceling J-style models custom wound for Sadowsky; single-coil J-style, PJ, and EMG pickups are also available. The active tone circuit (also sold as an outboard preamp) was designed by amp maker Alex Aguilar to meet Sadowsky's requirements; it has boost-only bass and treble controls centered at 40Hz and 4kHz, respectively. A passive tone control (treble cut) is available as an option. Roger is meticulous about the grounding and shielding of his electronics, which makes his basses especially resistant to 60-cycle hum and RF interference.

Sadowsky 4-strings are available with alder or swamp ash bodies; the ash bodies can be topped with bent maple, including strikingly beautiful pieces of quilted maple. When ordered with the Vintage Style option, they come with a pickguard and metal control plate, replicating the look of an old Fender Jazz Bass. Standard hardware includes a custom bridge (formerly from Gotoh; more recently Hipshot) and lightweight Hipshot tuners. Finishes range from natural and sunburst to a selection of such "classic colors" as candy apple red and Lake Placid blue. All Sadowsky basses are available left-handed or fretless (with or without a polyester fingerboard coating). Players can order virtually any combination of woods, pickups, and other components, depending on their needs.

The Sadowsky 5-strings are 34"-scale basses in either 24-fret or 21-fret configurations. The right-hand string spacing is wide, making it easy for 4-string players

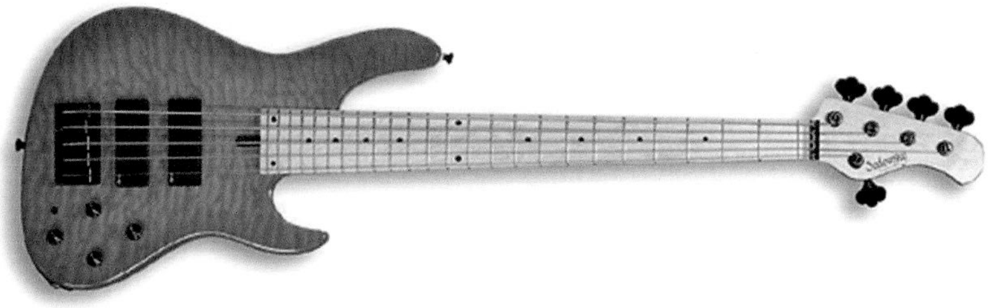

■ Sadowsky 24-fret 5-string.

to adjust. The 24-fret 5-string is equipped with two custom EMG 40-J pickups selected for their "tight, punchy" sound. The 21-fret 5 is available as either a Standard or Vintage model. The pickups on the Vintage 5 are custom single-coil J's, but others are available—including a unique PJ configuration that was developed with input from Nashville studio ace Michael Rhodes. It can be ordered with its P-style Basslines pickup flipped, reversing the coils. "Ken Fallon, who works with me, was a strong advocate of that," Roger says. "It tightens the *B*-string sound because it pushes the bass coil closer to the bridge, and it also helps popping on the *G*, because it puts the treble coil where a neck position J-Bass pickup would be. It's a good example of the little things that make what we do meaningful."

In 2002 Roger Sadowsky moved his shop from midtown Manhattan to Brooklyn and began to offer Ultra Vintage models that have full-size P- and J-style bodies, Brazilian rosewood fingerboards, and other features that make them as close as possible to vintage Fender basses—but with that characteristic Sadowsky attention to detail that can't be found in a production instrument.

SCHECTER

During the 1970s, many bassists upgraded their stock instruments with new pickups and better hardware, and some even replaced bodies and necks. The boom in the replacement-parts industry was driven by guys like David Schecter, who was one of the leaders in creating the products musicians needed to improve their axes. Schecter also assembled complete instruments from parts, creating basses that anticipated the "custom vintage" creations of such builders as Roger Sadowsky and Mike Lull.

In the 1980s, Schecter Guitar Research suffered through the cycle of growth, acquisition, decline, and reorganization that's a familiar saga in the music industry. The '90s were a time of recovery and a return to the basic principles that had fueled the company's initial success. In recent years, Schecter instruments have been divided between the imported Diamond Series and the USA Custom Series. The latter group includes Fender-inspired Traditional models (in P and J styles) and S Series 4- and 5-strings. The Model T Bass, created for Robert DeLeo of Stone Temple Pilots, combines the look of an early-'50s P-Bass with modern tapped-coil PJ pickups. The Baron has a single-cutaway body and one Basslines pickup; it's available as a 4- or 5-string. Two other Schecter basses feature Kent Armstrong pickups: the Tempest Bass, which is sort of a souped-up Gibson EB-3, and the Hellcat Bass, with three lipstick-tube pickups mounted in its angular double-cutaway body.

■ Schecter Baron 5-string.

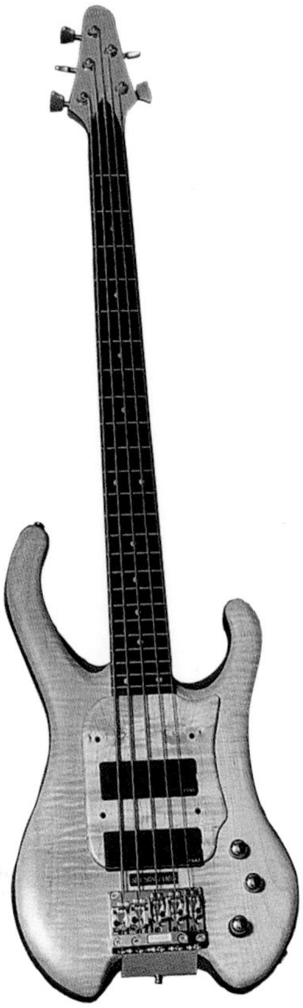

■ Simpson-James SJ-5 Custom.

■ Spalt Matrix.

SIMPSON-JAMES

"I started to build basses in 1971," says Christopher Simpson Mowatt. "It was one of those things where you experiment and see what happens. I learned a lot, made as many mistakes as one can make, and slowly refined my approach."

Mowatt dropped out of building for a while—he runs a repair service, Guitar-Tech, in Westfield, Massachusetts—but his interest was rekindled when he hooked up with Robert James Clarke in 1992. They began to design and build custom instruments branded with their middle names. "The first Simpson-James bass was a fretless 4-string that I built for myself," says Mowatt. "That lasted until I took it down to a local shop to fit it for a case, and the 'oohs and aahs' got the best of me." The design was altered in 1994 when Mowatt acquired a unique piece of body wood. "A friend gave me some maple from an old dining table built in the mid 1800s. There was a hole where the leg bolts came through, forcing me to change the shape of the bout—and the new SJ-5 Custom was born."

The next step was designing a production bass that could compete in the mid-price range. "That's when I came up with the Performer Series of bolt-on basses," says Chris. "I wanted to create a flexible bass that was solid, lightweight, and playable." The Performer is traditional in many respects, including its alder body, maple neck, single Basslines MM pickup, and 34" scale length. But it's got some interesting wrinkles, too. The body has been trimmed down to keep the bass light (about 7½ pounds). Three alternate capacitors are supplied, so the tonal response can be user-tweaked. The neck has a radiused edge where it meets the fingerboard, for better playability. And that maple or rosewood 'board sports frets of two different widths: .105" up to the 12th fret and .085" from 13 to 21. Mowatt says this provides better intonation—and it also makes upper-register playing easier. Production numbers have been modest because of Mowatt's busy repair business, but a few Simpson-James basses were still being made in 2002.

SMITH: SEE KEN SMITH

SPALT

It's not a bass—it's a modular bass system. The futuristic low-frequency instrument created by Michael Spalt has an aluminum "mounting platform," to which various pickups, electronics, bridges, body extensions, and wooden necks can be attached. He came up with the idea in 2000, after experimenting with modular guitars. "They weren't accepted in today's vintage-dominated market," says Michael, "but they had a beautiful, clear, low-range sound, so I decided to build a bass prototype. It took off from there."

The Spalt line includes the 34"-scale Matrix 4-string and Terminator 5-string, both with bodies and headstocks of chromed or black-anodized aluminum. The Matrix's neck is made of maple or goncalo; on the Terminator, it's wenge or bubinga. Fingerboards are cocobolo. The body extensions feature various exotic woods, including wenge, padauk, and zebrawood. Pickups and electronics come from EMG or Bartolini. Even closer to the cutting edge is the Magma, a 4- or 5-string equipped with the LightWave optical-pickup system. "With the LightWave, you can detune to 8Hz and still get great usable tone," says Michael, "if your amp can handle it."

SPECTOR

Inspiration comes in many forms. For Stuart Spector, it was a banjo. "One day in 1974 I was sitting in my friend Mike Kropp's apartment," recalls Spector. "Mike is a fabulous banjo player, and he was playing a pre-war Gibson 'hearts & flowers' Mastertone flathead banjo. I'm listening to him play and thinking, Wow, that's a beautiful banjo. And Mike says, 'It's not the original neck—it's a reproduction. The original was a tenor neck; this one is a 5-string, which is what you want for bluegrass. The neck was made by my college friend Kix Stewart.' Mike tells me that Kix—who's the Stewart of Stewart-MacDonald Guitar Shop Supply—had made the neck in about a week and spray-painted it in his bathroom. I heard this story and thought, Well, if he can do that, I can make a guitar or a bass."

Soon after the banjo incident, Stuart set up shop. "I was living in a communal house in the Fort Green section of Brooklyn. I bolted a workbench to my bedroom wall and bought some hand tools at the local hardware store. I purchased wood at H.L. Wild & Company, which was a guitar-parts store in the depths of the East Village. It was this incredible old shop, and if you poked around in there you could find all kinds of amazing things."

Spector based his decision to become a luthier on simple financial reality: "I felt I could build something I couldn't afford to purchase." There were no lutherie books for electric guitars or basses, so Stuart learned by trial and error—with a little help from his friends. "When I was making my first instrument, somebody told me about some guys in the next neighborhood who had a wood shop. I went over there and met Billy Thomas, who became one of my closest lifelong friends. He was an experienced woodworker who also played guitar and bass. Billy was interested in what I was doing, and he offered to teach me how to run woodworking equipment without maiming myself. He was very proud that he came from three generations of woodworkers, all of whom had retained all of their fingers."

Spector soon completed his first bass: a fretless with an all-maple neck and a padauk/mahogany body. The decision to build a fretless was, once again, practical: it meant he didn't have to figure out where to place the frets. "There were no bass pickups available," Stuart recalls, "so I made a primitive one, using a sewing-machine motor to wind the wire. I remember getting little bar magnets and putting them in the middle of this wooden core and winding it. It didn't work great, but you could get a sound. I made a tailpiece out of a brass bar, and the bridge was a piece of ebony."

When Thomas and several colleagues rented a loft in an old factory building to set up the Brooklyn Woodworkers Cooperative, Spector got a space there and began to build instruments in earnest. "Eventually I worked up enough courage to go up to 48th Street and show a bass to Bernie Gracin at Gracin & Towne Music. He said, 'Yeah, I can sell these' and paid me $450 or something like that." Bolstered by his first commercial success, Stuart formed a partnership with a former furniture builder, Alan Charney, and went into business as Spector Guitars. His first employee was a novice luthier named Vinnie Fodera [see Fodera]. Their early offerings included the SB-1 neck-through-body bass, which had a black-walnut body and a DiMarzio pickup.

In 1976 Spector and some of his co-op friends visited a cabinet shop where the woodworking machinery was being sold off. "The guy was moving on to something else. He had an assistant named Ned Steinberger; Ned moved into our place, where he was designing and

■ Spector SB-1 (top left), ca. 1975, NS-1 prototype, 1977 (top right), and NS-2, 1985.

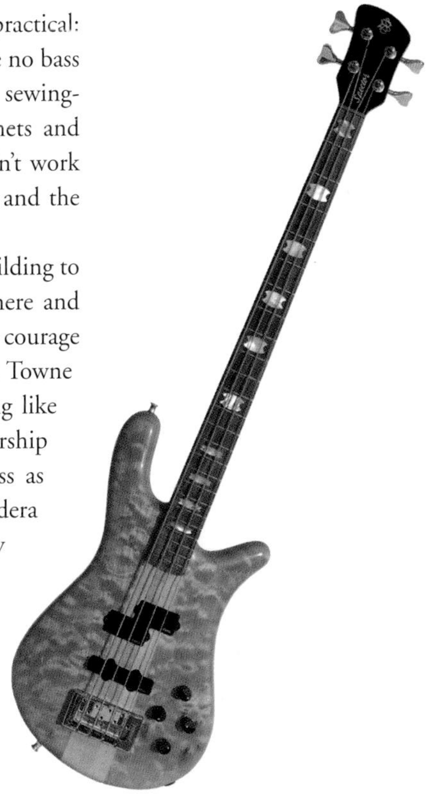

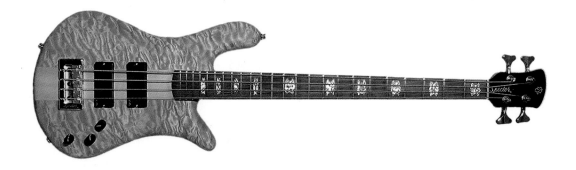

■ Spector NS-4.

■ Spector Rex-4.

building furniture. He became fascinated with the idea that we were nutty enough to make musical instruments, and he said, 'Hey, I think I could design a bass guitar.' I said, 'Great, be my guest.' He came back a week later with the first version of the NS carved-body bass, which we're still making to this day." The NS prototype had a maple through-body neck, walnut body wings, a single pickup (maker unknown), and a Badass bridge. Steinberger attached a lead weight to the lower part of the body to improve its balance—an inelegant solution that got him thinking about designing a bass with tuning machines on the body [see Steinberger].

Introduced in 1977, the Spector NS quickly became a favorite of pro bassists. The original single-pickup model was designated NS-1; dual-pickup versions were tagged NS-2. Spector offered many variations, but all featured a crisp, focused sound and the curved "ergonomic" body shape that makes them more comfortable to play than flat-bodied basses. For ease of production, Steinberger had designed the bass so the neck blank ran the full length of the instrument, with not only body wings but outer peghead sections glued on to create the finished shape. It was clever—and it worked.

As demand for the innovative NS heated up, Spector Guitars grew rapidly, and in 1985 Kramer acquired the company. Production was moved to Kramer's New Jersey factory in January 1986, and Stuart took on a consultant's role. Spector-by-Kramer basses were produced for the next five years, including thousands of budget-priced Spectors (most of them NS-2A models) made in Korea. Production ended in 1990, when Kramer went bankrupt. Stuart Spector soon began to build basses again, affixing the SSD (Stuart Spector Design) label while engaging in a legal battle to recover the Spector trademark—which he did in 1998.

The born-again Spector operation offers high-end basses made in Stuart's shop in Saugerties, New York, as well as Spector-designed production instruments built in the Czech Republic, Korea, and China. The U.S.-made instruments include the familiar neck-through NS bass, with various wood, pickup, and electronics options, and the bolt-on NS-2J, with its "deep inset" neck and EMG-J pickups, which revives a model first made in 1982. (Another bolt-on model, the B.O.B., was offered from 1996 to 1999.) The Spector 4-strings have a 34" scale length; 5- and 6-string basses have a 35" scale. A semi-hollow NS model, with piezo pickups, was added to the line in 2002.

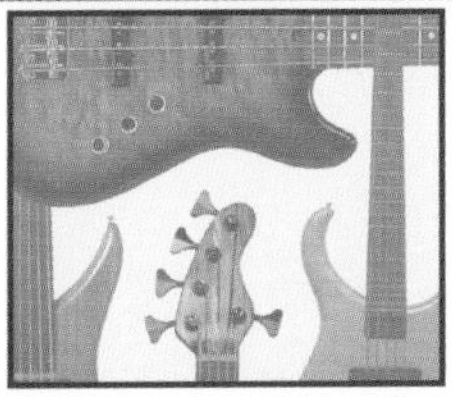

BOLT-ON vs. NECK-THROUGH

By Stuart Spector

The most common description of the difference between bolt-on and neck-through-body basses is that bolt-ons sound "punchier" and neck-throughs have "more sustain." If you compare the progenitors of these genres—a Fender P-Bass and, let's say, an Alembic neck-through—then this evaluation is probably true. However, I feel that these characteristics have a lot to do with all the materials and components used to make the instrument, not just the way the neck is attached.

There's no voodoo involving the transmission of sound through uninterrupted fibers of wood linking both ends of the string. It's physics, not magic. If you look at a typical bolt-on bass, it usually has a body made of a lighter and probably softer wood (alder or swamp ash) than the neck (hard maple). The bridge is attached to that body wood, and in many cases the bridge is lighter than the type found on neck-through basses. Both of these factors affect the resonant frequency of the bass and thus affect how much energy is either conserved in the vibration of the string or absorbed by the sympathetic vibration of the body and bridge.

Another important factor is the stiffness of the neck. Fender necks are typically made from one piece of maple and have a light, single-action trussrod. Usually this works fine—and if there's a problem with the neck, a bolt-on is much easier to replace. Replacement isn't possible with a neck-through, of course, so responsible builders make every effort to build a neck that's as strong and reliable as possible. This usually involves multi-laminated wood, more elaborate trussrod systems, and reinforcement with high-tech composites such as carbon fiber (graphite). The resulting stiffness raises the resonant frequency of the neck above the resonant frequencies of the strings. This keeps the energy of the vibrating string in the string and allows it to continue vibrating longer, thus enhancing sustain.

The construction of the pickups is yet another factor. On Fender pickups, the polepieces are placed on either side of the string. This arrangement accentuates the initial attack and lessens the sustain, as the string finishes its vibration at a greater distance from the polepiece than it would if it were directly beneath the string. A pickup that has a bar core running the length of its coil will sense the attack and decay of the note in a more even fashion, so the sound will have less attack and more sustain.

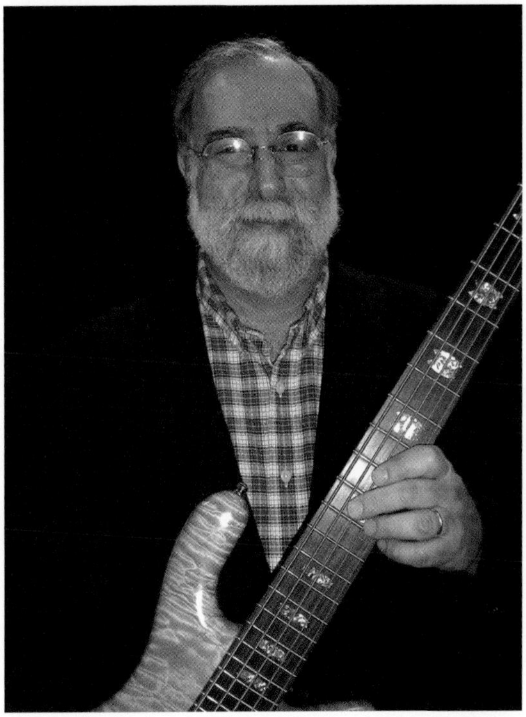

■ Stuart Spector with Spector NS-5.

I know from experience that it's possible to build a bolt-on bass that has virtually the same solidity of connection as a neck-through. You can craft a very tight-fitting neck pocket, use extra bolts, and apply a great deal of pressure to the connection. Will the resulting instrument have great attack or great sustain? In my opinion, that will depend on a number of choices in materials and construction that extend way beyond the method of neck attachment.

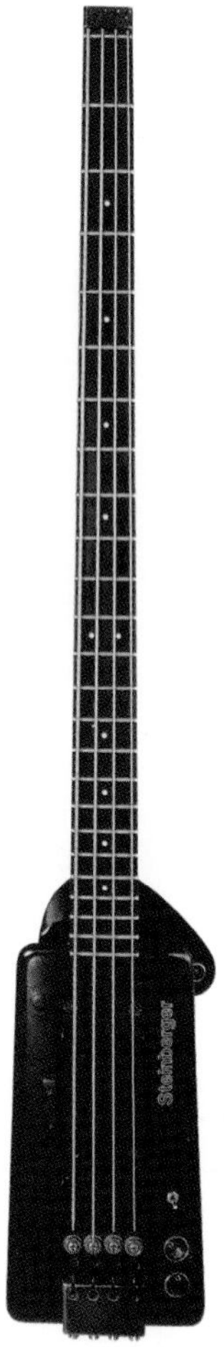

STEINBERGER

Ned Steinberger is a designer who happened to become an instrument maker. While working on furniture at the Brooklyn Woodworkers Cooperative in the mid 1970s, Steinberger became friends with Stuart Spector, who was renting a nearby loft space. Curious about the basses Spector was building, Steinberger decided to try his hand at designing one—and his concept became the Spector NS, an instrument so well conceived that it became an instant (and much-imitated) classic [see Spector].

But Ned wasn't satisfied. There were aspects of the NS that struck him as clumsy, especially the way he had to offset its neck-heaviness by adding weight to the body. Steinberger took out a clean sheet of paper and tried again, this time improving the balance by lopping off the peghead and moving the tuners to the body—creating the Steinberger headless bass.

The concept was simple, but the execution proved to be difficult. Ned at first experimented with a lightweight wooden structure, but it wouldn't produce a decent tone. Then he began to consider synthetics. "It was really a clear evolutionary path to graphite, because I was familiar with fiberglass," he says. "I'd used it on boats and furniture. So I covered the whole thing with fiberglass. It weighed twice as much and was four times as stiff—and it sounded pretty damn good."

Convinced that rigidity was the key to good sound, Steinberger began to build a bass from graphite. "When I first got it, I thought I'd been sold the wrong stuff. Graphite is very stiff and therefore brittle, but fiberglass—which has inferior properties when molded—is nevertheless very tough by comparison to graphite, in loose form. I thought, This stuff is no good—it's too fragile. I had a lot of learning to do. It took months of work to get a mold together, and I had no money at the time. Everything was done on a shoestring. On one of my early attempts, I ended up with everything glued together—it was an improperly released mold, totally inseparable, a 100 percent loss. That was a dark moment."

Undaunted, Steinberger forged ahead. Before the end of 1977, he had built a complete instrument. All he had to do was convince someone to play it. "I was still working in the furniture business, and I was down in York, Pennsylvania. Stanley Clarke was on his way through, playing with his band. I went to the show and showed him this new bass. I don't even know how I got in to see him, but he

■ Steinberger L-Series prototype, ca. 1979.

■ Steinberger L1, ca. 1980.

was really encouraging. He understood what I was doing, and even though it didn't suit his needs, he recognized that there was something going on. And he gave me a lot of helpful hints."

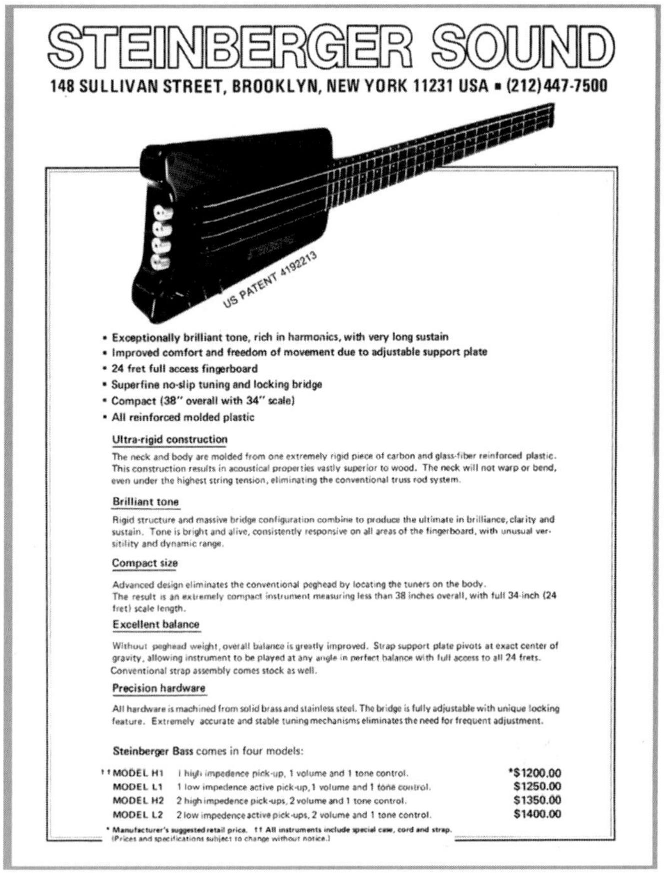
STEINBERGER SOUND

148 SULLIVAN STREET, BROOKLYN, NEW YORK 11231 USA • (212)447-7500

US PATENT 4192213

- Exceptionally brilliant tone, rich in harmonics, with very long sustain
- Improved comfort and freedom of movement due to adjustable support plate
- 24 fret full access fingerboard
- Superfine no-slip tuning and locking bridge
- Compact (38" overall with 34" scale)
- All reinforced molded plastic

Ultra-rigid construction

The neck and body are molded from one extremely rigid piece of carbon and glass-fiber reinforced plastic. This construction results in acoustical properties vastly superior to wood. The neck will not warp or bend, even under the highest string tension, eliminating the conventional truss rod system.

Brilliant tone

Rigid structure and massive bridge configuration combine to produce the ultimate in brilliance, clarity and sustain. Tone is bright and alive, consistently responsive on all areas of the fingerboard, with unusual versitility and dynamic range.

Compact size

Advanced design eliminates the conventional peghead by locating the tuners on the body.
The result is an extremely compact instrument measuring less than 38 inches overall, with full 34-inch (24 fret) scale length.

Excellent balance

Without peghead weight, overall balance is greatly improved. Strap support plate pivots at exact center of gravity, allowing instrument to be played at any angle in perfect balance with full access to all 24 frets. Conventional strap assembly comes stock as well.

Precision hardware

All hardware is machined from solid brass and stainless steel. The bridge is fully adjustable with unique locking feature. Extremely accurate and stable tuning mechanisms eliminates the need for frequent adjustment.

Steinberger Bass comes in four models:

†† MODEL H1	1 high impedence pick-up, 1 volume and 1 tone control.	*$1200.00
MODEL L1	1 low impedence active pick-up, 1 volume and 1 tone control.	$1250.00
MODEL H2	2 high impedence pick-ups, 2 volume and 1 tone control.	$1350.00
MODEL L2	2 low impedence active pick-ups, 2 volume and 1 tone control.	$1400.00

* Manufacturer's suggested retail price. †† All instruments include special case, cord and strap. (Prices and specifications subject to change without notice.)

■ 1980 Steinberger brochure.

Steinberger tried to sell his concept to a major instrument company, but there were no takers. Somewhat reluctantly, he went into business on his own. Hap Kuffner and Stan Jay of Mandolin Bros. were early believers in his design; along with plastics engineer Bob Young, they became partners in Steinberger Sound, founded in 1979. The new company began to produce instruments—about six a month at first—but acceptance was slow. "We went to Summer NAMM in 1980," Ned recalls, "and we were pretty much the laughingstock of the show. People would walk by the booth and start giggling." Then, at one of the show's evening concerts, Andy West of the Dregs demonstrated what could be done with a Steinberger L-series bass. His spectacular performance turned the giggles into gasps of astonishment. "The next day the booth was mobbed, and it was mobbed for years and years following. If there was ever any doubt about what you need to get people interested in musical instruments—well, it's musicians."

Steinberger's visibility was further boosted by Tony Levin, who played an early fretless prototype of the rectangular-bodied bass. "That instrument had a lot of hardened steel in it, mixed with the graphite—the thing weighed a ton," says Ned. "It had liabilities, but that super-stiff, super-heavy construction gave it a really sweet, dynamic sound."

The early Steinberger line included the H1 (with one DiMarzio high-impedance pickup) and H2 (two DiMarzio high-impedance pickups) models; the better-known L1 and L2 basses were identical except for their EMG low-impedance pickups. Because the tiny body made seated playing a problem, these basses had a hinged leg-rest that could be swung into place. The L2 model is much more common: about 1,500 L2s were produced compared to only about 50 L1s. A 5-string L-series bass joined the line in 1982; it's often referred to as a "narrow 5" because Ned designed the bridge to fit in the same space as the standard 4-string bridge.

By 1984, soon after Steinberger moved from Brooklyn to a new factory in Newburgh, New York, the L2 bass had evolved into the XL2. This is perhaps the ultimate expression of the Steinberger bass concept: a headless one-piece instrument made of molded graphite, with a small rectangular body (usually black but sometimes white) and a pair of EMG-HB active pickups. Ned cooked up some clever options over the next few years, including the DB detuning bridge, with a flip lever that drops the *E* string to a predetermined pitch (usually *D*), and the TransTrem pitch-shifting bridge. The XL5W ("wide 5") model offered the string spacing most 5-string players favor. The most radical version of all was the XL2GR, with a Roland synthesizer pickup and controls onboard. This was definitely *not* your father's bass guitar.

■ 1985 Steinberger XL2.

■ Steinberger XM2 with TransTrem bridge, ca. 1989.

The Steinberger bass got lots of attention and collected awards by the armful, but it still faced resistance in the market. Grudgingly, Ned Steinberger acknowledged this problem by introducing less radical models. The XP basses, conceived as a sort of bargain line, had V-shaped wood bodies with bolt-on Steinberger Blend necks and passive pickups. They weren't very successful and disappeared after a couple of years. The XM2, with a more "guitar-like" double-cutaway wood body, joined the line in 1986. In that same year, tired of trying to be a businessman instead of a designer, Ned sold his company to Gibson. Production at the time was about 3,000 instruments a year. Ned stayed on as a consultant, eventually helping Gibson shift manufacturing from Newburgh to a new factory in Nashville that was shared with another corporate acquisition, Tobias.

Gibson continued to move Steinberger toward more "normal" designs. In 1990 the company introduced the Q4 (4-string) and Q5 (5-string) models; they had contoured rock-maple bodies that were available in such un-Steinbergerish colors as bright red. In the mid '90s these basses were restyled and renamed the XQ2 and XQ2-5, causing further market confusion. At least one bass, possibly a prototype, was made with EMG PJ-style pickups and called the XQ3.

Even the XL2 model got a new name under Gibson, becoming the XL Standard. (The XL Pro had a DB bridge; the XL Elite added active electronics and a snazzy gold Elite logo; the XL Standard 5 was—you guessed it—a 5-string.) More and more production was moved offshore, and by the time the Nashville factory was shut down in 1998, most of the Steinberger basses being sold were all-wood "Spirit" knockoffs made in Korea. Gibson has announced its intention to revive the classic Steinberger basses, but whether that happens or not, there's no doubt that Ned Steinberger's creation has left an indelible mark on the future of bass design.

SEE ALSO: NS DESIGN

■ Steinberger XQ2, mid-1990s.

STEVENS

Cowboy poet, horse trainer, songwriter, ranch hand, and master builder—Michael Stevens is one of a kind. He got his start as a luthier in 1967, working with Larry Jameson at Guitar Resurrection in Oakland, California. Then, in 1974, Michael abruptly switched careers, leaving the musical-instrument business to pursue another passion: training Arabian show horses. He reunited with Jameson in 1978 at a new Guitar Resurrection in Austin, Texas, and then moved on to his own shop.

In 1986 Fender lured Stevens to California, where he and John Page headed the newly established Fender Custom Shop [see Fender]. While there, Michael built instruments for many of Fender's most famous endorsers and played a key role in the revitalization of R&D under Bill Schultz. After four years, he returned to Texas and founded Stevens Electrical Instruments, where he builds basses and guitars that showcase his design chops and meticulous craftsmanship.

The Slant 4 bass gets its name from a pair of Stevens double-J pickups, mounted at an angle, with the bass side closer to the bridge. It has an alder body, a 22-fret graphite-reinforced maple neck with a kingwood fingerboard, and a strings-through-body bridge. Scale length is 34". Stevens believes that a lighter bridge is better for tone, so his are made from aircraft-grade aluminum. The Slant's electronics are passive, but there's a 3-way pickup-selector switch plus two hidden mini-switches, for maximum tonal flexibility. Stevens also builds Slant 5 and Slant 6 models, with 24 frets and a 35" scale length. His basses have a classic look, with double-cutaway bodies, pickguards, and Fender-style headstocks, but they have many subtle refinements and are carefully tailored for maximum player comfort.

■ Stevens Slant 5; detail photo (left) shows the control setup, with mini-switches hidden in body recesses.

STICK

While it's true that the invention of a new instrument can inspire new ways of playing—and the bass guitar is a prime example—the reverse can also be true. Consider the Stick.

The origin of the technique known as "touch style" or "two-hand tapping" dates back to the late 1940s or early 1950s, when several guitarists, including Merle Travis and Jimmy Webster, pioneered the idea of using both hands to tap

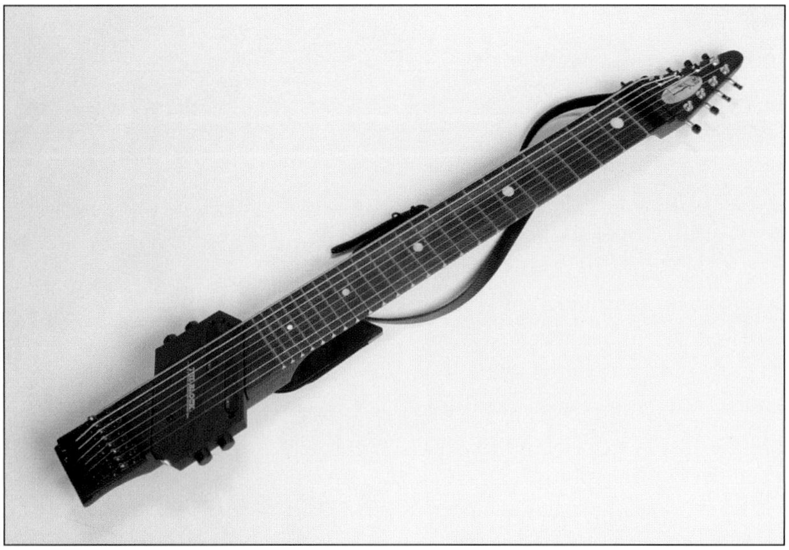

■ Stick Bass (8-string), rosewood.

on the strings, creating melodies, chords, and bass lines simultaneously. In the late '50s, Dave Bunker took a different approach, building a doubleneck guitar-and-bass instrument that he played using the touch technique [see Bunker]. The idea hung around and eventually got a big boost from the two-handed virtuosity of such artists as guitarists Eddie Van Halen and Stanley Jordan and bassists Michael Manring and Victor Wooten.

In 1969 a guitarist named Emmett Chapman was experimenting with new sound-production ideas and trying out different modifications on the instruments he'd built. (At one point, he was playing a 9-string guitar that had a "gear shift" lever for retuning the highest string.) "Then one evening," Chapman later wrote in *Electronic Musician*, "a sudden impulse struck from out of the blue, and I started to play the full two-handed technique. Realizing the implications this would have for my music sent me leaping around the house in sheer delight."

At the time, Chapman was unaware of the earlier two-handed tappers—but his approach was different, anyway. He moved his guitar to a near-vertical position and placed his right hand perpendicular to the strings, rather than in the normal picking position. "All fingers of both hands were now locked in and matched the frets anywhere on the board . . . [and] the musical result is that you can play two, three, and even four notes on a single string with only finger manipulation and no arm movement."

Chapman soon realized that a standard guitar wasn't the ideal instrument for applying his piano-like technique, so he began to invent a new one. Between 1970 and 1974 he built a series of prototypes, each one evolving a little further away from conventional guitar design and toward the Stick. The final product looked something like a 10-string neck-through-body bass—without the body. The strings were divided into two groups, with five melody strings tuned in descending fourths (*DAEBF#*) and five bass strings tuned in ascending fifths (*CGDAE*). The lowest-pitched string in each group was in the center of the flat fingerboard, so each hand moved up in pitch as it moved outward. Because of this tuning and string configuration, patterns learned in one position could be moved easily up or down the fingerboard.

■ Stick XG (10-string), graphite with 36" scale length.

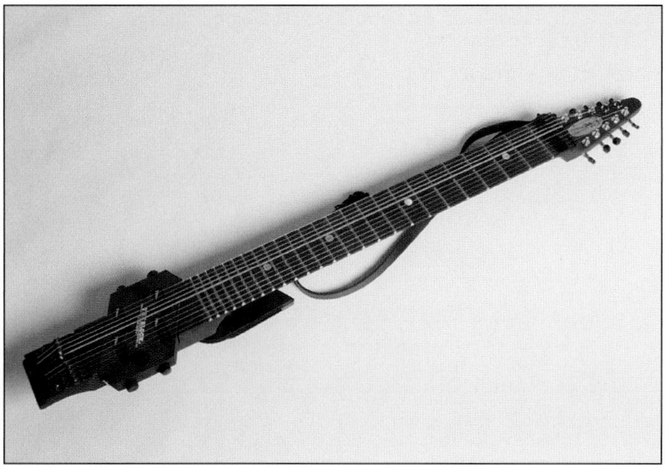

In 1974 Chapman begin to build a production version of the Stick. It was made from Brazilian ironwood (pau ferro), had 25 frets (plus a zero fret), and a pair of humbucking pickups, one for each string group. The pickups were mounted on a sliding block, and the wiring was stereo, so each string group could be run through its own amplifier. Because it had bass

■ Grand Stick (12-string), mahogany.

strings, scale length was 34". Bass players were immediately drawn to it; the Stick's early acceptance owes much to the work of Tony Levin, Alphonso Johnson, and Miroslav Vitous. Levin, in particular, opened people's ears to the Stick's potential by playing it with Peter Gabriel and King Crimson; his ingenious parts often covered the bass function and added richness to the upper-register textures at the same time.

In 1985 Chapman began to build another version of the Stick, made from polycarbonate resin and equipped with stainless-steel rods as frets—these eventually became standard equipment on the wooden models as well. A MIDI-interface option was added a year later.

Almost from the beginning, musicians requested different tunings and string configurations, and in 1991 the possibilities became more complex with the introduction of a 12-string model called the Grand Stick. It can be configured with seven melody and five bass strings, or six of each. There's also an 8-string all-bass model, the Stick Bass. Its strings follow the usual bass-guitar setup, with the lowest string closest to the upper edge of the fingerboard; standard tuning is *BEADGCFB♭*, but there are many possible variations. A mid-'90s collaboration with Ned Steinberger produced the NS/Stick Guitar-Bass, an 8-string instrument with a small alder body. The strings are tuned in fourths, beginning with low *B*; in the upper register, they can remain in fourths or be tuned in a guitar relationship, with a major third between the 2nd and 3rd strings—or something else, if that's what you want.

Current Stick models are made in laminates of several different hardwoods, including Indonesian rosewood, canarywood, purpleheart, and padauk. The large shell inlays on the fingerboard can be white pearl, black pearl, abalone, or paua. In 2001 all-graphite Sticks, with neck beams made by Moses, debuted. The graphite models have a 36" scale length and one additional fret. A Roland MIDI-interface system is available for all Sticks, and Emmett Chapman continues to refine the features and capabilities of the family of instruments derived from that "sudden impulse" he had back in 1969.

■ Victor Bailey with Pensa-Suhr J-style bass.

■ Sukop 5-string with 35" scale length.

SUHR

"I started playing guitar in the early '70s," says John Suhr, "but I really wanted to play bass. I was intrigued by the bass in the Beatles' music, and I wanted to be as melodic as Paul McCartney. I asked about lessons at my local music store, and I was told, 'You have to learn guitar before you can play bass.' To this day, I would like to go back to that person and say 'Wrong!'"

Suhr did learn guitar, though, and he was soon gigging as a club musician in his native New Jersey. He plunged into repairs, too, working in a couple of shops and "hanging around" with luthier Bob Benedetto. "After playing for a few more years and doing all my own repair work, I moved to Brooklyn and began cooking in a place in Soho," says John. "I worked with a guy named Carmine, and I was told to fire him because he sliced the meat too thick for the boss's sandwich. Carmine got a job at Rudy's Music Stop [on West 48th Street]. He told Rudy Pensa about my repair skills."

Pensa hired Suhr to set up a repair shop in his store, and it eventually took over two entire floors in the building. The customer list included many of the city's top studio players. Rudy and John also collaborated on a line of Pensa-Suhr instruments, Fender-inspired basses and guitars with electronics that were quite advanced for the 1980s. One of their customers was Victor Bailey, who bought a Pensa-Suhr J-style bass. "It's the most amazing bass I've ever played," he said in a 1989 *Guitar Player* interview. "The neck is perfect, and it's easy to play stuff that I was struggling to play on other basses. It sounds and feels great."

In 1991 Suhr moved to California to work with rack-gear guru Bob Bradshaw. Two years later, he was offered a position as a master builder at the Fender Custom Shop. "I worked there with J Black, a good friend from New York City who had worked with Roger Sadowsky. It was his prodding that convinced me to take the job." While at Fender, Suhr designed pickups and preamps for the new Precision and Jazz production models introduced in 1995 [see Fender]. "But I still wasn't doing what I wanted to do," he says, "which was to make everything myself and have 100 percent control over what I was making, from design to wood to paint to electronics."

With that goal in mind, Suhr left Fender in 1997 to establish JS Technologies Inc./Suhr Guitars. Since then he's been building guitars in several different styles—but he hasn't forgotten his early affinity for bass. In mid 2002 John stated plans to begin building basses, both vintage-style and "modern design," later in the year.

SUKOP

There's nothing like an early start. Stephen Sukop began playing bass when he was 10 and built his first instrument—a fretless acoustic bass guitar—when he was 16. "The wood came from an old TV console," says Sukop. "I bent the sides by soaking the paneling in a bathtub for almost a week, until my mom couldn't take it anymore." He moved on to a headless bass with a body hacked from an oak 2x6 and a neck hijacked from a Gibson Grabber.

While attending Berklee College of Music in 1984, Sukop made several more basses, including some with solid purpleheart bodies. In 1989 he moved back to his native Pennsylvania to begin building full time, and he's been at it ever since. He relocated to New Mexico in 1997, where he takes time off from carving and sanding to teach snowboarding. (He's a certified instructor.)

Sukop's handmade double-cutaway basses have five-piece or seven-piece maple and purpleheart through-body necks. Body cores are made of mahogany, ash, alder, or walnut. Stephen often uses curly, quilted, spalted, or burl maple for the tops; other woods, and semi-hollow bodies, are available. "Around 1994 I started making 'constant radius' instruments," he says. "I carve the top so the radius of the body matches that of the fingerboard." For maximum clarity, he favors custom bridges (made by Kahler or, more recently, Dingwall) with an independent section for each string. The 24-fret (or fretless) fingerboards are made of wenge, maple, rosewood, ebony, or purpleheart. Scale length can be 34", 35", or 36"; the number of strings can be 4, 5, 6, or 7. Bartolini pickups and electronics are standard.

Every Sukop bass is topped with a distinctive hourglass-shaped headstock with an inlaid centaur figure. But more important than any aspect of his basses' construction, says Stephen, is the feel: "If it feels right, you'll get the sound."

SURINE

At first glance, the wide bodies, long horns, and small pegheads of Surine basses look a little odd. But Scott Surine carefully considered their dimensions, and he emphasizes that he's as concerned with the ergonomics of his instruments—especially balance—as he is with their sonic versatility. In that respect, they're first-rate. As Tom Mulhern noted in a 1993 *Bass Player* review, "I'm not sure a 5-string can be much less neck-heavy than this, short of using a headless design."

Scott, who studied both music and graphic design in college, has been playing bass since 1971. He's the principal designer of the custom basses that bear his name; Kenneth Lofquist handles the lutherie chores. They've been in business in Denver since 1992. The Surine line has gradually expanded from the original Affinity and Protocol models to include four other styles: Esprit, Quest, Regency, and Homage. These neck-through-body instruments all have Bartolini electronics, and all have 24 frets except the semi-hollow Regency, which has an extended fingerboard that adds nine more. The standard scale length is 34".

Surine basses are made in four levels of construction. Series III basses have a two-piece hard-maple neck, rosewood fingerboard, solid-wood body wings, and passive electronics; wood choices include alder, mahogany, and rock maple. Stepping up to Series II brings a three-piece flame-maple neck with purpleheart streamers, active electronics, and more body-wood choices, including walnut and swamp ash. Series I models have a five-piece neck with purpleheart stringers, ebony fingerboard, exotic-wood top and back, and exotic-wood headstock cap with mother-of-pearl logo inlay. The top-of-the-line Series X level, added in the company's tenth anniversary year of 2002, have all of the Series I features and a seven-piece neck. Many different body woods are available for Series I and Series X basses, including bubinga, padauk, and cocobolo. The Regency is made only as a Series I or Series X instrument. All models except the J-style Homage and Series III basses are available as 4-, 5-, 6-, or 7-strings; Homage and Series III are made as 4-, 5-, and 6-strings. If that's not enough choices to ponder, there's a long list of options, including 35" scale length, custom string spacing, and lined or unlined fretless. The idea, says Scott Surine, is to build basses suitable for just about any playing technique or style of music.

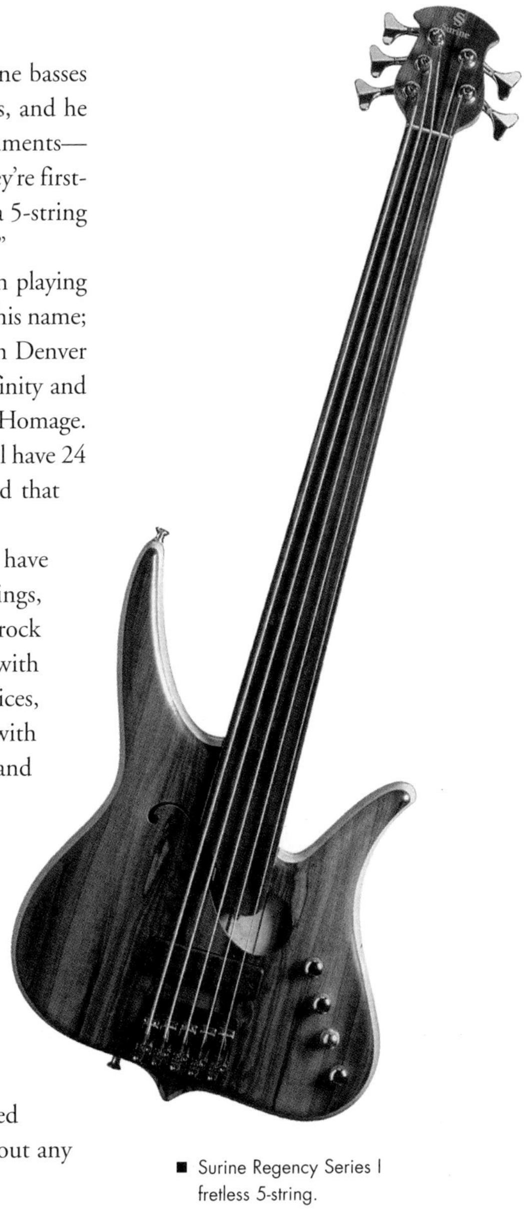

■ Surine Regency Series I fretless 5-string.

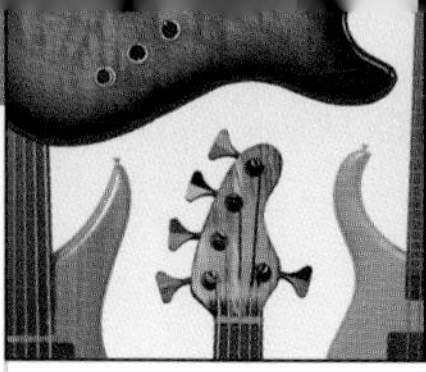

TACOMA

It's become common for an established U.S. instrument manufacturer to start an offshore operation, but the story of Tacoma Guitars turns that scenario on its head. The company's origin can be traced to a wood-processing mill in Tacoma, Washington, that was operated by Young Chang of Korea. The mill's output was shipped back to Korea, where it was used to build pianos and, later, guitars. In 1999, with the Asian economy in recession, Young Chang sold the mill to J.C. Kim, a Korean-American businessman and avid guitarist. Kim enlisted American music-industry veterans Ferd Boyce and Terry Atkins, and together they took over Tacoma Guitars. All of Tacoma's instruments are made in the U.S.

The line includes the Thunderchief, a 34"-scale, single-cutaway acoustic bass guitar with an off-center "paisley" soundhole. (Its teardrop shape recalls a typical pattern found on paisley fabric.) Relocating the soundhole allowed Tacoma to use a "VS" bracing pattern simpler than the ones on conventional acoustic guitars; according to the company's literature, this means "the entire top is free to vibrate as a sound generator, producing unsurpassed volume, bass response, and sustain." Another innovation is the two-bolt neck attachment, which makes adjustments easier than with a traditional set-in (glued) neck.

The Thunderchief was initially offered with a Sitka spruce top and mahogany back and sides; other back and side woods, including rosewood and figured maple, have become available. Elixir polymer-coated strings are standard. Options include 5-string, fretless, and several pickup/preamp systems.

■ Tacoma Thunderchief acoustic bass guitars, fretless (left) and fretted.

TAYLOR

Founded in 1974 by Bob Taylor and Kurt Listug, Taylor Guitars has grown from a tiny shop to one of the world's largest producers of acoustic guitars. By early 2002, the Taylor factory in El Cajon, California, was employing more than 400 workers using both modern computer-controlled equipment and traditional handwork to build 80 different models—including a unique acoustic bass guitar.

The design of the Taylor bass was a collaboration between Bob Taylor and Steve Klein. The most striking visual aspect is its off-center soundhole, which allows the strings to drive more of the top. Closer inspection reveals the body's "bi-directional" taper, which is wider on the treble side than the bass side and wider at the lower bout than it is at the upper bout. This shape creates a large air chamber—essential for a bass—without adding a lot of bulk. And because the top and back are not parallel, the design prevents the standing waves that can cause frequency-cancellation problems.

The Taylor bass has a bolt-on, graphite-reinforced mahogany neck with a sleek, comfortable soft-V shape. The peghead is actually a separate piece, matching the body wood, that's joined to the neck with finger joints. The ebony fingerboard extends over the body, creating a thumb rest for fingerstyle playing, and a graceful cutaway

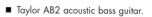

■ Taylor AB2 acoustic bass guitar.

provides easy access to the upper frets. The scale length is 34". For plugged-in playing, it's equipped with a Fishman piezo pickup and preamp.

When introduced in 1996, the Taylor bass was available with a Sitka spruce top and imbuia back and sides (AB1) or all imbuia (AB2). Taylor later added big-leaf maple versions, either with a Sitka spruce (AB3) or maple (AB4) top; the necks are also made of maple. In early 2003 Taylor had temporarily discontinued the AB series and was in the process of redesigning its acoustic bass line.

TOBIAS

Michael Tobias began his career as a repairman in Washington, D.C., and Orlando, Florida, building a few guitars and basses on the side. He moved to California in 1980, working in San Francisco and Costa Mesa before settling in Los Angeles.

The first Tobias Guitars shop was established in a converted storefront at 1614 Cahuenga Boulevard, Hollywood, in 1984. Assisted by Bob Lee and Kevin Almieda, Mike built both guitars and basses—but he soon discovered that most of his customers were bass players, many of them students and teachers at the nearby Musicians Institute.

The Tobias bass quickly garnered a solid reputation for impeccable craftsmanship, good sound, and excellent playability. The centerpiece of the instrument was a multi-laminate, through-body neck made of different combinations of maple, walnut, purpleheart, wenge, and bubinga. On the Basic and Classic models, the neck was five-piece; on the top-of-the-line Signature, it was seven-piece. This method of construction provided both excellent stability and sustain superior to that available with a bolt-on neck. Tobias carved the neck in an asymmetric "airplane wing" shape, wider at the top edge (lowest-pitched string) than the bottom edge. (Tobias says he got the idea from luthier Michael Gurian, who used it on his acoustic guitars.) This shape made the bass easier to play, especially on 5- and 6-string models. Fingerboards were made from rosewood or pau ferro, and the body wings were topped with beautiful pieces of flame maple or such rare woods as cocobolo or lacewood. Custom Bartolini pickups and active electronics completed the package.

■ 1990 Tobias Basic 5.

Many top players adopted Tobias basses, including jazz artists like Gary Willis and Jimmy Haslip and such gospel standouts as Freddie Flewelen and Andrew Gouché. As orders increased, Tobias added employees and stepped up production. Even so, by the time of the January 1988 NAMM show, Tobias Guitars had so many back orders it was unable to accept new orders. Unwilling to convert his operation to mass production, Mike Tobias sold the company to Gibson in 1990.

■ 1996 Tobias Growler 5-string.

Tobias basses beginning with serial number 1094 were produced under the new ownership. At first, the same crew built the instruments, working in a larger shop in Burbank and adding such new models as the Killer B (a 5-string with a bolt-on neck) to the line.

Gibson relocated Tobias Guitars to Nashville late in 1992. None of the California crew made the move; the last Tobias bass produced in the Burbank shop carried serial number 2044. In the 1990s Gibson hired subcontractors to produce more-affordable Tobias models, including the Model T (made in the U.S.), the Standard (made in Japan), and the Toby (made in Korea). Mike Tobias stayed on as a consultant until the end of 1994 before establishing a new business, MTD (Michael Tobias Design), in Kingston, New York. Gibson suspended domestic operations of Tobias Guitars in 1998, with production of all Tobias basses moving to offshore factories.

SEE ALSO: MTD (MICHAEL TOBIAS DESIGN)

TRAVIS BEAN

In the heady days of the early 1970s, a drummer and motorcycle racer named Travis Bean decided he could build better guitars and basses by using aluminum for the neck. With partner Marc McElwee, Bean founded his namesake company in Sun Valley, California, in 1974. When production ceased five years later, Bean had built more than 3,500 instruments, including 1,059 basses in two different models. While they had only a small impact on the market, they clearly demonstrated the viability of non-wood necks.

Travis Bean basses have almost-neck-through construction, with a solid piece of aluminum extending from the peghead, with its T-shaped knockout, to the bridge. The two pickups are attached to this unit, known as the "receiver." Most of the basses produced were TB2000 models, with double-cutaway, natural-finish koa bodies; options included fretless and a choice of scale length. (Bean built two short-scale basses for Bill Wyman of the Rolling Stones.) The company also produced three dozen TB4000 basses, with wedge-shaped bodies.

While the stability and sustain of Travis Bean basses impressed some players, their neck heaviness and the cold feel of the aluminum drew frequent criticism. The idea was picked up by Gary Kramer, who had been one of Bean's financial backers, although Kramer aluminum-neck basses had a more conventional bolt-on neck configuration [see Kramer]. In 1997 Travis Bean started up his company again, focusing on guitar models.

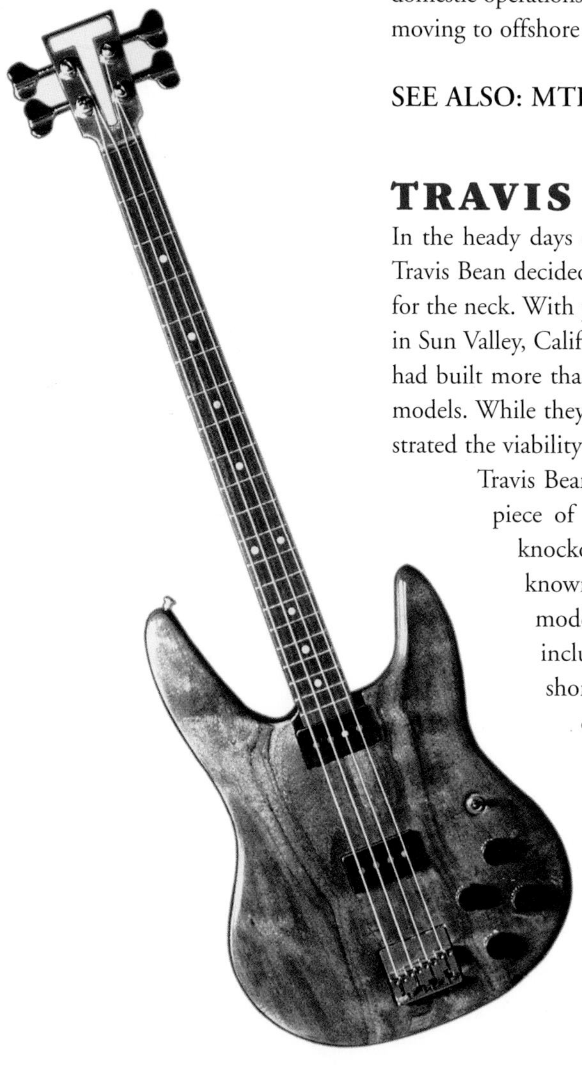

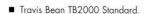

■ Travis Bean TB2000 Standard.

TURNER: SEE RICK TURNER

TYLER

James Tyler's basses are prized by a select group of L.A. and Nashville studio players, who won't leave home without them. "It all started in 1973 when Neil Stubenhaus asked me to build a bass for him. Then I made one for Abe Laboriel," says James, whose tongue is often lodged in cheek. "It's all gone downhill from there."

The Neil Stubenhaus Model is a 34"-scale 5-string. It's got an ash body, maple neck with pau ferro fingerboard, Seymour Duncan PJ pickups—and a huge, commanding sound. The oft-recorded Stubenhaus, who's played on more than 400 album dates (as of 2002), has three of them, plus a Tyler PJ 4-string. James Tyler also builds 34"-scale basses in standard 4- and 5-string configurations as well as the Abraham Laboriel Model, which has tighter string spacing and a different body shape. Other variations include the Paul Slagle Model, with a figured-maple top, and the multi-laminate Hippie Sandwich. For those who prefer longer scale lengths, there are 35"-scale 5- and 6-strings and the scary-looking triple-pickup 36"-scale XXL ("extra, extra long and extra, extra low") 6-string, tuned *F♯BEADG.*

One secret of the Tyler sound is the custom Demeter preamp that James installs. "Years ago, Demeter's preamp was only a simple 3-band EQ," says James. "I had him add buffered panning for the pickups and a gain control that added 10dB. We revoiced the EQ, and then added switches for each band to shift the frequencies up or down." (That said, it should be noted that Stubenhaus prefers to run his Tylers passive in the studio.) The wood is important, too. Tyler used to make his bass bodies from mamywo, a Malaysian wood with strong midrange properties. "Some people liked it, but I decided I wasn't happy with the bottom end," he says. "The basses are ash with an alder center now." All of his basses have an odd-looking stair-step headstock and an asymmetric neck profile, for better playability and less fatigue. Any of the models can be made fretless, and Tyler offers a large menu of custom options, including such unique finishes as "Jimburst" and "Psychedelic Vomit." Though Tyler took his basses out of production for a time, he had scheduled to reintroduce them in 2003.

■ Tyler Five-String with spalted top.

■ Tyler Abraham Laboriel Model 6-string.

U.S. MASTERS

■ U.S. Masters EP52 5-string with flame-maple top (right).

Wisconsin-based U.S. Masters was started in 1995 by brothers David and Richard Regenberg, veterans of musical-instrument retailing. They wanted to offer reasonably priced, American-made basses and guitars that placed a premium on playing ease and flexible sound. They created their EP bass, introduced in 1997, using computer-aided design and manufacturing tools. Available in both 4-string (34" scale) and 5-string (35" scale) models, the EP series has been offered with a wide variety of wood and electronics options. All basses feature the Compression-Set Captive Neck Joint, a patented bolt-on design utilizing threaded steel inserts and machine screws to create a tighter union; according to the company, this "improves attack, sustain, tone, and resonance."

U.S. Masters originally equipped its basses with Bill Lawrence pickups, but in 2000 the company switched to Kent Armstrong models. These are complemented with EMG active electronics on all models except the EP42 and EP52. The EP41p was introduced in 2001 at a direct-sale price of $800 (EP51p 5-string, $859). It features an oil-finished maple body, purpleheart fingerboard, Kent Armstrong P-style pickup, and EMG 3-band EQ.

VACCARO: SEE KRAMER

VALLEY ARTS

■ Valley Arts Custom Pro.

Valley Arts evolved from a teaching studio to a retail store with an extensive repair department to a custom-instrument shop. In the late 1980s and early '90s, the Valley Arts crew, headed by Mike McGuire, built well-regarded basses and guitars for many L.A.-area musicians. Most were Fender-inspired designs, but they featured choice woods, refined construction details, and state-of-the-art electronics. The VA Custom Pro 4- or 5-string bass was made of alder with a carved top of flamed or quilted maple, a bolt-on bird's-eye maple neck, and EMG or Bartolini electronics. The Lee Sklar Signature bass featured Sklar's favored array of two EMG-P pickups. The extensive range of options made virtually every bass a personalized model. Valley Arts was also one of the first outfits to give bassists the opportunity to plunge into the digital world with its MB-4 MIDI Bass.

In the late '80s Valley Arts began to farm out some production work to Japan, and in 1993 it was acquired by the huge Korean musical-instrument manufacturer Samick. Domestic operations were moved from North Hollywood to City of Industry, California, and Valley Arts has carried on as a sort of custom shop, doing R&D work for Samick and building a few instruments. Recent bass offerings include several versions of the Custom Pro and the California Pro, 4- or 5-string, with a swamp ash body and PJ pickups.

VEILLETTE

After the 1983 dissolution of his partnership with Harvey Citron, Joe Veillette worked as a musician and collaborated with Stuart Spector for several years before setting up his own business. Veillette at first concentrated on guitars but began to build basses, on a limited basis, in the late '90s. His instruments have an unusually clean look, devoid of inlay and other decorative flourishes. "I like to think of these units as tools for musicians, allowing music to flow as transparently as possible," says Joe. "My instruments are simple and very sturdy."

Simple, perhaps—but certainly not simplistic. Veillette MK IV acoustic/electric basses, available in 34"-scale 4-, 5-, 6-, and 8-string models, fretted or fretless, have a number of distinctive construction features. The single-cutaway poplar body is chambered and topped with figured maple. The graphite-reinforced neck is attached with a single large machine bolt threaded into a "tee-nut" inserted in the neck under the trussrod, a method Veillette chose because it enhanced sustain while retaining the punchy sound of a bolt-on. The rosewood bridge is dovetailed into the body and actually pulled into the joint by string tension; Joe says this helps to give the MK IV fretless a more "woody," upright-like tone. (Fretted models have a wenge bridge.) An Alvarez piezo system with 3-band preamp is standard, and a bridge-position magnetic pickup can be added. Best of all, the instrument is comfortable, well balanced, and light—only seven or eight pounds, depending on configuration.

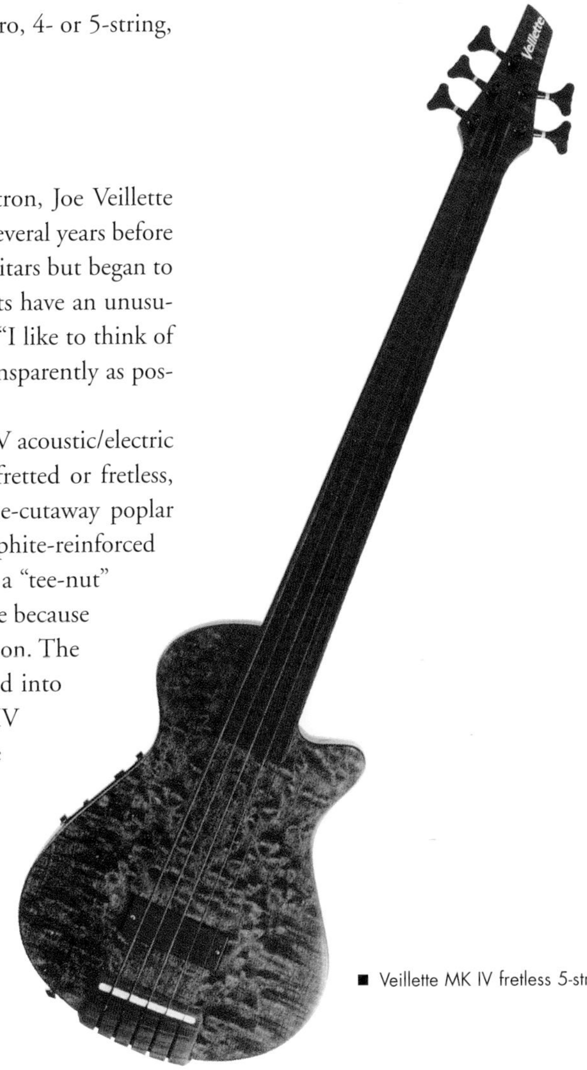

■ Veillette MK IV fretless 5-string.

SEE ALSO: CITRON

VIOLINGUITARMAKER

Peter Jay Huiras of Cedarburg, Wisconsin, is the ViolinGuitarMaker. He studied in the late 1970s with violinmaker August Ohshovy, but is self-taught in carving and inlay work. Huiras describes his elaborate stringed instruments as "storytelling works of art." His electric basses range from almost-conventional instruments such as the Glowaxxxe through-neck 6-string to the extensively carved Pair of Eagles fretless 5-string, with a body made of Jamaican blue mahoe. The Lightning Dragon is Hurais's most elaborate bass creation; carved from curly maple, with inlays of bone and bocote, it expresses his belief in "peace and love through music."

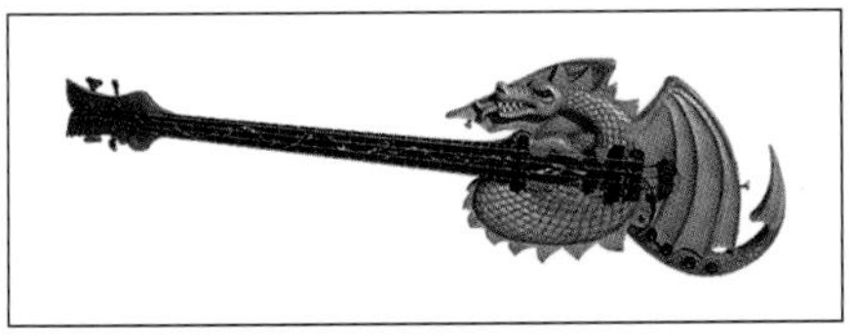

■ ViolinGuitarMaker Lightning Dragon.

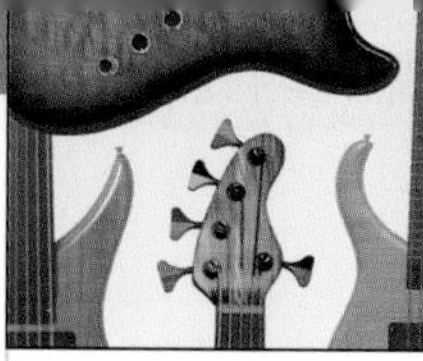

WARR

Since Emmett Chapman invented the Stick in 1970, a bunch of guitar-and-bass instruments have been created for playing in the two-hand tapping style. These have included Charles Soupios's Biaxe, Sergio Santucci's TrebleBass, the Mobius Megatar, and several others, some of which have been played only by their creators. The Warr Guitar joined the club in the late 1990s.

Inventor Mark Warr has declared, "I believe that the Warr Guitar is just that: a guitar"—but it's a bass, too. In fact, it's more like a standard bass than the other touch-style instruments because it has a full-size body, made from premium tonewoods, and can be played in a horizontal position as well as vertically. Warr Guitars are made in 8-, 10-, 11-, 12-, and 14-string models, bolt-on or neck-through, in a wide variety of tunings and string configurations. They incorporate the Buzz Feiten Tuning System. The Artist and Phalanx models have solid bodies; Artisan models are semi-hollow. The Trey Gunn Signature instruments have a number of design refinements, including an elongated body with the bridge placed closer to the center for a "drum effect." All Warr Guitars have a 34" scale length. Bartolini pickups and 18-volt electronics are standard, and there are many options, including piezo pickups and MIDI-interface capability.

■ Warr Phalanx (above) and Artisan (right).

SEE ALSO: STICK, MOBIUS MEGATAR

WARRIOR

Founded by J.D. Lewis in 1994, the Atlanta-area Warrior's first instrument was the neck-through Warrior Bass. A year later a bolt-on model called the Crusader joined the line; it was succeeded in 1996 by the Standard, a similar model with a more traditional body shape. Since then, Warrior has continued to refine its basses with numerous improvements in electronics and construction, including the "G Factor" through-body stringing system. Warrior places a sword inlay, rather than the conventional two dots, at the 12th fret. Custom "collectable art" instruments, many with unusual wood combinations and elaborate inlays featuring Biblical motifs, receive special attention. In addition to 4-, 5-, and 6-string models, Warrior offers extra-extended-range 7- and 9-string basses and multi-course 12- and 15-string instruments. In 2002 Warrior's luthiers were building bolt-on Soldier models and neck-through and set-neck basses in the Studio, Signature, and Dran Michael series, as well as one-of-a-kind King's Closet premium instruments.

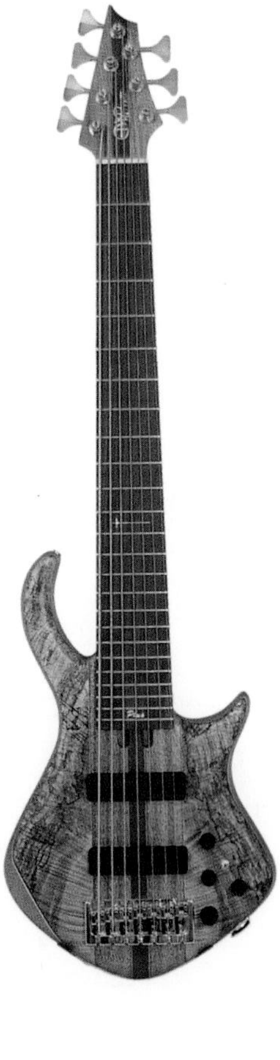

■ Warrior Custom 7-string.

WASHBURN

■ Washburn XB900.

Washburn is one of those music-industry brand names that just won't go away, making more comebacks than an aging heavyweight fighter. Its history stretches back to the late 1800s, when the Lyon & Healy Company of Chicago plucked the middle name of one of its founders, George Washburn Lyon, for its premium line of guitars. Lyon & Healy was one of the behemoths of its era, cranking out 100,000 instruments a year at one point, but by 1930 its fortunes were flagging. The Washburn name then passed to the Tonk Bros. distribution company, who farmed out production of Washburn-brand instruments to several Chicago-area manufacturers. The Washburn name disappeared after World War II but surfaced again in 1962, when Roland revived it for a line of guitars made in the Far East. In 1975 it was sold again, this time to Chicago businessman Rudy Schlacher, who has used it to market basses and guitars, the vast majority of them imported from Japan and Korea. There are also a few U.S.-made custom shop instruments.

Many Schlacher-era Washburn basses have been low- to mid-priced student models, but the company's AB series of acoustic bass guitars, with their unique slotted soundholes, found favor with pros in the 1990s. The most notable U.S.-made Washburn solidbody bass was the XB900 Bantam, designed by Grover Jackson and introduced in 1995 [see Jackson]. It featured a swamp ash body, 24-fret bolt-on neck, and custom Bartolini electronics with variable midrange control. It was later updated—the changes included an exotic-wood top in zebrawood, bubinga, or flame maple—and renamed the XB920. Washburn also offered U.S.-made 5-string (XB925), 6-string (XB926), and 8-string (XB928) versions.

WECHTER

Abraham Wechter has been designing and building acoustic instruments since the 1970s. He's best known for his 6- and 12-string guitars, but he has also made a small number of acoustic bass guitars, most notably for radical bass stylist Jonas Hellborg. Wechter's first ABG for Hellborg was a double-cutaway 4-string in the "Roman" style. "My interest in the bass was kindled by him," says Wechter. "His bass was built with a very stiff Sitka spruce top, bubinga back and sides, and a curly maple neck. We tried to maximize the volume and brightness of tone by the choice of woods and the stiff but very light bracing. After Jonas had the bass for a while, he asked me to put on a carved-maple arched back to replace the original bubinga back. At the same time, I raised the action with individual intonation-compensated saddles and filled the neck with steel reinforcing rods—all of this was to maximize the acoustic performance. Jonas was willing to make these modifications in pursuit of the ultimate tone and projection; most players would not be comfortable with such a high action and heavy neck." A second project for Hellborg, begun in 2002, is a 6-string ABG with a 32" scale length, designed in Wechter's patented "Pathmaker" body style.

■ Wechter Jonas Hellborg acoustic bass guitar.

WITTMAN

When someone stole his prized '61 P-Bass, Ken Wittman decided he'd just build a bass to replace it. (And that's why luthiers aren't like you and me.) Before long, he was building basses for other folks, too. Along the way, he came up with some interesting ideas—like a strap system that takes the shoulder pain out of those long gigs and a tuner built right into the instrument.

Wittman's mainstay model is the Aurora. Calling its contoured body shape a "double-cutaway" isn't quite right, because the lower portion of the body hasn't just been cut away—it's pretty much gone. This makes the bass much lighter; Wittman further enhances the ergonomics by making a headless or "pseudo-headed" Aurora (in a bridge-tuning configuration but with a small vestigial headstock). Ken builds most of his basses to order, and there are many choices: 4-, 5-, or 6-string; bolt-on or neck-through; fretted or fretless; domestic or exotic wood; EMG or Bartolini pickups (or something else). He'll even build you a doubleneck, or a bass with a traditional body shape and piezo pickups. About the only thing that's standard is the 34" scale length—and the Spinstrap.

Wittman created the patented Spinstrap system in response to that persistent post-gig complaint: My shoulder hurts! A plate attaches to the back of the bass, at the balance point, with a rotating pivot arm in the center. Both ends of the strap are attached to this arm, not the instrument, so the bass can move freely—even spinning in a circle (thus the name). Because twirling your bass can do interesting things to the cable, the output is connected to a jack on the pivot arm. With the system installed, the strap can be worn over either shoulder; Ken recommends the right, which frees the fretting arm. The Spinstrap really does reduce the physical strain on the body, as has been confirmed by a couple of scientific studies.

The other unique feature of Wittman's basses is the built-in ProTuner: an electronic tuner with an LED display inlaid into the side of the neck, just above the neck/ body joint. The circuit is mounted in the control cavity along with its own 9-volt battery; it's wired before the volume control and activated by a push/pull switch, so you can use it silently or with sound output. Both the ProTuner and the Spinstrap are sold separately and can be retrofitted to many other basses.

- Wittman Aurora 5-string.
- Wittman Aurora fretless 6-string (right), with built-in ProTuner on side of neck (detail below).

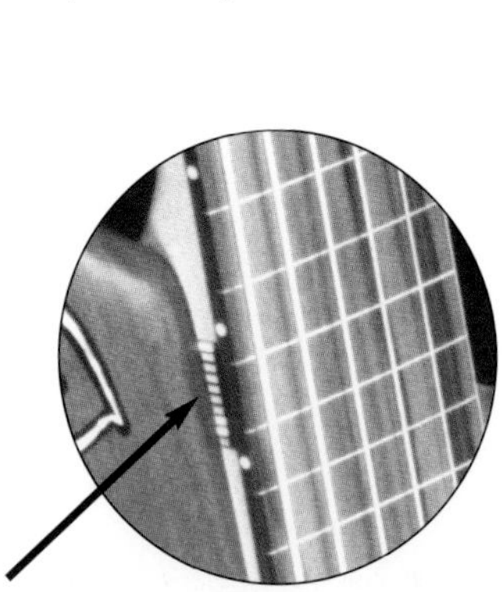

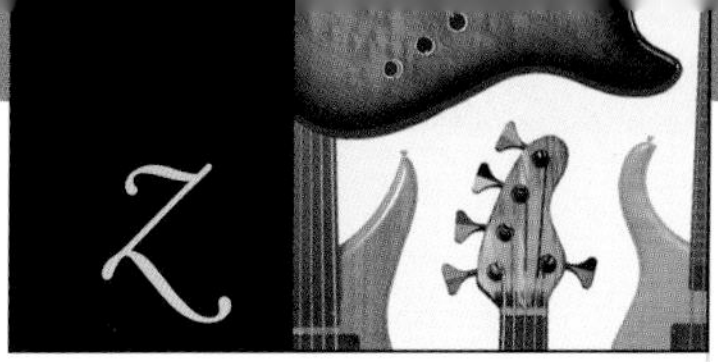

ZETA

Zeta Music Systems of Oakland, California, is best known for its family of electric string instruments, which includes violins, violas, cellos, and upright basses in several different body styles. Zeta also makes the Crossover Bass, a "hybrid" fretless that can be strapped on like a bass guitar or played upright, pizz or arco, on a telescoping endpin. It's made from traditional bass guitar materials—alder, ash, and maple—and Zeta created it as a bridge to upright playing for some electric bassists. Thus the name.

When introduced in the mid 1990s—as the Cross-Over Bass—there were 4-string, 5-string, and Rob Wasserman signature 6-string models, all with a 34" scale. The 6-string was later dropped, and Crossover models were offered at two price levels: Educator (4-string with 34" scale) and Performer (4 string with 34" scale; 5-string with 35" scale). Zeta has made technical and aesthetic upgrades over the years, including better piezo pickups, 18-volt electronics with a "Silent Practice" headphone amp, optional MIDI capability—and no hyphen in the name.

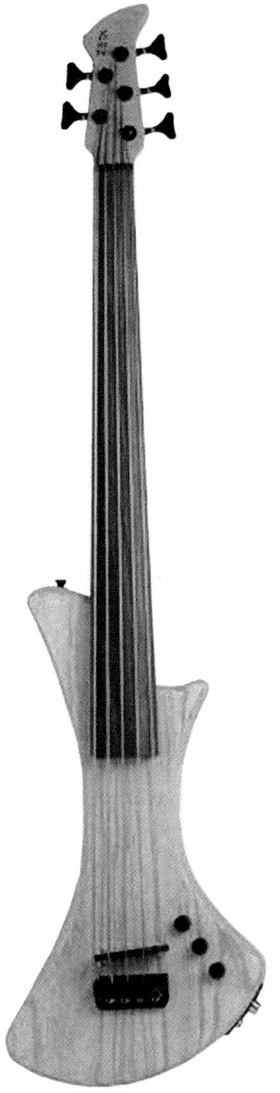

■ Zeta Crossover Bass 5-string.

ZON

"It's quite simple—I woke up one morning and decided I wanted to build an instrument for myself." And that's how Joe Zon became a luthier. End of story.

Well, not quite. Zon's path to building basses and running his own company began on the bandstands of Buffalo, New York, where he often found himself struggling to keep his bass in working order. "When I started playing, I had an old Beatle Bass copy," Joe recalls. "As a kid, I had been good with my hands, building bicycles and fixing things, so it was natural for me to work on my instrument. Things would rattle loose, and I'd take it apart and fix it."

In 1977 Zon decided he was ready for the next step. "My dad had a buddy who worked at a mill, so he had access to wood machines—planers, jointers, all kinds of stuff. And my best friend's dad worked in a lumber yard. At the time, I was working for an auto-parts company, so I swapped a set of brakes for a slab of mahogany and some maple and other stuff. I drew the shape I wanted, and my dad's friend cut it out for me. Then I started carving it by hand."

Zon is quick to note his first two attempts at lutherie were "pretty crude"—and they both ended up as firewood. But on his third try, he came up with a finished instrument. "It's got a reverse Thunderbird body design, because I was quite an Entwistle fan. The body is made of oak, and the neck is birch. There are three pickups: a Guild humbucker in the neck position, a Jazz in the middle, and a P-Bass at the bridge. The P-Bass pickup is reversed, because I thought the bass side should go toward the bridge—I wanted more treble out of the bass strings

■ Zon Legacy Elite V.

■ Zon Sonus 4/1.

■ Zon Sonus Studio 5.

and more bass out of the treble strings. It's got on/off switches for each pickup, plus phase switches and two output jacks. One is stereo and one is mono, so I could run it through three amplifiers."

The multiple-output design of the proto-Zon bass recalls the experiments of another Buffalo bass notable: Billy Sheehan. (Sheehan's modified '69 P-Bass, "The Wife," featured Gibson humbucking and P-Bass pickups wired to separate output jacks.) "I met Billy during my high school years," notes Joe. "We got together on a couple of occasions, just yakking about ideas for instruments, and I took a couple of lessons from him. I was doing my thing and he was doing his, but we had some similar ideas."

Building on what he had learned fixing his own basses, Zon began to develop his repair skills. At first he worked out of his parents' house during the day while gigging at night. His reputation for quality work spread quickly, and soon he had a steady job as a repairman at the Buffalo Guitar Outlet. "It was on-the-job training, and over a few years I learned an awful lot. Eventually I decided I was going to start using all the things I had learned to build my own line of instruments."

Zon Guitars was founded in 1981. Two important discoveries shaped the sound of the early Zon instruments: The first grew out of Joe's work on modular synthesizers at Polyfusion Electronics; what he learned there led to experiments with active circuits, which provided the flexible tone he wanted. And then he encountered graphite necks. "At a NAMM show I came across the Modulus Graphite basses. I played one and really liked what I heard. It had the clarity and brightness of a bass I'd put together using a Kramer aluminum neck, but that bass wouldn't stay in tune. So when I played the Modulus, I thought, Hey—this is interesting! It sounds like that Kramer neck, but it's supposed to be more stable. Soon after that, Modulus started making necks for us, based on masters I carved."

The graphite-neck Zon basses debuted at the 1982 Summer NAMM show. Their distinctive look and clear sound were received enthusiastically by players and dealers, as well as fellow builders such as Ron Wickersham of Alembic. "I really respected Alembic's quality and innovation," notes Joe, "so for Ron to give me positive feedback meant a lot." The early Zon offerings included the futuristic Scepter bass, but Joe really established himself as a builder when he created the Legacy, a mainstay of his line since 1982. An intelligent blend of traditional (wood body, set-neck construction) and high-tech (graphite neck, active electronics) concepts, the Legacy had a distinctive look that immediately set it apart from the many copycat basses on the market.

In 1987 Joe Zon moved his company from Buffalo to Redwood City, California, and Zon's annual output began to grow steadily. The OEM deal with Modulus ended in the early '90s, but Joe found another supplier of composite necks made to his specifications. In 1992 he introduced the Sonus, a new model that represented a contemporary update on the Jazz Bass concept. It was a hit, and Zon has created many variations, including 5- and 6-string versions, the single-pickup Sonus 4/1 and 5/1 models, a Sonus 8-string, and the bubinga-topped Sonus Special. In 1999 he introduced the Sonus LightWave, which has an infrared optical pickup system. "The tone is almost a cross between a solidbody bass and an acoustic bass guitar," says Joe. "This instrument has a different voice—another flavor, another color."

Joe Zon has had a long and productive relationship with virtuoso bassist and

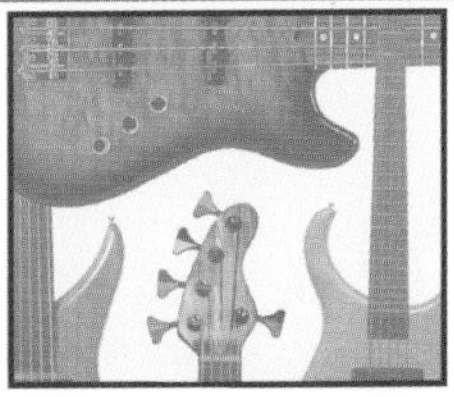

STRING ANGLES & TONE

By Joe Zon

Neck, headpiece, and bridge angles all have an influence on a bass's tone. When I'm designing an instrument, I keep those angles in mind since they have a direct relationship to the string's vibration.

The study of string angles on acoustic instruments dates back to the early 19th century, when the need arose for instruments of increased volume and sound intensity. The electric descendants of those instruments, including the electric bass, still benefit from the principles learned in those days. If an electric bass doesn't sound good acoustically, amplification won't do much to make up for its inadequate tone.

I've found that by increasing the back angle of the non-vibrating portions of the string at the witness points (the points of contact) of the bridge and nut, more downward pressure is created on the section of the string between each witness point and the point of termination. This increase in pressure provides additional sustain and clarity of tone while adding desirable tension. While there's a point of diminishing returns in the amount of tonal improvement that can be achieved by increasing the back angle, varying degrees of angle seem to correlate with given results. By balancing the amount of downward pressure at both string ends, for example, I can achieve a more even open-string response.

The string trees on a non-angled headstock do not produce the same result as an angled headpiece. With a non-angled headstock, some strings have trees imposing pressure to keep them in the nut slots while other strings do not, causing unequal string-to-string downward pressure. Additionally, the uneven string length produced by tuning-key placement results in strings that are unbalanced in tension and, consequently, open-position clarity. I've found that a headpiece with an angle of 11 to 14 degrees creates better string-to-string clarity and sustain, especially if the tuning-key position balances the tension on both sides of the headpiece, as with a 2+2 configuration.

Neck angle is set to provide proper string height (action) in relation to the fingerboard. The higher the bridge is set, the more neck angle is required, causing the strings to be positioned farther from the body. My experience has shown that by keeping the strings as low and parallel to the body as possible, more energy is reflected back into the string, increasing sustain and giving the instrument a warmer, darker tone. Conversely, increasing the neck angle and raising the strings away from the body affects sustain and produces a brighter and more "nasal" tone.

■ Joe Zon with Zon Sonus LightWave fretless and one of his early basses, a three-pickup model wired for "tri-phonic" sound.

Bridge angle refers to the angle at which the string intersects the saddle's witness point. Achieving good tone involves striking the right balance: The back angle needs to be steep enough to produce the desired downward pressure without excessive saddle height. The bridge design itself plays a key role. Saddles with a profile very low to the bridge plate may not provide enough back angle between the saddle and the termination point; when that happens, the downward pressure is minimized, impairing sustain or clarity. Bridges with a separate saddle plate and tailpiece offer good downward pressure, but they tend to require a neck angle that raises the strings farther off the body, causing a brighter, less warm tone.

A strings-through-body design is a more extreme approach to achieving good downward pressure. This method increases tension by having the string extend through the body and bridge plate. The string intersects the saddle at a fairly severe angle, which pulls the string downward across the saddle and provides more downward pressure. The resulting acoustic coupling enhances sustain and clarity of the instrument. The shortcomings of this design are the difficulty of finding strings long enough to work and the somewhat cumbersome operation required to install them.

The subject of string angles has been debated over the years, and many aspects of it are subjective. The ideas I've suggested here are guidelines derived from my years as a designer and builder of basses. Ultimately, the characteristics that string angles affect are also influenced by other design aspects and instrument components. In the end, it's how all of these characteristics are integrated that determines if the bass produces the tone the builder is striving to achieve.

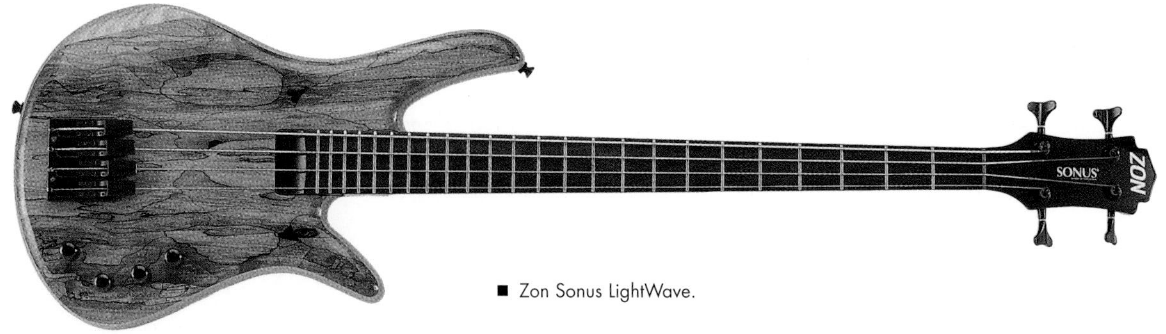

■ Zon Sonus LightWave.

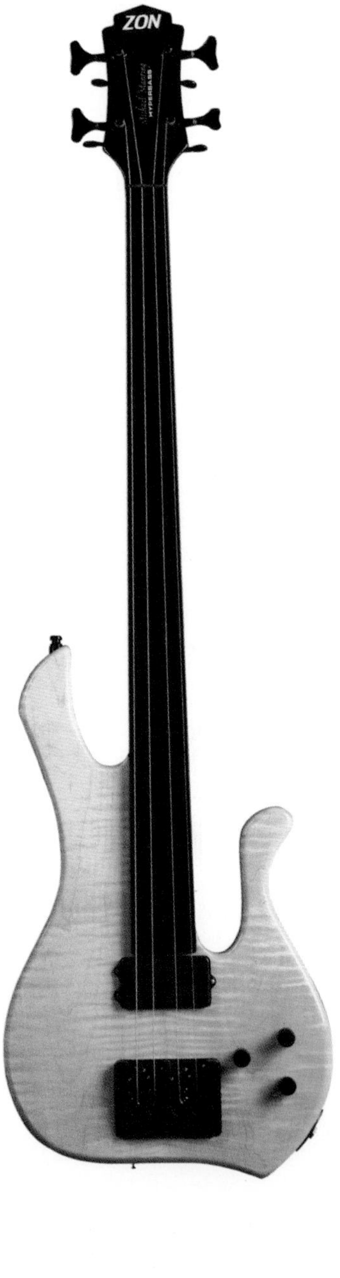

■ Zon Hyperbass.

composer Michael Manring, whose compositions frequently employ unusual tunings. Late in 1989 he collaborated with Zon on the design of a radical new 4-string called the Hyperbass. The first instrument was delivered to Manring in October 1990. Although it shared some characteristics with Zon's standard models, including a graphite neck glued to an alder body, the Hyperbass was essentially designed from the ground up. It has a three-octave phenolic-resin fingerboard and an unusually deep cutaway that gives Manring access to the instrument's full range. To facilitate quick retunings, the headstock is fitted with four Hipshot keys and the bridge has two levers: one raises and lowers all four saddles together; the other can be "assigned" to one or more saddles with set screws. By flipping the detuners and bridge levers, Manring can choose among thousands of possible tunings. Because many of these tunings are quite high in pitch, he uses very light strings (.020–.052). The Hyperbass's quadraphonic electronics are as unusual as the tuning mechanisms. In addition to a single custom-wound Bartolini magnetic pickup, there are four Fishman transducers mounted inside the instrument: one is in the neck, between the nut and the first fret; the others are mounted in the body just beneath the ¼" curly-maple top. The Hyperbass is wired with a quad/mono output option, controlled by a mini-toggle switch. In 1992 Zon introduced a production version, with the retuning hardware and quad/mono electronics available as options.

Zon has built several other custom basses for Manring, including a headless 4-string ("Vinny"), a bubinga-topped Legacy Elite II fretless 4-string ("Bub"), a Legacy Elite II fretless 6-string, a Legacy Elite II 10-string, and a Sonus/Hyperbass hybrid with a "bee's wing" bubinga top ("Junior"). The creative thinking behind these Manring instruments has helped to fuel the expansion of Zon's regular line of basses, many of which express their creator's quest to figure out where everyone else in the industry is heading—and then go the other way.

ACROSS THE POND(S)

A Brief Look at the International Scene

The bass guitar is an American invention, but it has become an international phenomenon. Bass guitars are now heard around the world, in styles that range from Brazilian samba to West African highlife to Japanese enka. Bass guitars are also made in many countries, with overseas production numbers steadily rising in recent years.

The early days of non-American bass building were largely characterized by instruments that were either knockoffs (faithful and not-so-faithful copies of U.S.-made basses) or original designs that were often, well . . . weird. There were few non-American bass guitars available until the 1960s, when the burgeoning popularity of rock & roll pumped up demand. One of the first companies to jump into the low-end market was Germany's Höfner, which introduced its violin-bodied 500/1 model in 1956. A few years later, Paul McCartney would make it one of the most familiar bass guitars of all time. Another German company, Framus, entered the fray in 1959 with its Star Bass, a semi-hollow single-cutaway 4-string that was adopted by Bill Wyman of the Rolling Stones. (In his search for easy-to-play basses, the small-handed Wyman later moved on to a signature model made by England's Vox; it had one of the dinkiest bass necks ever.) During the 1960s and '70s Framus offered several bass guitar models, as well as an EUB called the Triumph Bass. In the 1980s Framus was succeeded by Warwick, whose extensive line of 4-, 5-, and 6-string basses has been imported into the U.S. by Dana B. Goods of Santa Barbara, California. Turnabout being fair play, the Framus brand name has been revived on basses made by Warwick.

■ Warwick Streamer ProM.

Germany is a bass crazy nation, with many builders both large and small. While Warwick is the best-known brand in the U.S., other companies have made inroads in recent years, including Auerswald, Bogart, Clover, Esh, Human Base, and Marleaux. Because of an unfavorable rate of exchange between the deutschmark (and now the euro) and the U.S. dollar, prices for these basses have been relatively high in the States, limiting their sales. They sell well in Europe, though, and German bassmakers produce high-quality instruments in a wide range of styles, from back-to-nature ABGs to experimental extended-range models with as many as ten strings.

The United Kingdom has a bass-building history that stretches back to 1960, when Burns of London introduced its Artiste. The better-known Burns Bison, with pointy horns and "Wild Dog" switch, followed two years later. Often overlooked is the Burns TR2 of 1962, which has a legitimate claim to being the first active bass, although its simple boost controls were far less sophisticated than what Alembic was soon to offer. Many British bassmakers have taken a high-tech approach. During the 1970s and '80s, neck-through Jaydee basses emulated the multi-laminate construction and active electronics pioneered by Alembic. Rob Green of Status has used graphite extensively for necks and even entire instruments, including the radical Buzzard Bass he created for John Entwistle. MIDI entered the picture at Wal, which has been making premium basses since 1978; the Wal MIDI bass was one of the first bass guitars to use the wired-fret system that later appeared on the Peavey Midibase. Tony Zemaitis, who died in August 2002, was a respected custom builder whose one-of-a-kind basses often have engraved-metal pickguards. Across the Irish Sea, Chris Larkin of County Kerry

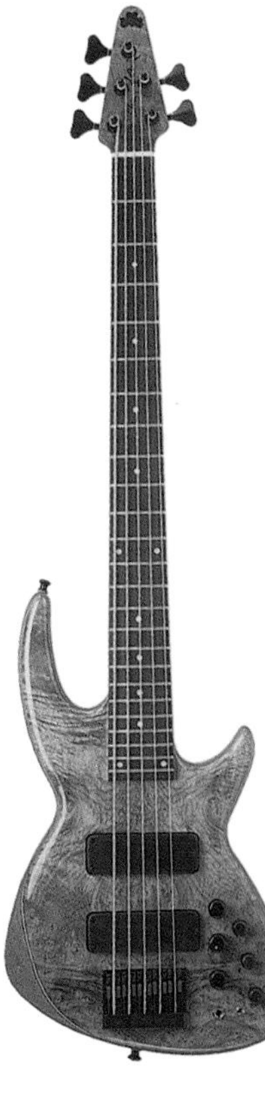

■ Chris Larkin 5B Bass.

■ MTD Grendel GR4fl.

builds excellent instruments; he came up with the clever idea of using switchable circuit boards, one for stage and one for studio, in his onboard preamp.

Sweden's Hagstrom gained bass fame in the late 1960s with its 8-string, which was adopted by studio players and featured by the Jimi Hendrix Experience on *Axis: Bold as Love*. Hagstrom also built basses that were imported by Ampeg and made pickups for the early Guild basses. Denmark's Johnny Mørch was one of the first European custom-bass builders, and his work influenced American luthiers like David King. More recently, the Danish company Celinder has produced appealing axes such as its Fender-inspired J Series.

Farther south, France's Vigier is known for such unusual instruments as the Arpege, with active electronics featuring 12 EQ presets in ROM. Jerzy Drozd of Spain builds elaborate bolt-on and neck-through models, including the Obsession Signature, which has 13 neck laminates. Italy's Eko was one of the first companies to produce an acoustic bass guitar, back in the 1970s, and one of its odd-looking Fiddle Basses was a Les Claypool favorite in the 1990s. Current Italian builders like Frudua and Manne produce sleek contemporary designs. The Austrians got into the act with the wild-looking Andreas Basking Shark, with Alembic pickups and an aluminum fingerboard. In recent years, the craftsmen of the Czech Republic have distinguished themselves with contract work for such well-known American builders as Michael Tobias (MTD Grendel basses) and Stuart Spector (Spector CR Series basses). Luthiers in Slovakia build instruments for Neuser, which has its sales office in Finland; the extensive line includes the unique Claudia or "clawbass," with a key-and-hammer mechanism for striking the strings.

Go East, Young Man

The rapid growth of the Japanese guitar industry in the 1960s was the death knell for American companies like Harmony and Kay, which couldn't compete with the bargain-basement imports pouring into the country, bearing exotic names like Guyatone, Sekova, Teisco, and Zim Gar. Many of these Japanese basses were poorly made Fender knockoffs, but the quality of the instruments improved during the 1970s. One of the biggest breakthroughs was the 1979 introduction of the Ibanez Musician, a neck-through-body bass that rivaled the best American-made instruments in its price range. Ibanez has since become one of the world's largest producers of bass guitars, and its Soundgear basses are favored by many amateur and professional bassists.

The import boom continued in the early 1980s, with well-made basses by Aria, Tokai, Tune, Yamaha, and other companies grabbing U.S. market share. Yamaha's BB series was especially well received, and the BB5000 was one of the few production 5-strings available in the late '80s. In recent years Yamaha has worked

■ Ibanez Soundgear SR800A.

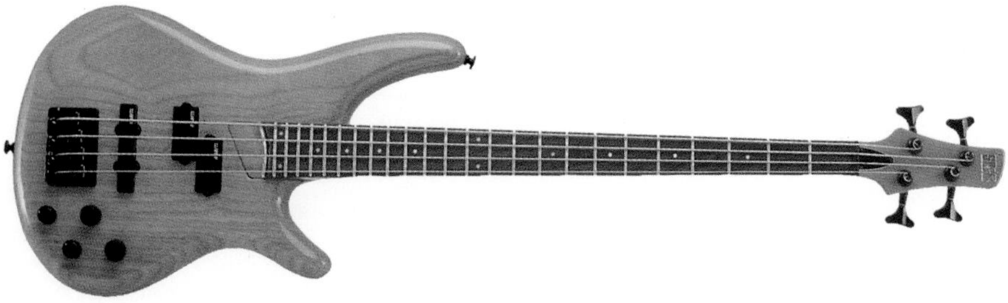

closely with such leading American bassists as Nathan East, Billy Sheehan, John Patitucci, and John Myung to develop signature-model instruments (and increased credibility). Many of Yamaha's custom instruments are made at its Los Angeles R&D facility, giving them the ironic distinction of being American-made basses carrying a Japanese brand name.

Fender paid the builders of Japan the ultimate compliment by establishing an operation there in 1982. Made at the Fuji-Gen Gakki factory, which also produced Ibanez basses, the instruments were sold under the Heartfield and Squier names as well as Fender; the Heartfield brand later disappeared, but many Japanese Fender and Squier basses are still being made today. Fender also set up manufacturing operations in Korea and (briefly) India. After acquiring Guild in 1995, Fender began to produce Korean-made copies of Guild instruments that are sold under the DeArmond name. (Once upon a time, DeArmond was a U.S. pickup manufacturer. As Hartley Peavey has observed, "In this industry, companies die but names never do.")

More good Japanese basses arrived on American shores in the '90s, bearing such brand names as Alvarez, Atlansia, Fernandes, Kawai, Moon, and Riverhead. As these instruments moved up both in quality and price, more budget basses began to arrive from Korea. With the cost of materials low and plenty of skilled labor available, Korean musical-instrument factories could churn out large numbers of inexpensive axes—and they did just that. Many were made at the huge factories of Samick, which sold basses under its own name (and that of its acquisition, Valley Arts Guitars) as well as subcontracting for American companies. Jack Westheimer, who had been a pioneer in the importing of Japanese instruments, has been operating his own Korean factory since the '70s, building instruments for his Cort brand and other companies. Westheimer also works with U.S. builders like Bill Conklin and Greg Curbow to build "authorized copies"—budget-priced Korean versions of their designs. Some U.S.-based companies, like DiPinto of Philadelphia, offer original instruments that are built to order in Korea and given final setup in the States.

■ Cort Artisan Bass B-4.

"If you can't lick 'em, join 'em" has been the rallying cry for many American bass companies. Gibson sells piles of Korean-made instruments under the Epiphone, Kramer, Tobias, and Steinberger names, and other U.S. makers have moved to establish parallel operations in the Far East. Even Peavey, which for years touted its "Made in USA" reputation, joined the party in 1996. As this book is being written, it's possible to buy Korean-made basses that carry the labels of a raft of U.S.-based companies, including Hamer, Jackson, Lakland, MTD, Schecter, and others. And China is rapidly emerging as the new Korea, with both U.S. and Japanese companies ramping up instrument production there. Many American-made basses have foreign components (especially tuners and other hardware), and the question "Where was it made?" is increasingly hard to answer. The bass guitar has conquered the world.

SOURCES

Every issue of *Bass Player* magazine includes product information and reviews, and my complete collection of *BP* was an invaluable resource for writing this book. The listings in every edition of the *Bass Buyer's Guide* (1992–1994) and the *Guitar & Bass Buyer's Guide* (1994–2002) were also helpful. I also consulted dozens of websites, from the bogus to the brilliant, and many books on instrument lore, including:

Babiuk, Andy. *Beatles Gear.* San Francisco: Backbeat Books, 2001.

Bacon, Tony with Dave Burrluck, Paul Day & Michael Wright. *Electric Guitars: The Illustrated Encyclopedia.* San Diego: Thunder Bay Press, 2000.

Bacon, Tony & Paul Day. *The Fender Book: A Complete History of Fender Electric Guitars* (revised edition). London: Balafon Books, 1999.

———. *The Gibson Les Paul Book: A Complete History of Les Paul Guitars.* London: Balafon Books, 1993.

———. *The Gretsch Book: A Complete History of Gretsch Electric Guitars.* San Francisco: Backbeat Books, 1996.

———. *The Rickenbacker Book: A Complete History of Rickenbacker Electric Guitars.* San Francisco: Backbeat Books, 1994.

Bacon, Tony & Barry Moorhouse. *The Bass Book: A Complete Illustrated History of Bass Guitars.* San Francisco: Backbeat Books, 1995.

Black, J. W. & Albert Molinaro. *The Fender Bass: An Illustrated History.* Milwaukee: Hal Leonard, 2001.

Freeth, Nick & Charles Alexander. *The Electric Guitar.* Philadelphia: Courage Books, 2000.

Greenwood, Alan & Gil Hembree. *Vintage Guitar Price Guide 2002.* Bismarck, ND: Vintage Guitar Books, 2001.

Gruhn, George & Walter Carter. *Gruhn's Guide to Vintage Guitars* (2nd edition). San Francisco: Backbeat Books, 1999.

———. *Acoustic Guitars & Other Fretted Instruments: A Photographic History.* San Francisco: Backbeat Books, 1993.

———. *Electric Guitars & Basses: A Photographic History.* San Francisco: Backbeat Books, 1994.

Hopkins, Gregg & Bill Moore. *Ampeg: The Story Behind the Sound.* Milwaukee: Hal Leonard, 1999.

Moseley, Willie G. *Stellas & Stratocasters.* Bismarck, ND: Vintage Guitar Books, 1994.

———. *Vintage Electric Guitars: In Praise of Fretted Americana.* Atglen, PA: Schiffer Publishing, 2001.

Moust, Hans. *The Guild Guitar Book: The Company and the Instruments, 1952–1977.* Breda, the Netherlands: Guitarchives Publications, 1995.

Smith, Richard R. *Fender: The Sound Heard 'round the World.* Fullerton, CA: Garfish Publishing, 1995.

Washburn, Jim & Richard Johnston. *Martin Guitars: An Illustrated Celebration of America's Premier Guitarmaker.* Emmaus, PA: Rodale Press, 1997.

Wheeler, Tom. *American Guitars: An Illustrated History* (revised and updated edition). New York: HarperCollins, 1992.

White, Forrest. *Fender: The Inside Story.* San Francisco: Backbeat Books, 1994.

ADDRESSES

Listed below is contact information for builders in this book that were producing bass guitars at the time of publication (2003). In most cases, the best way to get more information is to visit the website first; the sites listed here (with a couple of exceptions) are all official company sites, not unofficial or "fan" sites. A check with any good search engine, such as Google, is likely to turn up unofficial sites for most well-known companies, but the content may not be accurate or comprehensive.

A Basses
152 Clark Lane
Waltham, MA 02451
(781) 891-1134
albey@abasses.com
www.abasses.com

Acacia Instruments
www.acaciainstruments.com

Alembic
3005 Wiljan Court
Santa Rosa, CA 95407
(707) 523-2611
info@alembic.com
www.alembic.com

Ampeg
Division of St. Louis Music
1400 Ferguson Ave.
St. Louis, MO 63133
(314) 727-4512
www.ampeg.com

Axtra Guitars
P.O. Box 724
Kenosha, WI 53141
(262) 654-7900
lstolars@acronet.net

Azola Music Products
P.O. Box 1519
Ramona, CA 92065
(760) 789-8581
jill@azola.com
www.azola.com

B.C. Rich Guitars
Division of HHI
4940 Delhi Pike
Cincinnati, OH 45238
(513) 451-5000
sales@bcrich.com
www.bcrich.com

Benavente Guitars
388 SW K St.
Grants Pass, OR 97526
(541) 472-9451
chris@benaventeguitars.com
www.benaventeguitars.com

Bolin Guitars
4021 North 36th St.
Boise, ID 83703
(208) 344-1260
bolinguitars@aol.com
www.bolinguitars.com

Born To Rock Design, Inc.
470 West End Ave., #8A
New York, NY 10024
(800) 496-ROCK
mail@borntorock.com
www.borntorock.com

Breedlove Guitar Co.
19885 8th St.
Tumalo, OR 97701
(541) 385-8339
info@breedloveguitars.com
www.breedloveguitars.com

Brian Moore Guitars
P.O. Box 540
LaGrangeville, NY 12540
(845) 486-0744
info@brianmooreguitars.com
www.brianmooreguitars.com

Brubaker Guitars
900-A Leidy Rd.
Westminster, MD 21157
(410) 857-7600
brubakerguitars@erols.com
www.brubakerguitars.com

Bunker Guitars
17624 15th Ave. SE, #108-A
Mill Creek, WA 98012
(425) 483-1217
info@bunker-guitars.com
www.bunker-guitars.com

CA Guitars
P.O. Box 3100
Lafayette, LA 70502
(337) 291-2642
sales@caguitars.com
www.caguitars.com

Carl Thompson Basses
171 Court St.
Brooklyn, NY 11201
(718) 852-1771
www.ctbasses.com

Carvin
12340 World Trade Dr.
San Diego, CA 92128
(800) 854-2235
info@carvin.com
www.carvin.com

Chandler Musical Instruments
P.O. Box 3637
Chico, CA 95927
(530) 899-1503
paul@chandlerguitars.com
www.chandlerguitars.com

Citron Guitars
282 Chestnut Hill Rd.
Woodstock, NY 12498
(845) 679-7138
harvey@citron-guitars.com
www.citron-guitars.com

Clevinger Bass
1243 Bates Rd.
Oakland, CA 94610
(510) 444-2542
clevbass@pacbell.net
www.clevinger.com

Conklin Guitars
P.O. Box 1394
Springfield, MO 65801
(417) 886-3535
conklin@conklinguitars.com
www.conklinguitars.com

Curbow String Instruments
P.O. Box 309
Morganton, GA 30560
(706) 374-2873
info@curbow.com
www.curbow.com

Dammann Custom Basses
2958 Barrsden Farm
Charlottesville, VA 22911
(804) 973-6413
ralph@dammannbasses.com
www.dammannbasses.com

Dave Maize Acoustic Guitars
P.O. Box 2129
Cave Junction, OR 97523
(541) 592-6217
dave@maizeguitars.com
www.maizeguitars.com

David J. King Bass Guitar Systems
4805 N. Borthwick Ave.
Portland, OR 97217
(503) 282-0327
david@kingbass.com
www.kingbass.com

De Lacugo Basses
TDL Guitar Works
903 Moody Court
Paso Robles, CA 93446
(805) 237-0200
info@TDLGuitars.com
www.TDLGuitars.com

Dingwall Designer Guitars
P.O. Box 9194
Saskatoon, Saskatchewan S7K 7E8
Canada
(306) 242-6201
sales@dingwallguitars
www.dingwallguitars.com

Don Grosh Custom Guitars
26818 Oak Ave., Unit F
Santa Clarita, CA 91351
(661) 252-6716
info@groshguitars.com
www.groshguitars.com

Elrick Bass Guitars
3814 N. Mozart St.
Chicago, IL 60618
(773) 588-2017
rob@elrick.com
www.elrick.com

Ernie Ball Music Man
151 Suburban Rd.
San Luis Obispo, CA 93401
(805) 544-7726
info@ernieball.com
www.ernieball.com

F Bass
16 McKinstry St.
Hamilton, Ontario L8L 6C1
Canada
(905) 522-1582
george@fbass.com
www.fbass.com

Farnell Guitars
1009 Brooks St., Suite C
Ontario, CA 91762
(909) 629-9111
webmaster@farnellguitars.com
www.farnellguitars.com

Fender Musical instruments Corp.
8860 E. Chaparral Rd., Suite 100
Scottsdale, AZ 85250
(480) 596-7108
www.fender.com

Fleishman Instruments
1533 Welter Court
Sebastopol, CA 95472
(707) 823-3537
guitars@sbcglobal.net
www.fleishmaninstruments.com

Fodera Guitars
68-34th St.
Brooklyn, NY 11232
(718) 832-3455
info@fodera.com
www.fodera.com

Fury Guitar Manufacturing
902 Avenue J North
Saskatoon, Saskatchewan S7L 2L2
Canada
(306) 244-4063
info@furyguitar.com
www.furyguitar.com

G&L Guitars & Basses
c/o BBE Sound Inc.
5381 Production Dr.
Huntington Beach, CA 92649
(714) 897-6766
info@glguitars.com
www.glguitars.com

G. Gould Music
1315 23rd Ave, #200A
San Francisco, CA 94122
(415) 759-5199
geoff@ggould.com
www.ggould.com

Gibson USA
1818 Elm Hill Pike
Nashville, TN 37210
(800) 4GIBSON
www.gibson.com

GMP Guitars
510 E. Arrow Hwy.
San Dimas, CA 91773
(909) 592-5144
gmp@gmpguitars.com
www.gmpguitars.com

Godin Guitars
19420 Avenue Clark-Graham,
Baie D'Urfé, Québec H9X 3R8
Canada
(514) 457-7977
info@godinguitars.com
www.godinguitars.com

Gould Guitars & Basses
P.O. Box 302132
Escondido, CA 92030
(760) 747-7272
rebel@gouldguitars.com
www.gouldbasses.com

GR Basses
12169 Kirkham Rd., Suite B
Poway, CA 92064
(858) 637-8523
webmaster@grbasses.com
www.grbasses.com

Gretsch Musical Instruments
P.O. Box 2468
Savannah, GA 31402
(912) 748-7070
lena@gretsch.com
www.gretsch.com

Guild Guitars
8860 E. Chaparral Rd., Suite 100
Scottsdale, AZ 85250
(480) 596-9690
info@guildguitars.com
www.guildguitars.com

Hamer Guitars
Kaman Music Corp.
P.O. Box 507
Bloomfield, CT 06002
(860) 509-8888
info@kamanmusic.com
www.hamerguitars.com

Jackson/Charvel
4710 Mercantile Dr.
Fort Worth, TX 76137
(817) 831-9203
info@jacksonguitars.com
www.jacksonguitars.com

James Trussart Custom Guitars
2658 Griffith Park Blvd., #262
Los Angeles, CA 90039
(323) 665-4405
jt@jamestrussart.com
www.jamestrussart.com

Jerry Jones Guitars
P.O. Box 22507
Nashville, TN 37202
(615) 255-0088
sales@jerryjonesguitars.com
www.jerryjonesguitars.com

Johnson's Extremely Strange Musical Instrument Co.
119 W. Linden Ave.
Burbank, CA 91502
(818) 955-8152
xstrange@ix.netcom.com
www.xstrange.com

J.T. Hargreaves Basses & Guitars
P.O. Box 13301
Des Moines, WA 98198
jay@jthbass.com
www.jthbass.com

Ken Bebensee Electric/Acoustic Stringed Instruments
18001 Salmon Mine Rd.
Nevada City, CA 95959
530-292-0156
ken@kbguitars.com
www.kbguitars.com

Ken Smith Basses
P.O. Box 199
Perkasie, PA 18944
(215) 453-8887
sales@kensmithbasses.com
www.kensmithbasses.com

Kenneth Lawrence Instruments
1055 Samoa Blvd.
Arcata, CA 95521
(707) 822-2543
lawrence@reninet.com

Kinal Guitars and Basses
3239 East 52d Ave.
Vancouver, B.C. V5S 1T9
Canada
(604) 433-6544
guitar@istar.ca
www.kinal.com

Klein Electric Guitars
P.O. Box 247
Linden, CA 95236
(209) 887-2651
kleinelectric@yahoo.com
www.kleinelectricguitars.com

Kubicki Technology
726 Bond Ave.
Santa Barbara, CA 93103
(805) 963-6703
info@kubicki.com
www.kubicki.com

KYDD Basses
P.O. Box 2650
Upper Darby, PA 19082
(800) 622-KYDD
kyddbass@aol.com
www.kyddbass.com

Lakland Musical Instruments
2044 N. Dominick
Chicago, IL 60614
(773) 871-9637
dlakin@lakincorp.com
www.lakland.com

Landing Guitars
4015 Fairfield Ave.
Munhall, PA 15120
(412) 462-8999
landing@ix.netcom.com
www.landingbass.com

Lieber Instruments
6439 State Highway 28
Fly Creek, NY 13337
(607) 547-7072
info@lieberguitars.com
www.lieberguitars.com

Linc Luthier Instruments
1318 N. Monte Vista Ave., Suite 11
Upland, CA 91786
(909) 931-0642
basses@lincluthier.com
www.lincluthier.com

Little Guitar Works
18038 Fair Oaks Dr.
Penn Valley, CA 95946
(530) 432-7701
jerome@littleguitarworks.com
www.littleguitarworks.com

Liutaio Mottola
46 Wyoming Rd.
Newton, MA 02460
(617) 965-8006
rm.mottola@verizon.net

Martin Guitars (C.F. Martin & Co.)
P.O. Box 329
Nazareth, PA 18064
(610) 759-2837
info@martinguitar.com
www.mguitar.com

Matt Pulcinella Guitars
500 West Sellers Ave.
Ridley Park, PA 19078
(610) 558-7313
matt@mpguitars.com
www.mpguitars.com

Michael Dolan Custom Guitars
3222 Airway Drive, #4
Santa Rosa, CA 95403
(707) 575-0654
MNDolan@aol.com
www.dolanguitars.com

Mike Lull Custom Guitars
13240 NE 20th St., #2
Bellevue, WA 98005
(425) 643-8074
service@mikelull.com
www.mikelull.com

Mobius Megatar USA
P.O. Box 969
Fairfax, CA 94978
(415) 435-8803
tappers@megatar.com
www.megatar.com

Modulus Guitars
8 Digital Dr.
Novato, CA 94949
(415) 884-2300
info@modulusguitars.com
www.modulusguitars.com

Moonstone Guitars
P.O. Box 757
Eureka, CA 95502
(707) 445-9045
steve@moonstoneguitars.com
www.moonstoneguitars.com

Moses, Inc.
P.O. Box 10028
Eugene, OR 97440
(541) 484-6068
orders@mosesgraphite.com
www.mosesgraphite.com

Mouradian Guitars
1904 Mass. Ave.
Cambridge, MA 02140
(617) 547-5454
dadman4250@attbi.com

MTD (Michael Tobias Design)
3 Lauren Court
Kingston, NY 12401
(845) 246-0670
mike@mtdbass.com
www.mtdbass.com

Mudge Basses
P.O. Box 21279
Oakland, CA 94620
(510) 581-2825
mudgebass@aol.com

National Reso-phonic Guitars
871C Via Esteban #C
San Luis Obispo, CA 93401
(805) 546-8442
natres@nationalguitars.com
www.nationalguitars.com

New York Bass Works
178 N. Beech St.
N. Massapequa, NY 11758
(516) 799-5160
david@newyorkbassworks.com
www.newyorkbassworks.com

Novax Guitars
940A Estabrook
San Leandro, CA 94577
(510) 336-1426
Novax@netwiz.net
www.novaxguitars.com

NS Design
42 Hilltop Road
Nobleboro, ME 04555
(207) 563-7700
email@nedsteinberger.com
www.nedsteinberger.com

Ovation
P.O. Box 507
Bloomfield, CT 06002
(860) 509-8888
info@ovationguitars.com
www.kamanmusic.com

Parker Guitars
P.O. Box 388
Wilmington, MA 01887
(978) 988-0102
support@parkerguitars.com
www.parkerguitars.com

Peavey
711 A St.
Meridian, MS 39301
(601) 483-5365
info@peavey.com
www.peavey.com

Pedulla Guitars
P.O. Box 226
Rockland, MA 02370
(781) 871-0073
christin@pedulla.com
www.pedulla.com

PRS (Paul Reed Smith)
380 Log Canoe Circle
Stevensville, MD 21666
(410) 643-9970
custserv@prsguitars.com
www.prsguitars.com

Ray Ramirez Basses
20 Esmeralda St.
Humacao, PR 00791
(787) 852-1476
rramirez@coqui.net
www.rayramirezbasses.com

Read Custom Instruments
P.O. Box 859
Bolton, MA 01740
(978) 779-0075
jread@readcustom.com
www.readcustom.com

Reverend Musical Instruments
27300 Gloede, Unit D
Warren, MI 48088
(586) 775-1025
sales@reverenddirect.com
www.reverenddirect.com

Rick Turner Guitars
Renaissance Guitars
815 Almar Ave.
Santa Cruz, CA 95060
(831) 460-9144
rturner466@aol.com
www.renaissanceguitars.com

Rickenbacker International Corp.
3895 S. Main St.
Santa Ana, CA 92707
(714) 545-5574
info@rickenbacker.com
www.rickenbacker.com

Rob Allen Guitars
511 E. Gutierrez St., #2
Santa Barbara, CA 93101
(805) 965-9053
robal1@earthlink.net
www.roballenguitars.com

Robin Guitars
3526 East T. C. Jester Blvd.
Houston, TX 77018
(713) 957-0470
sales@robinguitars.com
www.robinguitars.com

Roscoe Guitars
P.O. Box 5404
Greensboro, NC 27435
(336) 274-8810
info@roscoeguitars.com
www.roscoeguitars.com

Sadowsky Guitars
20 Jay St., #5C
Brooklyn, NY 11201
(718) 422-1123
roger@sadowsky.com
www.sadowsky.com

Schecter Guitar Research
1840 Valpreda St.
Burbank, CA 91504
(800) 660-6621
info@schecterguitars.com
www.schecterguitars.com

Simpson-James Basses
c/o Guitar-Tech
17 Spruce Circle
Westfield, MA 01085
(413) 568-6654

Spalt Basses
1316 Manzanita St.
Los Angeles, CA 90027
(800) 328-0136
info@spaltbasses.com
www.spaltbasses.com

Spector Basses
1450 Route 212
Saugerties, NY 12477
(845) 246-1385
info@spectorbass.com
www.spectorbass.com

Steinberger
645 Massman Dr.
Nashville, TN 37210
www.musicyo.com
www.steinbergerworld.com

Stevens Electrical Instruments
P.O. Box 1082
Alpine, TX 79831
(915) 364-2487
acowboy@stevensguitars.com
www.stevensguitars.com

Stick Enterprises
6011 Woodlake Ave.
Woodland Hills, CA 91367
(818) 884-2001
stick@earthlink.net
www.stick.com

Suhr Guitars
18650 Collier Ave., Unit A
Lake Elsinore, CA 92530
(909) 471-2334
johnsuhr@suhrguitars.com
www.suhrguitars.com

Sukop Instruments
57 Crooks Ave.
Clifton, NJ 07011
info@sukop.com
www.sukop.com

Surine Basses
P.O. Box 6440
Denver, CO 80206
(303) 388-3956
mail@surinebasses.com
www.surinebasses.com

Tacoma Guitars
4615 E. 192nd St.
Tacoma, WA 98446
(253) 847-6508
ferd@tacomaguitars.com
www.tacomaguitars.com

Taylor Guitars
1980 Gillespie Way
El Cajon, CA 92020
(619) 258-1207
sales@taylorguitars.com
www.taylorguitars.com

Tobias Basses
1840 41st Ave., #102
Capitola, CA 95010
www.musicyo.com

Tyler Guitars
6166 Sepulveda Blvd.
Van Nuys, CA 91411
(818) 901-0278
tylerguitars@tylerguitars.com
www.tylerguitars.com

U.S. Masters Guitar Works
2324 Pinehurst Dr., Unit 3
Middleton, WI 53562
(608) 836-5505
guitars@usmasters.com
www.usmasters.com

Valley Arts Guitars
18521 Railroad St.
City of Industry, CA 91748
(626) 964-4700
info@samickmusicus.com
www.samickguitar.com

Veillette Guitars
2628 Route 212
Woodstock, NY 12498
(845) 679-6154
joe@veilletteguitars.com
www.veilletteguitars.com

ViolinGuitarMaker
8611 Highway 60
Cedarburg, WI 53012
(262) 375-2738
PeterJay@ViolinGuitarMaker.com
www.ViolinGuitarMaker.com

Warr Guitars
572 Lotus Ave.
Thousand Oaks, CA 91360
warr@warrguitars.com
www.warrguitars.com

Warrior Musical Instruments
93 Direct Connection Dr.
Rossville, GA 30741
(706) 891-3009
anointed@warriorinstruments.com
www.warriorinstruments.com

Washburn International
444 E. Courtland St.
Mundelein, IL 60060
(847) 949-0444
washburn@washburn.com
www.usmusiccorp.com

Wechter Guitars
P.O. Box 91
Paw Paw, MI 49079
(269) 657-3479
info@wechterguitars.com
www.wechterguitars.com

Wittman Basses
691 Woodland Ave.
Williamsport, PA 17701
(570) 327-1527
wittbas@uplink.net
www.wittman-spins.com

Zeta Music Systems
2230 Livingston St.
Oakland, CA 94606
(510) 261-1702
info@zetamusic.com
www.zetamusic.com

Zon Guitars
780 Second Ave.
Redwood City, CA 94063
(650) 366-3516
customerservice@zonguitars.com
www.zonguitars.com

PHOTO CREDITS

All photos were supplied by manufacturers and *Bass Player* magazine (photos by Paul Haggard), except as noted below.

Page VII: courtesy David Pomeroy

Page 1: courtesy Ned Steinberger

Pages 4, 5 (Mike Tobias):
© 2003 Backbeat Books

Page 13 (Alembic #1):
courtesy Balafon Image Bank

Page 20 (Ampeg AUB-1):
photo by Evan Sheeley

Page 20 (3 Ampegs):
courtesy Bruce Johnson

Page 31 (Carl Thompson):
courtesy Balafon Image Bank

Page 32 (Carl Thompson #5-15-2000):
courtesy Aaron Beharelle

Page 32 (Carl Thompson #7-31-02):
courtesy Casey Paquet

Pages 37, 39:
© 2003 Backbeat Books

Pages 45 (Danelectro), 49 (Epiphone):
courtesy Balafon Image Bank

Page 52 ('51 Fender Precision):
photo by Bill Adams

Page 52: ('56 Fender Precision):
photo by Michael Sandy

Page 53 ('60 Fender Jazz):
photo by Michael Sandy

Page 54:
courtesy Jim Roberts

Page 55 and 56 (Fender Mustang):
courtesy Balafon Image Bank

Page 58 (Fender Musicmaster):
photo by Bill Adams

Page 64:
photo by Neil Zlozower

Page 66:
photo by Michael Sandy

Page 71 (G&L L-1000):
courtesy Willie Moseley

Page 73 (all photos):
courtesy Balafon Image Bank

Page 74 (Gibson EB-3):
courtesy Balafon Image Bank

Page 74 (Gibson Melody Maker):
photo by Bill Ingalls

Page 75 (Gibson SB-450):
photo by Bill Ingalls

Page 76 (Gibson Ripper and Victory Standard):
photos by Bill Ingalls

Page 77 (Gibson Les Paul Bass):
courtesy Balafon Image Bank

Page 81 (Gretsch Model 6070):
courtesy Balafon Image Bank

Page 84 (Guild Starfire Bass I):
courtesy Balafon Image Bank

Page 85 (Guild B-302A):
photo by Bill Ingalls

Page 85 (Guild SB-602 Pilot):
courtesy Willie Moseley

Page 86 (Guild Ashbory B-100):
courtesy Balafon Image Bank

Page 88 (Harmony):
courtesy Balafon Image Bank

Page 94 (Kay catalog page):
courtesy Balafon Image Bank

Page 94 (Kay K5965 Pro Bass):
photo by Bill Ingalls

Page 95 (Ken Smith BT Bustom VI):
courtesy Balafon Image Bank

Page 98:
© 2003 Backbeat Books

Page 100 (Kenneth Lawrence Chambered Brase 6):
photo by Frank Bevans

Page 100 (Kenneth Lawrence 5-string):
photo by Rudy Gillard

Page 101:
photo by Rudy Gillard

Pages 102, 103:
photos by Frank Bevans

Page 106 (Kramer Duke Deluxe):
photo by Bill Ingalls

Page 106 (Kramer Ferrington):
courtesy Balafon Image Bank

Page 107 (Kramer Stagemaster):
photo by Bill Ingalls

Page 113 (Joe Osborn/Dan Lakin):
© 2003 Backbeat Books

Page 116 (Little Torzal 434):
photo by Melissa Prado Little

Page 122 (Mike Lull):
photo by Richard McNamee

Page 128 (both):
photos by Bill Ingalls

Page 132 (Music Man StingRay):
photo by Bill Adams

Page 133 (National B-5):
photo by Willie Moseley

Page 138 (Ovation Elite 5):
courtesy Balafon Image Bank

Page 138 (Ovation Typhoon V):
photo by Bill Ingalls

Page 148 (PRS Bass-4):
courtesy Balafon Image Bank

Page 154:
© 2003 Backbeat Books

Pages 156, 157:
courtesy Balafon Image Bank

Page 158 (Rickenbacker 4001S):
courtesy Balafon Image Bank

Page 163:
© 2003 Backbeat Books

Page 167 (Spector SB-1 and NS-1):
courtesy PJ Rubal

Page 167 (Spector NS-2):
courtesy Balafon Image Bank

Page 169:
© 2003 Backbeat Books

Page 170 (Steinberger L-Series prototype):
courtesy Balafon Image Bank

Page 170 (Steinberger L1):
courtesy Andy Yakubik, SteinbergerWorld.com

Page 171 (brochure):
courtesy Andy Yakubik, SteinbergerWorld.com

Page 171 (Steinberger XL2):
photo by Michael Sandy

Page 172 (Steinberger XM2):
courtesy Balafon Image Bank

Page 172 (Steinberger XQ2):
courtesy Andy Yakubik, SteinbergerWorld.com

Pages 174, 175:
photos by Mark Lee

Page 176 (Sukop):
photo by GallantPhotography.com

Page 179 (Tobias Basic 5):
photo by John Loy

INDEX

T

U

WHEN IT COMES TO THE BASS, WE WROTE THE BOOK.

The Jazz Bass Book

Technique and Tradition

By John Goldsby

Bassists get expert guidance on mastering proper technique, practice methods, and improvisation, plus new insight into the theoretical and conceptual aspects of jazz. The companion CD featuring bass plus rhythm section allows readers to hear technical examples from the book, presented in slow and fast versions.

Softcover with CD, 240 pages, ISBN 0-87930-716-1, $24.95

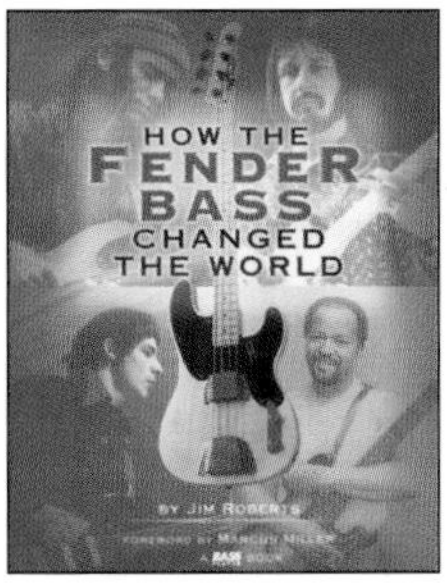

How the Fender Bass Changed the World

By Jim Roberts

Introduced in 1951, the Fender Precision Bass had completely transformed the sound of popular music by the early '60s. This is the first book to show you how and why. It tells the story of technological and artistic evolution, of basses and players—and of their profound influence on the world around them.

Softcover, 192 pages, ISBN 0-87930-630-0, $27.95

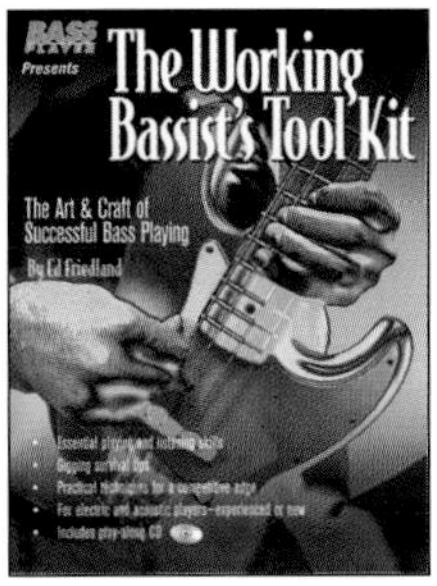

The Working Bassist's Tool Kit

The Art & Craft of Successful Bass Playing

By Ed Friedland

Whether you're just starting out or already working, this book/CD set is your ultimate guide to successful gigs in rock, jazz, blues, R&B, and more. You'll learn key skills for going pro, techniques for staying hot, and tips for tackling any gig—electric or acoustic. Packed with musical examples and exercises.

Softcover with CD, 120 pages, ISBN 0-87930-615-7, $19.95

Jaco

The Extraordinary and Tragic Life of Jaco Pastorius

By Bill Milkowski

This biography has become the classic portrait of the troubled genius who revolutionized modern electric bass. Featuring reminiscences from artists who played with him, it reveals how Jaco played melodies, chords, harmonics and percussive effects simultaneously, while fusing jazz, classical, R&B, rock, reggae, pop, and punk—all before age 35, when he met his tragic death.

Softcover, 272 pages, ISBN 0-87930-426-X, $14.95

The Bass Player Book

Equipment, Technique, Styles, and Artists

Edited by Karl Coryat

Whether you're a novice or seasoned bassist, acoustic or electric, you'll find instruction and inspiration here. This all-in-one handbook covers theory, positioning, groove, slap, harmonics, and more, providing in-depth musical examples in all key styles. You get expert advice on choosing equipment, plus personal insights from Paul McCartney, Stanley Clarke, Les Claypool, and other bass innovators.

Softcover, 224 pages, ISBN 0-87930-573-8, $22.95

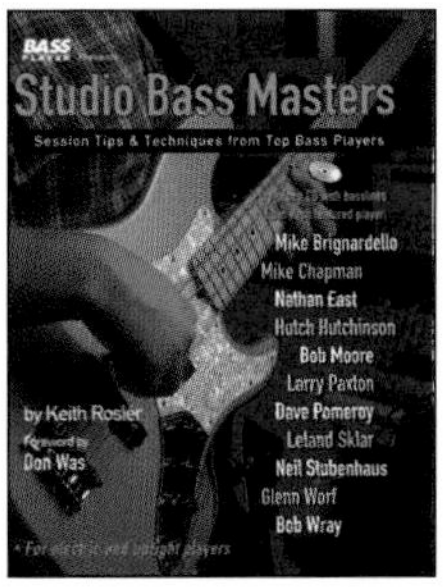

Studio Bass Masters

Session Tips & Techniques from Top Bass Players

By Keith Rosiér

Foreword by Don Was

Eleven top electric and upright bassists reveal their secrets of session success in this enlightening and practical book/CD set. Session aces like Leland Sklar and Hutch Hutchinson discuss recording experiences, studio techniques, style and chops, favorite basses, setup, and more. The play-along CD provides bass lines from each player, illustrating their diverse musical styles.

Softcover with CD, 128 pages, ISBN 0-87930-558-4, $19.95

Backbeat Books

AVAILABLE AT FINE BOOK AND MUSIC STORES EVERYWHERE, OR CONTACT:

Backbeat Books • 6600 Silacci Way • Gilroy, CA 95020 USA
Phone Toll Free: (866) 222-5232 • Fax: (408) 848-5784
E-mail: backbeat@rushorder.com • Web: www.backbeatbooks.com

Backbeat/Bass Player Lakland Flag Bass Giveaway

Total retail value: $6,100

Backbeat Books, *Bass Player*, and Lakland Musical Instruments have teamed to bring one lucky winner this beautiful custom 5-string, the same instrument featured on the cover of Backbeat's *American Basses: An Illustrated History & Player's Guide*, by *Bass Player* founding Editor Jim Roberts. Built exclusively for *American Basses*, the Flag Bass features Lakland's legendary tone, playability, and workmanship, plus a stunning finish designed by acclaimed Chicago artist Gary Weidner. In addition, if you choose to subscribe to *Bass Player* magazine with your entry, you will receive a 50% discount on your subscription.

Lakland Model 55-94 Flag Bass with ash body, quartersawn graphite-reinforced maple neck, and bird's-eye maple fingerboard. Equipped with Lakland Bartolini MM/J pickups and NTMB-L preamp with adjustable midrange and MM-pickup coil tap. The bass also features Hipshot Ultra-Lite tuners and Lakland's Dual Design bridge, which allows through-body or through-bridge stringing. Includes a vintage-style crème-colored case. Retail value: $4,100.

Custom finish by Gary Weidner: textured flag collage in a style that salutes America's great abstract expressionist painters. Retail value: $2,000.

Remember, you don't have to subscribe to *Bass Player* or purchase *American Basses* to enter the Giveaway, but you're always a winner when you take advantage of the great musical instruction and inspiration you'll find in Music Player Network publications.

See official rules on attached entry card. You may also enter online at www.backbeatbooks.com/flagbass. Contest deadline is March 31, 2004.

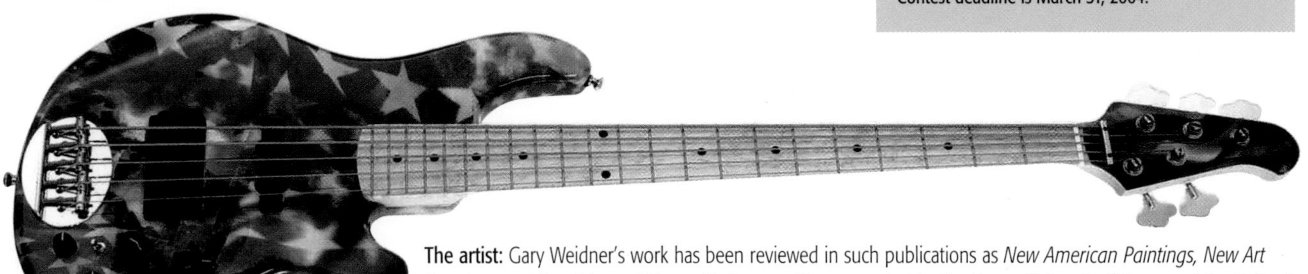

The artist: Gary Weidner's work has been reviewed in such publications as *New American Paintings, New Art Examiner,* and the *Chicago Tribune*. He is currently represented by the Gruen Gallery in Chicago and the Cultural Exchange Gallery in Scottsdale, Arizona, and his work has recently been auctioned by Sotheby's in New York City.

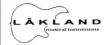

Backbeat Books | BASS PLAYER | LĀKLAND musical instruments